by LEO DUROCHER

Nice Guys

WITH **ED LINN**

Finish Last

Simon and Schuster   New York

Designed by Irving Perkins
Manufactured in the United States of America
1 2 3 4 5 6 7 8 9 10

Portions of this book were
serialized in
Sports Illustrated magazine.

Library of Congress Cataloging in Publication Data

Durocher, Leo Ernest, 1906-
    Nice guys finish last.

    Includes index.
    1. Durocher, Leo Ernest, 1906-
2. Baseball.   I. Linn, Edward.   II. Title.
GV865.D83A36   796.357'092'4 [B]   75-1462
ISBN 0-671-22057-8

I dedicate this book to my parents—to Mom, who came to understand my love for baseball and to enjoy my success—and to Dad, who encouraged me from the beginning and who was probably my greatest fan—and I his.

CONTENTS

BOOK I: THE GOOD OLD DAYS

BOOK II: THE DAYS OF TRIAL AND GLORY

BOOK III: THE NEW BREED

BOOK I

The Good
Old Days

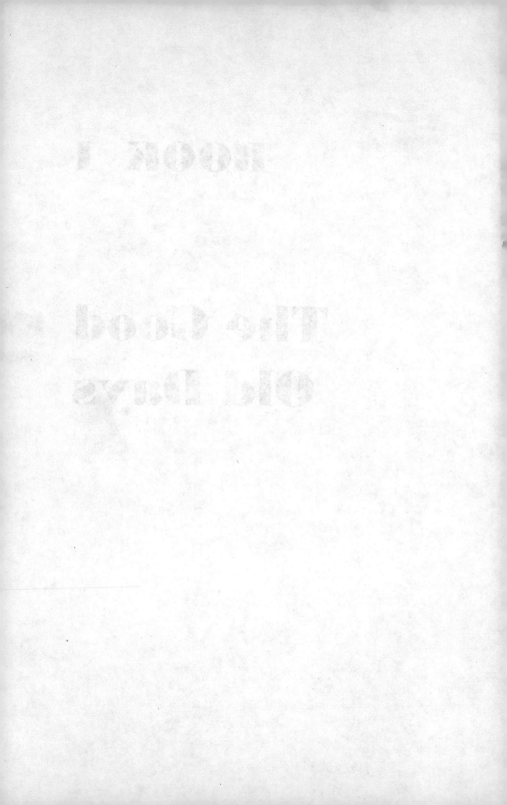

I COME TO KILL YOU

MY BASEBALL CAREER spanned almost five decades—from 1925 to 1973, count them—and in all that time I never had a boss call me upstairs so that he could congratulate me for losing like a gentleman. "How you play the game" is for college boys. When you're playing for money, winning is the only thing that matters. Show me a good loser in professional sports, and I'll show you an idiot. Show me a sportsman, and I'll show you a player I'm looking to trade to Oakland so that he can discuss his salary with that other great sportsman, Charley Finley.

I believe in rules. (Sure I do. If there weren't any rules, how could you break them?) I also believe I have a right to test the rules by seeing how far they can be bent. If a man is sliding into second base and the ball goes into center field, what's the matter with falling on him accidentally so that he can't get up and go to third? If you get away with it, fine. If you don't, what have you lost? I don't call that cheating; I call that heads-up baseball. Win any way you can as long as you can get away with it.

In the olden days, when I was shortstop for the Gas House Gang, I used to file my belt buckle to a sharp edge. We'd get into a tight spot in the game where we needed a strikeout, and I'd go to the mound and monkey around with the ball just enough to put a little nick on it. "It's on the bottom, buddy," I'd tell the pitcher as I handed it to him.

I used to do it a lot with Dizzy Dean. If he wanted to leave it on the bottom, he'd throw three-quarters and the ball would sail—*vroooom!* If he turned it over so that the nick was on top, it would sink. Diz had so much natural ability to begin with that with that kind of an extra edge it was just no contest.

Frankie Frisch, our manager and second-baseman, had his own favorite trick. Frank chewed tobacco. All he had to do was spit in his hand, scoop up a little dirt, and twist the ball in his hand just enough to work a little smear of mud into the seam. Same thing. My nick built up wind resistance on one spot; his smear roughed up a spot along the stitches, and the ball would sail like a bird.

We used to do everything in the old days to try to win, but so did the other clubs. Everybody was looking for an edge. If they got away with it I'd admire them. After the game was over. In a week or two. When Eddie Stanky kicked the ball out of Phil Rizzuto's hand in the opening game of the 1951 World Series I thought it was the greatest thing I'd ever seen. Not because it was the first time I'd seen it done but because it was my man who was doing it. Before the 1934 World Series began, the St. Louis scouting report warned us that Jo-Jo White of the Detroit Tigers was such a master at it that he would sometimes go all around the bases kicking the ball out of the fielders' hands. Sure enough, the first chance he had, he kicked the ball out of Frankie Frisch's glove and practically tore his uniform in half. A couple of innings later, Jo-Jo was on first again. "I got him," I told Frank.

"No you don't," Frisch said. "He's mine. I'll get him; you step on him."

White came into second, and while Frank was rattling the ball against his upper incisors I was dancing a fandango all over his lower chest. I guess Jo-Jo was no *aficionado* of the

Spanish dance because he did nothing at all during the rest of the Series to encourage an encore. Or maybe he just didn't like the idea of having to make an appointment with his dentist every time he slid into second base.

When *my* man Stanky does it, he's helping me to win. When *their* man White does it, he's helping them. I can't be any more explicit about it than to say that you can be my roommate today and if I'm traded tonight to another club I never saw you before if I'm playing against you tomorrow. You are no longer wearing the uniform that has the same name on it that my uniform has, and that makes you my mortal enemy. When the game is over I'll take you to dinner, you can have my money and we'll have some fun. Tomorrow, you are my enemy again.

The Nice Guys Finish Last line came about because of Eddie Stanky too. And wholly by accident. I'm not going to back away from it though. It has got me into Bartlett's Quotations—page 1059, between John Betjeman and Wystan Hugh Auden—and will be remembered long after I have been forgotten. Just who the hell were Betjeman and Auden anyway?

It came about during batting practice at the Polo Grounds, while I was managing the Dodgers. I was sitting in the dugout with Frank Graham of the old *Journal-American,* and several other newspapermen, having one of those freewheeling bull sessions. Frankie pointed to Eddie Stanky in the batting cage and said, very quietly, "Leo, what makes you like this fellow so much? Why are you so crazy about this fellow?"

I started by quoting the famous Rickey statement: "He can't hit, he can't run, he can't field, he can't throw. He can't do a goddam thing, Frank—but beat you." He might not have as much ability as some of the other players, I said, but every day you got 100 percent from him and he was trying to give you 125 percent. "Sure, they call him the Brat and the Mobile Muskrat and all of that," I was saying, and just at that point, the Giants, led by Mel Ott, began to come out of their dugout to take their warm-up. Without missing a beat, I said, "Take a look at that Number Four there. A nicer guy never drew breath than that man there." I called off his players' names as they came marching up the steps behind him, "Walker Cooper, Mize, Marshall, Kerr, Gordon, Thomson. Take a look at them. All nice guys. They'll finish last. Nice guys. Finish last."

I said, "They lose a ball game, they go home, they have a nice dinner, they put their heads down on the pillow and go to sleep. Poor Mel Ott, he can't sleep at night. He wants to win, he's got a job to do for the owner of the ball club. But that doesn't concern the players, they're all getting good money." I said, "You surround yourself with this type of player, they're real nice guys, sure—'Howarya, Howarya'— and you're going to finish down in the cellar with them. Because they think they're giving you one hundred percent on the ball field and they're not. Give me some scratching, diving, hungry ballplayers who come to kill you. Now, Stanky's the nicest gentleman who ever drew breath, but when the bell rings you're his mortal enemy. That's the kind of a guy I want playing for me."

That was the context. To explain why Eddie Stanky was so valuable to me by comparing him to a group of far more talented players who were—in fact—in last place. Frankie Graham did write it up that way. In that respect, Graham was the most remarkable reporter I ever met. He would sit there and never take a note, and then you'd pick up the paper and find yourself quoted word for word. But the other writers who picked it up ran two sentences together to make it sound as if I were saying that you couldn't be a decent person and succeed.

And so, whenever someone like Ara Parseghian wins a championship you are sure to read, "Ara Parseghian has proved that you can be a nice guy and win." I've seen it a thousand times. They don't even have to write "Despite what Leo Durocher says" any more.

But, do you know, I don't think it would have been picked up like that if it hadn't struck a chord. Because as a general proposition, it's true. Or are you going to tell me that you've never said to yourself, "The trouble with me is I'm too nice. Well, never again."

That's what I meant. I know this will come as a shock to a lot of people but I have dined in the homes of the rich and the mighty and I have never once kicked dirt on my hostess. Put me on the ball field, and I'm a different man. If you're in professional sports, buddy, and you don't care whether you win or lose, you are going to finish last. Because that's where those guys finish, they finish last. *Last.*

I never did anything I didn't try to beat you at. If I pitch pennies I want to beat you. If I'm spitting at a crack in the sidewalk I want to beat you. I would make the loser's trip to the opposing dressing room to congratulate the other manager because that was the proper thing to do. But I'm honest enough to say that I didn't like it. You think I liked it when I had to go to see Mr. Stengel and say, "Congratulations, Casey, you played great"? I'd have liked to stick a knife in his chest and twist it inside him.

I come to play! I come to beat you! I come to kill you! That's the way Miller Huggins, my first manager, brought me up, and that's the way it has always been with me.

I'm just a little smarter than you are, buddy, and so why the hell aren't you over here congratulating me?

After the Dodgers had lost the final playoff game to San Francisco in 1962, I couldn't even bring myself to do that. And I wasn't even the manager, I was only the coach. Still, I should have been the second Dodger over there, right behind Walter Alston. Alvin Dark, the Giants' manager, was one of my boys. He had played for me and he had been my captain. Many of the Giants players were close friends, and there was Willie Mays, who is as close to being a son as it is possible to be without being the blood of my blood and the flesh of my flesh.

But, dammit, we had gone into the ninth inning leading by two runs. With the ball club we had, we should have run away with the pennant. All right, that's baseball. I could remember that Jackie Robinson, whom I had been feuding with all year, had been the second Dodger player in our locker room in 1951 after we had beaten them on Bobby Thomson's home run. I knew Jackie was bleeding inside. I knew he'd rather have been congratulating anybody in the world but me. And still Jackie had come in smiling.

But I sat there without taking off my spikes, and I just couldn't do it. We had lost with one of the best teams I had ever been associated with. My kind of team. This was the year Maury Wills stole 104 bases and won the Most Valuable Player award. Tommy Davis, who hadn't broken his ankle yet, had the most incredible year in modern baseball. (Would you believe .346, 230 base hits and 153 rbi?) Plus 27 home runs. Willie Davis, who could outrun the world, had 21 home runs and 85 rbi. Frank Howard was giving us the long ball, 31 home runs and 119 rbi. And *good* pitching. Don Drysdale was having the best year of his life, 25 victories and the Cy Young award. Sandy Koufax had been going even better until he was knocked out by a circulatory blockage in his finger shortly after the All Star game. And still Koufax led the league in Earned Run Average. Ed Roebuck was having a fabulous year in relief.

Seven key players having the best seasons of their career, and we couldn't shake the Giants. Three guys who could run like ring-tailed apes, and we had a manager who sat back and played everything conservatively. *Forget the signs.* Speed overcomes everything. *Let them run.*

After Koufax went out, I just thought, *To hell with it.* Alston would give me the take sign, I'd flash the hit sign. Alston would signal to bunt, I'd call for the hit-and-run.

They were throwing the first pitch right in there to Maury Wills, knowing he was willing to get on with a walk. "Come on," I told him. "Swing at the first one, don't let them get ahead of you. You're not just a runner, you're a hitter. Rip into it." Goddam, when he wasn't bouncing the ball over the third baseman's head he was ripping line drives down the right-field line, something he had never done before. I was letting him hit on the 2–0 and 3--1 counts, something he had never done before either. The more he hit, the more he ran, and before you knew it his fielding had got better. I never "saw" a take sign from Alston with any of the speedsters— and how they loved it. The whole team knew what I was doing, and they were saying, "Just keep going, Leo. Goddam, we never played like this before. It was always played tight to the vest around here before but now, Christ, we're playing wide open."

All that talent wanting nothing more than to express itself. The players were so loose; oh, God, that's the way it's supposed to be, everybody laughing, everybody relaxed. We won 17 out of 21 games and took a 5½-game lead with maybe five or six weeks to go. And then we lost two games in a row and Alston called a meeting. "As of tonight, starting with this ball game," he said, "I will take complete charge of this ball club. And Leo, that means you. If I give you the bunt sign, that's what I want. The bunt. And if I give you the take sign, I want that hitter to take. Any sign that I give and you miss," he said, "I will fine you two hundred dollars and the player at bat two hundred dollars."

There was not a thing I could do any more. "I'm gone, fellows. All I can do is stand there like a wooden Indian and give you the signs. If he gives me the bunt you got to bunt. Because it won't just be me who'll be fined if you don't. You'll be fined, too."

And, boy, he took the bats right out of their hands. He took the bats out of their hands and, brother, their assholes tightened so that you couldn't drive a needle up there. In the pressure of a pennant race you can really tighten them up, and the tighter they got the more conservative he became.

And every day he held a meeting, which is the worst thing you can do when a team is going very bad or very good. If they're going good, who needs a meeting? "Just keep going, fellows," that's all the meeting you need. If they're going bad, you can only look for the opportune moment to relax them.

Whenever I held a meeting on a team that was that tight it would be to say, "Come on, for chrissake, you're playing like a lot of two-dollar whores. Swing the bat if you hit the ball ten feet in the air. If I didn't know you fellows and I wasn't seeing it, I wouldn't believe this. I know you're a good ball club, what the hell are you doing? Come on, let's slash and rip at 'em. And no curfew tonight. Go out and get drunk. I don't care what you do. Just show up at the park in time for tomorrow's game."

Every day Alston would hold a meeting and go over the opposition. You know what they say at meetings? On seven of the eight starters, they say, "Push him back and curve him on the outside." The eighth guy is hitting .220 and they say, "Throw it by him."

Day by day it got worse and worse. The only reason we didn't blow the lead was that San Francisco was losing right along with us. With eight games left we were still four ahead. We lost four out of five—couldn't score a run—and with three games left we were two ahead. All we had to do was win one of them. We lost all three. With a team like that, it was criminal.

In the third game of the playoff series, we were leading by two runs in the last of the ninth. And that was the inning that almost got me fired.

Ed Roebuck had come into the game in the sixth inning and pitched out of a jam. Got by the seventh and struggled to get through the eighth. Pitching has always been one of my strong points, and I could see that his arm was hanging dead. "How do you feel, buddy?" I asked him, as he was coming off.

He said, "My arm feels like lead. Man, I am tired."

I didn't go to Alston. I went to the pitching coach, Joe Becker, who was standing practically alongside him at the corner of the dugout near the bat rack. That's the right way to do it. You don't go over the pitching coach's head. "Get somebody ready," I said to Becker. "Don't let this fellow go out in the ninth inning. He can't lift his arm."

Becker didn't say a word. Alston didn't say a word. It was like I wasn't there.

I said, "Walt, he told me he was tired. He's through." And Alston said, more to Becker than to me, "I'm going to win or lose with Roebuck. He stays right there."

All right, I went out to the third base coaching box, we got the bases loaded with two out and Roebuck is supposed to be the hitter. I was so sure Alston was going to send up a pinch hitter, that I was making hitting motions from the coaching line. And here comes Roebuck out of the dugout with his batting helmet on.

When I came back in and took my seat at the other end of the bench, Drysdale, Koufax and Johnny Podres—who had started the game—were standing right there. "Don't let them send Roebuck back out," they pleaded. "Tell him he's got to make a change. Don't let him do it, Leo."

Don't let him? "What the hell do you want me to do, I'm not managing the club. There's not a goddam thing more I can say than I've said."

Worst inning I ever saw in my life. The first batter singles, and he's forced at second. One out. And now Roebuck is so tired that his control deserted him. He walked Willie Mc-Covey, who was pinch-hitting, and then he walked Felipe Alou. The bases are loaded and here comes Willie Mays. Alston didn't make a move and I'll be a sonafagun if he almost didn't get away with it. Willie hit a bullet back at

Roebuck. Waist high, practically into his glove. If it had stuck it probably would have been a double play. As it was, the ball was hit with such force that it tore the glove right off his hand. A run was in and the bases were still loaded, but we were still one run ahead.

And now Walt called me over from the other side of the dugout to make a pitching change. When I got to the bat-rack, he said, "Bring in Williams."

I put one foot up on the bench and I hollered back, "What? Did I hear you right? You're bringing in Williams?"

"That's what I said. Williams."

Stan Williams was a big, wild right-hander. He had pitched very well toward the end of the season, but in a spot like this? Williams?

I went out and I brought in Williams, and then I said to the boys on the bench, "We may as well go in. If I had ten pitchers this would be the tenth one I'd bring into a spot like this. He'll walk the ball park."

Orlando Cepeda hit a long fly to right field bringing in the tying run and advancing Felipe Alou to third.

Two out. Men on first and third, and, sure enough, Williams uncorked a wild pitch that Roseboro was able to block just enough so that only Mays could advance. With men on second and third, Alston ordered an intentional pass to load the bases again. Nobody on the bench said a word. Nobody had to. The same thought was on everybody's mind. He's loading the bases with Williams pitching, and right after Williams has shown that he hasn't got his control.

Another walk is going to bring in the winning run.

Williams walked Jim Davenport.

Kiss the pennant goodbye.

I wasn't the only one slumped at my stool after the game. The players told the clubhouse man to lock the door, and while Alston was over in the San Francisco dressing room congratulating Dark, something happened that I had never seen in any clubhouse or ever expected to see. Where they came from I will never know, but whiskey bottles were handed around to the players. For almost an hour, they sat there, stunned. Except for an occasional shouted curse, nobody said anything. They sat like I was sitting, in their sweaty uniforms, and tried to get themselves drunk.

Three hours later, I did manage to heave myself over to the Grenadier Restaurant, which was run by the same man who ran the Stadium restaurant at Chavez Ravine. A party had been scheduled for the Dodger officials, and while neither Mr. O'Malley nor Mr. Bavasi showed up, almost everybody else connected with the club did. The hilarity, as you might well imagine, was restrained.

During the course of these solemn rites, I was called over to the big table where most of the Dodger officials were seated. By then, everyone had had a few drinks and, although I am not normally much of a drinker, I'd had a few myself. While we were commiserating with each other, someone at the table said to me, "If you'd have been managing the ball club, we'd have won it."

I just looked this man right in the eye and I said, "Maybe." And then I said, "I know one thing. I'd have liked to go into the ninth inning with a two-run lead. I'd take my chances." Period. End of quote.

That's all I said. It wasn't exactly a call to mutiny and it wasn't exactly the most revolutionary idea since the movies discovered sound. Who wouldn't like to go into the ninth with a two-run lead? And, you will notice, I hadn't called a press conference to say it. I was replying to a question put to me, among friends, at a time when everybody had been drinking.

It didn't come out that way in the newspapers, though. The way the papers had it, I had publicly second-guessed Alston. The way the newspapers had it, I had said that if I had been the manager we'd have won the pennant.

Buzzy Bavasi, the Dodger's general manager, read the reports and told the newspapers that if I had said those things I was fired. When I was finally able to get him on the phone, he said, "Well, I see you were popping off again."

I said, "Who popped off, me or you? Why didn't you call me, Buzz? Why didn't you ask me if I said what they printed? I wouldn't have lied to you. If I'd have second-guessed Alston I'd have told you I second-guessed Alston. So what? You'd have fired me. That's the worst you could do to me."

Buzzy, not quite convinced, told me he was going to check my version out. A couple of nights later, I met him at a Friars Club stag for Maury Wills. His investigation, he said, had backed me up in every detail. "Buzz," I told him. "I'm surprised at you. You gave me an awful going over."

"Well" he said, "I was mad."

"I'll tell you something," I said. "I didn't feel too good that night myself."

Everybody was disappointed and so they pounced upon the one thing that had come to hand—a distorted story about Durocher. And so Durocher was up the creek again, a neighborhood I have come to know rather intimately through the years.

I will admit, however—if you press me hard enough—that I had said just enough to bring on everything that happened. I've been in that neighborhood before, too. Branch Rickey once said of me that I was a man with an infinite capacity for *immediately* making a bad thing worse.

Carve it on my gravestone, Branch. I have to admit it's sometimes true.

As far as Rickey was concerned, I was sometimes able to make a bad situation worse even when I'd have sworn I was making it better. During the last year of the war, when the Dodgers were playing anybody who could fit our uniforms, one of the fittees was Tom Seats, a left-handed pitcher who had labored through the years in the minors, not wholly without success. A year earlier, he had been doing his bit by working in an airplane factory in San Diego.

Pitching only over the weekend, he had won 25 games in the Pacific Coast League.

For us, he couldn't get by the third inning. Over and over it happened—I couldn't understand it. He was strong as a bull; he had a good curve; his control wasn't that bad. And he kept getting his jock knocked off.

Charlie Dressen, who could get information about everybody, finally came to me and said, "You know, Leo, they tell me this guy drinks. Can you get any whiskey around here?"

That was a good question. Whiskey was in such short supply by then that not even Mac Kreindler of "21," who had been a good friend of mine from back in the old days, could get any for me. The best he could come up with was two dozen of those little half-pint bottles of brandy.

Just before Seats was ready to warm up for his next start, I invited him into my office for a man-to-man talk. "Tom," I said, "you've got to be a better pitcher than you're showing me. You can't win twenty-five games against nine girls unless you're a better pitcher than this."

He didn't have the slightest idea what was wrong. All he knew was that he didn't seem to have any strength when he went out there.

I said: "I know you drink."

"I sure do."

I asked him if he drank brandy.

"I drink anything," he said.

Out of my desk came one of the little bottles of brandy. As I poured him a shot, his eyes got that big. He took one gulp, and I could see that the next time I wouldn't have to worry about the glass. He warmed up, and I want to tell you something; by the time the game was ready to start the brandy was pouring out of him. That sonofagun pitched five scoreless innings. They couldn't touch him. And then I took him into the clubhouse, let him get into a dry uniform and gave him another big belt.

From there on in he was the best pitcher we had.

At the end of the season, Mr. Rickey called me into his office for the specific purpose of congratulating me on the fine job I had done with Tom Seats. "I have never seen such a transformation," he said. "From a Class C pitcher to a fine major-league pitcher. I don't know what you said or did to the man, but whatever it was I'd like to hear it from you."

I said, "Well, Mr. Rickey, I gave him a shot of brandy— about this much—twenty-thirty minutes before he warmed up. And then I gave him another shot in the fifth inning."

Rickey's eyebrows always seemed to become twice as thick when he was angry. He just kept staring at me, and then his eyes began to squint, and I knew I was in trouble. "You . . . gave . . . a . . . man . . . in . . . uniform . . . whiskey?"

I didn't think he'd appreciate the distinction between whiskey and brandy, and so all I said was, "Yes, sir."

He said: "He will never pitch again for Brooklyn." His eyes got even smaller. "I should fire you right now."

I was in trouble, all right. "Mr. Rickey," I said. "I thought when I signed the contract I signed for one thing. There is a 'W' column and there is an 'L' column. I thought it was my obligation and duty to put as many as I could under that 'W' column. I saw nothing unethical about what I did. I just gave a man a little drink of brandy. I think it gave him more confidence, loosened him up. It must have done *something*, Mr. Rickey, or he couldn't have had what you just called such a transformation. Now what it was, Mr. Rickey, I don't know. But it certainly got the job done."

Branch didn't buy the medicinal angle at all. Seats never pitched another game in the major leagues, and I never came closer to losing my job.

As long as I've got one chance to beat you I'm going to take it. I don't care if it's a zillion to one. As long as I can be on the ball field with you I have a chance. In 1954, the year I won my second pennant with the Giants, we were playing the Dodgers late in the year, at a time when they were making a run at us. We won the first one, and in the second game, Carl Erskine had me beaten, 5–4, in the ninth. We had the bases loaded with two out, and Wes Westrum, my catcher, was coming to bat. Poor Wes was in a horrible slump. He was only playing because we had no other catcher. The way he was going he couldn't have hit me if I ran by slow and ducked a little bit. I called time and yelled for Dusty Rhodes, who was having the greatest season any pinch hitter has ever had. Before Dusty took two steps, my coaches came running in from first and third, and Frank Shellenbach, my pitching coach, was on the phone from the bullpen.

"You can't do that, Leo," they were all shouting. "You have no catcher."

And Rhodes is hollering. "He don't need a catcher. Don't worry about it, I'll win it right here."

I called Westrum back, and I told Rhodes there was an automatic $200 fine if he walked or got hit by a pitch. "I can't stand a tie score, Dusty," I said. "You got to hit the ball. I don't care if you hit it ten feet straight up over home plate. But swing."

The first pitch Erskine threw was a high change-up, which Dusty always had a tough time with. He started to swing nine different times, and almost fell on his face. The next pitch was a high, fast ball, and Dusty hit a bullet into center field and won the ball game.

Back in the clubhouse the newspapermen gathered around me. What would have happened if he'd walked or got hit? Or got on with an error? "You'd have had no catcher, did you think of that?"

Yeah, I'd thought of it. And I'd also thought that I'd rather be in the tenth inning without a catcher than in the clubhouse with a loss. "Once I'm in the clubhouse and the door is locked I can't win it. As long as I'm out on that green stuff out there, playing against you, I'll find somebody to catch."

I'd have found somebody, and if we had lost on a passed ball they'd have been calling me the dunce of all time.

I've been called that before, too. If you're afraid, go home. How badly do I want to win?

During my early years as a manager, some guy got up at a banquet after I had spoken and kept asking me that same question. Nothing I said seemed to satisfy him until, finally, the perfect illustration flashed into my mind. "If I were playing third base and my mother was rounding third with the run that was going to beat us," I told him, "I would trip her. Oh, I'd pick her up and I'd brush her off, and then I'd say, 'Sorry, Mom.' But nobody beats me!"

I was on my way home for a visit and, just my luck, they wrote up that part of it in the paper. My mother was a little woman, and while she knew nothing at all about baseball she knew enough to know that she didn't relish the idea of being tripped by her youngest son. She was ready for me as soon as I walked through the door. "You said that about your own mother? You'd trip me, son, your own mother?"

I tried to explain that it had only been a figure of speech, that it was just an illustration I had picked out of the air as a way of showing this man how far I would go to win.

She looked at me, and her eyes bugged out. "Then you *would* have tripped me," she screamed. "You would have *tripped* me. You *would!* You *would!*"

For the rest of my visit, she walked around with an injured air. And I guess she had a right to. God rest your soul, Mom, I'm afraid I would.

THE DRUMMER BOY

I WAS BORN on the kitchen table on the top floor of a three-decker wooden house on Merrick Street in West Springfield, Massachusetts. Two days later, my mother was back at her work. That's the way it was done in that kind of neighborhood, at that time.

I was the youngest of four sons, spaced two years apart. My brothers, in order of their age, were Clarence, Raymond and Armand. Not very long after I was born my father, who had been an engineer for the Boston and Albany railroad, suffered a heart attack. Not serious enough to completely disable him but enough to wipe out whatever small savings he might have had and to limit his activities.

And so my earliest memory is quite probably of my mother leaving the house to work as a maid in a downtown Springfield hotel.

We were so poor, I sometimes say, that we didn't live on the wrong side of the track, we lived in the middle of the track. A joke which has a certain bite to it, in our case, because my father had gone back to work for the railroad. His job was to go from locomotive to locomotive and make sure the fires were properly banked.

We never had a Christmas tree; I remember that particularly. Christmas was always held on the linoleum floor in the kitchen in front of the old iron stove. When I was five or six, I wanted a drum. Oh, Lord, how I wanted that drum. More than anything I have ever wanted before or since. When I went to bed on Christmas Eve, I remember my mother and dad saying, "Well, you've been a pretty good boy; not the best but pretty good. Santa Claus may stop by."

When I woke the next morning there was a drum right there alongside me on the bed. Well, let me tell you, no rich kid ever got a Mercedes-Benz that meant so much to him as that drum meant to me. That's something poor people have on rich people. Anything my parents gave me I knew they were giving me out of sacrifice and sweat and love.

Not, as you may have guessed, that I didn't give them immediate cause to regret it. I started banging on that drum as soon as I woke up, and I never stopped. For three days, I went marching around the neighborhood with the drum hanging from around my neck, whacking away at it. At night I went marching around the house. The three-decker houses that were so common in those days had two apartments to each floor, six families in all. After a couple of days, five families in our house and twelve families in the adjoining houses were screaming to shut that kid up.

The shouts were in French, because it was a neighborhood of French Catholics. My mother, whose maiden name was Clara Provost, was born in a little town just outside Montreal. My father, George, came from the little French community of Cohoes, in upper New York. He was a small man, possibly five feet four inches. My mother was barely over five feet. Nothing except French was spoken in our home, or, except for the Latin liturgy, in church. I didn't know one word of English when I started public school. Until I began to play professional baseball, my name was always pronounced the French way; not De-*roach*-er but Doo-roe-*shay*. When I began to mix more with the other kids in town, socially and in athletics, their nickname for me was

Swamper. After a while it was, anyway. It developed something like this: Frog . . . Bullfrog . . . Swamp . . . Swamper. Jeez, do you know the last time I heard that name? I was sent to Atlanta in the Southern Association in my second year of organized baseball, and we were playing the inmates at the Atlanta prison. I hit a ground ball and was running to first when I heard some guy in the stands holler out, "Hey, Swamper." One of my classmates had got out of Springfield the hard way.

In a neighborhood of poor Catholics like that, the Church played an enormously important part in our lives. My brothers and I were all altar boys. Many a Sunday the four of us were on the altar together in our little white surplices, serving mass. Frequently two masses in a row, although there was never any shortage of boys anxious to take our place. We enjoyed it, and none of them more than me. It's odd the things that stay with you through life. One Sunday, my oldest brother, Clarence, backed into a candle and the surplice went up like that—*phhhhfffft*—and in that one second, while everybody was standing there paralyzed, a man in the front row jumped the rail and pulled it off him. Clarence wasn't so much as scorched, and I stared at that man through the rest of the mass, marveling—as I still marvel—that anybody could have reacted that quickly in an emergency.

You don't ever really get away from that kind of an upbringing. Not that I was ever in any danger of joining the priesthood, but in all the years I was traveling around playing ball I very rarely missed a Sunday morning mass. When I was divorced, I lost the right to have my confession heard and receive communion, and that hurt me. I found it very painful to sit there and watch everybody else get up and file up to the altar. And so, while I still feel the urge to go to church from time to time, I always leave without a sense of real fulfillment.

My mother ran the house, there was never any doubt

about that. As far as I can remember, my father hit me only once. When I was about ten or eleven. He had been transferred to Cambridge, Mass., a few months earlier, but we were living in the same kind of a house, the top floor of a three-decker, almost directly across from the streetcar barn. One Sunday after church, I thought it would be a good idea to hide behind the car barn and smoke a cigarette. To show how smart I was, I had picked a spot that was visible from our kitchen window. In those days, a beating meant that the old man took off his belt and let you have it. I was one of that kind of kid who couldn't be made to cry. The more he hit me, the madder I got. I just kept looking over my shoulder at him, as if to say, *Go on, hit me harder; I dare you!*

The beating I knew I had coming to me, but when my mother told me to go to bed without supper that night I went running out of the house and was gone all night. All night they looked for me. Know where I was? I had sneaked back into the house and was hiding under the second-floor staircase. At five in the morning, my father finally found me huddled there, half asleep, and picked me up and carried me up the stairs, kind of nuzzling me and sneaking in a kiss here and there. I suppose I knew from that time on that there was nothing I could do wrong as far as my father was concerned.

After a year in Cambridge we moved back to a big house on Elm Street, on the other side of Springfield. It was like moving into a whole new world. The boys were beginning to contribute toward the house by then, but mostly my mother was able to swing it by taking in boarders. For the rest of the time that I was at home, we'd all sit down together, family and boarders, and the food would be passed around on steaming platters.

I always worked at something or other. It was expected. All the usual things that kids did; I had a paper route; I was right there knocking on doors with my shovel when it snowed. I mowed lawns. I worked in an ice-cream parlor. Springfield was really a small city within a rural setting. There was farmland all around us. When I was in high school, I'd work the tobacco fields in Agawam, the town just to the south of us. During the harvest season, we'd work from seven in the morning until six at night. They'd roll back the cheesecloth that had been protecting the field from the frost and, goddam, you'd go up and down those rows as fast as you could. On a good day you could make yourself maybe $3.50.

There was no organized activity for kids. We were on our own, and we did everything. Crazy things. As soon as the Connecticut River would freeze over, eight or ten of us would put on our racing skates and skate all the way up to Boston. A hundred miles back and forth. We'd start out early in the morning, staying close to the shore where the ice was safe, and when we'd get to the Harvard Rowing Club, we'd just turn around and head back.

Almost all the kids could ride horses, because horses were all around us. I myself learned how to ride—are you ready for this?—by playing polo. Springfield College had a polo team, I knew a couple of the guys from high school, and after I had got to where I could sit a horse, I'd go galloping around the grounds whacking away at the hard little ball.

Through it all, I had one steady job. By the time I was twelve or thirteen, I was already very concerned about my grooming. Although you wouldn't think it to look at me now, I used to have a great mop of blondish hair. My hair was so thick that I couldn't run a comb through it, I had to put my head under the faucet and smooth it back with a towel. The local barber happened to have three pool tables in his back room, and so I made a deal with him. I would wait for him to open every Saturday morning, he would cut my hair for me and then I would go back and sweep the floor, clean the tables and set out the chalk in preparation for the big Saturday afternoon crowd. Well, the poolroom didn't open until one o'clock and I would be finished by noon. That gave me an hour to practice. At the beginning, I was so small that I had to stand on a box to reach the balls. By the time I was in high school I was so good that I was the "house man." I'd come in after school and go to work racking balls, and if anybody wanted a game, either for "time" or for a side bet I would take them on. When any hustler breezed into town looking for a game, the older guys would back me, sometimes for as much as $100. With the money on the line, I didn't lose.

When I began to make some money, hustling pool, I'd save up $75 for a custom-made suit (easily the equivalent of $500 today). I don't know what it was that made me so clothes-conscious; nobody else in my family was, certainly. We were the kind of family where my mother washed all the clothes, shirts included, and hung them on the line in the kitchen to dry overnight. My shirts she had to starch. I can still see my mother, God rest her soul, dipping the collars and cuffs of my shirts in a little can of starch, letting them dry for a few minutes, ironing them out and hanging them up on a hanger. Leo wouldn't stand for any wrinkles.

There was one other athlete in the family. My oldest brother, Clarence. Clarence was a wonderful center fielder and, something I never was, a hitter. I used to think of him when I'd see that little Albie Pearson who played for the California Angels in the early sixties. Clarence was just about Pearson's size, he could field every bit as good and he had a lot more power. Enormous power for a little man. But Clarence was also a brilliant student, and he had the sense of responsibility that you find in oldest sons. He studied business administration at Springfield College, went to work at the bottom rung of one of the biggest manufacturing companies in Springfield and ended up as executive vice-president.

I can't say that Clarence was my first hero, though. When we moved to Elm Street, we were living only two blocks from

Rabbit Maranville, the shortstop for the Boston Braves. Rabbit was not only the great hero of all of Springfield, he was a fellow Frenchman—and my father knew him. Actually could go up to him and talk to him. The Rabbit was a little fellow, that's how he got his nickname, but he was smart and he was colorful. My father took me to Boston a couple of times to see him play, and everybody would wait for a high pop fly to be hit in his general direction so they could see his "vest-pocket" catch. Sheer logic tells you that the best way to catch a fly ball is up over the eyes so that you are watching it all the way. Rabbit would catch it beneath his belt buckle. *Plop!* Followed by laughter. Followed by applause.

The guy I will never forget, though, was Heinie Groh, the third baseman for Cincinnati. Groh had the oddest batting stance I have ever seen. The best way for you to visualize it —and I have never seen it described quite right—is to picture a soldier standing at present arms. That was Groh. He would stand there facing the pitcher head-on, with his feet together and the bat held straight up in front of him. To complete the picture, just in case you couldn't recognize him, you know, he used what was always referred to as "Heinie Groh's bottle bat," the shortest, thickest bat I have ever seen. By the time the ball was at the plate, of course, he had swung around and was in a normal hitting stance—and the sonofabuck could really hit.

Although Rabbit Maranville never had a chance to see me play, my father was quick to tell him I was the best young player in town, and a shortstop at that, and he took a certain amount of interest in me. What that meant was that I was getting tips about playing shortstop from the man who was going to become the first shortstop to be elected to the Hall of Fame, and I was getting them at a time when I was eager to learn. Know the hitters, he would say. Study them. Anticipate where the ball was going to be hit. Get rid of the ball quick. Rabbit didn't have the best arm in baseball, but he was known for being able to get the ball away faster than anybody in the game. I became faster. Ask anybody who saw me play and they will tell you that it looked as if I was throwing the ball before I caught it. Pee Wee Reese tried to imitate me when he first came up, and for four or five games he was throwing the ball all over the place. What you can learn at thirteen or fourteen, you just can't learn at nineteen and twenty. "Do it your way," I'd tell him. "Not mine. I was doing it this way when I was just a baby, and it's part of me. With your arm, you don't have to get the ball away that fast."

We little guys had to make up in brains and toughness what we lacked in size, Rabbit would tell me. "Never take a backward step out there. The first backward step a little man takes is the one that's going to kill him."

He gave me something more tangible than advice, too. A brand-new glove. And then he took a big scissors and cut a hole right in the middle of it, just the way he did with his own glove. You were catching the ball really against the bare skin. It stung like hell at first, but it was surprising how quickly my hand hardened. In a very short time, I felt nothing at all except when I'd catch a hot line drive. (The gloves in those days were so much smaller than they are today that you can't really call them the same thing. In those days, the player had to make the play, not the glove.)

I used Rabbit Maranville's glove on through the minors and during my first couple of years with the Yankees. I kept it until it was such a rag that I could fold it up and stuff it in my pocket. When the time finally came when I had to get myself a new one I picked up a scissors and got ready to cut out another hole. And then I asked myself why. I was doing it because Maranville did it, and that was no reason at all. Instead of cutting a hole in the glove, I slit the inside, took out all the padding, and kept a layer of leather between the ball and my hand. That one was in tatters by the time I was through; it was practically falling apart. But I held onto it to the end of my career. They were the only two gloves I ever had.

Maranville was playing for the St. Louis Cardinals the first year I went to spring training with the Yankees, and by coincidence both clubs trained in St. Petersburg and we played each other often. The first time Rabbit saw me play, he said to me, "You do things backwards right now better than a lot of guys that have been here for years." Boy, that was praise from on high. I considered myself the Rabbit's protégé, and I waited for him to tell me how well I had learned my lessons. Instead, he said, "Where did you learn to get the ball away like that?"

Where did I—? *From you, Rabbit! From you!* That's how I came to understand that all the time I had looked upon myself as his protégé, he had looked on me as a neighborhood kid who was always being brought around by his father. *And who would have thought the kid was actually going to make it?* One of those things.

By another coincidence, I was on the field when Rabbit played his final game. I was with the Cardinals myself then, and Rabbit, at the age of forty-five, was making a comeback with the Boston Braves. It may very well have been the first exhibition game of the spring season. I know it was at St. Petersburg, and Rabbit was being thrown out at the plate. Exhibition game or not, forty-five years old or not, the Rabbit came barreling into the catcher and you could hear the ankle crack. He was lying there in agony, with the ankle twisted completely around. The batter on deck for the Braves was Shanty Hogan, their big catcher. "Don't stand there looking at me," the Rabbit rasped at him, "Knock me out."

And just as quick as that, Hogan whacked him on the chin and knocked him out cold. That was my teacher, Rabbit Maranville, one hell of a little guy.

I wasn't just a baseball player in high school, I was a good all-around athlete. In season, I played football (140-pound halfback on offense, end on defense); track (sprinter) and basketball (guard). Baseball was where I was outstanding, though, and I was good enough so that I was offered a scholarship to Holy Cross, which has always been the baseball college in that section of the country.

It all went out the window, high school career, college, everything, when—speaking of stupid—I hit a teacher. I had been clowning around in the back of the science class, making a pest of myself, and he had made me come down to the front of the room and sit with my knees pressed together under the desk and my hands folded on top of the knees, an uncomfortable and ludicrous position. OK, I had it coming to me. But then, out of a clear blue sky, he came over and slapped me across the face. Well, punishment is one thing but nobody had a right to hit me except my parents. Certainly not a grown man while my hands were tucked away so that I didn't even have a chance to defend myself. Remember those big window-lifter poles they used to have in school rooms? Well, I went to the back of the room, grabbed ahold of it and belted him across the back. The principal suspended me for thirty days and I just never went back.

Instead, I went to work for the Boston and Albany railroad at thirty dollars a week because they wanted me for their ball club. Springfield had a very strong twilight league, with tremendous local rivalries. I was maybe fifteen years old, and I was put in charge of a crew of about two dozen colored guys. Our guys would unload the long, uncut four-by-eights that were used for railroad ties, and another crew would come by and cut them down to size. My job was to sit there and keep count.

After a while, Wyco Electric Company, which manufactured motorcycle batteries, offered me five cents an hour more to come and work—meaning play ball—for them. Boston and Albany got me back by offering me five cents more than Wyco was paying me, Wyco went up another five cents and I kept shuttling back and forth between them until I wound up at Wyco making $57.50 a week, a man's wage.

The owner of Wyco, Mr. Staughton, really liked me. Right from the beginning, he made it clear that he was offering me not just a chance to make some easy money by playing ball for him but to learn the business from the ground up. He got to like me so much that on Saturday night he would let me take his Cadillac to drive up to Kookamongo Lake, where they had a barn with a big dance floor and a band. I'd pile some of my friends into it and we'd dance, drink beer and take a shot at the girls. And then I'd bring the car very quietly into his garage at around two thirty in the morning.

I had learned to drive on Clarence's Model-T, not always with his permission. Boy, that was a big event when Clarence came home with a Model-T. He kept the car in a wooden shed which sat on top of a little knoll right across the street from us. What I'd do was to open the door, stand on the running board (ask your father what a running board is, kids) and let it roll back off the knoll and down the street as far as its momentum would carry it. That was because you had to crank it up to get the motor started, and if it didn't start up right away (and it never did) it could make a tremendous racket. A couple of times I stole the car when Clarence had a date himself and—oh, Christ—I thought he was going to kill me.

The one thing I wasn't so cocky about in those days was my baseball ability. Oh, I knew I could do a lot of things on a ball field, but I thought professional baseball players were a lot better than they really were. The two best players in the twilight league in my opinion were Bunny and Eddie Trauske, who played shortstop and second base. Both of them had been given tryouts at Waterbury in the Eastern

League for three straight years and hadn't been able to make it. If they couldn't make it, I'd say, what chance did I have?

There were two people in particular who kept telling me I was far better than the Trauskes. One, of course, was my father. My father took great pleasure in everything I did; the custom-made suits, the pool playing, everything. And nothing gave him more pleasure than to watch me play ball. He was a very quiet man around the house—he'd had a heart attack, remember—but when it came to standing up for me he had a very short fuse. His friends would start to talk about how good the Trauskes were, and immediately my father would become pugnacious. "What about my boy? What about my boy Leo?"

"No question about it," they'd say. "Bunny Trauske is two to one a better ballplayer than your boy. And so is his brother Eddie."

"Pa," I'd say, tugging at his elbow. "They're just needling you. Let it go. Forget it."

No chance. "They can't talk that way. You can outplay both of them Trauskes." And—boom—off he'd go.

They could do it to him even when I was in the big leagues. First thing we'd do when I came home to visit, he'd take me down to Boyle's restaurant for a cup of coffee and a sweet roll. The guys there would pretend not to see us and pretty soon they'd be talking about the shortstops. "That Dick Bartell has got to be the best young shortstop around," one of them would say. "Fields. Hits. Scrappy."

"What's wrong with my boy? Leo's just as good as Bartell."

I'd tug at his elbow. "Just relax, Pa, they're only having fun. They're just needling you a little bit."

So I'd step out for a minute, and when I came back he'd be saying, "Jurges? What's wrong with my boy? Jurges never saw the day he could field with my boy."

To the end of his life they could do it to him, God rest his soul. Twice a day.

God rest his soul, how he loved me. Back home in Spring-field there was a picture of me that I've tried to find for years. A baby picture of me sitting in the high chair, wearing a dress and covered with blond curls. It was one of those old-fashioned pictures in a huge round frame, and it never left his side. Wherever the bed might be, whatever side he was sleeping on, that was where the picture had to be hung. My mother tried to move it once, and he had a fit.

He took such pleasure in me, and I was such a rotten son. It's not a nice thing to have to say, but it's true. He would come to New York when I was playing there to spend four or five days with me, and we'd walk around Times Square. That's all he wanted to do. Couldn't take him to a movie show. He didn't want to go to any fancy dress-up restau-rants. I suppose he'd have felt out of place there, and the truth is that I felt he'd be out of place too.

We'd come out of the subway, and I'd forget he had a bad heart, step out a couple of strides in front of him and look back impatiently. "Come on, Dad." "Don't worry," he'd say. "Just take your time, I'll be there." After a while I got sick of walking around Times Square every night and he'd go out by himself.

There was a famous grill on Seventh Avenue, near where the Palace Hotel used to be. They had a chef right in the window, and he loved that. He loved their roast beef. The Automat fascinated him too. When it came time for dessert he would say, like a happy kid, "Let's go to the Automat." Coffee and a slice of pie. Unvarying. And always he'd take a bus when he was ready to go home. "I ride the trains all day long," he'd say. "This is my vacation."

As proud as he was of me already, his great ambition for me was to be a manager. And he never got to know. When Larry MacPhail appointed me manager of the Brooklyn Dodgers, to my own great surprise, during the winter meet-ings in Chicago, he told me to be quiet about it for a few

days. He wanted to hold the announcement for a press conference when we got back to New York.

The press conference was being held on Monday. On Sunday night, my brother called to tell me that my father had
just died. It had been his dream for me, and I hadn't thought
to call him from Chicago. Just thoughtlessness. Sure. But
you're only thoughtless about things that don't mean that
much to you. Absolutely unforgivable. But that's the way it
happens in life, isn't it? The way of the world. The parents
do everything for the child, and the child is ungrateful.

There was one other man who encouraged me constantly
—David Redd, a black man I worked with at Wyco. "You're
better than all of them," David Redd kept telling me. "The
Trauskes are what you see when you look at them. Good
players for around here. You've got something they haven't
got. You do things."

He encouraged me enough so that when I was seventeen
I tucked my glove in my back pocket and went to see Art
Sheean, the owner of the Springfield ball club, added a year
to my age and asked for a tryout. He took one look at me,
told me I was too small and ran me right out of the park.

A year later, after I had grown a couple of inches and put
on six or seven pounds, Jack O'Hara, my tailor, arranged for
me to go to Hartford during their two-week tryout period
with the understanding that when I made the Club I'd be
signed to a contract for $150 a month. I still had so little
confidence in myself that I merely asked Wyco for a two-
week leave.

My father couldn't have been happier. My mother was so
mad she threw me out of the house. Playing ball had been
all right if it could get me a college scholarship and she had
taken the same attitude about the twilight league. Because
I was a ballplayer I was making a good salary at Wyco, with

prospects of being moved into an executive position. But to throw away a $57.50 salary to become a professional ball-player—a bum—and at less money at that, was more than she could take.

"Ma," I said. "I'm only taking a two-week leave. I talked to Mr. Staughton, and he's all for it. If I don't make it, he says I can come right back to work."

"Bum!" she said.

"Pa," I said, looking to him for support.

But my mother was boss in that house, and we both knew it. "If you're going to be a bum all your life, then I'm just as glad you're getting out of the house," she told me. "Go on, pack up your clothes and get out of here."

Since I would be staying in Hartford for the two weeks anyway, she was only kicking me out in a manner of speaking. But she had made her point all right. From that moment until I left she wouldn't speak to me. Not a word.

The manager of the Hartford club was Paddy O'Connor, a tough, gruff Irishman. I played very well; in fact, I had some glowing writeups in the Hartford papers. But no glowing words came from O'Connor or any of his coaches. They didn't encourage me, they didn't discourage me. They didn't seem to know I was there. At the end of two weeks, which was a Sunday night, I knocked on the door of Paddy O'Connor's room.

"Mr. O'Connor," I said, clearing my throat. "I have to go back to work tomorrow if I'm not going to make the club. So I have to know how I'm doing."

He didn't so much as look up.

"Mr. O'Connor," I said. "Like I said, my two-week leave from my job is up, and I want to know what my chances are. If I'm not going to make it here I don't want to be out on the street altogether."

Paddy O'Connor finally opened his mouth and spoke. He said, "Agggggwwwrrr." Just growled at me like a big bear.

Frightened the hell out of me. I took it to mean I hadn't impressed him very much, and so I packed my things and went home. My mother was pleased to let me back in the house, and at seven o'clock the next morning I was back at work.

A few days later, I was there at the bench with David Redd when Jack O'Hara came bursting in. It was seven-thirty in the morning. "Get those overalls off," he said. "We're opening the season at Bridgeport today, and you're going to be in the starting lineup."

O'Hara had come back from the Florida training camps the previous night, asked for me and had been told that I had been let go. "You let him go?" he had screamed. "What do you mean you let him go, you dumb Irishman? Isn't there anybody in this camp who knows a ballplayer when he sees one?"

He had a Hartford uniform for me in his car. He drove me home to get my spikes and gloves, stopped off for a few minutes at his tailor shop, and we were off to Bridgeport. It was about a 75-mile ride over small roads and through practically every city and town in between. When it became clear that we were going to be lucky to make it in time, he had me change into the uniform in the car. We got there, honest to God, just as the game was about to start. O'Connor shrugged at me and put me in the lineup—I'll never forget it. I had nine or ten chances in the field, and I had a couple of hits. A month and a half later, Paul Kritchell, the chief Yankee scout, came down to look the club over and bought me.

In September, five months after I had left the Hartford camp with my dreams of a baseball career behind me, I was wearing the uniform of the New York Yankees and sitting in a dugout alongside Babe Ruth, Lou Gehrig, Bob Meusel, Earl Combs and the rest of that crew.

I even got to bat a couple of times as a pinch hitter.

It was not the World Champion Yankees I was joining. The year the Yankees bought me was the year of Babe Ruth's famous bellyache. The Babe had been out most of the season, and the great team that had won three straight pennants in the early twenties was falling apart. Particularly at shortstop and second base. They had bought Tony Lazzeri (who had been a minor-league shortstop) from the Pacific Coast League, where he had hit 68 home runs in their 160-game season. They had bought Mark Koenig, who was considered to be the best shortstop in the Midwest, and had brought him up to finish the 1925 season. And they had bought me.

A year earlier I had been overimpressed by anybody who was a professional ballplayer. I took one look at the shortstops around the league and I knew there wasn't one of them could field any better than I could.

The next year the Yankees sent me to Atlanta and the year after that they optioned me out to their top farm club in St. Paul. Although you can't tell it by looking at my statistics in the record book because I didn't get in any games, I was back with the Yankees at the end of both years and was sitting on the bench through both World Series. The 1926 Series in which old Grover Cleveland Alexander came shuffling in from the bullpen to strike out Tony Lazzeri with the bases loaded. And the 1927 Series, in which the team generally acknowledged to be the greatest of all time demolished the Pittsburgh Pirates in four straight games.

STRONG MINDS AND WEAK BACKS

I HAD BEEN WITH THE YANKEES for only a couple of days when Miller Huggins, the manager, tested me. The way it has always been in baseball, the humpty-dumpties, the substitutes, come out early to take their batting and fielding practice, and then the bell rings and the hitting cage belongs to the regulars.

When the bell rung, I had already been working out for about thirty minutes fielding ground balls that were being hit to me by Wally Pipp, who had lost his job to Lou Gehrig during the season and was helping out where he could. Wally was great when it came to that kind of thing because he could hit ground balls a mile a minute, and nothing pleased him more than to drive one through you. After another ten minutes or so, I came into the bench for a drink of water, and Miller Huggins said to me, "Go on up and hit."

I grabbed a bat from in front of the dugout, went into the batting cage and, boy, did I get a blast. Ruth and Gehrig and the rest of them all started to scream, "Get out of here, you busher! Get out to the field where you belong!"

Let me tell you, I just dropped the bat and got out of there and ran back for my glove.

Miller Huggins said, "I thought I told you to hit."

I said, "Well, they wouldn't let me."

Very firmly he said, "I told you to get up there and hit!"

OK! I grabbed a bat and I strode to the cage holding the bat in one hand like a club. Nobody was going to run me out of there the second time. Nobody.

As luck would have it, Babe Ruth was waiting to hit next. I jumped in from the right side and Ruth moved in the left side. "Get out of here, you humpty-dumpty," he roared. "Get lost!"

I said, "You better talk to the Man over there because he told me to hit next and I'm hitting."

And all around the cage, the regulars were hollering, "Get out, you busher. . . . Break your bat over his head, Babe. . . . Knock the cage down on him."

Well, he was going to have to do something like that to get me out of there. I just stood my ground and yelled to the pitcher, "You're gonna have to pitch to both of us because I'm not getting out of here."

With that, Mr. Huggins called in, "Let him hit, Babe. Get out of there."

Babe growled and snorted and let me know I was "fresh as paint" but later, in the locker room, Mr. Huggins patted me on the back. He had a way of sitting next to me and talking very softly, as if we were in it together. As if it was *us* against *them*. "Never lose that self-assurance that you're the best," Mr. Huggins would tell me again and again. "There are a lot of fellows around here with strong backs and weak minds," he would say. "You have a strong mind and a weak back. Let them do all the hitting, you use your head. And as long as you live, there will be a place for you in baseball. You'll be here when they're all gone."

I was Miller Huggins' boy from the first. My father and Rabbit Maranville, the other two important men in my life up to then, had both been small men. Miller Huggins was an itty-bitty man, no bigger than a jockey. He couldn't have stood more than five feet three, and he weighed maybe 120 pounds. Tiny as he was, he had been a big-league second baseman for twelve years, and from what everybody told me, one of the very best. He had managed the St. Louis Cardinals for three years, and the Yankees for eight. With the Yankees he had won three straight pennants, had suffered the humiliation of being hung out of a speeding train by Babe Ruth when the Babe was in his cups, and had fined the Babe an unheard of $5,000 and made it stick by surviving Babe's "me or him" ultimatum.

He loved me like a father, and I loved him like a son. I couldn't hit worth a damn—Babe Ruth nicknamed me "the All-American Out"—but Mr. Huggins kept telling me I'd stick around for a long time if I kept my cockiness and my scrappiness and that fierce desire to do anything to win. "Little guys like us can win games," he would say. "We can beat 'em," he would say, tapping his head just like Rabbit Maranville, "up here."

The only time he really got mad at me came during my first trip to spring training. I had already been called up to New York at the end of three straight seasons by then, you have to remember, and being a friendly sort of guy I had been getting around the nightclub and debutante circles pretty good. Among the people I had become acquainted with were a very wealthy Michigan family with a very charming daughter. They had come down to St. Petersburg on their 125-foot yacht, and, having taken care to pack a tuxedo in my trunk, I became her escort for the Florida social season. The big debutante affair in those days was the Blossom Festival at the Vinoy Park Hotel. As befitted my wardrobe, if not my station, her father sent his chauffeured limousine to pick me up.

A couple of days before the ball, it had suddenly occurred to me that if there should happen to be a delegation of my teammates in the lobby of the Princess Martha Hotel when I walked through, I stood an excellent chance of being down to a pair of shorts by the time I got to the door. With my native shrewdness I had therefore questioned the bellboy and discovered that it would be possible to take the freight elevator down, duck out into a side alley and emerge about fifty feet from the front entrance.

I came sneaking out of the alley and—oh, God—sitting right there on one of the street benches were Miller Huggins and his two coaches, Art Fletcher and Charley O'Leary. One thing I'll say for myself—I brought their conversation to a sudden halt. I bowed politely, murmured "Lovely evening, gentlemen," and with no aplomb at all, dove into the limousine and told the chauffeur to get me out of there.

Naturally, I stayed out well beyond the curfew—one doesn't leave that kind of an affair early, does one?—and in the morning I found a note tucked into the top of my locker. Mr. Huggins, it seemed, was anxious to see me.

"Son," he said quietly, "did you come down here to wear evening clothes?"

"No, *sir*, Mr. Huggins. I came down here to play baseball. But, Mr. Huggins, this was a very fine affair and I had an invitation and, of course, it was a black-tie affair so I had to wear evening clothes and—"

He cut me off with the most disgusted look I have ever seen in my life. "And you *had* them, didn't you? You had them packed into that fancy trunk of yours, didn't you? Let me give you a tip. You put them right back in that trunk and don't you ever let me see you with those things on again. Do you understand?"

"Yes, *sir*, Mr. Huggins."

I packed my tuxedo away and toward the end of spring training got my chance to break into the lineup when Tony Lazzeri broke a couple of ribs. "Ever play second base, son?" Miller Huggins asked me. Never having played a game there in my life I said, "Sure. Lots of times." What was I going to say, no?

And would you believe that at the end of the first couple of weeks I was leading the league in hitting? Mr. Huggins had turned me into a switch hitter by then on the theory that I just might be able to beat out some infield hits leaving from the left-hander's side of the box. It was funny. Batting right-handed, I had never been able to keep myself from pulling away from the ball. Not even on the sandlot. Batting left-handed, I just stood there paralyzed when a ball came at me. But I did very well for a while hitting left-handed. Little ping hits over the infield, mostly to the opposite field or through the middle. Just slapping at the ball. And right-handed, everything was falling in for me, too. The first time I faced Lefty Grove, who threw nothing but fast balls at that time, I choked way up on the bat to make sure I'd be able to get out in front of the ball. *Whooosh.* The ball was by me anyway, but I got a little piece of it and it went skidding off the other way, between the first baseman and the bag for a base hit. Before the day was over, I had another hit off Grove. A little blooper over second base.

While I was leading the league, Babe Ruth, who had started very badly, was close to the bottom. "The league is upside down," he said. "But don't worry about it, kid. When the season's over I'll be near the top where I belong and you'll be near the bottom where you belong."

The Babe was still telling me I was fresh as paint, only now he was saying it with a smile. As well he should have, because he was always agitating me to get on the opposing players. In those days, the umpires let you ride opposing players far more than they do today. I was a cocky kid with a booming voice and—yeah, I guess I was as fresh as paint—when Babe or anybody else would tell me to yell something, I was only too happy to oblige. Everybody got a great kick out of it, and I almost got a few punches on the nose.

Many stories have been written about the "fight" I had with Ty Cobb the first time I ever played against him, and I always read them with great interest because no fight ever took place. What happened was that Cobb, who was just finishing out his career with Connie Mack's Athletics, was on first base, and Tris Speaker, who was also finishing out his career in Philadelphia, hit a line drive through the pitcher's box. I dove for the ball, got my glove on it and slowed it down enough so that it stopped in short centerfield just off the dirt. While I was scrambling after it I happened to get in Cobb's way—accidentally, of course—forcing him to pull up just enough so that I was able to throw him out at third to end the inning.

Now, in those days, the Yankee dugout was behind third base—not first base as it is now—and as I'm passing Cobb on the way in, he says to me, "You get in my way again, you fresh busher, and I'll step on your face."

I hadn't said a word to Cobb, and I still didn't. Hell, this is Ty Cobb. But Ruth, who was coming in from left field, wanted to know what Cobb had said. "Well, kid," Ruth said —he called everybody kid—"the next time he comes to bat call him a pennypincher."

I'd never heard that word before, but just from the way everybody on the bench started to laugh I had a pretty good idea what it meant. What I didn't know was that Cobb had a reputation for being a very tight man with a dollar and had been ready to fight at the drop of a "pennypincher" for years.

Well, naturally, I can't wait for him to get up again so I can go to work on him and, holy cow, he turns in the batter's box, pointing his finger, and the umpire has to restrain him. Now, the game is over and the umpires don't care any more. Both clubs have to use the third-base dugout to get to the locker room, and Cobb races over to cut me off. He's out to kill me and I'm looking for a place to run because I am not about to tangle with Mr. Cobb.

Finally, Babe came running in and put his arm around Cobb, and he's kind of grinning at him and settling him down. "Now what are you going to do? You don't want to hit the kid, do you?" And while Babe has his attention—boom—I'm up the stairs like a halfback and into the locker room.

Babe saved me again from being either hit or smothered to death by Fatty Fothergill, one of the great forgotten hitters of that era. Fothergill was a short, stocky fellow, about as wide as he was tall, and he used to hit line drives you could hang your wash on. Rattle them off the walls. (Just to give you an idea, in the three previous seasons he had hit .353, .367, .359.) Fothergill was very sensitive about his weight; so sensitive that he kept telling the sportswriters that he'd really appreciate it if they'd forget that Fatty stuff and call him Bob. The other fellows on the Yankees would tell me to whistle sharply and holler, "Hey, taxi!" when he came up, and I had embellished enough on that theme through the year so that I had poor Fatty looking to sit on me. As the season was coming to an end, we came into Detroit for a five-game series: a single game and two doubleheaders. And what a season it had been! After two months we were running so far ahead of the record set by the 1927 Yankees that we were being called the greatest team to have ever set foot on a diamond. And then everything began to go wrong. We couldn't win, and the Athletics, who had one of the great teams of all time themselves just coming into its own that year (Foxx—Simmons—Cochrane—Dykes—Grove—Earnshaw), couldn't lose. By September, having blown a 13-game lead, we had actually fallen into second place.

When we got to Detroit, we were in a flat-foot tie. We won the first three games, the Athletics had lost one, and as we took the field for the second game of the Sunday doubleheader we knew that a win would clinch a tie for the pennant.

I had a personal reason, above and beyond the purely competitive one, why it was essential that we win. Although

I had only been in New York for five months, I had already managed to get myself $7,000 in debt—which wasn't bad, considering that my salary was only $5,000. I needed that Series money to even think about getting even.

As Detroit came up in the sixth inning, we were ahead by one run, and it was getting so dark that everybody knew the game was going to be called. Detroit got two runners on base, there were two outs, and up to the plate comes Fatty Fothergill, who has been wearing us out all day.

Now, Mr. Huggins was always after me to keep my wheels spinning out there, to do anything that might give us a little edge. Just as our pitcher, Henry Johnson, was getting the sign, I hollered "Time!" and went racing in toward the plate as if I were absolutely furious about something. When I got to within ten feet of the plate, I yelled just as loudly as I could, "There's a man here hitting out of turn!"

The umpire pulled out his lineup card, studied it carefully and shouted back, "What's the matter with you? Fothergill is the hitter."

"*Fothergill?*" I said, squinting. "Ohhhhh, that's different. It's only *Fothergill!* From where I was standing, it looked like there were *two* men up there."

Well, Fothergill was so mad that the veins stuck out on his neck. He started to curse me. When they finally got him back into the batter's box he was so blind with rage that he took three straight strikes, dropped his bat and started after me. Now, it's the same in Detroit as it was in Yankee Stadium. Both teams had to go through the third-base dugout to get to their dressing rooms. I made a mad dash for the dugout but Fothergill had the angle on me and he cut me off. I ran out into shallow left field, faked one way and made a dash the other, but Fothergill, who was pretty quick for a man who was built like a fireplug, kept cutting me off. He's going to whack me, and whack me good. But, once again, it was the Babe who finally got ahold of him and put his

arm around him, and once again, while the Babe was talking
to him, I slipped up into the runway and skedaddled into
the clubhouse.

Boy, the clubhouse was in an uproar. Mr. Huggins came
over and whispered, "That was great. That's the way I want
you to play, son." And to me that was praise from heaven.
No question about it, it was my greatest day as a New York
Yankee.

My first season in the big leagues and I'm with a pennant
winner and a World Champion. In the World Series, we
beat the St. Louis Cardinals in four straight games. I got in
all four games but only to spell Tony Lazzeri at second base
in the late innings. And though I didn't get any base hits
in my two times at bat, I did back the right fielder up against
the fence, batting left-handed against Grover Cleveland
Alexander, in the fourth game.

Of course, it was a very short fence.

In fact, with short porches in right field at both ball parks,
you knew that Ruth and Gehrig were going to go wild. In
the first three games, Gehrig had a slight edge. Three home
runs, and when he wasn't hitting the ball out of there they
were walking him. In the fourth game, Babe Ruth took over.
You knew he was going to. Everybody in the park knew he
was going to. Gehrig had his fourth home run. The Babe
hit three.

You think of the Yankees and you think of Babe Ruth. And
you're right. He thrived on pressure. He enjoyed it. He and
Dizzy Dean were two of a kind in that respect. They'd come
to the big game, say exactly what they were going to do and
then go out and do it. When the Philadelphia Athletics, who
won 98 games themselves that year, came to the Yankee
Stadium for a Labor Day doubleheader, they were half a
game ahead of us. They had Grove and Earnshaw ready.
You couldn't get near the Stadium; the place was jam-

packed. The perfect setting for Babe Ruth. As the A's came up the dugout steps to get onto the field, the Babe was waiting for them. "Well, how does it feel to be in first place, fellows? Take a good look at it, you bums, because you'll be in second place when the day is over."

He was laughing at them. He couldn't wait. The whole club just relaxed, and when the day was over the Yankees were in first place.

The same thing happened with Lou Gehrig, who had got off to a tremendous start and was far ahead of everybody else in home runs. By the middle of the season he was still something like 17 home runs ahead of Babe. "Don't worry about it, kid." Babe told him. "When it's all over you'll be behind me."

He was.

Now that I think of it, it was the only time I ever did hear them speak to each other. The way I'd characterize their relationship is that they were not overly friendly but neither did they dislike each other. What you have to remember is that although everybody brackets their names together, Gehrig was far closer to me in age than he was to Ruth. When Gehrig joined the Yankees in 1925, the same season I first came up with them, Babe had already been in the big leagues for 11 years. Gehrig was twenty-two years old, Ruth was thirty. Ruth was loud and rowdy. Gehrig would sit in the clubhouse, smoke his pipe and play bridge.

Babe Ruth dominated that team totally. He dominated it on the field, and he dominated it even more off the field. He made more money by far than anybody else, and nobody resented it, because we knew he was putting money in all of our pockets. There has never been anything like Babe Ruth, because everything about him was bigger than life.

As far as I am concerned, there is only one all-time home-run champ and that's Babe Ruth. All right, Henry Aaron went to bat 2,890 more times in order to hit one more home run. All you have to do is use your common sense. I'm not

trying to take anything away from Henry Aaron. Long before anybody even thought he had a shot at the record I had
been saying that they ought to put Henry Aaron in the Hall
of Fame right now. While he was still playing. Henry Aaron
is a great all-around ballplayer who, among his other accom-
plishments, hit a lot of home runs. If you appreciate baseball,
in all its finer aspects, he has been a pleasure to watch.

Babe Ruth was ***The Sultan of Swat***

Babe Ruth was ***THE BAMBINO***

Babe Ruth was what you came to see!!!!

It was like going to a carnival, with Babe as both the star
performer and the side-show attraction. Hell, that's what we
called him: "You big ape." He was what a home-run hitter
was supposed to look like. Wide, flat nose. Big feet. Little
ankles. Belly hanging over his belt. All he had to do was
walk onto the field and everybody would applaud. The air
became charged with electricity. You just felt that something
great was going to happen.

He'd twirl that big 48-ounce bat around in little circles up
at the plate as if he were cranking it up for the Biggest Home
Run Ever Hit—*you felt that*—and when he'd hit one he
would hit it like nobody has hit it before or since. A mile
high and a mile out. I can see him now, as I did so many
times, just look up, drop the bat and start to trot, the little
pitter-patter pigeon-toed, high-bellied trot that seemed to
say, I've done it before and I'll do it again, but this one was
for you. (Henry Aaron has a good home-run trot too, it's
probably the most colorful thing about him. He holds his
elbows up high, if you've ever noticed, and kind of swaggers
from the waist up while he's kind of shuffling from the waist
down.)

The Babe didn't even have to hit a home run to thrill you.
He would hit infield flies that were worth the price of admis-
sion. The fielder would holler, "I got it," and he'd wait . . .
and wait . . . and then he'd begin to stagger and finally he'd

make a wild lunge. The ball would land fifteen feet away from him, and the Babe would be standing on second base with a big grin on his face.

You'll think I'm exaggerating when I say that it was a thrill to see him strike out. But not if you ever saw him. He would take that big swing of his and you could hear the whole stands go *Whooooossshhhh!* And then break out into wild applause as he was walking back to the bench.

Charisma counts. Charisma is what takes a superstar and turns him into a super-superstar. I've never seen a charismatic ballplayer who didn't make the team better than it figured to be, for the same reason that a charismatic actor makes any play he is in better than it should be. There is just something about these people that carries everybody else along with them.

There's no question about it, Babe Ruth was the greatest instinctive baseball player who ever lived. He was a great hitter, and he had been a great pitcher. The only thing he couldn't really do was run, but when he went from first to third—or stole a base for you—he invariably made it because he instinctively did the right thing.

All of which proves, in case you have ever wondered, that you don't have to be a mental giant to be a great baseball player. In anything that took any intelligence, like remembering a sign, the Babe was dumb. Which is why Mr. Huggins never bothered to give him a sign. If not being able to remember the names of teammates he had been playing with for years is a sign of dumbness, then the Babe has to be the dumbest man I have ever known.

A great big boy was what he was, alternately generous and mean. And, unlike me, born under a lucky star. A Saturday afternoon exhibition game in New Orleans was rained out and so Babe went to the racetrack and won about $9,000. The players didn't get paid until the season started in those days, and so naturally everybody was broke. Babe walked into the clubhouse on Sunday, threw the whole wad of money on top of the equipment trunk and said, "Well, boys— come and get it."

Boy, it was like feeding time at the zoo.

After everybody had taken what they wanted, Babe just picked up what was left, put it in his pouch and dropped the pouch into the money trunk. The Babe would give you anything, but he was funny about one thing. If you took the money you had better be there when you got your next pay- check. Because if you weren't, he'd come around with a bat in his hand and tell you to get it up.

He could be a mean drunk, although even there it was the meanness of a big, backward child. What else can you say of anybody who would hang anybody out of a speeding train? He very quickly cured me of my penchant for wearing silk pajamas when we were on the road. You'd be asleep in your berth, and all of a sudden you'd think a train had hit you. The Babe would be roaring up and down the aisle knocking the younger guys out of their berth and ripping the pajamas off you. After the first couple of trips, I'd just go down to the army-navy store and buy a dozen pair of pajamas at fifty cents apiece. By the time we came back home, I'd be lucky if I had one left.

But who the hell was going to say anything to him? Not me. He was the great Babe Ruth, and I was the All-American Out.

In certain ways, though, I was as good a friend as he had on the team. The Babe had a big brown Packard roadster, and we used to ride to the Stadium together almost every day. And there was many a time I put him to bed on the road after he had been out on the town. That's what made the run-in I had with him when I was finishing out my play- ing career with the Dodgers so sad.

Larry MacPhail, who had just taken over the club, wanted to hire Babe in the hope of drawing a few fans into the park. During the game Babe was to coach at first base, but his real job would be to take early batting practice so the fans could come in and see him belt the ball out into the street.

Before MacPhail signed him, though, he asked me to find out whether Burleigh Grimes, the Dodgers' manager, was willing to take Babe on, and, if he was, to bring him up to his apartment so that Larry could discuss terms with the Babe and his business manager, Christy Walsh.

Babe, of course, had always wanted to be a manager himself. After the contract had been signed, he drew me into the bedroom of MacPhail's suite for a drink. "Stick with me, Leo," he said. "I'm going to be taking this club over." In a way it was sad, because whatever Babe might have thought, he didn't have a snowball's chance of getting the job. He had been hired as a freak attraction, with about the same standing as Bill Veeck's midget.

Still, it burned me up. I was Grimes's captain, he had given me a great deal of responsibility, and I knew he hadn't wanted Babe in the first place. "Dammit, Babe," I said. "You've got a lot of gall plotting to undermine this man after he's been good enough to bring you in and give you a job. You are insulting me by even thinking I might be willing to help you."

Well, Babe came right back at me, and there were some pretty blunt words flying around for a while.

The blowoff came after I had won a ball game by throwing my bat at a pitch out. I had only been protecting the runner, since I had given him the hit-and-run sign, but by one of those freaks the bat hit the ball solidly and the ball landed right on the first-base line. Afterwards a newspaperman asked me whether the Babe had given me the sign. My answer was one word: "No."

The writer was apparently blessed with extrasensory perception, though, because he managed to get a full column out of that one word. It came out sounding as if I had criticized the Babe for not giving signs.

Babe came into the clubhouse before the next game,

breathing fire. As soon as Grimes's daily meeting was over, he opened up on me before the whole squad. "You were always a fresh punk as far as I'm concerned," he bellowed, waving my explanations aside. "And I'm going to give you a whack in the mouth. I should have done it years ago."

Well, you can't take that in front of all the players unless you're ready to hang up your uniform and go home. We were seated right across a narrow aisle from each other, with me on a stool and the Babe sitting backwards on a high-backed iron chair. "Just hold it a minute," I said. "Number one. I did not say what was written in the paper. What I said was that you did not give me the hit-and-run sign. If the truth of the matter were to be known," I said, "you don't give signs to anyone on this club, do you?"

"Maybe I don't," he said, beginning to rise. "But I know enough to give you a whack across that big mouth of yours."

I've been around enough clubhouses to know that no fight is going to last more than ten seconds. I also knew I wasn't going to let Babe use that ten seconds to whack me around. So I took a leap at him and bulled him back into his locker, chair and all. Before he could disentangle himself, there were about twenty-five guys between us.

After everybody else had gone out onto the field, Grimes came over to me and said, "The next time you do that, I'll fine you. He belongs to *me!*" That was when I knew Grimes had heard that Babe was gunning for his job. Because what he was saying was that if anybody belted Babe, it was going to be him. Babe went out with a little bruise under his eye, and the word got around that I had hit him. But I didn't, and I didn't want anybody to think that I had. *"Me hit the Babe? You've got to be crazy!"*

By the next year, I was manager of the Dodgers, and the Babe had been let out. Let me be perfectly frank about this. MacPhail didn't consult me. If he had I would have said, "Get rid of him." Hell, this was my first shot at managing and I needed all the help I could get. I loved Babe. We were friends until the day he died. Off the ball field, I'd have given him anything I had. On the ball field at that stage of the game, he was no good to me. If he had been my own brother, I've have got rid of him. He couldn't help me *win*.

And so, in the end, Miller Huggins was right. With all those strong backs on that greatest of all Yankee teams, little Leo outlasted them all.

Huggins' plan for that second year was to make me the regular shortstop and move Mark Koenig over to third base. In the first week of the season we went to Boston, where they had a big lefthanded rookie outfielder named Russ Scarritt. I had played against Scarritt when I was at St. Paul, and he had always made a star out of me because I had discovered that he invariably sliced a left-hander's curve right down the left-field line. With Lefty Heimich, a mediocre curve-baller, pitching for us, I told Koenig to play Scarritt deep and over toward the line and I'd cover him. Koenig, who wasn't too happy about being shifted to third, told me to take care of my position and he'd take care of his. Sure enough, Scarritt comes to bat and hit a rocket, a yard or two to Koenig's left, that went right under Koenig's glove. I had positioned myself a long way over towards third, of course, despite what Koenig had said, and I had already been moving even further that way with the pitch, and so I was able to make the play and *be in position to throw*.

It wasn't only Huggins who congratulated me. After the game, even the Boston writers came into our locker room to tell me it was the best play they had ever seen. "If you were watching," I told them after I had told them how I knew about Scarritt, "you'd have seen that I didn't have to go that far. I was already there. Maybe if some of the other guys on this club would stop calling me Lippy and listen to what I was saying for a change they'd be in position too."

Koenig, who thought I was making myself look good at his

expense, was a little mad with me for a while. So what? I'm a man with an opinion, and if that didn't make me the most popular man to have around, it didn't bother me a bit. I wasn't running in any popularity contest. Not as a player, and not as a manager. Off the field, Koenig and I were good friends; we'd go out together from time to time. On the field, if you can help me, great. If you can't, you're going to hear about it. That's the way Miller Huggins brought me up, and that's the way I've always been.

And, make no mistake about it, I was training myself to become a manager even then. I kept a little black book in my pocket, and when I wasn't playing I would sit beside Mr. Huggins and write down every move he made. At night, I would study the more interesting situations that had come up, and then I'd give myself a test by writing and rewriting exactly what he had done and what the thinking had been behind it.

Not that I ever discussed his strategy with him. Miller Huggins was not a talkative man. He would sit on the bench inning after inning, hardly moving. He always had a package of loose Beechnut tobacco in his pocket and he would reach in from time to time, take out one or two leaves and put them into his mouth. The floor of the dugout was made of wood but it was constructed more or less like a duckboard so the water would run out when they washed the bench down. Huggins would just sit there, and every now and again he would look down and spit right into the crack. That was all. He never said or did much of anything except when there was a purpose to it, but when there was a purpose to it he could be tough.

Tony Lazzeri, for instance, was a player who had to be shaken up from time to time. Huggins would wait until Lazzeri was picking up his bat, and then he'd give me the wink and say, "Get your glove and warm up. You're going in at second base."

Hooooo, it was like setting off a bomb under Lazzeri. "*He's* going to play second! HE's going to play in my place! That humpty-dumpty? The All-American Out!"

"That's right," Huggins would snap. "I've seen all I want to see of you for the day. I don't want to have to look at you any more."

And just about that time, Lazzeri would go up and rip one. Hit it about 30 miles. And come back to the bench swaggering, look right at Huggins as if he were going to spit in his eye and say, "How do you *like* it?"

Basic psychology that went right into the black book. Twenty years later, a pitcher named Sal Maglie came back from the Mexican League to rejoin the New York Giants, and it was positively eerie. He not only looked a little like Tony, he gave off the same vibrations. Over and over, I'd do the same thing to Sal, and over and over Sal would pitch himself out of the trouble. Get him mad and he'd play better. *Play better.*

My second season with the Yankees, which had started so promising, ended up with everything falling apart. The Athletics were coming on strong, they were on their way to winning the first of three straight pennants, and we kept falling farther and farther behind. About two weeks before the end of the season, we were playing a doubleheader at home. It was a cold, misty day, one of those days that seems to seep into your bones. Everybody else had gone out to the field for the second game except Mr. Huggins and me, and I noticed that he was looking in the mirror and picking at a sore on his face. He looked sick, and he had a wracking cough. He looked tinier than ever, like he was shrinking away.

"Mr. Huggins," I said, "Why don't you go home? We're not going anyplace. We can't win the pennant and we've got second place clinched. You're sick. Please. Why don't you go home?"

"Maybe you're right, son," he said. "Maybe I should." And he did. He went home and he never came back. He went home and he had a stroke and he died.

And there's an odd thing about that. Although the records say that he died during the last week of the season, I am absolutely sure in my mind that he didn't die until after the season was over. I mean, I'm looking right at the newspaper report, and I can't believe it. The only explanation, I suppose, is that the season ended for me on the day Mr. Huggins left the club.

And so, as it developed, did my career with the New York Yankees.

In a roundabout way, it could be said that I was sold because of all those debts I kept running up. Although actually it was another case of Little Leo opening his big mouth at a time when it would have been a helluva lot smarter to keep it shut. After two seasons with the Yankees, I still owed money all around town. Instead of using my World Series check to pay off the old debts the previous year, I had blown it on a new Packard. What the hell, I deserved it. In particular, I owed the Picadilly Hotel around $800. My plan, therefore, was to ask for $7,000, a thousand-dollar raise, with the thousand being paid to me in advance so that I could get myself out of hock at the hotel.

In those days the Yankee offices were on 42nd Street, overlooking Bryant Park and the old Sixth Avenue El. When we got together to sign the contract, Mr. Barrow informed me I wasn't going to get either the raise or an advance. I was going to sign for $6,000 again, he said. Take it or leave it.

"Don't hold your breath," I snapped. "Because that's never going to happen."

Mr. Barrow just turned around in his swivel chair and stared out the window, his back firmly to me, as much as if to dismiss me. As if, you know, I wasn't worth his time. Boy, that burned me. I turned away and went stalking off, and if it had been an ordinary-sized office I might have got out of there without any more trouble. It was a huge office, though, and by the time I reached the door I felt the urge to make it clear to him that I meant what I had said. That I was never going to sign for any lousy $6,000.

When I still found myself talking to his back I said, "Ahhh, go and fuck yourself," taking care to make it just loud enough so that he could hear me but still soft enough so that he could pretend he hadn't.

Unfortunately, Mr. Barrow wasn't playing by my rules. He came spinning around in his chair—now I had his attention all right—and he yelled, "What did you say?"

"Didn't you hear me?" I yelled back.

"Yes, I did hear you."

And so I looked him right in the eye and I said, "And it still goes."

Mr. Barrow raised up out of that chair, leveled his finger at me and said, "And so do you!"

The next morning I picked up the paper and learned I had become the property of the Cincinnati Reds. He had sent me out of New York, out of the league and onto a last-place club.

"WHAT IF IT DOESN'T RAIN?"

THE QUESTION ARISES, I suspect, as to how I managed to run into so much debt so quickly. Ahhhh, it was easy. Let us remember that I was first called up to New York at the tag end of 1925, right smack in the middle of the Roaring Twenties. And while the standards could hardly be any looser than they are today, it seems to me that they were considerably gayer. Or could it be that I was younger? I had just turned twenty myself, and Little Leo and Little Old New York roared together.

Let us consider clothes. My teammates nicknamed me "Fifth Avenue," with Lyn Lary, another snappy dresser, completing the entry as "Broadway." I was never a flashy dresser, understand. I was just what my nickname indicated: class. Flashy comes cheap. Class costs. I did all my shopping at Sulka's, then as now one of the great luxury stores of the world. My shirts cost a minimum of $25. I'd pay $10 or $12 for a necktie, and $5 a throw for socks. Well, when you're making $5,000 and then $6,000, it becomes very easy to run out of money. So I'd have the clothes sent to the Picadilly Hotel and have it put on my bill, utterly confident that something good was going to happen tomorrow that would enable me to pay it off.

Those were the days of the great clubs in New York, and

I touched all the bases. I'd go to the Stork Club, where Arthur Brown, the maître d', was a great baseball fan and always put me at the best table. Toots Shor at the Tavern was another great fan. The great place to go afterwards was the Cotton Club in Harlem, which was being run by Connie Immerman (remember the name). They had late shows, and you'd run home, get into evening clothes and run back to watch Cab Calloway and Bojangles Bill Robinson. Robinson was a great Yankee fan and a great friend of mine. His favorite stunt was to sprinkle salt on top of the opposing team's dugout (that was putting salt on their tail to hold them down, see?) and then jump up on it and do his soft-shoe routine.

Clayton, Jackson and Durante were at what they called the Chez les Ambassador on top of the old Winter Garden. There was one stretch where I was there every night to see Jimmy Durante, who was the hottest thing in town, do his famous number "Wood." That was the number in which he'd break up everything that had wood in it, starting with the piano, and pile it in the middle of the floor. He'd pull out the fixtures, everything, and every night he'd seem to find something new. And all the time he'd be chanting like a maniac: "Wood . . . wood . . . woood. . . ." To close the act they'd bring out a wooden outhouse. Sitting inside would be Eddie Jackson wearing a raccoon coat and reading the telephone book: "Wood . . . wood . . . wood . . ."

Billy Rose had the Diamond Horseshoe, with the most beautiful showgirls in New York. I was also inspecting the ladies of Ziegfeld's Follies, George White's Scandals and Earl Carroll's Vanities closely. I had no more difficulty getting a date in New York than Man O'War—who also came to beat you—had in Kentucky.

On New Year's Eve, I remember as through a mist, wearing tails, a top hat and a pair of gray spats with pearl buttons (which was what your well-dressed man about town was wearing that year), I took my girl to a party; and, for this special occasion, I was also sporting a cane. Thank God, Miller Huggins couldn't see me.

I was a ballplayer with the New York Yankees, and everybody seemed to want to be seen with me, to invite me out, to pat me on the back. I was traveling in pretty fast company for a utility infielder, sure. And if when the party ended and the music stopped, I was a little further in debt, so what?

I could say that I had been counting upon another World Series check to get me out, but that would be giving me credit for thinking more than twenty-four hours ahead. When you're a kid and you do something that seems wrong, they say, Well, he's inexperienced. And if you do something good, they say, Aha, he's finally matured. It wasn't a matter of maturity or immaturity with me. It was a matter of philosophy. Joe E. Lewis had a line which I thought expressed it perfectly: "They're always asking me why I don't save my money for a rainy day. Well, what if it doesn't rain and I'm stuck with all that money?"

I always used to say that if I had seven dollars and I was hungry, I ate seven dollars. My stomach has always been more important to me than my wallet. I'm not going to worry about tomorrow morning while I'm eating tonight's meal. If I had twelve dollars, I ate twelve dollars, and if I only had the price of a hamburger I ordered a steak and signed for it.

To put it bluntly, I have lived above my means all my life. When I was making $5,000, I lived $10,000. In the fifties, when I was working for NBC and making twice as much money as I had ever made in baseball, I was more in debt than ever. And when the president of NBC, Robert Kintner, whom I despised, hollered at me in a restaurant to come over to his table, I said, "I told you once, twice and for the third time and last: I don't table-hop, I don't eat with drunken bums and as far as I'm concerned you should be eating out of a trough." That left me to live beyond my means while earning nothing.

I had still another life during my stay with the Yankees.

Away from the ball park, away from the nightclubs, away from the broads. Pool was a big sport around New York, and I'd pick up pocket money during the winter by going to the big Broadway pool halls like the Strand or Jack Doyle's and doing a little hustling. Or, rather, letting myself be hustled. I'd just sit around until somebody asked if I wanted to play a friendly game. At the worst, I'd pick up ten or twenty dollars, and if after a little preliminary fumbling the guy wanted to make the game a little more interesting, I could make myself a score.

But that wasn't where the real action was. In the early morning hours when the good folk were tucked away, all the hustlers would tuck their custom-made cues into their leather cases and head for Scabouche's, a not very imposing pool hall over a cigar shop right next to the Palace Theatre. They were all pool hustlers, yes; but they were also the top tournament players in the country. On a good night, there might be as many as a hundred people who had paid twenty-five cents apiece just to sit in the wooden grandstand and watch them lock horns. Ralph Greenleaf, Willie Mosconi, young Marshall Camp from Detroit, Frank Taberski, Chicago Slim (a big colored fellow) and Major White. The Major wore glasses that looked like the bottoms of Coca-Cola bottles, and he had a short little stroke. He looked like the easiest mark you ever saw, and he was one of the world's great pool players. I made a lot of money backing the Major.

One game stands out in particular. I had barely walked through the door when Major White called me over. He was going to play Chicago Slim, 115–100, and he was $300 short. "Go ahead," I told him. "I'll back you." The score was 102–94 when Chicago Slim missed with eight balls on the table. The Major stepped up and cleared the table but left himself with a very tough break shot. If he goes for it and makes it, he scatters the balls all over the table and runs the game out. If he misses, Chicago Slim is home free. So he turned to me and said, "What do you say, kid?"

I said, "You've got the cue, Major. If you think you can make it, just go to racking them up." And he hit it, and it went in like a bell.

So I collected my money and split it with him. Because you'd do that. Here you had the greatest hustlers and angle men in the world, and yet you'd back another player even though you were only going to keep half the money if he won. You'd do it for him, and he'd do it for you because although every game was for blood, there was a great camaraderie about it. Or maybe it was only because you were there for action and you'd take whatever action you could get.

The pool playing turned out to be quite valuable to me in another way. You can walk into any pool hall and find some kid who can make great shots. What separates the shot-maker from the tournament player is generalship. The top players know when to play safe, when to play the more difficult shot in order to leave their opponent without a good shot, and when to go for broke. And, most of all, they know how to pick the table apart. Ralph Greenleaf, who liked me very much, impressed upon me very early that I was only thinking two or three balls ahead. "If there are eight balls on the table," he said, "you should know where you are going to be to make the fifth one before you start shooting."

This was the same time, remember, that I was keeping my little black book on Huggins. The two meshed together perfectly. As a manager, I always knew what I was going to do at least one pitch or one batter ahead, keeping all possible alternatives and variables in mind.

When I left the Yankees, I pretty much left my pool playing behind me. The sale to Cincinnati turned out to be a blessing because Sidney Weil, the owner of the club, turned out to be the nicest, kindest man I have ever known. He started by giving me a raise in salary to $7,500, and then arranged to pay off all my debts and take a specified amount out of my salary every month. In every way he was a second father to me.

Not that it did any good.

Given my personality, everything about the Cincinnati situation lent itself to irresponsibility. We were a very bad ball club with a succession of highly paid, over-aged hitters like Harry Heilmann, Edd Roush and Babe Herman. Of all the things we didn't have, the two things we didn't have the most of were pitchers and customers. (In my first year with the club, I did give our handful of fans something to root for by combining with our second basemen, Horace Ford and Tony Cuccinello, to set a record in double plays. We should have. With our pitching staff and heavy-legged outfielders, there were always men on base waiting to be doubled up.)

The manager was Dapper Dan Howley, whom we all loved because he was everything a manager shouldn't be. We'd lose eight straight, and after every game Howley would say, "Don't worry, boys, we'll get 'em tomorrow." Then we'd win one and he'd do everything except throw a party for us.

I'd come directly to the park after a night on the town, something I wouldn't have dreamed of doing in New York. And it was stupid. There were players like Paul Waner and Hack Wilson and my old teacher, Rabbit Maranville, who were known around the league for playing just as well, and sometimes better, when they were drunk. I never drank enough to get drunk, and I just couldn't play very well without sleep. (The only time I did was when I was with the Cardinals. I had gone four or five days without a base hit and was in such a deep state of depression that when we got to Chicago I spent the night wandering from one club to another, hardly knowing where I was at. I got to the park and just kind of floated through the game, feeling quiet and peaceful, went 4 for 4 and wasn't depressed any more.)

Sidney Weil was a remarkable man himself. He had become a millionaire as the owner of a Ford agency and a string of garages and, just as I joined the team, was going broke in the stock market crash. (The ball club was taken away from him a year after I departed. So Mr. Weil went to night school, studied how to become an insurance agent, and in no time at all was a millionaire again.)

With all his other troubles, Mr. Weil loved me. It didn't matter what I did, he could never get mad at me. He'd pay off a stack of debts for me, and then I'd go up to New York and hit Sulka's, or run up some bills in Chicago. Look, it's possible to spend money anywhere in the world if you put your mind to it, something I proved conclusively by running up huge debts in Cincinnati.

Mr. Weil did everything humanly possible to keep me out of debt but by the time I was traded to St. Louis three years later I owed more than ever. Still, you know, if there is one thing I firmly believe it is that everything happens for the best. Because I was always in trouble through those early years, I came to know Judge Landis, the commissioner of baseball, rather intimately, a pleasure denied to those players who met every roll call and paid all their bills.

Judge Landis would send you a telegram ordering you to appear in his Chicago office at a specific time, on a specific date, and it would always work out so that you could catch a plane or a train, grab a cab and just make it to his office on time, breathing heavily. He'd never tell you what he wanted you for either, so by the time you got there you were a nervous wreck.

The legend has been spread that the owners hired the Judge off the federal bench. Don't you believe it. They got him right out of Dickens. He'd be waiting for you in an old torn sweater, a pipe in his mouth, his mane of gray hair all awry and the back of his hands blotched with age. His desk, which was always piled high with stacks of paper and assorted junk, seemed to be in complete disorder, but the word had got around the dugouts that if you were ever foolish enough to lie to this man he would reach into the middle of that mess and pluck out the one document that would incriminate you.

Let me tell you something. If a ballplayer owes you any money, all you have to do is write a letter to the commissioner, and I guarantee that you'll get paid right now. Because if he can't pay it, the commissioner is going to order the club to pay it and take the money out of the player's next paycheck. Landis would send for me. "What's this?" he would say. "What's this? You're back again? You owe a bill here and there, don't you?" And then his finger would come shooting out and he'd say, "Mr. Smith in Cincinnati says you owe him five hundred dollars and Mr. Jones of the Jones Company in Chicago says you owe a bill there of six hundred dollars. That's right, isn't it?"

And you knew that somewhere in that pile of papers were copies of those two bills. "Now why haven't you paid these bills? Don't you know bills have got to be paid? You're short of money, aren't you? You'd be only too happy to pay these bills if you had the wherewithal, isn't that right?" He'd give me a stern lecture about living within my budget, and then he'd put his arm around me and say, "Now when you run short and need some money, what are you worried about? Come to me. I'm the place to come, that's what I'm here for. I'm your man."

The only thing about him was that he was an absolute fanatic when it came to gambling. As far as Judge Landis was concerned, it was a gambler who had undoubtedly set Sodom and Gomorrah on the road to ruin. Other than that, he was always on the side of the ballplayer; he had no use for the owners at all. "Don't worry about them," he would tell me. "They're not out to help you. You know where your friend is. Right here. *I'm* your man."

Whenever I visited him, and, as I say, I got to be practically a member of the official family, he would never fail to put his arm around me and walk me to the door. And the last words ringing in my ears as I was leaving were always "I'm your man."

I didn't always make it easy for him. During my first year at St. Louis, I found myself standing before the Judge because I had cheerfully postdated a check, and had then blown my paycheck somewhere else. The Judge, who was beginning to lose patience with me—possibly because I had been before him for doing exactly the same thing a dozen times before—ordered me to turn all my affairs over to the club and never write another check again.

The next time I got fined for a fight with an umpire, the club automatically made out the check and sent it in. Now one of the rules of baseball has always been that the player must pay a fine by personal check within five days of notification, because it comforts the commissioner's office to think it is the player and not the club who is paying it. (I have never been on a club that didn't let its players know they'd be reimbursed. I wouldn't faint from the shock if some clubs still do it today.)

We happened to be playing in New York a few days later, and—oh-oh—I get a call giving me ten minutes to report to Judge Landis, who happened to be a few blocks away at the Roosevelt Hotel. I ran right up there and I found him steaming. "You, of all people, should know the proper procedure for paying a fine. How dare you let the club send it in for you?"

But this time I jumped right back at him, because I had him good. "Because," I said, "*you* told me never to write another check."

The Judge just lay his head down in his arms, and when he looked up again he was a beaten man. "You dolt!" he cried. "I didn't mean *me*."

The best example of the Judge in action is the Babe Phelps case. Babe was one of the players I inherited when I was managing at Brooklyn. A catcher. He was called "Blimp" because of the truly remarkable shape he presented in silhouette, but don't let that fool you. He was some kind of hitter, with the smooth powerful swing you only seem to find in these big left-handers.

In 1940, MacPhail—always the innovator—had made us the first team to travel by commercial airline, a move which brought on an enormous amount of public debate. Babe Phelps, who was terrified of flying, didn't bother to debate anything. He absolutely refused to get on any plane, thereby earning himself the new name of "The Grounded Blimp."

Babe was the worst hypochondriac I had ever come across, anyway. He would come dragging into the clubhouse and tell us he hadn't slept a wink. Why not? Well, he had been up all night checking his heartbeat. It was Babe's theory that the body could continue to function if your heart missed one beat, or even two or three, but that if it missed four beats in a row you were dead. He had stayed up all night, you understand, to make sure that he was going to be alive in the morning.

The rest of the team traveled by air; Babe Phelps took a train and caught up with us.

The next spring, which was the year we won the pennant, we trained in Havana, Cuba. Babe traveled by train to Miami, took a cab to the dock to catch the boat and then apparently decided that he wasn't cut out to be an amphibious Blimp either. The excuse he gave us, when we finally were able to reach him at his home back in Odenton, Maryland, was that he had started out with a mild cold, which had got so bad by the time he reached Miami that he had decided to go home to recover. Larry MacPhail, somewhat alarmed at discovering that he had a player on his payroll who went north to recover from a cold, hired a specialist at the Johns Hopkins Hospital in Baltimore to examine him. The report came back that Phelps was "in great shape," which, considering Babe's shape, was . . .

Actually, he was in better shape than I was. We had bought another catcher, Mickey Owen, from St. Louis over the winter—which may have been what Phelps was really pouting about—and Mickey was holding out. That left me in Havana through spring training without a big-league catcher.

Phelps had recovered well enough to join us when we returned to the United States, and since the wartime regulations made it impossible for MacPhail to reserve airline space for us any more, we counted upon having the pleasure of Phelps's company on our trips. Except that when we counted heads at the railroad station on our first western trip, Phelps wasn't there. His roommate, Lew Riggs, a journeyman third baseman we had picked up that year, told me that Babe had come down through the lobby with him, got into a cab with him, and had then told him he didn't feel well or something and wasn't going to make the trip.

I called the Tower Hotel in Brooklyn and they told me that Mr. Phelps was in his room but wasn't taking any calls.

So I called Larry MacPhail and told him the story and off we went. The next thing I heard MacPhail had fined Phelps $1,000 and suspended him. Suspended him? He didn't have the idea at all. I didn't want him to take Phelps away from me, I wanted him to put Phelps on a train and get him out to me as fast as he could. Phelps announced he wasn't going to pay any fine and appealed to Landis. Landis, who loved nothing more than to overrule fines and suspensions, called a hearing for the day we arrived in Chicago.

All I could do as the hearing got underway was tell Landis what Riggs had told me, being careful to drop in the information that Babe had been bothered for some time by a heart condition.

So we go around a little and finally Landis turns to Phelps with a sympathetic smile: "Were you sick, Babe? Was your heart bothering you? Is that the reason you didn't make the trip? Did you feel you were having a slight heart attack? Was that it, that your heart was bothering you?"

And Babe Phelps says, "No."

Landis takes a look at him, sniffs a couple of times and starts again from the beginning. "Well, I was told, Babe . . . you heard your manager, Mr. Durocher, tell me that you had got in a cab with Lew Riggs and told him that you didn't feel well and couldn't make the trip. That you didn't feel well and went back to the hotel and got into bed because *you didn't feel well* and that's why nobody could get in touch with you."

Babe Phelps says, "That's not so. I didn't get into any cab with Lew Riggs."

The words were hardly out of his mouth before Landis' hand shot out for the phone and he was telling his secretary to get Mr. Riggs at Wrigley Field. He asked Riggs to tell him what had happened, got his answer and then he said, "Now you speak just as loudly as you can. Go ahead. Answer my question again." He holds the phone out so we can all hear while Lew Riggs repeated the story exactly as he had told it to me.

"Thank you, Mr. Riggs." Very quietly he put the phone down and all the time he's just looking at Phelps. "Well," he says. "Do you think Mr. Riggs is lying? Do you care to answer that? You don't have to if you don't want to, but I'd be interested in anything you have to say."

No, Phelps says. Riggs wasn't lying.

All right, then. Landis starts over again. Only this time, instead of putting it in question form, he's making flat statements. "Well, then, your heart was bothering you. . . . You didn't feel well and as far as you were concerned your health came first. . . . You decided it would be very dangerous to your future well-being to make this trip because of your heart condition."

Babe Phelps keeps saying no. Every time he'd say no, Landis would just look at him, look down and shake his head. And finally he's looking at me as if to say, "Well, what do I have to do with this fellow, hit him over the head with a mallet?" I swear that he went over it half a dozen times, trying to just get Babe to say that he wasn't feeling well. Babe wasn't admitting anything. Judge Landis had to let the fine and suspension stick, of course, and would you believe that Phelps was indignant? Indignant! He had been told that Landis was always for the player, and look what Landis had done to him. He was so mad that he quit the team and went back home to Maryland.

Half a dozen times I thought I had his promise to return to us on my word of honor that I'd get that fine rescinded before the year was over. And every time he'd change his mind again. He was getting $10,000 for the year, I'd point out, a pretty good salary. And since it had become obvious by that time that we had a hell of a shot at the pennant (why else do you think I was on my knees to him?) there could also be another $7,000. What was he doing in Odenton, Maryland, that could match that?

He was loading baggage, he said.

"Oh, how much can you make loading baggage?"

"Fifty bucks a week."

We finally traded him to Pittsburgh at the end of the year, just to get something for him. He played there for one year and then quit and went home to resume his fascinating career on the baggage platform.

But that was Judge Landis. The only way a player could lose with him was to be daft. Nobody has accused me of being daft, and with Landis and Weil both in there pitching for me, it didn't matter very much how much debt I got into.

When I left Mr. Weil, it broke my heart.

It was a Sunday morning, very early in the season, a day I never will forget. Cincinnati was in New York to play the Giants. I had just got back to the DeWitt Clinton Hotel from early mass when I got a call from the traveling secretary telling me that I was now the property of the St. Louis Cardinals, who were also in town playing the Brooklyn Dodgers. I said, "I'm not going to go. There's no way I will ever leave Mr. Weil."

He said, "What do you mean you're not going? You've been traded, you go. You belong to the Cardinals."

"Two things," I said. "One, I'm not going. Two, goodbye."

A few minutes later, Mr. Weil called me. By then I had been thinking not so much about Mr. Weil as about Leo. If Mr. Weil was known to be the nicest operator in the league, Branch Rickey, the general manager of the Cardinals, was even more widely known to be the worst. The cheapest, the shrewdest, and the most hardhearted. When Mr. Weil came up to the room, he explained to me that Mr. Rickey had offered a trade that he simply couldn't refuse—two young pitchers, including Paul Derringer, who was already one of the best pitchers in the league, plus a pretty good hitting infielder, Sparky Adams, to take my place. Just what Cincinnati needed, Weil felt, to become competitive.

Why Mr. Rickey, who was not in the habit of giving up young talent, was willing to be that generous was obvious. The Cardinals' shortstop, Charlie Gelbert, had shot himself in the leg over the winter while hunting, and for once Rickey's farm system had not been able to produce a replacement.

I'd play for less money, I pleaded. I'd mend my ways. I'd become a sterling citizen. Anything. "I don't want to leave you, Mr. Weil," I said, knowing that would get him. "I don't want to play for anybody except you."

"You at least owe Mr. Rickey the courtesy of going to visit him," Mr. Weil insisted. "And I will go with you."

Although I had never met Mr. Rickey in my life, I had heard all kinds of stories about his operation, more popularly known as the Chain Gang. "I know how I'll kill it," I told Mr. Weil, with an appropriate curl of the lip. "I'll tell the old skinflint he's got to give me a thousand-dollar raise." If I couldn't kill the deal, I was already thinking, I'd at least get something out of it for myself.

Mr. Rickey was at the Alamac Hotel. The first time I saw Branch Rickey, who was to become the great man in my life, he was propped up in bed, wearing a white hospital nightgown, and nursing a cold. He had a cigar stuck in his mouth, his glasses were perched on the edge of his nose and he was reading—so help me—the Bible.

I don't think Mr. Rickey ever forgot that first meeting either. I came bursting into the room in front of Mr. Weil, pulled up a chair, swung my feet up on his bed, leaned back comfortably and said, "How are you, Branch?"

Wow! Mr. Rickey raised up, bolt straight, in his bed. No ballplayer, as I well knew, had ever called him by his first name before. I could see that I had made a very promising beginning. "Branch," I said, "you might as well kill this deal right now because nothing can make me play for a cheapskate like you."

I wouldn't let him get a word in, either—another novel experience for him. I threw everything I'd ever heard about him at him. I told him his players were nothing but chattels to him, just replaceable parts on his assembly line. I told him I knew all about the way he swindled his players by out-talking them during salary negotiations. I dredged up every slander and rumor I had ever heard about him with a little free and fancy hemstitching of my own thrown in for good measure.

Mr. Rickey lay back and listened, letting me talk myself out. When he was sure I was through, he stuck a fresh cigar in his mouth and chewed on it thoughtfully, his eyes never leaving me. Now it was his turn. "You've said a lot of things about me since you sat down in that chair," he said. "You know something, son, I've heard a lot of things about you, too . . ." (oh, oh, that was a low blow). "You know," he said, "it has always been my opinion, as it seems to be yours, that where there is smoke there is generally a little bit of fire connected with it somewhere."

Now, I hope you realize—as I did not—that I was witnessing a typical Rickey performance. He had not only taken the offensive completely away from me, he had, in the same stroke, disarmed me by admitting that at least part of what I had said about him might be true.

He leaned toward me, and in that rich, rumbling voice that makes everything he says sound like a pronouncement from on high, he said, "But I'm not interested in that. Your reputation doesn't worry me one bit, son. I made this trade because I think the St. Louis ball club can win a lot of pennants with you at shortstop. This deal was made because in my opinion *you're* just what we need. *You* can do it for us, *you* can turn the trick for us, *you* can make us go, *you* can be the spark. With *you* on the team, we can win pennant after pennant after pennant."

Well, by now I've got my feet off the bed and I'm listening to this fine man with great interest. The more this man talks, the smarter and the nicer he becomes. In fact, I'm beginning to become just a little indignant about all the vicious slanders that certain people have been spreading about this brilliant baseball man, this keen judge of talent. This biblical scholar.

Before long, I was regarding Mr. Rickey with such affection that, although I was obviously being underpaid, I decided it would be in very poor taste to ask for anything more than the token $1,000 raise in salary. But somehow, you know, Mr. Rickey kept waving all talk of money aside, as if $1,000 was too insignificant to worry about with all that World Series money I was going to be collecting.

I know it doesn't sound possible that anyone could shower all that praise upon a man and then simply dismiss the question of extra money. And, of course, nobody *could* do it except Mr. Rickey. It's only three days after a session with Mr. Rickey that you suddenly snap out of the trance and say to yourself, "Hey, wait a minute. . . ."

When we left the room, Sidney Weil told me he'd give me the extra thousand himself if it would make me happier with the deal. To show what a great kid I was, I took it.

Once that was settled, I took a cab to Ebbets Field, dressed quickly and reported to the manager, Gabby Street, on the bench. Gabby sent me right out to shortstop. Frankie Frisch, who was playing second base, stared at me in amazement. "Where," he asked, "did you come from?"

"They just made a trade for me, buddy. Here I am."

And that's how I became a member of what was to become known as the Gas House Gang, the roughest, rowdiest, most colorful team of all time.

Branch Rickey had his own system for seeing that I remained solvent. At the end of the year, I would always owe the club something around $2,000 or $3,000. "Forget it, son," he'd say, "We'll call it a raise. But we'll leave the contract the same, and while we're at it we'll sign next year for the same salary." It amounted to an annual bonus for me, but since my base salary never did go up a dollar it wasn't exactly a bad deal for him, either.

THE GAS HOUSE GANG

IN ANY VOTING on the Greatest Teams of All Time I have seen, the 1927 Yankees have been ranked first and the 1934 Cardinals second. Which shows what the passage of time can do. In sheer talent, we weren't in the same class with a dozen teams I could name. We were a one-shot champion, and they were saying that we weren't even the best team in the league that year. To win the pennant, we'd had to win 20 of our last 25 games, and even then the Giants had to lose their final two games to a second-division team. I can tell you one thing, though. We may not have been the best, but there were 25 players on that team who thought we were, and that's half the battle.

The best thing we had going for us, as far as posterity is concerned, was our name. The Gas House Gang. It gave us an identity, it gave us a personality, and in both cases it was an accurate one. You say those words and you think of Dizzy Dean and Paul Dean and Pepper Martin and Joe Medwick and Frankie Frisch and Rip Collins and Bill DeLancey and, let us not forget the captain and shortstop, Leo Durocher.

I remember it so clearly that we came into the Polo Grounds to play a doubleheader late in the season. We were still 5½ games behind the Giants with 14 games to go, but we had been coming on strong, we had been unbeatable on the whole trip through the East, and the place was jam-packed. Ballplayers are a superstitious breed, nobody more than I, and while you are winning you'd murder anybody who tried to change your sweatshirt, let alone your uniform.

To complete the picture, we had played on a couple of wet fields during the trip and so our uniforms were not only dirty, they were caked with dry mud. Pepper Martin and Frankie Frisch were already being called our "diving seals." They would put on a double steal, and just as Martin—who had invented the head-first slide—would be diving into third base, Frisch—who had been the first to copy it—would be diving into second. DeLancey and Medwick would dive half the time, and so would Rothrock and Orsatti, our other two outfielders. By the time we got to New York the uniforms were so filthy that we could have thrown them in the corner and they'd have stood up by themselves. The bills of our caps were all bent and creased and twisted. We looked horrible, we knew it and we gloried in it.

We swept the doubeheader at the Polo Grounds to stay alive, and the next day I saw a cartoon in the *World-Telegram* by Willard Mullin. It showed two big gas tanks on the wrong side of the railroad track, and some ballplayers crossing over to the good part of town carrying clubs over their shoulders instead of bats. And the title read: "The Gas House Gang."

Whether it was Willard Mullin who coined the name for us with that cartoon I can't say for sure; all I know is that it was the first time I ever saw it. And that I just loved it.

I think people of a certain age remember the Gas House Gang so fondly because we typified what big-league baseball was in those days. It was a rough-and-tumble no-holds game played predominantly by farm boys. Generally unschooled, generally unspoiled, generally unsophisticated. Right off the farm or down from the hills. Today, the battle cry is "This is my office; this is where I work. I've got a private life and interests off the field." In the olden days, they had only one interest: baseball. We'd go into a small town to play an exhibition game and Dizzy Dean and Pepper Martin would station themselves at opposite corners of the main street.

"Howy'a Pepper Martin?" Dizzy Dean would holler.

"Howy'a Dizzy Dean?"

First thing you know they'd have hundreds of people gathered around, trying to decide whether those two nuts could really be Pepper Martin and Dizzy Dean.

"You pitching today, Diz?"

"Yeah," Diz would say. "I want all you people to come on out and watch me, hear?" And then Diz would ask Pepper if he was going to put on his pre-game pepper-game show.

"Sure am," Pepper would say. "I sure hope you folks can come out real early so you can watch."

They had themselves a great time, and they'd be packing the stands for the club. But mostly it was that they were full of themselves and their sense of who they were. They enjoyed being Pepper Martin and Dizzy Dean. The day wasn't long enough for them.

All over the National League, the real fans would be out early to see the Pepper Martin pepper show. The best way to describe it, I guess, would be to say that it was the baseball version of the Harlem Globetrotters warm-up routine.

They'd line up in foul territory, throw the ball to the guy with the bat, and then it would be back under their arm, through their legs, around the other guy's back; bounced off their arm, elbow and shoulder.

A constant succession of fakes, feints, misdirection and sleight of hand. Once every two or three minutes a roar would go up as someone actually threw the ball to the batter, who would wake up just in time to hit it back.

After it was over, Pepper would put on a personal exhibition, which consisted of keeping the ball in the air by bouncing it off the bat like one of those paddle-ball games—except that there was no elastic. To end it, he'd walk all the way across the field, keeping the ball in the air all the time, and tip his hat with one hand as he got to the dugout while the bat was kept moving with the other. He was just marvelous, that Pepper. He was a wonder.

And, do you know, I don't think it's the players who'd frown on that kind of thing these days so much as the owners. How would anybody know they were running a multimillion-dollar industry if the players were actually having fun out there?

The philosophy on the field was totally different than it is today. Baseball was a form of warfare played under a set of rules that were not necessarily drawn up by the league officials and certainly not by the Marquis of Queensberry. Today a pitcher gets fined if the umpire *thinks* he threw at a batter. In the olden days, the umpire didn't have to take any courses in mind reading. The pitcher *told* you he was going to throw at you. Pat Malone of the Cubs used to get insulted if a hitter like me just took a good swing at the ball. He'd come halfway down to the plate snarling, "You're swinging *pretty good* for a humpty-dumpty. I think I'd just better knock your cap off." The next pitch would come at my head and—boom—down I'd go. "Throw at me again, you dumb Irishman," I'd bray. "I got a better chance getting on base by getting hit than by hitting the ball."

Usually Pat would be only too happy to oblige.

In Cincinnati, I played with Edd Roush, a great hitter. Since Edd didn't have to get hit by a pitch to get on base, he took a very dim view of being flattened. The old Roush game was that if a pitcher knocked him down, he was going to take a piece out of somebody, somehow, somewhere, before he sat down on the bench again. I once saw him slice Charlie Grimm's leg completely down the back. Laid it open like a side of beef.

Later, when I was with the Cards, Hal Schumacher of the Giants threw two pitches in a row behind me. Well, that's considered very bad form, because the same reflexes that normally would get you out of the way will tend to drop you right into the path of the pitch. When I lifted myself up out of the dirt that second time, I was mad—though not so mad that I couldn't remember all those stimulating conversations I'd had with Edd Roush. I hit a little weak ground ball to the shortstop—par for me—and as I was crossing first base I kicked out with my spikes and tried to do to Zeke Bonura what Roush had done to Grimm. Instead, I barely caught his heel. That left Zeke mobile enough to wheel around and fire the ball at me. I turned around and—whoosh—the ball was whistling past my ear. Right behind the ball came Big Zeke himself, bearing down on me like a freight train. Boy, I took a lunge at him and held on for dear life so that all those calmer heads which are supposed to prevail could get a chance to do their job.

I had nothing against Zeke. Fine fellow. I had cut him and he was perfectly entitled to take whatever measure of reprisal seemed best to him. If I had met him outside the park that night, I'd have been happy to buy him a dinner. When the bell rang, everybody took their best hold, that's the way we played in those days. We fought and we yelled and we jockeyed. Everybody had a great time, and nobody ever squawked.

Dizzy Dean's special hatred was the batter who dug a hole for his back foot as he stepped into the box. Diz would just stand there nodding his head until he was finished and then he'd yell, "You all done? You comfortable? Well, send for the groundkeeper and get a shovel because that's where they're gonna bury you." And—boom—down he'd go.

I once saw Diz hit seven straight Giants in Miami early in the exhibition season, because the Giants had had the nerve to score seven runs off him in one inning. Diz was so mad he was stomping all over the place. "They're not gonna hit *the Master* that way." The last batter was Bill Terry, the manager. Terry got as far out of the box as it was legal to get, and kept looking down at our catcher, Bill DeLancey. "Come on," he said, "What's the matter with you guys? Are you guys crazy?"

"Because you're the manager you're no better than the rest of them," DeLancey told him. "Get up here, because you're going to get yours too, you know."

Diz got him twice. Hit him in the back and the ball bounced up and hit him again in the neck. When Cy Pfirman, the umpire, finally went out and told Frisch he was going to have to take Diz out, he was almost apologetic about it. "I got to do it, Frank," he said. "He's gonna kill somebody."

The Giants didn't beat him a game all that year. I always had a feeling they didn't really look forward to hitting against him. But today if you just yell "Put it in his ear," to loosen the batter up a little, off comes the umpire's mask and you're in the clubhouse.

In the Gas House Gang, we fought as much among ourselves as with the opposition. Joe Medwick once knocked our pitcher, Ed Heusser, cold in the middle of a game because Heusser told him he hadn't hustled after a fly ball. Laid him out right there in the dugout with half the crowd looking in. Another time, he belted Tex Carleton in the batting cage because Carleton, who was supposed to be our starting pitcher, wouldn't get out of there after the bell rang. Hit him a shot that blackened his eye and knocked him back against the cage. That Medwick was a mean sucker, he came to play.

So, in his own way, was Dizzy Dean. Diz was pitching one day in Pittsburgh, and they loaded the bases on him very early in the game. Somebody hit a high fly along the left line, I took out after it and ran and ran and just missed catching up to it. The ball hit fair, three runs scored, and when we got to the bench, Diz accused Medwick of loafing on the play. One word led to another, and Medwick said, "You do the

pitching, loudmouth, and I'll take care of the outfielding."
And Diz said, "I'll give you a punch in the mouth."

Diz had been down by the water fountain at the end of
the dugout, and as he started toward Medwick, his brother
Paul got up and came with him. In those days, you may
remember, the bats were laid out on the ground right in
front of the dugout. Medwick just reached over and picked
up a bat. "Keep coming, brothers Dean," he said. "Come on,
both of you. I'll separate you real good."

Everybody jumped between them, of course, and a couple
of innings later, Medwick hit a grand-slam home run right
out of Schenley Park. Through the trees and over everything.
A ton. Medwick came back to the bench, filled up his mouth
with water and just spat it all over Diz's shoes. "See if you
can hold that lead, gutless." And then we were separating
them again.

Just don't let an outsider step in, though, or there were
twenty-five guys on his back. We were playing an exhibition
game in Tampa, Florida, during spring training, and when
we came back to the Tampa Terrace Hotel, Irv Kupcinet,
the Chicago columnist, was there with some other writer.
We were all lined up at the desk trying to get our keys, and
Kupcinet was standing a few feet away, alongside a huge
potted palm. Either Kup or the other guy had just written a
magazine article about Diz, and there was something in there
Diz didn't like. Something he had said about his wife, Pat.
The first thing I knew, Diz took out after them, and Kup came
right back at Diz. Now, Kup is a big man. He had been an
NFL football player and he was still in good shape. And
while Diz and Kup were hollering at each other Medwick
walked over and—boom—hit him a shot out of nowhere and
knocked him right into the flowerpot.

Boy, I'll tell you, that Medwick never lost a debate in his
life, mostly because he didn't bother. He was a one-man
rampage.

Kup had a radio show and who do you think his lucky guest was that evening? That's right, Leo Durocher. Kup's eye was so far out by then that you could have hung your hat on it. He took it good-naturedly, though. "I'll say one thing about Medwick," he said. "He's got a pretty good punch."

Frankie Frisch, our manager, was rough and tough, and the team took its personality from him. He and I fought and we cursed each other out, but it was only because he wanted to make me a better hitter. He was always on me to hit the ball to right. "Hit the ball to right, you humpty-dumpty!" And he was right, so right. Miller Huggins had told me, "The way you play shortstop you don't have to hit over .250, but be a *tough* .250 hitter." In other words, get the hits when they mean something, move the man around, knock in some runs. And I became that at the end of my career. A .260 hitter who would knock in his 70 runs. But there were things I couldn't do that a .250 hitter should learn to do. "Wait on the inside pitch, wait on it, and you'll hit it to right," Frankie would scream at me. "It's easier to hit the inside pitch to right than the outside pitch."

If I had paid more attention to Frisch I would have been a better player.

The other thing about Frisch was that he had been brought up under John McGraw, and he wasn't interested in having you come in and tell him where it hurt. The only injury I had in all the years I played ball came when I reached over casually for the last ball being hit during infield practice. The ball hit me right in the web of the hand between the thumb and the index finger and split it wide open. They took me to the hospital, and put fourteen stitches in. I came back to the ball park, slapped a piece of gauze around it, taped it real tight, and I was playing again in three days. Pepper Martin played with a broken finger and nobody knew it until he threw the ball across the diamond and yards of bandage came following behind it. When the writers asked him about it after the game, Pepper said, "It's only a small bone."

Frisch? Pepper could have walked past him in the locker room with a sign reading "Broken Finger" hung on it, and Frankie wouldn't have noticed.

Pepper was the only player I ever worried about on the field. Listen to what I'm saying now: Pepper played without a cup or supporter. He didn't wear any underwear either, and he didn't put on the sanitary socks. Just the uniform stockings that loop under the arches, his pants, his shirt, his shoes and his cap.

This was the man they called "The Wild Horse of the Osage," one of the greatest nicknames that has ever been put on a player. He ran like a wild man, he belly-flopped into the bases and he played third base, which wasn't his natural position, with his body. Chick Hafey, who kept all the third-basemen in the league black and blue, once hit a ball off Pepper's leg that left it numb for a full week. Pepper kept his mouth shut and stayed in the lineup.

I shuddered every time Hafey came to bat. Jeez, if one of those scorchers had ever hit Pepper there, he would have become instantly eligible for a job in the best-stocked harem in Arabia. Half the time I'd be playing shortstop and I'd look up and Pepper would have his glove under his arm and he'd be getting a chew of tobacco. Or, since his shoe was always torn, he'd be shaking the dirt out from under the sole. I'd holler, "Pepper," and he'd put the glove on just as the pitcher was ready to pitch the ball. But God apparently watches over drunks and third-basemen who play without any protective gear. Pepper must have been hit in every other portion of his body at one time or another except the crucial one.

Not that Pepper Martin couldn't make the other side shudder too. There was a series in Boston where Pepper's back was so sore that he could hardly bend. Naturally, the Braves began to bunt on him. Naturally, Pepper felt they were trying to show him up. He went to the mound, called Rip Collins over and told him, "The next guy that bunts on me, forget the bag and back up the runner. I'm going to bounce one off his noggin."

He missed the first one, got the second one, and that ended the Braves' bunting for the day.

Frisch screamed and he hollered and he used all the four-letter words, but he took command of the ball club and the players respected him. It always happens, though, that certain guys can get away with things that others can't. On the Gas House Gang, it was Bill DeLancey, our young catcher. DeLancey was a big, handsome kid from North Carolina. He was just a rookie in 1934 but he could say anything to Frisch, and Frisch would beam all over him. Frisch had a habit, when we were playing badly in the field, of coming back to the dugout and groaning, "I can't look at this any more. I'm going to throw up, I'm going to puke. I got to go get a couple of aspirin, you guys make me sick."

DeLancey would say, "Get in the clubhouse, you dumb Dutchman, we can do better without you."

And always, it seemed, that as soon as Frisch disappeared we'd score some runs. Frisch would come back and DeLancey would say, "Who *sent* for you? Who *needs* you?"

Frisch wouldn't say a word. DeLancey was the player, above all others, that Frisch loved.

And he played only one more year. What happened was that he caught cold or something on a hunting trip, and it developed into an eye infection. The club brought him into St. Louis from Springfield, Missouri, in an ambulance, and while Dr. Heyland, the club physician, was clearing up the eye infection he discovered that Bill had a very bad case of TB. Five years later, he tried to make a comeback but it was just too much for him. Poor Bill, he had all the tools to have developed into one of the great catchers of all time, and he died on his thirty-fifth birthday.

Frisch was one of the rare college graduates in baseball in

that era. He was the "Fordham Flash," he had majored in baseball, football and soccer. Most of the players, as I have said, were farm boys and their roots remained in their home soil. Half the energy over the last month of the season would be spent in planning the hunting and fishing trips. They never saw themselves as anything except visitors in the big cities.

Pepper Martin and Dizzy Dean, who roomed together on the road, got us put out of three different hotels in Philadelphia alone. I think it was the Bellevue-Stratford which had the dining room for women only, where the Main Line dowagers would hold their society luncheons. They'd all arrive in chauffeur-driven cars, the cars would be lined up along the curb—nothing but Rolls-Royces, Lincolns and Cadillacs—and you just knew something was going to have to be done about that sooner or later. What Pepper did first was to go to a trick store for a handful of smoke bombs. What he did next was to go down to Wanamaker's with a couple of the others to buy firemen's uniforms. The lunch hour ended, the dowagers filed out into their cars and from there it was nothing except explosions and smoke and jumping hoods. The women went running back into the dining room in panic to mix with the women who were trying to leave and a whole new group that was trying to get in. In the middle of all this pandemonium, Pepper and his crew arrived in their firemen's uniforms to enforce the fire regulations. Well, they had women moving from one table to the other, they had three women standing up here and five others sitting down there. They had the manager and the captains running all over the place.

It wasn't until a year later, however, that the management asked us to leave. That was Pepper and Diz too. Pepper, who was a mechanical wizard, spent half his time on the road shopping for new gadgets. A micrometer in the window of a pawnshop had caught his eye, and once he was inside his eyes lit upon a pile of overalls. Out of the pawnshop came four ballplayers wearing overalls. After that it was only a matter of stopping off at a hardware store to pick up the basic carpentry tools, including a huge curved saw.

As soon as they walked into the lobby, they were spotted by Rip Collins, who marched them down to the kitchen and announced that they were going to redecorate the whole place. The chef found that kind of bewildering because the kitchen had just been redone in copper. "That's right," Pepper said, rapping his hammer up and down the shiny new copper walls. "They've found out that when the steam from your cooking hits the copper it gives off poisonous fumes. We're here to redo it in aluminium."

The next thing they knew, the chef was chasing them up the stairs with a meat cleaver trying to redecorate their heads.

Directly across from the stairs was the biggest banquet room in the place. A boy scout meeting was in progress, with a mixture of adults and kids. Pepper and his crew cleared everybody away from the very first table they came to— "Excuse me. . . Excuse me—" threw the chairs back and stood the table on its end. While the head speaker was being introduced, Pepper was hunched down taking sightings along the table with his micrometer, Dean was slapping a level here and there, and the others were arguing noisily and pointing up to the ceiling and down at the floor.

Finally, a couple of men came down from the head table to find out what was going on. "We're redecorating," Rip Collins told them. "Gonna do over the whole place. Go right ahead with your speech, though. You're not bothering us."

Through it all, the main speaker was just standing there. Speechless, you might say. "Well," Diz said, "If you're not going to make a speech, I will. Sit down, I'll take care of this."

Immediately he was recognized. "It's Dizzy Dean . . . it's Dizzy Dean." Everybody began to cheer and applaud, and Diz made a speech that just rocked the place. The kids were in heaven, the adults couldn't have been more pleased, and we were put out of the hotel.

We were put out of hotels in other cities, too. The Governor Clinton for one. They had a big wind fan there that cooled off the whole lobby, and Pepper strolled over in front of it with some sneezing powder folded into the crease of his newspaper. He opened the paper, and well . . . the whole lobby was cleaned out in two minutes. Bar and all.

Their favorite trick, to show how juvenile they could get, was to drop a bag of water out of the hotel window within a reasonable distance of some innocent passerby. To show how juvenile I can get, I was usually right there with them. We used two bags really, one inside the other. We just barely missed a Philadelphia policeman once; that's what got us thrown out of the Benjamin Franklin Hotel. We came even closer to Frisch at the Kenmore Hotel in Boston. Frisch was standing in front of the hotel, talking to one of our coaches, Mike Gonzales, and the bag hit the sidewalk with a crash and went splattering all over them. Jeez, if it had hit Frank it would have driven him right into the ground. Diz and I ran bravely out of the room, and by the time Frank got there, he found Pepper all alone except for an open window and a windowsill that was soaking wet. Didn't faze Pepper a bit. "Who, me?" he said. "I wouldn't do that to you, Frankie."

When I say that Pepper was a mechanical wizard, I mean it. Among other things, he built himself a midget racing car and raced it every night out at Walsh Stadium. Actually, it was his partner, a former Indianapolis winner, who raced it. What Pepper did was to push it. I was out there many a night to watch him. He had built it with a hyped-up outboard motor, which meant that he had to get behind it with the driver inside and work up a pretty good head of speed before it would start. We were in a pennant fight, and Pepper would show up fifteen minutes before game time, dead tired. He never took batting practice, never showed up for meetings. Frank was raising hell about it. Every time he and Pepper's wife, Ruby, got together they'd be hatching plots to push the damn car into the river.

Now we're in the last week of the season, and Pepper, who had been ordered by Rickey to give up his racing career, doesn't show up. Everybody's calling all around town. Where's Pepper? Have you seen Pepper? About ten minutes before game time, here comes Pepper into the clubhouse covered with dust from head to foot. I never saw anybody look so dirty; he looked as if he had just climbed out of a coal bin. Frank hit the roof. "Where the hell have you been?"

Well, you can't say that Pepper didn't have a good excuse. A neighbor of his who also had a racing car had bet Pepper he could beat him in a race through the streets of their village. The honor of the Gas House Gang had been at stake. "And," Pepper said with his big grin, "I won, Frankie-boy."

"Oh," Frisch said, weakening a little. "How much did you beat the bum for?"

"A gallon of ice cream."

I thought Frisch was going to kill him.

There was nothing Pepper wouldn't do. He once told the director of the St. Louis Zoo that he was going to go on a hunting trip at the end of the season and he'd catch a rattle-snake for him. The director thought he was kidding. He didn't know Pepper the way we did. Pepper got himself a forked stick and some rope and went out looking for a rattler. When he found one, he trapped it in his stick, hopped on its back—or whatever you do with a rattler—and grabbed it by the throat. Or wherever you grab it. While Pepper was trying to get the rope around it, the snake kept shaking loose and Ruby, who was along on the trip with him, danced around screaming for him to let go. Finally, she placed her rifle over his shoulder and blew the snake's head off—blowing Pepper back about twelve feet in the process.

Listen, when he was forty-four years old he visited us in spring training and demonstrated how he could leap on top of the dugout roof from a standing start. Rickey was forming the Brooklyn Dodgers professional football team in the old All-American Conference that year and he promptly hired Pepper to be his place-kicking specialist. It didn't matter that Pepper had never place-kicked in his life. As far as Mr. Rickey was concerned Pepper could do anything he put his mind to. Besides, Mr. Rickey was always a great believer in technique. He hired all kinds of experts to instruct Pepper on the proper form and knee action, probably the aerodynamics of a spheroid too, for all I know. Before long, Pepper was booting the ball through consistently from 30 and 40 yards out.

"You see how you've profited from the instruction, Johnny," Rickey beamed. "Which of the advice did you find to be most valuable?"

"Well," Pepper said, "I listened to them all and tried everything they said, and then I figured it out that what you were supposed to do was give the ball a good kick."

He'd probably have led the league in scoring too, if he hadn't ripped a muscle in his kicking leg just before the season started.

If Martin was the spirit of the Gas House Gang, Dizzy Dean was what Babe Ruth had been to the Yankees, our Big Man and our good-luck charm. The guy who would tell you what he was going to do when all the marbles were on the line and then go out and do it.

You know, Diz was just a big rawboned twenty-two-year-old kid out of the Ozarks when I joined the Cardinals. He was having his first twenty-game season, the writers were just starting to come around, and Diz loved the attention so much that he'd give them all a different story. I mean from the ground up. Different age, different birthplace. Even a different name. One writer would come in and Diz would tell him his name was Jerome Herman Dean and he was born in Arkansas. The next day, he'd tell another writer that he was really Jay Hanna Dean from Tennessee and had adopted the other name when he signed his first baseball contract in memory of a cousin who had drowned in a swimming hole. I'd sit there and listen to him, and I'd say, "Diz, why do you tell these people you were born in all these different places? You're gonna run out of states south of the Mason-Dixon line pretty soon." He'd say, "They got to write a story, partner. I'm big news now. If I gave this one the same story, what's there left for him to write? That ain't news."

The season that was to make the Gas House Gang famous began with the Great Dean Holdout. Let me see if I can put this so it will be believable. Diz had already signed his contract for something like $7,500, even though he had won twenty games the year before. But he wasn't holding out for himself. His brother, Paul, who had never pitched a big-league game in his life, was coming up that year, and when Diz got to camp and learned that Paul had signed for $3,000 he told Rickey, "You cheated my brother," and refused to put his uniform on.

All the while that Diz was holding out to get Paul more money, Paul, who wanted nothing more than a chance to pitch, was in uniform working out.

It finally got settled with Paul maybe getting another $500, although there were different stories about that, too. The other story being that he didn't. Still, it could have been a very profitable holdout for Diz if he had just listened to me. All the time he had been holding out he had been playing golf against a fellow named Mort Bright, who owned the inn where we were staying. Diz is one of those fellows who will play you any game for any amount of money, and beat you. The higher the stakes go, the surer you can be that he's going to win. By the time he put the uniform on, he had beaten Mort Bright for $16,000 or $17,000. Twice his salary. And I told Diz then not to play the guy any more. "Because, boy," I said. "You've got the uniform on now and that putter won't be the same in your hand."

"I'll still beat him," Diz said.

Mort Bright followed us north. Every morning, wherever we were playing, they'd be out at the local links. Bright followed us all the way to St. Louis, and got all his money back.

That's how Diz's greatest season started, though. Holding out for his brother and playing golf. The greatest argument against spring training ever made.

The day he finally put on his uniform, a group of newspapermen took him into the lower bleacher stands at Daytona Beach to interview him. Some of us were holding a pepper game right in front of them, with our backs to the bleachers, and we're all on the ear because everybody on the team got a kick out of Diz.

"Don't worry about me," Dean told them. "My arm is made of rubber. I'll be ready to pitch in two days." (That's what Diz always said: "My arm is made of rubber. I'll be ready in two days.")

"What about your brother Paul?"

"Don't worry about Paul. He'll do all right."

"Well, he never pitched in the major leagues."

"Yeah, but he's a fine pitcher. He's gonna do real good."

"How many games do you think you and your brother will win, Diz?"

And Diz said, "Forty-five."

We could hear the sportswriters snicker, which was all right because we were snickering too. "Forty-five, huh? That's pretty good, Diz. How many you going to win, Diz?"

"Whatever Paul don't win."

So I started to laugh. I looked at Frisch and said, "Well, let's go fishing for a month and a half. We've got forty-five won. We don't have a worry in the world."

Frank looked at me sourly. "Let's win them first. Then we'll talk about it."

And Diz hollered down: "Forty-five, Frankie, it's a cinch."

Some joke. He underestimated himself. Look it up in the records and you will see that Diz only won 30, and Paul won 19. And then they won two apiece in the World Series.

Five days after we won that doubleheader in the Polo Grounds we and our dirty uniforms were still in New York to play a doubleheader against Brooklyn. Dizzy pitched a three-hit shutout to win the first game, and Paul pitched a no-hitter to win the second. Those were the games that got us within striking distance and left no doubt in any of our minds that we were going to win. "The only thing that makes me mad," Diz said afterwards, "is I didn't know I hadn't given them any hits in the first seven innings. I should have knowed that. Then I'd have really breezed 'em in there and we'd both have had a no-hitter."

With the season coming to a close we were playing a three-game series against Pittsburgh and a three-game series against Cincinnati, and we were still two games behind the Giants. The Giants were going to close against Casey Stengel's Dodgers, and that was the year Bill Terry, the Giants' manager, had asked the famous question: "Is Brooklyn still in the league?" Diz had been pitching down the stretch with only two days' rest, and after Paul had lost the first one (the Giants had also lost that day), Frisch called a meeting to discuss the pitching rotation for the final five. I can see Diz like we were in the clubhouse right now: "I'll pitch today, and if I get in trouble Paul will relieve me. And he'll pitch tomorrow, and if he gets in trouble I'll relieve him. And I'll pitch the next day and Paul will pitch the day after that and I'll pitch the last one. Don't worry, we'll win five straight."

For once Diz was wrong. They only pitched in four of them.

You talk about fellows like Dean and Ruth, and people always say, "How did the other pitchers take that? Didn't they resent it?" How did the other players act when a Dizzy Dean or a Babe Ruth got up and bragged about what they were going to do? In the first place, that's not bragging in my book. They always called Diz a great popoff. To me a popoff is someone who brags about what he is going to do and then can't make good on his brag. Or who does his popping off after he's already done it. Diz would tell you what he was going to do before the game. After it was over it was never "Didn't I tell you?" or "I'm the Great Dean." He'd be around patting everybody on the back and saying, "That's the way to hit, Joe," and "That's the way to get me the runs, Pepper."

So in answer to the question of how the other players felt about it, we loved it. These were the guys who were putting money into our pockets. These were our bellwethers. We'd heard them make good on their boasts so often that we'd sit there and think, *Boy, this is great. The Big Man is really ready.*

With three games to go, Diz shut the Reds out to put us in a flatfooted tie with the Giants. The next day Paul Dean beat them 5–1, while Van Mungo, whose name is going to come up again, beat the Giants. We were a game ahead with one game to play. If we lost and the Giants won, baseball would have its first playoff. Because of the difference in time, we knew the Giants had lost again before our game started. Not that it mattered. With his chance to tie down the pennant and become a 30-game winner, there was no chance whatsoever that Dizzy Dean was going to lose. He pitched another shutout.

The World Series opened in Detroit and Diz was down to pitch the opening game with his usual two days' rest. We walked into the ball park on the day we arrived in town to look the place over, and the Tigers were out on the field taking batting practice. "Get the bats," Diz said. And then he walked down to the field in his regular street clothes, picked out one of the bats and jumped into the cage in front of Hank Greenberg, the big gun for the Tigers. "I'll show you how to hit the ball, Mo," he said.

The "Mo" was just what you think it is, the casual anti-Semitism of the locker room. That was part of the era of the farm boy too. What did it mean? Well, it meant what it meant. Depending on who said it and how you chose to take it. I was at a banquet with Joe DiMaggio the year he came back from a bad ankle injury and limped up to the plate at Fenway Park to bury the Red Sox. I was telling Joe I didn't think the Yankees could possibly have won the pennant without him. "No," DiMaggio said. "The *Little* Dago is the only player the Yankees can't afford to lose. He's the one who holds the team together."

The Little Dago was Phil Rizzuto. The Big Dago was DiMaggio himself. That's what they were called in their own locker room, and you can see that they took it as a compliment. For as long as I have been in baseball every Italian has been called "Dago," and every Jew has been called "Hebe." It's like anything else. Given a certain inflection, it can be a sign of affection. Given another inflection, it can be something else again.

There was never anything vicious about Diz, though. Greenberg just laughed at him. Diz hit a couple of pretty good drives, and then Greenberg stepped in and hit one a ton and a half. "That's the way to hit the ball, Mo," Dean said.

Outrageous but never vicious.

The final game is where the action was. Before we get there, I have to tell you that after we had taken a 2–1 lead in games (Diz had won game #1 and Paul had won game #3) Frisch decided that he could afford to give Diz another day of rest. The result was that we got slaughtered 10–4, and Diz almost got killed when he put himself into the game as a pinch runner. It happened in the fourth inning while we were still in the ball game. Spud Davis, a big, slow-footed catcher, came up to pinch-hit for the pitcher and lined a single to right. One run scored, and I went racing around to third with the tying run. When I looked around, Diz, who fancied himself a great base runner, was pulling off his jacket and dashing onto the field to run for Davis. I assume that he put himself in because he had been doing it all year. The first time it happened, Frisch had looked over to me and asked, "Who told him to run?" That was because I was his captain and, since he was a playing manager, he would leave a lot of these routine decisions to me. I thought Frisch had sent him in but, as I told him, "What difference does it make, Frank?"

Let me ask you something. How many times have you seen a base runner hit by the relay from second base? I played shortstop for years, and whenever a man was coming in high on me I always aimed the ball right between his eyes. Never hit a man in my life because the reflex action is to duck.

Pepper Martin hit a moderate hopper toward second base, and the way Pepper could run there was no chance at all of doubling him at first. I look toward second and see that Billy Rogell, the Detroit shortstop, is throwing the ball anyway. Instead of ducking, Diz jumps straight up and the ball hits him flush on the forehead.

They carried him off the field with his head out to here, and the first thing he said when he came to in the clubhouse was, "They didn't get Pepper, did they?"

Get him? Pepper had been across the bag when Rogell threw.

Diz pitched the next day anyway and although he pitched well enough, he wasn't the same Dizzy Dean. We lost, 3–1. And that sent us back to Detroit needing to sweep the final two games.

Paul won the first one. The whole World Series was coming down to the final game.

The question was whether Diz could come back on one day's rest, plus whatever ill effects there might still be from the beaning, or whether to pitch Wild Bill Hallahan, who had pitched a great eight innings in the second game, which

we had lost 3–2 in twelve innings. Hallahan was supposed
to be a great World Series pitcher because he had beaten
the Philadelphia A's twice in 1931, and the consensus of
opinion in the newspapers was that it was going to be him.
The way we had done it all year long was that Frank would
dictate the starting lineup to me and, depending on how he
felt, either he or I would go out and hand the card to the
umpires. Frank ran down the eight regular positions, and
when he got to the pitcher's spot he said, "Let's have a
meeting."

The first thing he did was to look at Diz. "How do you
feel?"

Diz was indignant. "You wouldn't think of pitching anybody else with the greatest pitcher in the world sitting
here?"

Great. As far as I'm concerned, that's all I have to hear.

Frank gives him a sour look and snaps, "Pay attention.
We'll go over the hitters."

We had already gone over the Detroit hitters about three
times that week, and Diz is lounging against his locker looking bored and half asleep and saying, "Yeah . . . yeah . . .
sure. . . ." Frank gets to the #3 hitter, Mickey Cochrane, their
playing manager. He's telling Diz that you have to get the
ball inside to him because Cochrane loves to line the outside
pitch to left, but before he can finish Diz stands up and
throws his scorecard down on the floor. "What the hell you
going over the hitters for? They're not going to get any runs
off of me."

With that, Diz reaches into the trunk where the Mudcat
Band kept their instruments and begins to hand them
around. In a couple of seconds, Pepper is strumming away
at his guitar and singing, "She'll Be Coming 'Round the
Mountain," at the top of his voice, the others are joining in,
and I never heard so many four-letter words in my life as
came streaming out of Frisch's mouth. Frisch looks at Diz,

who is doubled over with laughter, and yells, "Hallahan is the pitcher!"

I don't want Hallahan. I want Dean. I was still $6,000 in debt, which is just about what the winner's share is going to come to. The loser's share, I'm not interested in. I follow Frisch back to his locker, but I can't do a thing with him. "Hallahan's the pitcher," he keeps saying. "Write his name in. Hallahan."

The lineup card stays right in my pocket. Hallahan, hell! Instead, I go running over to Dean's locker and I say, "Diz, I don't care what you do, but you got to go over and apologize to this man. He is not going to let you pitch."

Diz can't believe it. "He wouldn't dare pitch anybody else."

"Diz, he's already told me he isn't going to let you pitch. You know he wants the Old Master, and I know he wants the Old Master. All you got to do is go over and apologize. Give him a left-handed apology. Anything at all, and I'm sure he'll let you pitch."

Frank was seated on one of those little round stools in front of his locker and he was bent over tying his shoes. He had already developed a little bald spot on the back of his head, and Diz walked over and said, "Frankie-boy . . ."

Frank looked up, real mad. Like he still wanted to throttle him. "Yeahhhh?"

And Diz said, "Let me tell you something, Frank . . ." and he reached over and patted him on the bald spot. "If you listen to me, Frank," he said, "I'll make you the greatest manager in the game."

That was his apology.

Well, Frank blew his top and I was ready to blow my top, too. I pulled Dean away from there and I said, "You dirty . . ." and added whatever words Frankie had missed.

Diz just grinned. "He'll let me pitch. He wants to win, don't he?"

When we were ready to go out, I said to Frank, "He's going to pitch, isn't he?"

Frank said, "That dirty sonafa—"

I said, "He'll be great, Frank. Isn't he great? He's ready today, you can see how ready he is, can't you, Frank?" And when Frank didn't say anything, I whipped the card out, wrote J. Dean in the pitcher's spot and shoved it back in my pocket.

After batting practice, I run back into the trainer's room where Diz is getting his arm rubbed. I don't know what I'm doing there. What am I going to do, tell him how to pitch? So I give him a pep talk. Knute Rockne at the top of his game never worked any harder. "No fooling around out there today, Diz. The loser's share is no good to me." The Great Dean. The Old Master. Bear down. "Pitch like I know you can pitch, and after today when they talk about the great pitchers they'll have to start with the name of Dizzy Dean."

Diz was paying no atttention at all to me, of course, but when he walked out to the field to warm up I was still at his elbow yacking away. We had to come out through the Detroit dugout, though, and all of a sudden I'm talking to myself. I look back, and he's standing behind the Detroit pitcher, Eldon Auker, watching him warm up. Auker was an underhanded pitcher. Not sidearm, but all the way under like a softball pitcher. He had already beaten us a game, the game where Diz got hit on the head, but Diz is standing there with his arms behind his back as if he's scouting him. He hollers down to Cochrane, "Are you going to pitch *this* guy today? You must have given up." Then he breaks out laughing, the most insulting laugh I've ever heard in my life. "Is that the best he's got? He's nothing. Nothing. My slow stuff is better than that."

Auker turns around and hollers, "Get out of here, you blowhard! You loudmouthed—" Auker is ready to pop him, he's so mad, and Cochrane is screaming at me, "Get him out of there!" He's ready to come charging up and take a whack at him himself.

I grabbed Diz by the elbow. "Come on, you donkey." The last thing I want right now is to have Diz bruise his right hand in any scuffle. Tomorrow you can take on Joe Louis, Dean.

Diz warmed up and didn't throw a fast ball until the last minute. Five or six fast balls, throws his glove down and comes walking in. Nothing worried this man. The more important the game, the more fun he had.

And luck? I've always said about Dizzy Dean that if the roof fell in and Diz was sitting in the middle of the room, everybody else would be buried in the debris and a gumdrop would drop into his mouth. In the third inning, I led off with a little pop fly to the infield. Diz came up and hit a high foul behind the plate which just barely dropped into the front row of boxes. Easily playable, should have been an out, except that Mickey Cochrane, a Hall of Fame catcher, the catcher picked on everybody's all-time All-Star team, didn't bother to go after it. The one time in his life probably that he so completely misjudged that kind of a foul ball. On the next pitch, Diz hits a little Texas Leaguer over third base. Goose Goslin, the Detroit left fielder, started in slow, because he never figured on a pitcher running, but Diz was a real good base runner and, of course, he was crazy, he'd take all kinds of chances. Diz rounded first in high gear and everybody in the ball park could hear Buzzy Wares, our first-base coach, yell, "Whoa! Whoa!" Goslin, who had a great arm, fired to Gehringer at second, and Gehringer had the ball waiting for him two feet away. There was no way for Diz to get around him, and Gehringer, a Hall of Fame second-baseman, hadn't missed a tag or said a word in fifteen years.

As Diz would say, he "slud" into second, there was a big cloud of dust, and I don't know how, why or whether Gehringer missed him, but the umpire is signaling that he's safe.

Pepper Martin is the next hitter. He tries to get away from a high inside pitch, the ball hits his bat and trickles down between first base and the pitcher. Greenberg gets the ball and starts to throw to Auker, who is racing over to cover, then decides to take it himself and then doesn't know what he wants to do. The next thing you know Pepper's on first and Dean is standing on third, laughing his head off. "Hey, Mo," he hollered. "Come on in the clubhouse after the game and get your meal money, you're the best player we got."

Now, Pepper Martin had picked up a lot of expressions from Branch Rickey. Pepper used to listen to Rickey, write down a word and use it at every opportunity. You haven't lived unless you've been to a banquet and heard Pepper Martin answer the inevitable question about how he knew when to steal a base. "I believe in intuition," Pepper would say. "As Mr. Rickey says, 'Intuition is the subconscious acting in a time of duress.'" His favorite Rickey word, though, was "initiative." Pepper would drive Frisch crazy by getting up in meetings and saying, "Frankie-boy, if you'll let me run on my own initiative I'll steal a base every time."

"You'll run when I tell you," Frank would yell.

"Frankie-boy, a good manager cultivates initiative."

"When I tell you, and not before!" Frank would scream.

Well, Rothrock is at bat, and Frisch is coming up next. As Frank leans over to pick out his bat, Pepper steals second. First pitch. Clean as a whistle. Frank looks up, and he still doesn't know what happened. Mike Gonzales, the third-base coach, has his hands spread wide as if to say, "I didn't give him any sign." Martin is grinning in from second base as if to say, "See, Frankie-boy, if you'd let me run on my own initiative I could do this every time."

The count goes to two balls and no strikes on Rothrock, and they decide to walk him to get to Frisch. Frank is coming to the end of his career, and when Auker gets two quick strikes on him he's up there swinging like a woman with four bales of laundry in her arms. Just guarding the plate.

But he keeps fouling off pitches, and he finally rips one down the right-field line, just fair, and scores all three runs. That's the end of Eldon Auker. Schoolboy Rowe gets Medwick for the second out, but Rip Collins singles. DeLancey doubles, scoring Collins. Orsatti walks. That brings me up for the second time in the inning with runners on first and second and I hit a ball to right on which DeLancey has to hold up at third.

Get the picture? The bases are loaded, and here comes Dizzy Dean again. This time, he tops a ball down third, and they can't make a play on it. Two hits in one inning. He's tied a World Series batting record. The sixth run of the inning has scored and the bases are still loaded. Pepper Martin walks and that makes the score 7–0. Thirteen men come to bat before Tommy Bridges comes in and gets Rothrock out.

Now, it was a cool day. But when we come in again, Dizzy won't sit down or put on a jacket. He's having too much fun walking up and down the dugout kidding with everybody. This is his day and he knows it and he's going to enjoy it. Frank is telling him that it's only the fourth inning. Sit down. Keep your arm warm. "It's all over," Diz says. "I told you at the meeting, one was all I needed. They're not going to get any." And he was right. One was all he needed, and Diz had scored it himself.

Now comes the fifth inning and Hank Greenberg is leading off. Our book on Greenberg was that he could really powder a high outside pitch but that he couldn't handle a good fast ball high and tight. For once, the book had been right. Diz was pitching him three-quarters sidearm so that his fast ball would run in on him, and he was handling him with such ease that day that he was actually laughing at him.

DeLancey goes down and gives the signs, and Dean is shaking everything off. Now, you caught Diz like a high school catcher: one finger for a fast ball, two for a curve, three for a change-of-pace curve. DeLancey puts down one finger, puts down two fingers, puts down three fingers, and Dean shakes him off every time.

So DeLancey starts all over. One, no; two, no; three, no. And I'm thinking: So what are you going to throw, Diz? *That's all you got!*

DeLancey calls time and walks out to the mound. Frank and I are running in too. Before we're halfway there, Dean has turned his back on DeLancey and he's waiting for Frisch. "Where did you say this fellow's strength was?"

"You're pitching great," Frisch says. "Just don't get the ball out and away from him. Come on."

"I don't think he can hit *me* out there," Diz tells him.

I thought Frisch was going to explode. "You bear down in there!" he yells. "Bear down or I'll have someone warming up in the next five seconds. Get the ball inside," he screams. "Inside!"

Diz wound up and threw a high, fast ball on the outside of the plate, and Greenberg hit a bullet right back through the box that almost took Dean's cap off.

Diz turned to Frisch and nodded his head. "You're right, Frankie. He can hit the hell out of the ball if you get it out there."

A couple of innings later we're leading, 11–0. Same thing. DeLancey goes down, runs through Dean's entire repertoire: 1, 2, 3. Dean won't pitch the ball. Frisch and I come trooping in again. All right, Diz, what's the matter now?

"Frank," he says. "Do you think Hubbell is a better pitcher than me?"

No, Diz, Hubbell's no better than you. Nobody's no better than you. You're a better pitcher than God. Come on, you're going great. Throw the ball and let's get this game over with.

Diz is satisfied. "If Hubbell's no better than me," he says, "then I ought to be able to throw a screwball."

He never threw a screwball in his life, and he wants to experiment in the seventh game of the World Series.

Something else had happened between those two brainstorms, as anybody who remembers that Series knows. In the sixth inning, we scored two more runs and the key hit was a triple by Joe Medwick. Medwick had a way of sliding with one leg underneath and the other foot up in the air. He couldn't slide any other way when he was coming in feet first, and he had been known to cut a man every now and again.

Medwick came into third base with his shoe pointed at Marv Owen's chest, and Owen, who was about as happy as you would imagine he would be at the way things were going, reached his own foot over and tried to stomp on him. You could have bet me right there that Medwick was going to get up and take a whack at him.

Medwick got up and took a whack at him.

At the end of the inning when Medwick went out to left field, the Detroit fans, who were no happier about losing the World Series than Owen, threw everything they could get their hands on at him. Fruit, vegetables, pop bottles, seat cushions, spare automobile parts. As soon as the ground crew had cleared it all away the barrage started all over again.

There was no way we were going to continue the game. Judge Landis, who was seated in the commissioner's box, sent for Medwick, Owen, Mickey Cochrane and Frisch. And also Bill Klem, the umpire behind the plate. I walked in with Frisch and I'm standing a little behind them, you know, so that I can hear what's going on.

Landis looks at Medwick and says, "Mr. Medwick, did you take a punch at Mr. Owen?"

Joe Medwick and I were roommates, and I never heard him tell a lie in his life. "Yes, sir," Joe said.

Landis looked at Owen. "And did you try to step on Joe Medwick?"

And Marv Owen said, "No, sir."

Landis just kept looking at him. "I ask you again, did you try to step on Joe Medwick?"

Marv Owen said, "No, sir."

Landis just kept looking at him. After a long silence, he turned to Medwick with a look that I had seen often. A very kind, almost affectionate look. "For your own good, son," he said, "I think I'll have to remove you from the game. You might get hurt. And we do have to continue the ball game."

And, do you know, Frisch raised up about six feet and told the commissioner that he would not take Medwick out. "I am the manager of the St. Louis baseball team," he said. "And I say who plays and who doesn't play." If Judge Landis ordered Klem to throw Medwick out of the game, he said, then there was nothing he could do about it. "But I will not take him out myself."

In the same quiet, gentle way, Landis told him, "Now you will take him out. You will take him out. You will do as I direct you, Mr. Frisch. You will take him out."

Judge Landis was right. There was nothing else to do. If Klem had thrown Medwick out of the game, Joe would have been automatically fined $200. If Medwick had stayed in the game, there would have been a riot in that park. The only thing Joe was disappointed about was that he had been having such a great Series that he only needed one more hit to tie Pepper Martin's World Series record of twelve base hits. Chuck Fullis, who went in to replace him, came up in the eighth inning and did get a base hit. As it was, Pepper Martin, who has to have the greatest World Series record of all time, had eleven hits too.

I had a great Series myself, and there is not only a story that goes with it, there are two. One of the stories involves Branch Rickey, and the other Babe Ruth.

Five days before the end of the season I got married. While the other Gashousers were rollicking around the town, I had been traveling in a different kind of company entirely. I had made some very good friends in the business community of St. Louis, partly through Branch Rickey and partly through some people I had met in the shoe business and the dress business. I first met Gussie Busch of Budweiser during this period, and this was twenty years before Busch got involved in baseball.

One of the women in the circle was Grace Dozier, a beautiful and brilliant woman who was the head designer for the Forest City Manufacturing Company. She was such a genius at designing cheap dresses that she had the exclusive accounts for Sears, Roebuck, J. C. Penney's, Grant's and Woolworth's. They wouldn't have anybody else design for them and the company gave her a percentage of every dress of hers that was sold. Eventually, she designed her own line, Carol King, which many of the women in the audience will recognize. To sum it up, Grace Dozier was one of the most astute and successful women in the country.

With the season coming to an end, we decided to get married. Just as soon as the season was over. Mr. Rickey thought it was the greatest thing that could happen to me. But why wait until the season was over? he wanted to know. Do it now. Right now. I could tell him what we were waiting for. All that had to happen was for me to get married on a Tuesday (which was when I did get married) and go out there and make two or three errors on Wednesday. Can you imagine what would have been yelled at me? I'd have never heard the end of it. "The marriage will be good for you," Rickey said. "You'll do well on the field. I can sense it. Believe me. Do it now. Don't wait until the season is over. Be the master of your own fate. Seize fortune by the forelock. The time is now. Trust me." What a promoter that man was.

So I got outvoted 2–1. And he was right. I played great during the drive to the pennant. And with the help of Babe Ruth, even better in the World Series.

Babe had just played his last game with the Yankees and he was covering the Series for a national newspaper syndicate. And who did he pick to be the star of the Series but his old pal, Leo Durocher. After the first four games, I had made the name he had tagged me with—the All-American Out—look a helluva sight better than his prediction. Fifteen times at bat without a hit before I finally got a meaningless single. "What are you trying to do," Babe said, "make a chump out of me? Come on, I'm going to take you and your bride to dinner and straighten you out."

He took us to a restaurant out in Bush's Grove. A great restaurant where you dined in little screened-in huts, the 1934 version of air-conditioning. "If you don't start hitting tomorrow," Babe told me, "I'm going to have to pick another star. But tonight I'll put you on stride."

I never will forget it, he ordered scallions for me. I had never eaten scallions before in my life, but at that point I would have been willing to try anything. "Greatest cure for a batting slump ever invented," the Babe said. "They've never failed me yet." He made me order a big dinner to go with them, and I could see why. I want to tell you something, I could taste them for days. He sat over me until I had eaten every last one of them, and then he said, "You'll get some hits tomorrow."

First time I came to bat, I drove a Tommy Bridges curve ball into left field for a base hit.

That was only a warm-up. The sixth game was the key game, because that was the one we had to win to stay alive. Mickey Cochrane sent his ace, Schoolboy Rowe, against Paul Dean to wrap it up. Rowe had won sixteen straight games during the regular season and he had already beaten us in game #2. The first time I came up, Marv Owen made a great play to rob me of a hit. They didn't get me out again. In the fifth, I singled over second to start a two-run rally that put us ahead, 3–1.

Detroit came back in the sixth to tie it up, and almost went ahead. With two out and runners on second and third, Owen hit a sharp ground ball in the hole. That was the play that had kept me in the big leagues for seven years. I made the play behind Martin, made the long throw to first and we were out of the inning.

In the seventh, I came to bat with two out, caught a Rowe fast ball and drove it to the fence in right center for a double. Paul Dean, who was a terrible hitter, then hit a ground ball between first and second to score me with what proved to be the winning run.

In the ninth inning, it looked as if we were going to get an insurance run. I came up with Orsatti on first, lined a single to center and took second on the throw to third. We had men on second and third with one out, but we couldn't get Orsatti home.

In the final game I had two more hits. In addition to that single in the big seven-run inning, I hit the fence again in right center for a triple and scored our tenth run.

By that time, all we were really trying to do was preserve Dizzy Dean's shutout. And, do you know, Diz was still so charged up that he almost blew it himself in the ninth. With Gehringer on first base, Goose Goslin hit a perfect double-play ball down to Rip Collins at first base. Rip speared it moving to his right, threw the ball to me and raced back to cover first base. I whipped the ball back, Rip reached for it, but Diz, who had come charging off the mound as soon as the ball was hit, cut right in front of him and took it away from him. What a beautiful double play! What a great fielding pitcher! The only trouble was that the umpire was signaling safe. Rip's foot had been on the bag and Diz's foot had been on top of Rip's.

Rogell promptly singled to put a run in scoring position. But Diz struck out Greenberg for the third time of the day, and then good old Marvin Owen hit a ground ball to me. I flipped it to Frankie and the St. Louis Cardinals were champions of the world.

The Gas House Gang.

Three years later, I was traded because Frisch demanded that Rickey get rid of me. And I couldn't understand why. Frank and I had always been close. Almost from the first, I had been his captain. Just before I was ready to leave for spring training that season, Frank came to St. Louis for a banquet and told me that if I'd wait a couple of days he'd drive down with me. It was a rough trip. The whole South had been hit with floods and half the bridges were washed out. Although we somehow made it to Florida, no trains were able to get through. Fortunately I had sent my trunk down early and Frank was actually wearing my clothes.

That's what made it so bewildering when Mr. Rickey called me in a couple of months into the season to tell me that Frank had given him an ultimatum *at the end of spring training*. Either I went or he went. Rickey had been sitting on it for two months, hoping that he'd be able to get Frank to change his mind. All Frisch would say, Rickey told me, was: "It's me or Durocher."

Rickey did tell me one thing, though. The only other player Frank had ever laid down that kind of an ultimatum on was Jimmy Wilson, who had been the catcher the year I came there. Wilson had always been considered a managerial prospect too, and when Frank was named manager during the season, some of Wilson's friends on the club didn't hesitate to let it be known that they thought the job should have gone to him.

"I think," Rickey said, "that he's afraid you're after his job."

To me, that kind of thinking is silly. Nobody can take a manager's job while he's winning and nobody can save it if he's not. When I'm managing a team I want the best baseball minds around me that I can find because they're going to help me win. What do I care who gets the job after I'm let go? When I was managing the Giants, Horace Stoneham called me in California to ask how I'd feel about taking Frisch on as coach. I thought it would be just great. Couldn't think of anybody I'd rather have. Stoneham asked me to fly to New York and tell Frank that myself. I flew right in and personally dictated a contract that made him the highest-paid coach in baseball. And then got Stoneham to raise my other coaches' salaries, just so there would be no jealousy.

And Frank was great. Just great, But even then, as close as we were again, I never asked him why he wanted me out of St. Louis.

THE MANAGER OF THE
BROOKLYN DODGERS

In order to become a big-league manager you have to be in the right place at the right time. That's Rule #1. There were 150,000,000 people in the country in 1939, and there were sixteen jobs for managers. To look at it another way, there were sixteen men in the country who were in a position to hire me for one of those jobs.

The main thing I had going for me was that it was the era of the playing manager. In the National League a playing manager had won the pennant for seven straight years. In the American League, only the Washington Senators, under the boy manager Joe Cronin, and the Detroit Tigers, under Mickey Cochrane (twice), had been able to break the dominance of Joe McCarthy's Yankees. To make the timing even better, Gabby Hartnett had taken over from Charlie Grimm with six weeks left to go in 1938 and brought the Cubs from far back to win the pennant, just as Grimm himself had done seven years earlier when he had taken over from Rogers Hornsby.

Everything runs in cycles, though, and by the end of the war the playing manager had somehow fallen into disrepute. The new wisdom was that playing and managing was simply too much for any one man to handle.

Ridiculous. I loved being a playing manager. It was easier

than managing from the bench. Christ, I was into everything; my wheels were spinning all the time. The two things
a manager does when his team is on the field are move players
and decide when to take the pitcher out. It's much easier to
move a player when you're right in the middle of it, and you
also have a far better sense of when your pitcher is beginning
to lose it. The only other thing I like to do is call a pitch,
one pitch, in a clutch situation, maybe ten or twelve times
over a season. The hitter fouls it off or takes it for a ball,
that's it. Now you're on your own, buddy. When you're on
the bench you have to call to the catcher to look over. When
I was playing shortstop, he was looking right at me. If I left
my glove open, I wanted a certain pitch. Direct communica-
tion. Otherwise, in a jam, I'd just make a fist. What that
meant was: You call it, buddy, go on. You're catching, you
know him better than I do, you're my captain, you run the
show, I've got all the faith in the world in you. When the
team is at bat, you're in the dugout anyway. Except when
you're on base, leading the club by example. Is that so bad?

I get a kick out of reading how difficult it is going to be
for Frank Robinson to manage the Cleveland Indians and
also serve as their Designated Hitter. Since when has swinging a bat every half hour or so become so taxing on the
brain? My bet is that Frank's very presence in the lineup will
give the club a shot in the arm. The Cleveland situation was
made for Frank Robinson, and Frank Robinson was made
for them. A good baseball city, hungry for a winner. A city
which has become predominantly black. There's no way
they're not going to turn out to root Frank on, and if he
begins to develop a winner, boy, that big Municipal Stadium
on Lake Erie is going to be jumping again. And that's where
the presence of a playing manager will really begin to help.
That isn't a script they're acting to out there, you know. It's
fifty men whose lives are on the line every day. Do you think
a game-winning home run by Frank Robinson isn't going to
have more drama than a game-winning home run by any-

body else? The players will react to the drama, the fans will react to them, the players will react to the fans, and it will just build and build. Just as it did in Brooklyn.

I always said that when it came to naming the first colored manager, Rule #1 would still apply. It was going to be the man who was in the right place at the right time. Robinson was hired because Phil Seghi was the man at Cleveland who had the power to do the hiring. As simple as that. Seghi had been the head of the Cincinnati farm system when Frank Robinson came up and he had seen Frank grow up from a wild kid to a confident clubhouse leader. You never know what kind of a manager anybody is going to make, but you'd have to be crazy to bet against him.

I thought for sure that Maury Wills was going to make the breakthrough in San Diego last year for the same reason. Because Buzzy Bavasi was there to give it to him. Buzzy had been the general manager in Los Angeles through all of Maury's years as field captain and clubhouse leader of the Dodgers. He couldn't help but know that Maury has everything it takes to make a good one. I don't know what happened.

My man was Leland Stanford (Larry) MacPhail. What Mr. Rickey didn't tell me when he sent me to Brooklyn was that the Brooklyn Trust Company, which had pretty much taken over the ball club, had offered him a fabulous deal to run the Dodgers for them. In the end, Branch had decided to stay in St. Louis, and it was he who had recommended Larry MacPhail. What he had done was to bring his two pet reclamation projects together.

MacPhail was a wild man. A big, beefy redhead. Like Rickey, he was a man of great imagination. Unlike Rickey, he was a man of physical action. Shortly after the Armistice in World War I—to give you an idea—he had led a group of fellow officers into Holland to kidnap the Kaiser. They had succeeded in getting into the castle where he was staying, too, and it was only through an accident of timing that they had missed him—and probably averted an international incident and saved themselves a court-martial. As a souvenir of that great adventure, Larry had picked up an ashtray with the Kaiser's seal on it, and the ashtray was always displayed prominently on his desk.

He did things, and when you do things, other things, unexpected things, are always happening around you. As general manager of the Cincinnati Reds, he had persuaded the league to allow him to install lights and play seven night games, an innovation which the Old Guard viewed as a threat to the very fabric of baseball and quite probably an end to our way of life. The St. Louis Cardinals were the sixth team on the list, but we were the Gas House Gang, the defending champions, and so MacPhail had set up special excursion trains and buses from the entire Ohio Valley. That was a mistake. With the trains and buses arriving late, the people in the back of the grandstand rushed down and filled the empty seats. And then, when the buses hit the stadium, just before the game started, the people who had not been able to buy tickets stormed the gates.

Just as the game was about to get underway, half a dozen guys who had apparently never been in a major-league park before came strolling out onto the field, sat down right behind second base, opened their beer cans, and prepared to watch the game. While the police were clearing them out of there, everybody else came pouring over the barriers.

The field was completely encircled by fans. They were lined up three or four deep all the way down the foul lines, around behind the catcher and in massed ranks behind the outfielders. You could forget about chasing foul balls. No chance. Anything that went into the crowd in the outfield was an automatic double.

As matter of fact, they completely took over the Cincinnati dugout, forcing the players to sit against the backstop. They

knew better than to try to take over our dugout. I guess
they'd heard about Joe Medwick. But, of course, a lane had
to be opened up every time we came to bat so that we got
from the dugout to the plate.

I swear to God, it was a miracle that nobody got killed.
They were standing so close to home plate that you couldn't
swing without coming within a couple of feet of somebody's
head. Early in the game, a curving line drive hit one specta-
tor flush in the face. He was carted away, and nobody else
moved an inch.

As one inning was about to start, I looked around and saw
Medwick standing on the line a few feet behind third base
arguing with a gorgeous blonde. Paul Dean was already in
his motion, and since you couldn't hear anything from here
to there, I had to go running in and scale my glove past his
ear.

The best was yet to come. In the last of the eighth, we
were leading, 2–1. The first man went out, the next man
walked, and up toward the plate strode—who else would it
be?—Babe Herman. Before he got there, the blonde—who
had moved to within a few feet of the plate by that time—
stepped out of the crowd and plucked the bat from his hand.
She took her stance in the batter's box, high heels and all,
and motioned for Paul to pitch to her. You can look it up,
this is true. Best-looking strike zone I ever saw. She had been
telling Medwick all night that even she could hit better than
he could, and now she was going to prove it.

God knows what would have happened if Diz had been
pitching. He'd have probably said she was digging in on
him and knocked her down. Poor Paul didn't know what to
do. Two times in a row he went into a big exaggerated
windup and then stepped back and looked in toward the
homeplate umpire, Bill Stewart. What could Stewart do?
Judge Landis was there in his box, and even he had been
afraid to do anything. We were playing the game only
because:

(1) MacPhail wasn't going to give all that money back.

(2) If we didn't play it they'd have torn the park down.

With nobody making a move, Paul Dean bent forward as if he were throwing the ball to a little kid and flipped it up to the plate underhanded.

And she hit it. She hit a little twisting ground ball down between first base and the pitcher's mound and set out—lickety-split, clickety-click—for first base. Paul Dean, game to the end, fielded the ball and threw her out.

Turned out that she was a nightclub singer. Got herself a lot of publicity and was promptly hired by a Cincinnati nightclub, who billed her as the only woman ever to come to bat in a big-league ball game.

As soon as MacPhail came to Brooklyn, things began happening there too. He started by getting permission to play night games, making Ebbets Field the second major-league park to install lights. In our first night game, the opposing pitcher was Johnny Vander Meer, who had pitched a no-hitter the previous time out. So what does he do on the first night game played at Ebbets Field but become the only man ever to pitch two consecutive no-hitters. And now a question for all you trivia fans: Who do you think made the 27th out? Right. In the ninth inning, Vander Meer walked three men, and there I was facing Vander Meer with two out. And I hit the ball just as good as I could hit it, a line drive, which Harry Craft, their fine center fielder, caught right off his shoe tops.

The only thing Larry didn't have was a ball club. We were awful. With three weeks left in the season, Burleigh Grimes told me that he wouldn't be coming back. "Leo," he said, "why don't you apply for the job?"

I wanted it so bad I could taste it. Still, there are certain amenities that must be observed in baseball. I said, "No, you're the manager of this ball club, Burleigh. I can't."

To which he said, just as I had anticipated that he would, "I'm already gone, Leo. MacPhail just told me. Do as I tell you. I'll take you to MacPhail myself and tell him what a great job you did as my captain."

Larry looked at me like I had twenty-two heads. "What makes you think you can manage a ball club?" he roared. "You've never managed one before. What makes you think you can handle twenty-four other players? You can't even handle yourself. What makes you think you're *smart* enough to handle a ball club?" There were two other questions he asked me, too. I can't remember exactly what they were but I distinctly remember that he threw five different questions at me, all of them casting grave misgivings about both my temperament and my ability.

Well, there was one thing I know I had, and that was confidence. And that's the main thing you need when you apply for your first managerial job. When you walk in there like that, what you are really saying is that you have the brains, the experience, the ability of leadership and the luck to win. To win! Larry obviously didn't think I had anything but gall. "Well, I can't prove it to you sitting here in this chair," I told him. "The only way I can prove it is out there on the field."

I never had been able to handle myself responsibly? So what? That isn't what players look for or respect you for. They're not college students, they're professional athletes. Physical men. They respect the pitcher who knocks them down and the base runner who bowls them over. They respect the guy who picks up the big pots in the card games. They respect the guy who lives hard and flies high.

All I needed was the opportunity, I had told MacPhail, and he had made it perfectly clear that I wasn't going to get it from him. "You a manager?" he said. "That's the funniest thing I ever heard." But remember what I said. If you have never been a manager before, it's all a matter of being in the right place at the right time. Since I knew I wanted to manage eventually, I had got into the habit of going to the winter meetings whenever they weren't being held too far from my home in St. Louis. Just to show myself. Just to stand around and talk to the men who were going to be in a position to hand out one of those precious sixteen jobs.

By luck, the meeting was in Chicago that year. I had already spent a couple of days hanging around the lobby when a message came to me to go up to MacPhail's suite. I walked in and found him there with his brother, Frank. Larry turned to his brother and out of a clear blue sky he said, "I want you to shake hands with the new manager of the Brooklyn Dodgers."

I like to fainted dead away right there.

I am sure that he checked me out with Rickey. I know for a fact that he checked me out with Ed Barrow, and that Barrow, the man who could have killed it for me, had given me a tremendous recommendation. That didn't surprise me in the least. From the day he traded me after I told him to go and fuck himself, Ed Barrow had become the best friend I had in baseball. Every time he saw me he gave me a speech about saving my money. "You think you have a lot of friends in baseball, don't you?" he would say. "Just wait for the day you're in trouble and you try to borrow some money. That's when you'll find out different. If a man has two real friends in his entire life he's lucky."

But, still, given a man who acted as impulsively as Larry MacPhail, I have to doubt that he would have been asking anybody about me if I hadn't been right there in front of his eyes.

I think it has been pretty well established by now that between Huggins, Weil, Landis and Rickey, I had more fathers in my baseball career than Shirley Temple used to have in those pictures of hers. My relationship with Larry MacPhail was altogether different. Of course, Shirley usually had an irascible but lovable father in her cast too, a description that would have fit Larry MacPhail to perfection if only he had been lovable.

There is no question in my mind but that Larry was a

genius. There is that thin line between genius and insanity, and in Larry's case it was sometimes so thin that you could see him drifting back and forth. They always said this about MacPhail: Cold sober he was brilliant. One drink and he was even more brilliant. Two drinks—that's another story. Supposedly he had been fired from the job in Cincinnati after he had broken the jaw of a city detective in the lobby of a hotel.

During my four years as his manager, there was not one dull moment.

His first project, before spring training started, was for me to take all our pitchers and catchers to Hot Springs, Arkansas, to get them into tiptop condition. Kind of training for spring training. Artie McGovern, a fighter, was hired to get us into shape. We get in on a Friday. On Saturday morning we were in the gymnasium working out with the mats and the medicine ball and the calisthenics and the Indian clubs and all that jazz, then everybody put on their sweat-shirts and sneakers and over the mountains we went.

So after we shower and dress, what the hell are you going to do in Hot Springs, Arkansas? There's one good place to eat, I'm told. The Belvedere Country Club. So I take my coaches, Charlie Dressen and Andy High, the traveling secretary, John McDonald, and a couple of other people. It's a beautiful place, we have a wonderful dinner. We bumped into Gussie Busch and his party, which consisted of four or five other people from St. Louis whom I knew very well. Fellow members of the Bastard Club, which I'll talk about when we get to the wonderful story of how I wasn't hired to manage the St. Louis Cardinals twenty-five years later.

After dinner, they cleared the tables and the next thing I knew they were bringing Bingo cards around. Two dollars a pot. Maybe $100, $125 in a pot. I bought five cards, and all of a sudden I'm a Bingo player. Saturday night in Hot Springs.

At the end of the night, they announced the Jackpot Game. Instead of the usual 5-in-a-row, you had to cover the entire card, and the winner would get $660. I quickly covered every square except one, the caller hollered I-17—I will never forget that combination—and up I jumped, finger held aloft, and from my lips came the happy cry, "That's *me*."

Before I left there, I didn't have a dime of that $660 left. I bought champagne for everybody in the house. I strutted around, making a big joke about being the Bingo champion, although, if the truth be known, it seemed to me that it was a good omen to come up with the jackpot prize on my first day as a working manager.

Early Sunday morning, the ringing of the phone sounded in my ear.

"Hello," I said, barely awake.

"You're fired!" came the voice of MacPhail. (I'm fired? I've been a calisthenics leader for one day, and this is the end of my career as a manager? What's the matter, I don't lead calisthenics good?)

"For what?" I yelled, fully awake.

"You're a gambler!"

"What the hell are you talking about, Larry?"

"I just read it in this morning's paper. You won the big Bingo prize."

"Bingo? Larry, that's a game old women play at church socials." I explained to him that the cream of Hot Springs society had been there with us, including Gussie Busch, who he knew very well. To convince him I wasn't really a hopeless Bingo addict, I told him, with suitable humor, how I had been waylaid after dessert.

"See?" he said. "Just what I said. That's gambling, and you're fired. Turn the club over to Andy High right now."

"Turn the club over to High?" I yelled. "To *High?* Are you crazy? If you don't want me to manage, that's your business, but how the hell can you give the club to Andy

High when you've got Charlie Dressen, the best baseball man I know. You got to give the club to Dressen."

Would you believe it? I was on the phone for fifteen minutes trying to convince him that he should give my job to Dressen instead of High. Finally, when the sheer absurdity of the situation came to me, I screamed the same suggestion into the phone I had once made to Ed Barrow and hung up.

The next day I went right on managing the club. Never heard another word about my misadventures as a Bingo player.

The reason MacPhail dreamed up the pretraining conditioning for our pitchers was because he wanted us to do well in the exhibition season. We had a three-game series with the Yankees when we returned to New York, and he had been telling me all winter that if we looked real good down South we'd be able to draw enough people in the two games at Ebbets Field to get us off the nut.

And we did get off winning. Early in the exhibition season, we were playing the Cardinals at St. Petersburg, and I'm here to tell you that it was hot. I was still a playing manager at that point, and just as soon as I put my face into that blast furnace I decided that if I couldn't find a way to sit that game out I didn't really have the resourcefulness to make a good manager.

We had picked up a kid named Pete Reiser for $200, one of a gang of players Judge Landis had freed from Rickey's farm system. The kid had looked very good in batting practice at Clearwater, and although he was listed as an outfielder, it seemed to me that I had been told he had also played some shortstop. It also seemed to me like an excellent time to find out what the lad could do. "Ever play shortstop, kid?" I asked.

"No," he said. What's the matter with this kid? I'm thinking. You're the manager and you ask a raw rookie if he ever played anywhere, he's supposed to say yes.

"Well," I told him, "you're the shortstop today."

The Cards never got him out. For three straight games, nobody got him out. He got on base eleven straight times, with seven hits. Four of the hits were home runs, two batting right-handed and two left-handed.

I just kept staring at him, wondering if it was all a dream. Holy cats, I'm thinking. What have I stumbled on here? This is a diamond, Leo. All you have to do is polish him. Sit down and let the boy play. And I'm thinking, MacPhail must be flipping. They'll break the gates down at Ebbets Field just to see what this kid looks like.

So I get a wire from MacPhail: DO NOT PLAY REISER AGAIN.

Now, despite the general picture of me as a rebel, I am an organization man. The front office gives the manager the players, and the manager does the best he can with them. But it's my job to decide who I'm going to put on the field. If the front office wants to give me a reason why I shouldn't play somebody, I'll listen. Send for me and I'll come. I'll respect your position, but you've got to respect my position too.

You want to manage the club, Larry, you put on the uniform and I'll go upstairs and sit at your desk.

I played Reiser. And I played him in center field where he belonged.

The next day we were playing Detroit at Macon, Georgia. I was just drawing on the pants of my uniform when John McDonald came in to tell me MacPhail had flown in and wanted to see me right away.

I said, "Should I finish dressing?"

He said, "I wouldn't if I were you. Put your street clothes on."

As soon as I stuck my head through the door of his suite, MacPhail began to curse me. He called me every filthy name I had ever heard. It was awful. I am fired, I am through, and I am a dirty sonofabitch.

I said, "That's all right, Larry. You don't want me to manage your ball club, that's fine. You're the president, you're the general manager, you're the boss. I'm not mad, so don't you get mad."

He kept right on cursing me. Worse than ever.

I said, "Look, Larry, let's not be a couple of kids about this. You don't want me to manage the club, this is fine. But . . . stop . . . calling . . . me . . . those . . . names."

MacPhail went right on cursing me. In fact, the more he cursed me the madder he seemed to get. Between curses, he was pacing up and down dictating my resignation to McDonald. Now, there were twin beds in the suite. McDonald was sitting on one of the beds and the typewriter was on the other. Big tears were rolling down his face as he typed, because John was a great booster of mine and he had wanted very badly for me to make good. MacPhail couldn't get through two sentences before John would deliberately make a mistake, pull the paper out of the machine and drop it on the floor. MacPhail, his rage increasing, would turn to me with new pinnacles of invective and then back to McDonald to start all over again.

McDonald must have been pulling his sixth sheet out of the machine when MacPhail started to turn toward me again, then wheeled back to McDonald and screamed, "And you're fired too because *you can't type!*"

It would have been the funniest thing I ever saw except that MacPhail was out of his head. Having taken all I could, I jumped up out of the chair and warned Larry not to call me that name again. Well, that was like warning a hurricane to go back where it had come from. Fortunately, I still had just enough control left so that I was able to check myself at the last second and only give his chair a kind of shove. A hard enough shove, though, so that Larry went toppling over backward and landed flat on his back on the bed.

In two seconds, he was back on his feet with his arms around me. He's got tears in his eyes, and then I had tears in my eyes and then the three of us were walking out of the suite, arm in arm, like three blubbering Musketeers. I was

Little Miller Huggins, who managed the Yankees from 1918 to the end of 1929, was the first great influence in Durocher's career. Leo was "Mr. Huggins' boy," and when Huggins died Leo's days as a Yankee were numbered. (N.Y. DAILY NEWS)

In 1927, the year Babe Ruth hit sixty home runs. Leo had been brought up at the end of the season to sit on the bench. The rollicking Babe and the brash Durocher got along well, even though it was the Babe who nicknamed Leo "The All-American Out."

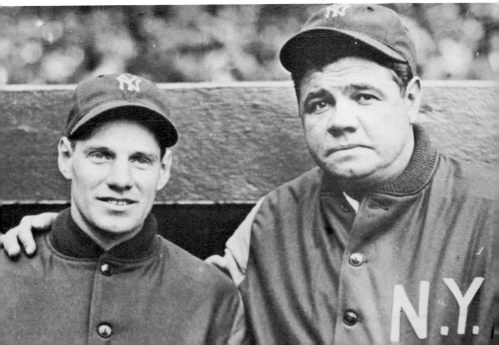

The young Durocher was a big-nosed, loudmouthed rookie short-stop in 1928. He got his chance to start the season at second base when Tony Lazzeri was injured, but he finished the season as a utility infielder. (ST. LOUIS POST-DISPATCH)

"Stern-visaged" was the description always applied to Judge Kenesaw Mountain Landis. He was hired by the owners after the Black Sox Scandal, and he was always the ballplayers' commissioner. He would forgive a ballplayer for anything except gambling. (N.Y. DAILY NEWS)

The captain of the Gas House Gang. The year is 1934, when Leo was at the top of his game as the premier fielding shortstop in baseball and about to start the season that was to imprint the Gas House Gang forever into the history of baseball. (ST. LOUIS POST-DISPATCH)

Frankie Frisch was a member of John McGraw's New York Giants before he went to St. Louis for Rogers Hornsby, in one of baseball's first great trades. He was the manager of the Cardinals, and Durocher became his captain. (N.Y. DAILY NEWS)

Paul and Dizzy Dean returning home in triumph after the 1934 seven-game Series. After winning forty-nine games between them during the season, they won two games apiece in the World Series. (N.Y. DAILY NEWS)

Dizzy Dean pitching and Leo Durocher at short. (N.Y. DAILY NEWS)

The batting order before the opening game of the World Series in Detroit. Reading from right to left: Pepper Martin, 3b; Jack Rothrock, rf; Frank Frisch, 2b; Joe Medwick, lf; Jim (Rip) Collins, 1b; Bill De Lancey, c; Ernie Orsatti, cf; Leo Durocher, ss; Dizzy Dean, p. (ST. LOUIS POST-DISPATCH)

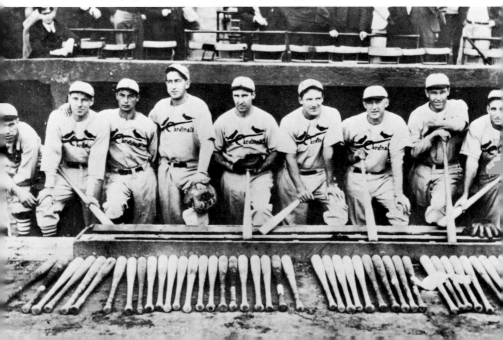

That's Durocher on the right, looking for all the world like the riverboat gambler he was sometimes accused of being. With him are Dizzy Dean (center) and pitcher Lon Warneke. Question: Do you think Leo ever really played cards over a glass-topped table? (ST. LOUIS POST-DISPATCH)

Dec. 13, 1938. The newly appointed manager of the Brooklyn Dodgers is presumably getting some pointers from a couple of his predecessors: Burleigh Grimes (right), the man he succeeded; and Casey Stengel (left), who had been fired three years earlier and was paid his full salary not to manage. (N.Y. DAILY NEWS)

(right) John McDonald, an ex-sportswriter and close friend of general manager Larry Mac-Phail, was an invaluable help in getting the first training camp organized. McDonald was not infrequently the third man in the fights between MacPhail and Durocher. (below) Before the last game of the 1939 season, general manager MacPhail congratulates his rookie manager on a third-place finish. Before the day was over, they had stopped smiling at each other. (both photos N.Y. DAILY NEWS.*)*

Charlie Dressen, shown here sitting with Durocher in the spring of 1940, was Leo's right arm and invaluable aide-de-camp for eight years. They continued to be tied together in subsequent years from opposite sides of the field; first, as the two men suspended by Happy Chandler, and then as opposing managers on the day Bobby Thomson hit THE home run. (N.Y. DAILY NEWS)

When Larry MacPhail spent $132,500 of the bank's money to buy Joe Medwick (left) and Curt Davis (right), the Dodgers were suddenly being looked upon as a contending ballclub. Before the week was over, Medwick was beaned by his former St. Louis teammate, Bob Bowman, and it was Curt Davis, the thrown-in pitcher, who proved to be the more valuable player in the deal. (N.Y. DAILY NEWS)

Before St. Louis left town, Manager Durocher, who had inserted himself into the lineup for the injured Pee Wee Reese, tangled with Cardinal catcher Mickey Owen. It started when Owen, sliding into second (left) slashed at secondbaseman Pete Coscarart with his spikes, and ended (below) with half the players from both teams in between them. Mr. Owen (far left) is being led to the St. Louis bench by the umpires. Mr. Durocher (upper right) has lost his hat. The hair went earlier. The fight was a draw. (both photos N.Y. DAILY NEWS)

Durocher is sitting out a suspension by watching his ball club from the press box. The baby-faced young man sitting alongside him is Pee Wee Reese, who is out this time with a broken bone in his ankle. (N.Y. DAILY NEWS)

Two MacPhail acquisitions who helped to bring Brooklyn its first pennant in twenty-one years. Dolph Camilli (left), the home-run-hitting, fancy-fielding first-baseman; and Billy Herman, the wise old head for second base. (N.Y. DAILY NEWS)

With three games left in the 1941 season, Clara Durocher came to Boston from Springfield, Massachusetts, to see her son clinch the pennant. She brought the Dodgers luck. They won, 5–0. (N.Y. DAILY NEWS)

After a wild train ride from Boston, and a few mixed signals around the 125th Street station, Durocher and his Dodgers found a mob waiting for them at Grand Central Station. (N.Y. DAILY NEWS)

Tommy Henrich swings and misses, and the Dodgers have won the fourth game of the World Series, 4–3. But—what's this?—Mickey Owen hasn't got his glove over quickly enough for Hugh Casey's sinker, and the game isn't over. The final score was New York 6, Brooklyn 4. (N.Y. DAILY NEWS)

Reese and Reiser. The Dodgers' babies try to relax while they are waiting for their first World Series to begin. As a twenty-two-year-old rookie, Reiser has just led the National League in batting. (N.Y. DAILY NEWS)

Fat Freddie Fitzsimmons was forty years old. His arm was so crooked that it threw him off balance when he walked. He could only work once a week, and his arm would tighten up so badly that he was rarely around at the finish. But he won the big games, and he was the player Durocher admired above all others. He was also "The Man Who Hated Johnny Mize." (N.Y. DAILY NEWS)

Pete Reiser, who may have had more natural talent than any ballplayer who ever lived but who broke himself up running into fences. Back from the service in 1946, Reiser immediately ran into the wall at Ebbets Field and lacerated his scalp. Number 6 is Carl Furillo. (N.Y. DAILY NEWS)

The announcement that Durocher was signing to manage the Dodgers again for the 1947 season had more than routine interest because of the stories that MacPhail was trying to hire him for the Yankees. The contract had actually been signed in Columbus, Ohio, a few weeks earlier. (N.Y. DAILY NEWS)

Albert Benjamin ("Happy") Chandler. In his first spring training, the new commissioner of baseball sees nothing but bright skies ahead. A year later, his investigation into a fight between Larry MacPhail and Branch Rickey ended with the suspension of Leo Durocher. (N.Y. DAILY NEWS)

Eddie Stanky, who couldn't do anything on a ballfield except beat you, joins the Happiness Boys to announce that he has signed his contract for the 1947 season. But when Durocher interceded for Stanky again a year later, it resulted in an explosion that blew both of them out of Brooklyn. (N.Y. DAILY NEWS)

But there is no joy in Flatbush . . . (N.Y. DAILY NEWS)

The Brooklyn fans are still letting their feelings be known as the season opens.
(N.Y. DAILY NEWS)

A sad-looking Durocher poses with Walter O'Malley shortly after the edict has come down from Chandler suspending him for a full year. Walter O'Malley, who was in a power struggle with Branch Rickey for control of the club, doesn't look quite so crushed, does he? (N.Y. DAILY NEWS)

(above) A dapper and obviously unrepentant Durocher visits the clubhouse before he leaves town. Sitting with Leo, left to right, are Pete Reiser, Gene Hermanski and Dixie Walker. Standing: Pee Wee Reese and Hugh Casey. (below) The next time Leo visited Ebbets Field, it was to watch the Dodgers take on the Yankees again in the World Series. Seated in the box with Leo and his wife, Laraine Day, is Danny Kaye. (both photos N.Y. DAILY NEWS)

no longer fired, I was no longer through, I was no longer even a dirty sonofabitch.

The next day in Atlanta, Larry dropped into my room just as I was getting ready to leave for the park. "I'm glad we had that little talk yesterday," he said. "I think we understand each other much better. Everything's going to be fine."

I never did find out why he didn't want me to play Reiser.

He fired me sixty times if he fired me once, and I was still there when he left. He even fired me the night we won Brooklyn's first pennant in twenty-one years. That one I had coming to me. Not for the reason he fired me but because I had allowed him to dictate a ridiculous pitching selection in a critical spot after I had refused to allow him to step into my domain over almost three full years.

It began early in my first season when he came raging into the clubhouse after Van Lingle Mungo had been beaten by an Ernie Lombardi home run, a tremendous shot that had knocked out half a dozen seats in the upper deck. He ran up to Mungo's locker, threw his panama hat on the floor and jumped up and down on it. Called Mungo everything. That was bad enough. What made it worse was that there has always been a unwritten law that the front office is not supposed to set foot in the clubhouse. Not the owner, not the president, not the general manager.

As quickly as I could, I ran everybody into the latrine and showers except Mungo. When only the three of us were left, I said, "Now you! Get out! Get the hell out of here, and don't you ever come in here again!"

He couldn't believe it. "You're running me out of here? You dare—"

"You don't belong here. You want to talk to one of my players, you send for him up in your office. This is our clubhouse, our home. Don't you come in here and start ranting and raving. If there's any ranting and raving to be done in this room, I will do it."

Well, he spluttered, he didn't have to send for me to fire me. "I can fire you right here! You're fired!"

Larry went stomping out, the players came filing back and we all looked down at his battered panama and went into hysterics.

Not the last time he ever came into the clubhouse. And certainly not the last time he tried to become the manager. I had taken a team that had finished in seventh place, and on the last day of the season we had to win only one game of a doubleheader against Philadelphia to clinch third place, the highest Brooklyn had finished in the memory of man. It was raining fairly hard and everybody knew we weren't going to be able to get in the second game. We got ahead of them by one run, and then in the ninth inning they got a man on first and third with one out. The rain was coming down pretty hard, I'm at shortstop and MacPhail is up in that little private box of his that hung down in front of the press box. I forget who was pitching for us, but we had two pitchers in the bullpen, Luke Hamlin, who was our ace, and Billy Doyle, a kid we had just brought up from Memphis. Luke Hamlin was a pitcher who had been perfectly happy to win his eleven and twelve games a year although everybody in the league knew he had the stuff to be one of the better pitchers. At the beginning of the year, I had told him he was going to win twenty if I had to pitch him every day. "If I have to kill you, you'll win twenty. If your arm falls off you'll win twenty." And I did work him blind and he did win twenty games, and MacPhail thought he was the greatest thing in the world.

Hamlin was a fast-ball pitcher, Doyle had a great curve ball, and in a spot like this I wanted the ball hit down in the ground. So I walked to the mound and brought in Doyle, and all over the park you could hear MacPhail hollering, "Hamlin, you dummy! Hamlin!"

I'm looking right at him. His hat's down over his eyes, he's more than a little bit drunk and he's giving me an awful going over. So I did what I had been wanting to do all year. I put my thumb to my nose and waggled my fingers at him. *Screw you, MacPhail. The season is over, I've taken enough from you.*

He's still screaming for Hamlin when Doyle throws his first pitch and—boom—a ground ball right back to the mound. Doyle throws to me, I throw to first and the game is over. We don't play the second game, but MacPhail is in front of the dugout in the rain, calling me everything for bringing in Doyle.

He was right even when he was wrong. In his own mind he never made a mistake. MacPhail would get into these tremendous holdout affairs with players, not because the money meant anything to him but because he took every dispute personally.

After that third-place finish we had high hopes going into 1940. Dolph Camilli wanted $15,000, which he richly deserved. He had played every game for me, knocked in 104 runs, and he was far and away the best-fielding first baseman in baseball. But he also wanted $1,000 to cover the traveling expenses of bringing his wife and four children to camp from San Francisco, a bit of information he imparted to MacPhail after he had flown in by himself. MacPhail immediately roared that he wasn't running any kindergarten here, and he wasn't responsible for Camilli's "eight kids."

Camilli was a quiet, gentle man but he was as strong as an ox. His brother, who fought under the name of Frankie Campbell, had been a leading heavyweight contender, before he was killed in the ring by Max Baer. Nobody knew how well Dolph could fight because, quite frankly, nobody had ever wanted to find out. Nobody, anyway, before Larry MacPhail. Every time he said "eight kids," Camilli corrected him, and every time he had to correct him you could see him get a little madder.

The next thing I knew I heard the usual MacPhail screaming followed by gurgling, choking sounds. I went running in and the first thing I noticed, being exceptionally observant, was that Camilli had both of his hands under MacPhail's chin and MacPhail's feet were a foot off the ground. Between gurgles, MacPhail was still screaming, to put it as delicately as possible, that he wasn't going to be held responsible for Camilli's indifference to the most elementary tenets of family planning.

Holy cats, I didn't know what to do. I was afraid that if I went after Camilli, Dolph would handle MacPhail with one hand and hoist me up with the other. I was also afraid that if I talked him into letting MacPhail down, Larry would start swinging. In addition to which, just between you and me, I didn't find the scene all that displeasing.

The outcome was that MacPhail refused to pay for the transportation of Camilli's "eight kids," Camilli refused to get into uniform, and I spent the greater part of spring training trying to convince MacPhail that we weren't going to win any pennant with a guy named Bert Haas at first. Finally, MacPhail instructed me—as he was later to do with Babe Phelps—that I could tell Camilli he'd get his thousand bucks but that if he ever found out the money was coming from him I was fired. "This is one argument," he said, pronouncing his final verdict, "I'm going to win."

Never mind that he had almost got himself a free tonsillectomy and was paying the thousand anyway. If he said he had won he had won. That left me to convince Camilli that I was personally guaranteeing he'd get the money before the year was over—"Trust me, Dolph"—and by this time Camilli was so mad that he wanted MacPhail to come crawling to him on his hands and knees with the money in his mouth.

To get back to my insistence upon naming my own lineup, the player we argued about mostly was me. Or, to put it another way, Pee Wee Reese. Larry always signed me to two contracts, one as a manager and the other as a player. The first one, if I remember right, totaled $17,500, so it was probably $12,500 and $5,000. It was the opportunity I had been looking for; I would have paid for the chance. Once MacPhail was convinced I could do the job he pushed me up very quickly.

Reese had been playing for Louisville, another dying minor-league franchise. The Red Sox, who had a working agreement with Louisville, had first rights on him, and the story is that Joe Cronin went down to look at him and came back to tell Tom Yawkey, the Boston owner, that Reese was a pasty-faced kid who would never make it. Translated freely, that means to me that Joe Cronin was afraid that if the kid came up and showed how the position was supposed to be played Yawkey might discover that Cronin wasn't much of a manager either. But maybe I'm jealous. Cronin became the second shortstop to be voted into the Hall of Fame and the first one to come in carrying a bat instead of a glove. The best way to describe him is to say that he played shortstop as if he were training for his later career as league president.

With Reese suddenly available, MacPhail sent Ted Mc-Grew, his chief scout, down to look him over, and McGrew came back talking in such superlatives that Larry got the bank to buy the Louisville franchise just to get him.

Pee Wee was twenty years old when I first saw him in spring training and he looked twelve. I took one look at him and I said to myself: "Leo, you can rest your aching tootsies." MacPhail wouldn't hear of it. Having bought a whole ball club to get a young shortstop, he kept firing me for not playing shortstop myself. He knew I was the premier fielding shortstop in the business, see, because everybody had told him that I was. "That was six years ago, Larry," I'd tell him. "I'm thirty-four years old."

"You can play another two or three years."

Sure I could. I could also see balls going by me by a yard that I used to get like nothing. "We're talking about something I know a little about, Larry. Reese would be in front of those balls, waiting. What we got here is a diamond that you found in Africa. What we got to do is polish the diamond up, and he is going to be as good a shortstop as they ever heard of in the major leagues."

"I'm paying you five thousand dollars to play shortstop!"

"Reese is going to be the shortstop!"

"If you're not out at shortstop tomorrow, you're fired!"

It went on like that for three years, and the only time I played shortstop was when Reese was hurt, which kept me very busy in his first year and practically retired me thereafter.

If it sounds as if I'm ridiculing MacPhail, that isn't my intention. I have only been trying to give you one facet of the man's personality. Another man might have said, "Well, why don't you split the job with the kid for a while, Leo? Take a little of the pressure off him. Break him in easy." With MacPhail, though, everything came at you like a royal command, and it is part of *my* personality that I would automatically gird myself to resist.

Branch Rickey, for instance, would call me in when things weren't going too well, and sooner or later he would get around to saying, "Jones isn't playing too well, is he, Leo? Not hitting very well."

I would have to admit that he certainly hadn't been playing up to his potential lately. I certainly couldn't deny that.

Rickey would say, "Now, do you think Smith, who is sitting on the bench, do you think this might be the propitious moment to see whether he can go in and do a better job?"

My instinct would be to defend Jones (which was, of course, defending myself for playing him). Jones had been doing the job for quite some time, I'd point out. He was a known quantity and, as far as I was concerned, still quite a ballplayer.

"Well," Rickey would say, "you're the boss. You do what you want to do. I just thought I'd put it in the hopper."

He never told me to play the other player, oh no, but I'd

go out of there with his opinion stamped on my forehead. And since Mr. Rickey was careful not to offer an opinion unless he was sure he was right, I can't think of one instance where he put something "in the hopper" that I didn't get around to following his advice.

The thing about Larry MacPhail, as should be evident by now, was that he did everything to excess. With Reese playing shortstop, we got off so well that we were leading the league at the end of the month. And then Pee Wee got beaned so badly that he was in the hospital for a full week and was out of the lineup for three weeks. During that period Larry went shopping for the hard-hitting outfielder we desperately needed, and Rickey sold him Joe Medwick for a barrel of money. Well, when Rickey is willing to let a contending team have that kind of a player you have a right to suspect that (1) he has spotted a certain decline setting in; and (2) that he really didn't think we had the pitching to remain in contention. But, Jesus, Ebbets Field had always been made for Medwick, and if he was only 80 percent of what he used to be I felt we had a real shot at the pennant.

Joe had been with us for exactly six days when the Cardinals came to town. Joe and I had always been great pals in St. Louis, and he had taken a suite at the New Yorker where I was staying. As we were leaving for the ball park, we found ourselves in the same elevator with Bob Bowman, who was going to be pitching against us. Given that opportunity, I made one of my lovable remarks about his chances for survival, which gave him a perfect opening to tell me that he was sure of at least one automatic out in the lineup. Me.

"You won't last long enough to get to Leo," Medwick snarled. "You'll be out of there before you get down that far."

The usual baseball byplay, sure. But also a little more than that. Bowman, like so many other St. Louis pitchers, had had a run-in with Medwick after accusing him of loafing after a fly ball and there was bad blood between them. (The first time my old pal Joe got lackadaisical in Brooklyn I slapped a $200 fine on him, and it was one of the very few fines I never returned. Just to impress upon him, you know, that I have no friends once the bell rings.)

"I'll take care of both of you guys," Bowman said. "Wait and see."

Both of them batted .1000 in the prediction department. Our first three batters got line hits, and up to the plate came Joe Medwick. Bowman's first pitch hit him right on the temple and he dropped like the trunk of a tree. Out cold. I went for Bowman, the benches emptied and there were fights all over the field. All right, that was to be expected. But Jesus, MacPhail came running down from his box, and while Medwick was being carried off on a stretcher, MacPhail was standing in front of the St. Louis dugout challenging the whole ball club. Screaming at them. Out of control. It was a miracle that there wasn't a riot.

All right, to lose Medwick like that on top of Reese is enough to get your dander up. Especially when you've just paid out $132,000 for him. With most people, they'll get mad and get over it. Not MacPhail. He demanded that Bowman be barred from baseball for life; he came up with affidavits from everybody who had been in the elevator about the "threats" Bowman had made. Do you know that within twenty-four hours he had the District Attorney, Bill O'Dwyer, conducting a criminal investigation. O'Dwyer had just broken up Murder, Inc. MacPhail demanded that he now go after "Beanball, Inc.," which he described as a conspiracy among National League pitchers to kill off the Dodgers' pennant chances by eliminating our leading players. Burton Turkus, the man who had been in charge of the Murder, Inc., investigation, was assigned to the case and he actually had us all in a couple of days later for a hearing.

Everything to excess, and yet underneath it all the genius

of the man was never lost. All year long he hammered away at "Beanball, Inc.," and before another year had started he had ordered plastic helmets made up for us. "Guaranteed," he announced happily, "to withstand baseballs propelled at a hundred miles an hour. Now let them throw at us all they want. They can't hurt us."

The helmets were a development that was long overdue. All that ranting and raving had come to an end in a stroke of sheer logic.

THE FIRST PENNANT IN 21 YEARS

WHEN I SAY THAT Larry MacPhail was half madman and half genius, I am not trying to say that he was two separate persons. Not at all. It was two different sides of the same personality. The opposite sides of the coin. Using myself as an example, I would suspect the same basic drive and outlook that has always got me into trouble also made me whatever I was as a player and manager. I know what I want, I don't kid myself about it and I go after it. If wanting what I want has always made for a certain irresponsibility in my life style, it also sent me out to the sandlots as a kid to practice endlessly the lessons imparted to me by Rabbit Maranville, the best shortstop in baseball; to sit on the bench and study the moves being made by Miller Huggins, the best manager in baseball; and, in my later years with the Dodgers, sit at the feet of Branch Rickey, the smartest man to ever turn his mind to the business and science of baseball. And to do whatever had to be done to get the most out of the collective talents of twenty-five players. Because I never kidded myself about that, either. A manager is no better than his players. If you haven't got the talent, you can go home.

With Larry MacPhail, the same total belief in his own infallibility, his refusal to let go of anything he got his teeth into, made him a manager's dream when it came to getting you the player you wanted. You told him once, he knew he could do it, and you never had to ask again.

Over the winter of 1940, we had agreed that our greatest needs were a strong young pitcher to go with our aging pitching staff and a right-handed catcher to go with Babe Phelps. The pitcher he went after was Kirby Higbe, a strong-armed right-hander who had been able to win a respectable number of games at Philadelphia. Getting him was relatively easy. Gerry Nugent, the owner of the Phils, was always in need of money. That's how Larry had been able to get Camilli. Larry agreed to pay Nugent $100,000 on condition that Nugent keep the deal secret. It was important to Larry that it be kept secret because he was negotiating with Branch Rickey for Mickey Owen, and he recognized that Rickey was willing to let us have a catcher as good as Owen only because he was sure our pitching wasn't strong enough to make us a real threat to take it all.

Keeping a deal secret isn't easy. Every contract, and every change of contract, has to be filed at League headquarters immediately, with a copy going to the commissioner's office, and all trades are reported automatically in the bulletin from League headquarters. We had picked up Pete Reiser for $200, you will remember, after Landis had freed 95 St. Louis farmhands whose basic contract with the Cardinals had been covered up. And right there perhaps was the opening that MacPhail saw. What he was counting on, I can only guess, was that Landis, that rock of integrity, hated Rickey so much for playing fast and loose with the rules that he would be willing to play fast and loose with the spirit of the rules this one time, himself.

The rule didn't say that you had to announce an exchange of contracts, it only said that the new contracts had to be filed. The announcement, naturally enough, had always come from the teams involved. The information in the League bulletins was a service, not a legal mandate.

Just to give us a thrill, the Giants went after Kirby Higbe while the negotiations for Owen were still going on. It took a full month before we got him, and in all that time not a word leaked out of either the commissioner's office or League headquarters that we already had Higbe.

In the end, MacPhail bought Owen for $80,000 and when he made the double announcement he was able to crow, "The New York Giants, despite what they have been saying, have no chance to land Kirby Higbe from Philadelphia."

Having spent $180,000 of the bank's money, Larry promptly got into a long holdout battle with Owen over a couple of thousand dollars. And there's a story that goes with that, too. At the hearing in the DA's office following the beaning of Medwick, Billy Southworth, the Cardinals' manager, had delivered a speech about the Cardinals' dedication to the principles of clean baseball that would have brought tears to the eyes of any Boy Scout leader, provided that it was a Boy Scout leader who had never seen the Cardinals play. The next day, Mickey Owen came into second base, spikes high, to take our second-baseman out of a double play. I hollered a few caustic remarks about that speech to Southworth, who was coaching at third base, and as Owen came running off the field he made his own contribution to the cause of clean baseball by taking a whack at me. In the interests of clean baseball, I whacked him back. In other words, my kind of a ballplayer.

During the press conference in Havana to announce that Owen had been signed, one of the writers asked me whether I thought Mickey was going to be able to hit enough to take the job away from Phelps.

"Well," I said, turning to Mickey, "what did you hit last year?"

Mickey, who was a bit of a flake, took a big puff on the big cigar that was always sticking out of his kisser. "It isn't *what* I hit," he said. "It's *who* I hit."

By that late in the training season, I was able to tell Larry we had a hell of a ball club there. "This is a *good* ball club," I told him. "We could win the whole thing with one other player."

And who was that? he wanted to know.

"Billy Herman," I said.

Billy Herman had been the premier second-baseman in the National League for nine years. He had become universally accepted as the classic #2 hitter in baseball, an absolute master at hitting behind the runner. A smart player who would be able to give Pee Wee Reese just the kind of help he needed. What made me think we had a chance of getting that kind of player? Sheer opportunism. For years, everybody had been saying that Billy Herman had everything it took to make a great manager, but when the Cubs had fired Gabby Hartnett at the end of the previous season they hadn't hired him. Instead, their new general manager, Jim Gallagher, had hired Jimmy Wilson, who had come out of virtual retirement at the tag end of the previous season when Cincinnati ran out of catchers and not only had a fine World Series at the age of forty but had captured the imagination of the baseball world by stealing second base. Common sense told you that Herman had to be very unhappy, and Billy had always been a convivial chap with a coterie of close friends and drinking companions on the club. Altogether a rotten situation which Gallagher, who had brought it on by hiring Wilson in the first place, should be only too happy to solve by getting rid of Herman.

About two weeks into the season, I was awakened by a call at about four in the morning. "Are you awake?" came the booming voice of Larry MacPhail.

"No, I'm bowling, Larry. I'm cruising down the Potomac on the Presidential yacht. I am *now*. What the hell's the matter with you?"

"Say hello," he said, "to your new second-baseman."

"Hello, buddy," came the weary voice of Billy Herman. "I'll see you at the ball park if this boss of yours will let me go back to sleep."

MacPhail had apparently been talking to Gallagher and Wilson about Herman, and as soon as the Cubs came to New York they had invited MacPhail up to their suite. Very quickly, Larry had deduced that they were trying to get him drunk. Possibly because they were pouring from a bottle of Napoleon brandy which, as everybody knew, was the magic potion that drove MacPhail mad. You should have heard him the next day as he was describing how he had kept emptying his drinks into flowerpots, toilet bowls and any other handy receptacle. "And every time they were pouring for me," he chortled, "I was pouring for them." How could anybody doubt it? For the best second-baseman in the league, he had given them a second-string outfielder and a utility infielder. And just to make sure they didn't renege on the deal in the morning he had made them write it out on the back of an envelope in their own wavering handwriting and sign it.

The deal for Billy Herman won the pennant for us. Or, to put it another way, the Brooklyn Dodgers won the pennant because Jimmy Wilson stole second base in a World Series at the age of forty. But that's one of the fascinations of baseball trading. You're going to find out later how the New York Giants won a pennant because an Army bomber trying to make an emergency landing at LaGuardia airport crashed into the bay.

MacPhail made one other important acquisition before the end of the season when he picked up an overaged, used-up pitcher, Johnny Allen, on waivers. We'll get to that. But first I want to tell you about another of our overaged, used-up pitchers, Fat Freddie Fitzsimmons.

Freddie Fitzsimmons was thirty-eight years old when I took over the ball club. He had already spent a full, meritorious career pitching for the Giants. In twelve years over there, he had won 170 games, and when he was picked up by Brooklyn the year before I got there everybody knew he was at the end of the line. Fitz was a knuckleball pitcher and his arm was so crooked that he literally could not reach down and pick anything up, he had to bend from the knees. It was so crooked that it threw his balance off and gave him a kind of rolling, swaggering gait. To put as little strain on his arm as possible, he only pitched once a week, and even then his arm would draw up, inning by inning, until you could see his hand disappear up his sleeve. Until finally it would stiffen up so much that you had to get him out of there.

And that was a problem, too. Off the field, Freddie was as nice a man as you would ever want to meet. Once he got out on the mound, you just couldn't talk to him. He'd snap his head at you and stomp around and snarl out his words like a lion chewing meat.

Still, Freddie knew how to pitch, and he was such a ferocious competitor that I had figured on keeping him around as a spot pitcher and coach until somebody better came along. Somebody better, huh? In 1940, at the age of thirty-nine, all Freddie did was set an all-time record for National League pitchers. Sixteen wins against only two losses.

In spring training his arm gave him so much trouble again that he had become little more than a coach until our pitching started to fall apart and we had to reactivate him. All he had done for us was win five straight games before Pee Wee Reese kicked a beautifully pitched game away for him against the Cardinals, the team we were fighting for the pennant. All right, we were ending the season by going on a long road trip, and by resting Freddie for eleven days I was going to be able to pitch him right back against the Cardinals in St. Louis. We came into St. Louis one game ahead of the Cards, and they had their best pitcher, Ernie White, ready for us. It turned out to be one of those ball games. But, then, the whole Western trip became a succession of beanball battles and fights with umpires. Fitz got into trouble in the very first inning when the base umpire, Lee Ballenfant, got in the way of the throw to first base on a double-play ball and got hit on the back, the only time I have ever seen that happen in my fifty years in baseball. A few innings later the Cards scored two runs when Pee Wee Reese dropped the throw from Fitz on an even easier double play. In the eighth inning, Al Barlick, the umpire behind the plate, almost beat us single-handed. He started by taking a base on balls away from Reese on a terrible call, which cost us the go-ahead run when Pete Reiser, the next batter, tripled. We were all up in the dugout screaming at Barlick. Reiser, who was the best I ever saw at stealing home, was jumping up and down the baseline. White became so rattled that he committed as flagrant a balk as it is possible to commit, and Barlick was so rattled that he didn't call it. You never heard such screaming. Jeez, I was all over him. And he gave me the most remarkable explanation I have ever heard. "I'm not going to let you win as important a game as this," he said, "on a technicality."

And just what the hell are you going to say to that?

In the last half of the inning the Cardinals loaded the bases with two out, and the batter was Big John Mize. Now, there is one thing I haven't told you about Freddie Fitz. For as long as I had known him, he had hated Johnny Mize, and I had never been able to get him to tell me why. He just didn't like him, the way some people just don't like other people. "He's a tomato-face," he'd growl. "He's a picklehead." He had all kinds of names like that for him. "I just don't like him."

I knew it was going to be a fight but I said to myself, "Goddam . . ." and started out to get him. As soon as Freddie saw me coming he turned his back and went stomping off in the other direction. By the time I caught up with him he was circling around in front of second base like a man on a bicycle. The umpires came closing in on me. "What are you going to do, Leo? Come on."

What am I going to do? I can't get to my pitcher. You go get him for me!

He was like a bear on a leash. *Awrrrrr.* Goddam, I'd never seen anybody stomp and growl like that. "You're not going to take me out of this fucken ball game, Durocher. Get back to the bench."

"Wait a minute, Freddie. . . ."

"*Back to the bench, Durocher.* I started this game and I'm going to finish it!"

When I was finally able to coax him back to the mound and quiet him down, I said to him, "Christ, Freddie, your arm looks like it's all choked up."

"Don't you worry about my arm. My arm's all right. *That picklehead*, he ain't going to hit me. I'm going to knock his cap off."

And all the time he was glaring in at Mize and talking loud enough so that he'd hear him. He would do that to Mize all the time, and Mize would never say a word. He'd just blow out his cheeks, like he was blowing wind, and dig in.

If you ever saw Freddie pitch you could never forget him. He would turn his back completely to the batter as he was winding up, wheel back around and let out the most god-awful grunt as he was letting the ball go—*rrrrrhhhhhooooo!*—like a rhinoceros in heat.

First pitch to Mize, he wound up, wheeled back—*rrrrrhhhhhooooo*—and threw a fast ball about six inches behind Mize's ear. Mickey Owen had to go flying behind Mize to catch the ball, and I fell right off the bench into the well of the dugout. Holy Jesus, a wild pitch lets in the go-ahead run and maybe beats us right there. He hits him and it's even worse.

Second pitch is a knuckleball right through the middle for a strike. Freddie comes waddling halfway down to the plate after he gets the ball back and snarls at Mize, "Get ready, picklehead, you're going down again."

I'm hollering at him from the bench and he's just staring at me, his eyes kind of glazed and smoky.

Another fast ball and down Mize goes. Then another knuckleball right through there. This time, Fitz walks even farther down to the plate. "Right at that thick picklehead skull of yours," he snarls.

I didn't believe it. There was no way he was going to a 3–2 count in that situation. On a 3–2 count, everybody would be running, the force play is gone, a hit brings in at least one extra run—and that's all aside from the risk of a wild pitch.

Rrrrrhhhhhooooo! Down goes Johnny Mize again, cap, bat and everything flying. Fitz has come stomping in right behind the pitch, and Owen runs out to meet him, trying to talk to him, to quiet him down. Fitz takes the ball away from him and snarls, "It's gonna be right there where you like it, tomato-face. And you're never going to get your bat off your shoulder."

Holy God . . . Mize's cheeks are out to here, and I'm on my knees on the dugout floor, practically praying. Fitz wheels around toward center field, swings back toward the plate—*rrrrrhhhhhooooo!* you can hear him in the center-field bleachers—and throws up a slow, slow, slow curve. Mize's eyes opened this wide and he started to swing about eleven times. The ball dropped right down in there for strike three, Freddie rolled his glove up, shoved it into his pocket and came strutting into the dugout. "I told you that picklehead could never hit me!"

Stayed in there, and we won it in eleven innings.

Johnny Allen's game was even more so. MacPhail had picked Allen up from the St. Louis Browns, after everybody in both leagues had waived on him, because our pitching was in such bad shape that we had nothing to lose. Johnny Allen was thirty-six years old, but he had been a winner for most of his life. Temperamental and terrible-tempered, but a winner. I said that Fitzsimmon had set the National League record for best pitching percentage in a season. Johnny Allen held the record for the majors. Fifteen wins and one loss while he was with Cleveland. Before that, he had led the league in his freshman year with the Yankees.

As a footnote to the records, he also brought on two changes in the rules, both of them sartorial. While he was with Cleveland he had cut the sleeve of his sweatshirt in ribbons so that when he swung his arm toward the plate the ball would come out of a flapping white background. Can't do that any more. Can't even have a loose thread. While he was with us, he brought on a change in the umpires' neck-wear—and if that doesn't give you a clue, it was also the last game he ever pitched for us.

Against our retread the Reds were pitching Paul Der-ringer, who had turned the deal for me into a great one for Cincinnati by becoming one of the very best pitchers in baseball. We could see how it was going to be when a strike was called on our leadoff man, Dixie Walker, before he stepped into the batter's box. Dixie, who almost never argued with an umpire, had flung his bat in disgust the previous day after being called out on strikes, and the League office was following our adventures so closely by then that the fines were being levied against us on a twenty-four-hour, day-to-day basis. Dixie had wanted to—uh—discuss that fine with Larry Goetz, and Goetz was so anxious not to fight yesterday's battle over again that he started a brand-new one by signaling Derringer to start pitching. Dixie was screaming at Goetz, Goetz was signaling to Derringer to keep pitching, and I came running out in front of the plate fully prepared to catch the next pitch in my teeth if I had to.

When their leadoff man, Billy Werber, came to bat, Allen shouted, "Down you go!" Oh yes, it was going to be another of those games. It was also one of those hot Cincinnati after-noons. Allen, who hadn't pitched that much for a couple of years, got locked into a scoreless pitching duel with Derringer, and by the third inning the beer and whiskey were pouring out of him. Every inning he'd come in and get a drink of water, and cool towels would be wrapped around his head. "Stay right with 'em, Johnny," I'd say whenever my pacing took me past him. "We'll get you a run."

At the end of nine innings, Johnny had pitched a one-hitter, and we had got him exactly no runs. "Stay in there, Johnny," I said. "We'll get 'em for you."

In the fourteenth inning, with the score still 0–0, Johnny walked the full length of the dugout and plopped himself down alongside me. Automatically I said, "Stay with 'em, Johnny. We'll get you a run."

He rolled his eyes to me and said, "You sure you're not shittin' me, Skip?"

I guess I'd have to say that I was. In the sixteenth inning he hit a ground ball that was bobbled and, great competitor that he was, ran so hard to beat the throw that he tripped over the base and went rolling and skidding across the dirt. We carried him off in such a state of exhaustion that he almost needed mouth-to-mouth resuscitation.

Our leadoff man in the seventeenth inning was Pete Reiser, and Derringer had been getting him out all day by pitching him tight. Now, for such a great control pitcher, Derringer had a peculiar way of pitching. At the very moment of his delivery he would take his eyes off the plate and focus on a point right in front of him, like a spot bowler. As Pete was picking out his bat, I told him to jump back in the batter's box just as Derringer was bringing his arm forward. Pete jumped back about a foot and hit the ball 450 feet into the right-field bleachers.

Before the inning was over, we had scored 5 runs. With considerable help from the Reds. The rules at the time didn't permit you to put on the lights after the game had started, and if it got so dark that we couldn't finish the game the score would have to revert to the previous inning. When it got so bad that Billy Werber, their third baseman, shielded his eyes and let a little pop fly drop in front of him, Goetz went over and warned McKechnie that the game was going to go to a finish. Regardless.

By the time we took the field, after a couple of our hitters had deliberately struck out, it was so dark that I couldn't see my outfielders. The only thing I could see out there was the fires being built by the bleacher fans so they could see what was going on.

And we almost blew it. In his haste to get the game over with before total darkness set in or the park burned down, Hugh Casey, our ace relief pitcher, began to pitch so quickly that he walked the first two men. Larry Goetz came out and told him, "We'll play this game to a finish if we have to put miner's lights on our caps. Don't let that worry you."

Five more minutes and we'd have needed them. With the bases loaded, the Cincinnati batter hit what looked like a hot line drive to me. I lost sight of it, but apparently the ball hit the ground because I could just about make out Reese bending over in the gloaming and throwing the ball to second.

Hugh Casey was perhaps the most important man on our pitching staff. He had been floating around the minor leagues for years before MacPhail brought him up. He had control and he had a natural sinker, and that was about it. His fast ball was used only to brush the hitter back, and he had a slider (called a nickel-curve in those days) which he used only to show the batter that he could throw something else. Given his limited repertoire, I had done something with him that was unique at that time. I had assigned him the job of late-inning relief pitcher, the guy who came in over the last few innings to choke off a rally. It was nine years before Casey Stengel came to the Yankees and began to use Joe Page the same way.

Hugh was another Southerner, a Georgian, and he drank enough so that he had a pretty good belly on him. But he had a great disposition, and for him to have panicked like he did in Cincinnati was so highly unusual that I didn't give it a second thought. And then in Pittsburgh it happened again. In the eighth inning, with a runner on third and two outs, Al Lopez pulled one of the shrewdest things I have ever seen on a ball field. As Casey was about to pitch, Lopez swung one foot out of the batter's box as if he were backing out, and when George Magerkurth, who was not the best umpire who ever lived, neglected to call time, stepped right back in again. Casey, of course, had hesitated in his delivery, and Magerkurth called a balk on him and waved the runner in from third with the tying run.

Well, I'm not strapped to the bench. I must have been out there for a good ten minutes, calling Magerkurth the kind of things that you can only get away with when the umpire knows he has blown one.

OK, when the game resumed, Casey got two quick strikes on Lopez. And then, instead of brushing Lopez back, he threw the ball at Magerkurth. Right at his head. Not a bad idea. Magerkurth was a huge man, and he made an excellent target. The only trouble was that Casey kept throwing at him. Three straight times the ball went flying over Magerkurth's head. The Maje, who didn't like the idea of being thrown at even once, whipped off his mask and came out screaming that he knew what Casey was doing. One more wild pitch, he hollered, and he was out of the game. I came running out, screaming at Magerkurth that I'd decide when to take my pitcher out for wildness, not him. All three of us were blind with rage, but when it was over I was the only one out of the game. There was a tunnel that led from the dugout to our dressing room, and I was so furious that I broke every light bulb along the way and then picked up the chair in front of the umpire's room and threw it right through the window.

When I got into our locker room, the clubhouse man, who had been listening over the radio, told me that the Pirates had scored another run. Casey had completed the job of walking Lopez, and a rookie shortstop named Alf Anderson, who was absolutely the worst-looking hitter I had ever seen in a big-league uniform, had driven him in with a triple.

"Anderson?" I yelled. "Anderson! What did *he* do to get a triple? Hit the ball into a hole?"

Nope. Casey had thrown one right down the pipe and Anderson—*Anderson?*—had hit it against the wall.

So now we went to Philadelphia with only a half-game lead to play a five-game series in three days. This was the series I had been saving up for. The Phils were deep in last place, and if we could sweep the series we might be able to go into the last four games of the season with a nice little cushion.

I take these pennant races very calmly, you understand. In the spring of 1934, I'd had more hair than anybody could want and by the end of the year I was practically bald. I'm not sure whether it was the pressure of the pennant race or heredity, and while I'd like to think it was heredity, I wouldn't give any odds. And that had been when I was only a player. As a manager, I hadn't had a good night's sleep in three weeks. I'd wake up at three o'clock in the morning and it would be in my mind that I had somehow made a decision on my pitching rotation.

Awake or asleep, it had come to me at the beginning of the road trip that it would be courting disaster to shave after a Dodger victory and fatal to change my clothes until we clinched the pennant. I had been wearing the same slacks and sport shirt for three weeks and—even more important—the same blue necktie. I knew absolutely that we couldn't win if anything happened to that blue necktie—but who's superstitious?

By the time we arrived in Philadelphia I looked like a bum. But I had my pitching rotation set. On Saturday it would be Wyatt and Higbe, who had already won twenty games apiece. On Sunday, it was going to be Johnny Allen and Curt Davis, who had come as a throw-in in the Medwick deal and had become a great clutch pitcher for us. And on Monday it would be Freddie Fitzsimmons. Wyatt and Higbe both won. The Cardinals won both games of their double-header, too. On Sunday, we made the season for the Phils. The largest crowd in their history jammed the park, and most of it had come down from Brooklyn. Johnny Allen won the first game with ease, and all Curt Davis had ever had to do was throw his glove on the mound to beat Philadelphia. Curt was already in the trainer's room getting his arm rubbed when Ted McGrew, who was MacPhail's crony (which meant that McGrew had a chance to get fired more often than I did), came sneaking into the clubhouse. "The boss thinks you ought to pitch Hamlin in the second game," he told me.

Well, that was like putting a torch to my fuse. "The boss *thinks* I ought to pitch Hamlin? We've come this far, and all of a sudden Mr. MacPhail is going to take over and become a genius? You go back and tell the boss to mind his own business. *Get out of here!*"

Hamlin! From the time we had become a pennant con-tender, Hamlin had shown nothing except a remarkable in-ability to hold a lead. Earlier in the year, after Hamlin had blown two big leads in a row, MacPhail had come barging into the clubhouse to call him a gutless so and so, and instead of running him out of there I had sat back and admitted to myself that I had never truly appreciated Larry's brilliant way with words before.

It was even worse than it sounds. I had told MacPhail what my pitching rotation was going to be on Friday night. He wasn't merely offering a suggestion, he was ordering me to make a change.

I ran McGrew out of the clubhouse, and then I got to thinking. *What if I pitch Curt Davis and he gets beat and we lose the pennant?* MacPhail would never forgive me. *But what if I pitch Hamlin and we get beat?* I would never forgive myself. There was one other consideration that I gave some little thought to. If my man pitched and we lost, MacPhail would fire me, and this time he might find out that he really meant it. If his man pitched and we lost, my job was safe. If you want to say that I lost my nerve, how can I argue with you? If you want to say that I used the better part of discretion, then you are a magnificent human being.

I did ask Curt whether it made any difference to him whether he pitched that day or the next one, but it was just going through the motions. Curt was the kind of a guy who was always agreeable to anything.

"I got a hunch," I told the players when they came around to ask what was going on. "Just a hunch, boys."

They knew I had hunches all the time, that I did things that went against the book. Enough of them had worked out so that over the last two months of the season the kind of situation had developed that a manager dreams of and almost never gets—twenty-five men who had absolute belief that any decision I made was the right one. Well, twenty-four anyway. I had sent Freddie Fitzsimmons down to tell Hamlin that he was going to be the pitcher, and Freddie told me later—oh, how I wished he'd have told me at the time—that instead of grabbing the ball, Hamlin had groused, "This is a fine time to tell a guy he's pitching. I don't care whether I win or lose now." And that he had just lobbed the ball while he was warming up until Freddie threatened to throttle him.

Hamlin's great trouble, I always felt, was psychological. He had a real good fast ball until he got into trouble, and then he'd let up a little on it to make sure he got it over. He loaded the bases in the first inning, and Danny Litwhiler jumped on one of those let-up fast balls and hit it up on the roof. Nobody was out yet, we were behind, 4–0, and to all practical purposes the ball game was over.

I had just taken off one of my spiked shoes back in the locker room when I saw McGrew stick his head through the doorway. I let it fly. Took the soft hat right off his head. Jeez, it could have killed him. "You miserable stool pigeon," I hollered after him. "You tell that MacPhail to keep his nose out of my business."

Sure. Better to call poor McGrew a stool pigeon than to call myself what I knew I was. With Hamlin, it was only a subconscious loss of confidence. I had turned myself into MacPhail's office boy, knowing exactly what I was doing and why.

On Monday, I pitched Curt Davis and he shut them out. With four games left in the season we were leading by one and a half games.

We won the pennant by winning two straight in Boston. In one way, the timing was perfect. We were heading back to New York that same night to play our final two games at Ebbets Field.

How all the champagne and whiskey got on the train I'll never know. But then, I'll never know where Dolph Camilli came up with a straight razor either. Dolph went through the train cutting everybody's belt or suspenders, and when they'd grab their pants to hold them up, Cookie Lavagetto would snip their tie off just below the knot. Not only the other players', anybody's who appeared on the horizon. Except for me. "My lucky tie, boys," I'd say. "You wouldn't dare to touch this tie." The same thing happened when everybody began to rip everybody else's shirt off. All I had to do was hold my hand up. "Tear my shirt, boys, and you're liable to damage the tie."

When we got to New Haven, I managed to sit everybody down. "That will be all, boys," I told them. "No more drinking." I had been getting reports from the conductor that they were estimating that there were going to be 25,000 to 30,000 people waiting for us at Grand Central Station. There were already so many of our fans there, I was told, that they had completely taken over the terminal.

I took the players into the dining car for the most beautiful steak dinner you have ever seen. Tony Martin, an old buddy, had been traveling with us as our good luck charm, and naturally he was invited to come in with us. They'd all had a lot to drink by then, and yet the adrenalin was running so strong that nobody was really drunk. In other words, they were all feeling just fine. Tony Martin got up, with just his trousers on—they'd ripped his shirt and undershirt off— and announced that he was going to sing a victory song. Pee Wee Reese, who looked all of fifteen by this time, put his hand right under his steak and hit him right in the chest with it. "Sit down, ya bum ya," he said. "We don't want any crooning. We're having too much fun."

Maybe you had to be there.

Now, all the time we were eating I was on the ear because I wanted to make sure nobody had any bright ideas about slipping away to finish off that champagne. And I kept hearing these murmurs all around me. "When the train stops at 125th Street we'll get off and take a cab and duck the crowd instead of going on to Grand Central."

Hey, what's going on here? I'm saying to myself. *What's all this about 125th Street?*

I got ahold of the conductor and he told me that it was true. We were going to be making a preliminary stop at 125th Street. "Oh no we're not," I said. "You tell them to go right on through to Grand Central Station."

The conductor didn't tell me that McDonald had got a wire from Larry MacPhail ordering him to stop the train at 125th Street. John McDonald didn't say a word about any wire to me either. MacPhail was waiting to board the train with Branch Rickey and a couple of other close friends, but I didn't know that. When we hit 125th Street we were going 50–60 miles an hour, and Mr. MacPhail and Mr. Rickey were left standing there with their coats just waving in the breeze as we sped by.

It took us a good two hours to get away from Grand Central, and somewhere underneath all the excitement I was thinking, where's MacPhail? All these cameras and no MacPhail? That's not the Larry MacPhail I know.

There was another crowd waiting in the lobby of the New Yorker, and as Medwick and I were trying to get through, the word was passed to me that the newsreel cameras were waiting upstairs in one of the club's suites. It seemed that they wanted to take some pictures of me before I shaved. When we got to the elevator, who did we find standing there but Larry MacPhail. Redder than a beet and breathing heavily. He didn't say Hello, Goodbye or Congratulations. Just a red, red face and breathing hard and not looking at anybody or anything.

Didn't say a word to me in the suite either. Not until the cameras were being taken away. "I want to see you," he said, pointing to McDonald. "And you. Come with me, both of you."

The three of us went into the bedroom and he closed the door and we were sitting in a tight little threesome. "Why didn't you have the train stopped at 125th Street as I ordered in my wire?" he asked McDonald.

That was the first I heard about the wire. Before John could answer, I told Larry exactly what happened, and all the time I was talking he just sat there and glared at me. "You're not satisfied being the manager of this club," he said. "You want to be president."

"No such thing. I figured the fans hadn't had a pennant winner in twenty-one years and they were entitled to see the players."

"You're fired!"

I said, "Here we go again. I'm fired. So I'm fired. Je-sus Christ." One word led to another, as it always seemed to do with Larry. He stopped cursing me only long enough to say, "We wouldn't have won any pennant if I hadn't straightened out your pitching rotation by making you pitch Hamlin."

After that, it became a cursing contest. It ended not unlike the first time the three of us had got together with him calling me everything under the sun and me giving his chair a good hard shove. Only this time I went barging out of the room.

Along about three in the morning, I was awakened from the first sound sleep I'd had in three weeks by a pounding on the door. John McDonald was standing there to tell me that the boss wanted to see me.

"Tell the boss to go to hell." I slammed the door in his face and for the rest of the night I was in one of those drifting states of sleep where I would doze off for about ten minutes, wake up and remember how mad I was and hit the pillow.

At seven thirty the phone rang. MacPhail. He wanted to know whether it was my intention to stop at his office on my way to the park.

"No, I had not intended to." Very formal.

"I wish you would."

"I would be glad to."

I walked into his office about two hours later and found him sitting at his desk signing checks. He was wearing a beautiful blue suit, the inevitable fresh carnation was in his buttonhole, and he looked as if he had just had 150 hours of sleep. He asked me very politely to sit down, finished signing the checks and then turned to me with a little smile on his face. "Got a little drunk out last night, didn't it?"

"Little bit," I said.

"Let's figure out how to beat those goddam Yankees!" he roared.

THE SECOND GUESS—
THE GREAT NATIONAL PASTIME

ONE OF THE QUESTIONS you are sure to get after any disaster —and I've lost 13½ game leads as well as overcome them— goes: "Thinking back on it now, if you could do it over again, is there anything you'd like to do different?"

It's an unfair question. It's a meaningless question, really, because what it really means is: "Knowing what you know now, would you do it different?"

Well, sure. If everybody on the *Titanic* had known that it was going to hit an iceberg, the ship would have left England with three passengers, all of whom would have just taken out a double-indemnity policy with Lloyd's of London.

I don't believe in second-guessing myself. I really don't. After something hasn't worked, I know that it hasn't worked. Period. If I had known it wasn't going to work ahead of time, I wouldn't have done it.

When I was on the NBC telecasting team with Lindsay Nelson, he would sometimes ask me after a play, "Well, Skip, what would you have done in that situation?" And I would tell him, "Lindsay, don't ever ask me a question like that after it's over. I can't be wrong now. I know what happened." Whenever he wanted to ask me anything, I would tell him—and I'd say this on the air—I wanted him to ask me before it happened. And even there, I'd always make it a point to add, "But of course I'm up in the booth, it's very easy for me to say to let him hit away. The manager is thinking down on the bench. Let's see what he does."

Managing a ball club is the most vulnerable job in the world. From the moment you take the job you're vulnerable. If you don't win, you're going to be fired. If you do win, you've only put off the day you're going to be fired. And no matter what you do, you're going to be second-guessed. The manager is the only person in the ball park who has to call it right now. Everybody else can call it after it's over.

At Ebbets Field, there was a guy who sat in the box seat right at the corner of the dugout where I always sat. If I stood up I could have reached over and touched him, that's how close he was to me. Every day he was there; and every chance he got he'd get on me something fierce. He got me so mad that I asked around to find out who he was, and do you know what I was told? I was told that he was Irwin Steingut, the political leader of Brooklyn.

There came one particular day when I was coaching at first and everything I did was wrong. When I called for a bunt, the batter bunted into a double play. When I hit-and-ran, the batter missed the ball and the runner was thrown out. Try to steal, same thing. By the seventh inning, Steingut had me so bananas that although we were only one run behind, I stayed in the dugout and sent somebody else out to coach. Immediately we got a man on first and second with nobody out. I gave the bunt sign. Follow me now—I had already given the sign and then I jumped up real quick and I said to him, "All right, smart guy. What would you do?"

He said, "I'd bunt."

"OK," I said. My man bunted—boom—double play. I jumped up again and just looked at him. Nose to nose. "Well, genius," I said, "what have you got to say?"

Nothing was what he had to say. Not then, not later, not ever. From that day on that man never said another word to me. And if he had just kept quiet and not told me to bunt, he'd have had me cold. "You idiot," he'd have screamed. "You stupid bum. Who ever told you you could manage?"

You'd think a political boss would know enough to keep his mouth shut until after the returns were in, wouldn't you?

I got MacPhail once, too, and I got him good.

When you're working for a man like MacPhail who is sure that he's right even after he has been proven wrong, you can imagine what a second-guess you're always getting from him. Any time a pitcher got knocked out, I'd kept him in too long. Unless, of course, the man I put in for him got bombed, in which case I hadn't left him in long enough. We had lost an important game to the Giants, and when I stopped at his office the next day, as I usually did, he began to tell me, at length, what I had done wrong. Which, in a word, was everything. "Look, Larry," I said. "You're taking a pretty good shot at me after it's all over. If you'll let me do these things the next day, I'll win 154. I'll never lose one because I'll never make a mistake. You're giving me a pretty good second-guess here."

He insisted that it wasn't a second-guess. No, no. He'd have done it his way the first time.

That fall, we were sitting together in the Brooklyn box watching the World Series. The Cardinals were trailing the Yankees by one run in the seventh inning, there was a man on first base, and Slaughter was the batter. I nudged Mac-Phail and said, "What would you do?" He was tongue-tied. Not a word out of him. I said, "What would you do, Larry? You can't go home and have dinner. *What would you do?* Would you hit or would you bunt?"

Before he could answer me, Slaughter hit a line drive to right center for a double. Tied the score. I nudged MacPhail again and said, "You'da hit, huh?"

MacPhail got all red in the face and said, "All right, I'll never second-guess you again."

In all honesty, I have to say that he never did second-guess me again. In all honesty, I also have to say that he went into the army before the month was over and never had another chance to.

Keeping all that in mind, I still have to say that we could have won the World Series in 1941. Every bad break that we could have got, we got. Which means nothing either. That's loser talk.

The whole Series revolved around two games. And those two games revolved around Hugh Casey. Going into the third game, we were all even. Freddie Fitzsimmons was my pitcher, the oldest man ever to start in a World Series. And Freddie was just tremendous. For seven innings he pitched scoreless ball. For seven innings Marius Russo, the little Yankee curveballer, matched him. The only trouble was that the final out in the seventh was a line drive off Russo's bat which hit Freddie square on the kneecap, bounced high in the air and was caught by Pee Wee Reese. Freddie had to be assisted back to the dugout, cursing every step of the way.

Casey came out to pitch the eighth inning, and they immediately got four hits and scored two runs. But it wasn't quite that simple. The second hit was a routine ground ball on which Casey failed to cover first base. Moments later, he stood paralyzed on the mound when he had Red Rolfe, who had got the first hit, picked cleanly off second.

When I asked him about it in the clubhouse after the game, he said, "I don't know what happened to me, Skip. I wanted to throw the ball but I just froze."

The next day was the day of the missed third strike. The game that was won and then lost. We were ahead, 4–3, in the ninth inning. Two out and nobody on. Two strikes on Tommy Henrich. Casey threw his bread-and-butter pitch, a hard sinker breaking low on the outside corner of the plate (which is the inside corner to a left-handed hitter like Henrich). Henrich missed the ball by a foot, the umpire yelled, "Strike three," and the ball got away from Mickey Owen.

How the story got started that Casey had crossed Owen up by throwing a spitball is something I will never know. Nothing was said about any spitter at the time, you know. It was months before I first heard it. Maybe as long as a year. I do know that nothing I can say here is going to change it. It makes a better story that way. The cheater outsmarts himself and virtue triumphs. Considering how often virtue gets to triumph these days, maybe I'd better leave it alone.

It just isn't true, though. Hugh Casey didn't even know how to throw a spitball. Why should he? Casey had a natural sinker—that's why he was a relief pitcher. A good spitball acts exactly the same way. It breaks down and away. Common sense tells you that a man wouldn't bother to develop a pitch that acts the same as the pitch he's already throwing. Since common sense triumphs about as often as virtue, future generations are still going to read how Casey's spitter got away from Owen.

What really happened was that Casey made a great pitch and then everything went wrong. Mickey Owen reached for the ball instead of shifting his feet, as he should have, and the ball went off the end of his glove and rolled behind him. It didn't roll that far, either. If there had been grass behind the plate, there is no question in my mind but that Henrich would have been thrown out at first base. Mickey spun around and went after the ball right away; Henrich was very slow in leaving the plate. But it was the fall of the year, there was a big stretch of dirt around the plate and, to make it worse, a slight downhill pitch. The ball not only kept rolling, it seemed to pick up speed. To complete the picture, the police had come running out of the dugout to hold back the crowd, and they were bouncing all around Owen's line of vision after he pounced on the ball and turned to throw.

It wasn't the pitch to Henrich that did it, anyway. There was still only a man on first with two out. It was what happened afterwards. And right there is where I do think it is possible for a manager to second-guess himself. Considering

Casey's actions within a very short period of time—pitching too quickly in Cincinnati, throwing those bean-balls at Magerkurth in Pittsburgh, and freezing twice within a matter of minutes the previous day—I should have called time and gone to the mound to remind him that he still only needed one out to end the ball game. To slow him down, in other words, until I was absolutely sure that he was in full control of himself.

He pitched to DiMaggio almost as soon as he had the ball in his hand, and Joe hit a bullet into left field. And right here is where I have to really give it to myself. A legitimate second-guess. The next batter was Charley Keller, a left-handed hitter. I had Larry French, a veteran left-hander who had been the last of the MacPhail pickups, warming up in the bullpen. Given everything that had been happening, the situation screamed for me to replace Casey with French. I did nothing. I froze. Casey slowed himself down, made two good pitches, and once again we were only one strike away. And now I had a thought of going out to remind him to brush Keller back with the next pitch. Maybe even the next two pitches. Not because I thought he needed to be reminded but only, again, to slow him down. Just as quickly as I thought about it I dismissed it. With Casey seeming to have settled down so nicely, I told myself, what was to be gained by going out and getting everybody jumpy? Defensive, timid thinking, it will kill you every time. Instead of going out, I did what I normally did. I whistled sharply to get his attention and drew my hand across my chest.

Hugh wound up and threw the ball right down the middle, the kind of pitch that Keller saw about once a year. His eyes opened wide as watermelons, his bat came jumping forward and the ball ended up high against the right-field wall. Suddenly, we were a run behind. Right there was where we lost the ball game.

I don't know whether Casey had grown mentally weary from the long, pressure-packed season or whether there was a latent instability in him that had been brought to the fore. Or whether he simply made a couple of very bad pitches at a very bad time. Except for that one stretch, he always seemed at least as stable as the average player, and I know that he had all the guts in the world.

The only other thing I can tell you about Hugh Casey is that a dozen years later he committed suicide. Stuck a gun in his mouth and pulled the trigger.

THE BALLAD OF VAN LINGLE MUNGO

IN MAKING THE TRANSFORMATION to a pennant-winning team we didn't completely lose the old-time Brooklyn flavor. We had our full share of oddballs, night riders and drinkers.

It always comes down to the same thing, though. Talent. Can he help me to win? If he's doing the job on the field, I'll tell you how great it is to have a "buffoon" in the clubhouse to keep everybody loose. If he isn't doing the job, I don't want "that drunk" around.

A buffoon is a drunk on a hitting spree (for further information please consult the story of Dusty Rhodes beginning on page 317).

A drunk is a pitcher who's lost his fast ball.

A confirmed drunk is a pitcher with a sore arm.

An incurable drunk is a pitcher who hasn't won a game all season.

I never minded having what are charitably known as "personalities" on any club of mine, though. It can help to have a character around, and I always felt that I could handle them. I had been there myself.

Right away, in the pretraining camp at Hot Springs, I came across a kid I loved. Red Evans. The whole squad would set out over the mountains together—six miles out and six miles back—and he'd be back thirty minutes before everybody else. I put a couple of spies on him, and they came back and told me he was running every foot of the way. He weighed 160 pounds and he was as big around as a cigarette. Never got tired. Same thing happened at the camp at Clearwater. He'd pitch, he'd run, he'd hit fungoes. He was always on the go.

A superbly conditioned athlete, you might say. I might have said that too, except that he was drunk every night. At Hot Springs, he'd get by Charlie Dressen and me and slip in somehow or other. I knew he was doing that because when I'd ask him how he had got in he'd tell me. He was such a good kid, he never lied to me about anything.

We had such fun with him. In the course of our first disciplinary meeting I asked him what time he had got in the previous night.

"Five o'clock," he said immediately.

"How many beers did you have?"

"Fifteen." That was pretty good; he not only drank them, he counted them.

"Were you drunk?"

"No."

"Well, for crissake," I said. "Charlie Dressen tells me it only takes about six beers to make you drunk."

He jumped up and he was ready to take Charlie on. "How dare you belittle my drinking?"

I thought so much of him I started him in the opening game. He may not have had the most talent on the staff, but nobody was in better shape. Opening game, he was doing great and then he threw a home run ball to Big Zeke Bonura and got beat. Another time he pitched nine innings of a scoreless game against the Cardinals. Pepper Martin on third base. Two out. I came in and told him, "Watch Martin. He loves to steal in this kind of a situation."

"I'll keep an eye on him, Skip."

He watched him all the while he was taking off from third and stealing home. Never took his eye off him. When his record got to 1–8, we had to let him go, but I made sure he got back all the money he had been fined. I loved the guy but he just couldn't win.

MacPhail had his own guy. A short-armed little curve-baller named Cletus Elwood Poffenberger. More commonly known as Boots. Larry had picked him up from Detroit, where he had been getting $4,000. He joined us while we were on the road, and MacPhail's instructions were to try to sign him for the same amount but under no circumstances to go higher than $8,000. Poffenberger boarded the train while we were on our way to Philadelphia and I ripped up his contract right in front of him and gave him the $8,000. And I was wrong. I always sided with the player in any salary dispute, and I was wrong. As a manager, I was part of management and my loyalty should have been to them. Why did I do it? *Because it wasn't my money.* I always figured that if a player felt I had got an extra thousand or two for him, maybe he'd play just a little harder for me. It had to hurt me sooner or later, and it did. At the worst possible time. You'd have thought that Cletus Elwood (Boots) Poffenberger would have taught me. My man, Red Evans, at least won one game for me. Larry's man didn't win any.

Poffenberger had a certain reputation when he came to us. I told him, as I was to tell so many others, "I've heard all the stories and now we can forget them. You're starting out fresh with me."

That was my second mistake. Apparently, Boots took that to mean that I was giving him permission to launch a whole new drinking career.

If you've ever been to the Bellevue-Stratford in Philadelphia, you know that they have a cluster of clocks above the cashier's desk. A big one with the local time, and smaller ones giving the times in various cities around the world.

The first night in Philadelphia, half an hour past midnight, Larry and I were sitting in the lobby and somebody almost stepped on my shoe. I looked up. Our new man, Poffenberger. Now, there was a funny thing about Larry. He could recognize very few of our players when they weren't in uniform, and I could see that he hadn't recognized his man, Poffenberger.

In the morning, I tapped on Mr. Poffenberger's shoulder and asked him what time he had come in. "Eleven o'clock," he said.

"You are a goddam liar," I said. "I was sitting right there in the lobby, and it was twelve thirty by the clock."

"Well," he said. "It depends which clock you were looking at. One of them clocks there said eleven, and that was the one I was going by."

The next morning he walked right past us again at one o'clock in the morning. MacPhail still didn't recognize him, and I waited until the next day again before I impressed upon Boots that he was all out of fresh beginnings.

On the third night, Larry and I left the lobby and started up to our rooms at two o'clock in the morning. Just before the elevator door closed, in steps Poffenberger. Just the three of us there. As soon as Poffenberger got off Larry wanted to know whether that wasn't one of our ballplayers.

"Sure, Larry. Poffenberger."

"Fine him!" Larry yelled. "You let him get away with that one time and he'll think he can do it every night."

We were leaving for Boston the next night on a sleeper train, and although the train wasn't pulling out until three in the morning, the players were supposed to be in their berths with the lights out by midnight. I was told that everybody had reported in and gone to bed, but something gnawed on me. Like boots walking over my head. I just decided it might be a good idea to tuck our wandering boy in and wish him pleasant dreams.

I opened the curtains, and there he was. Sound asleep under the covers. Boots Poffenberger with about two new sets of shoulders. I pulled the blankets back and, sure enough, there was Poffenberger's suitcase. He had put his clothes on over his pajamas and gone off into the night. When I woke up in the morning, I was told that he had just got onto the train as it was ready to pull out of the terminal.

He looked me right in the eye and told me he had been in bed at eleven.

"I'm not talking about the first time you went to bed," I said. "So it won't cost you. What time did you get back?"

"Twelve o'clock."

"Wrong. That mistake costs you one hundred dollars." What time had he got in?

"One o'clock."

"Wrong. It is now up to two hundred dollars."

"I'll give it to you straight, Skip. I got in at two o'clock. A few minutes before, I think."

"Three hundred dollars. Do you want to go for four?"

"Time," he said. "I can't afford this game, Skip. I got on board just as the train was pulling away."

He behaved himself when we got to Boston, which may be saying more about Boston than about Boots, and in the next few weeks he pitched well enough so that I was ready to give him a starting assignment against the Cincinnati Reds. It was another of those brutally hot Cincinnati days. I mean it was hot! Before we went out, I called a meeting so that I could go over the hitters with Poffenberger. The first thing I said was "Boots? Where's Boots? Where the hell is my pitcher?"

Dolph Camilli said, "I forgot to tell you, Skip. He told me it was too hot today, he wasn't coming out. He was going to stay in his room in the nice air-conditioning and think about his future."

I said, "I can tell him about his future. He don't have to look into any crystal ball, I can tell you that." It was going to cost him $200 for not showing up and another $200 for insubordination. After which I was going to tell MacPhail to send him so far away that he would be able to do all his pitching in front of Eskimos.

Dolph's forehead wrinkled, and so did his nose. "Well, he said something else, Skip. It sounded kind of funny. He said, 'Tell Durocher that I am tired of the way he is keeping me, like a bird in a gilded cage.' "

That did it. We sent him home and offered him around the League. Nobody wanted any part of him. After a couple of months, I got a letter from him. "I know you don't want me on the Brooklyn club," he wrote. "But can't you send me to Montreal? I know I can win there and I'm lonesome without any money."

It took a couple of weeks, but I finally was able to convince MacPhail that he should protect his investment by letting Boots pitch at Montreal. We sent him a check for $175 for his plane fare, and he never showed up. That was the end of Cletus Elwood (Boots) Poffenberger.

They pale into insignificance alongside Van Lingle Mungo. A song was written a couple of years ago, entitled "Van Lingle Mungo," which simply recited the names of major-league ballplayers of that period with each chorus ending with the rather melancholy refrain "Van Lin-gle Mun-go."

It wasn't the first song that was ever written about Mungo. There was a many-versed ballad which the poets of the New York press wrote on the ferry between Cuba and Miami to celebrate the exploits of Van Lingle Mungo with a certain Lady Vine and other assorted . . .

Well, let's go back to the beginning.

For four or five years in the early thirties, Mungo was the entire Brooklyn pitching staff. He had been considered as fast as Dean, maybe as good but nowhere near as funny. Mungo was from the hills of South Carolina, and he had a very peculiar way of talking. You could just barely make out what he was saying because he talked as if his mouth was always full of marbles. The best way to describe him is to say that he sounded like Edgar Bergen doing Mortimer Snerd from the bottom of a well.

They loved him in Brooklyn, though, and hope sprung

eternal that he was going to rise from the dead. For two years he had been taking up space on my roster, and I couldn't get MacPhail to get rid of him.

And he drank a bit. Anything. During one of those long road trips, I left the team right after the game and was meeting them in St. Louis. Mungo arrived with his hand in a sling. What had happened was that he had been using hair tonic either to comb his hair or wet his tonsils (choose one) and felt so good about it that he kept breaking up a card game in one of the compartments. The card players had finally pushed him out and locked the door, and Mungo, feeling hurt and lonely, had put his fist through the compartment window. The game had been called off on account of blood, and it seemed to me that even MacPhail would have to see that there was nothing worse than a sore-armed pitcher with his arm in a sling who bleeds all over his teammates' cards on the way to St. Louis.

To save himself, Mungo did the one thing I had never thought possible. He went on the wagon. Didn't touch a drop the rest of the season. All through the winter, MacPhail kept getting reports that Mungo was still on the wagon, and any report of MacPhail's had to be treated with respect. Larry was such a great believer in having detectives tail his players that there were probably more Pinkertons than revenooers roaming the hills of South Carolina that winter.

He showed up in Havana in great shape. Trimmer than he had been in years. Throwing the ball so good that I did what I had sworn I was never going to do. Count on Mungo. "Holy cow, look at him fire the ball. Just like the Old Mungo."

The resurrection of Van Mungo was so widely publicized that the Cleveland Indians, who were coming to Havana for our first Sunday exhibition game, sent word to me that if I'd pitch Mungo they'd pitch Feller and we could pack the park with a Battle of Speedballers.

On Thursday, Mungo asked me for late leave. Fine. My

rule was that if you wanted late leave, for any reason at all, all you had to do was ask. So that if the front office came to me with a report that you had been seen somewhere at two in the morning, I'd be able to say, "I know it. I gave him permission."

On Friday, he asked me again. I had never had anybody come up with an emergency two nights in a row. But: Fine. As long as you ask, Van.

Saturday was a rather trying day for me, what with being escorted off the field by a squad of Batista's soldiers and all, and so MacPhail and I put on our dinner clothes and drove out to the International Casino, about twenty miles away. We had dinner and played a little roulette. A very pleasant night in Havana. All of a sudden I told Larry, "I'm going back to the hotel. I'll send the car back to you." I was going back to check on Mungo. All of a sudden this hunch had come to me that Mungo was cheating on me.

I got back to the Nacional Hotel at about twelve twenty, maybe twelve thirty, and Charlie Dressen was sitting in the card room, waiting for me. He said, "Mungo's looking for you."

That made it even.

Now, as you entered the Nacional Hotel, the card room was off to the left and the lobby extended straight back. I sat there for a few minutes looking around, and as I came back out, there was Mungo coming out of the bar. Walking down the lobby and hitting both walls, that's how loaded he was. As I said, he talked like he had a mouthful of marbles even when he was sober. Drunk as he was, he was almost impossible to understand. "Eyus Chri, wha'euya? Eyinookin awova faya." ("Jesus Christ, where were you? I been looking all over for you.")

"Yeah, you been looking for me! I've been lost. You couldn't find me. *I was here all day!* You saw me at the ball park. What is it?"

He says, "Gee, Leo, I want a little late leave."

Late leave, huh? "You'll get late leave! You got five minutes to get up those stairs and get to your room. Five minutes. Or it's two hundred dollars."

"Jesus Christ. Two hundred dollars."

"Yes, and it will be four hundred. Get up there right now. What the hell's the matter with you?"

He grumbled something completely unintelligible and went staggering up to his room.

Immediately I went running up to my suite. My window overlooked the driveway, and that was the only way he could get out of the hotel. For thirty minutes I sat on the window and, just as I had anticipated, here he comes. On one arm he had Lady Vine, who was the star attraction at the hotel. A singer and mistress of ceremonies. On the other arm was the woman half of the dance team of Gonzales and Gonzales. A Latin dish.

I said to myself, "That dirty——"

I thought to myself, "Both of them?"

I thought, "What the hell do they see in him, either of them?"

I thought, "As drunk as that, *both* of them?"

I said out loud, "To hell with it," and went to bed.

We had so many players down there that it took two buses to get us from the hotel to the ball park. Mungo, my starting pitcher, wasn't on either of them.

The clubhouse in Havana was built down the left-field foul line, 600 feet from home plate. The clubhouse itself was divided into four separate dressing rooms. I had my locker in what was really the trainer's room, along with about a dozen other players. I held my meeting, the players went out on the field and Mungo still hadn't shown up.

I was still playing, and so I stayed behind to get a rub from our trainer, Wilson. That was a joke, too. Our regular trainer had gone into the army, and Wilson had been recommended to me in St. Louis. He knew as much about training, it turned out, as your pipe cleaner does. (During the regular season, he almost lost a game for us—to say nothing of our star pitcher—when Whitlow Wyatt asked for a glass of bicarb, and Wilson gave him a glass of mouthwash.)

Anyway, I was lying flat on the trainer's table, and I could see somebody walk by who by his general lumbering gait looked like it might be Mungo. A couple of minutes later he came back, still in street clothes. Without getting off the table, I said, "Where the hell were you? Why didn't you make the bus?"

In his mushmouth way, he said, "Ya bush wen'of alevme." ("The bus went off and left me.")

"That's right. I got fifty-five players here. Everybody's out of step but you. We all make the bus but you."

"Jesus, the bus went off and left me."

"Well, it cost you two hundred dollars for last night's episode, that's all I got to tell you. For breaking training rules." Which was a joke. A joke. He hadn't broken them, he had spit on them, trampled them and left them for dead. "And another two hundred for not showing up at the park on time."

With that, he mumbled something and clomped over angrily to his locker. I want to ask you something. Have you ever seen a guy who's been out in the cold and his fingers have gone numb? Like when you were a kid, maybe, and you were trying to unbutton your sweater? Can't even unbutton your shirt, your fingers are so cold?

I finally raised up and took a good look at him, and he was still fumbling with his shirt button. I said: "Hold it. Ho–o–o–ld it. You're drunk!"

I came up off that table like a shot. "Get out of here! Put your coat back on and get up that hill! Get back to the hotel. It costs you two hundred more now for coming to this ball park drunk."

And with that he challenged me. "You've been pretty fresh with me," he said. "And now I'm going to slap you right in the mouth."

I said, "You'll never have a better time than right now."

And I looked over and there's Wilson with an ice pick in his hand ready to help me.

I said, "Put the ice pick down and get out of here." I locked the door behind us and turned back to Mungo. "Now. You want to slap me in the mouth, go ahead. It's me and you." I said, "Yeah, you're gonna whip me, no question of that. Unless you're too drunk. But I warn you, before you do, I'm going to sink this Coca-Cola bottle into that numbskull of yours." I said, "You're not going to get away lightly either, don't forget that. You're going to know that you were in this room with me."

I'll tell you something. I don't know whether I had intended to make it that kind of a battle when I locked the door, and I don't know whether I'd have used the Coca-Cola bottle if he'd have come at me. But it's the way it always is. The more you talk the madder you get. If I hadn't used the bottle I'd have broken a chair or something over his head, you can be sure of that. I was mad.

Before it could come to a test, Mungo said, "Ah now, Leo . . ."

"Don't talk to me!"

Then it got to where he was trying to apologize, and I just told him to get back to the hotel.

I hadn't been out on the field fifteen minutes, and here comes MacPhail running lickety-split down the left-field line with his coattails flying. "Leoooo," he's hollering. "Leoooooo."

I came running down the line to meet him. "What the hell's the matter?"

"What happened to Mungo?" he said. Huffing and puffing.

After I had given him a complete rundown, he said, "You sent him back to the hotel, huh? Well, he just hit a cabdriver up on top of the hill, and I now fine him four hundred dollars more, and he's now sent to Macon, Georgia." Macon was where our Montreal farm club was training. All's well that ends well. I have finally got rid of Mungo.

Not yet. Not by a long shot. Mungo was supposed to leave on the seven o'clock boat back to Miami that night. Need I say that he missed the boat?

That night, at a little after midnight, I'm standing outside the door of the hotel, leaning against the wall. Mungo comes walking out, looks around and sees me. "What the hell," he says. "Don't you ever go to bed? Every time I look around I run into you."

"Yes, and you'd a been a lot better off if *you'd* of went to bed last night. And a lot better off if you'd of made that boat, too."

Off goes Mungo into the night.

At about six o'clock in the morning I got a call from the manager of the hotel. Will I please come down to Mungo's room right away?

What now? I put on my house slippers and my robe, ran down the stairs, and, Holy Christ, there are two policemen and a couple of soldiers with bayonets there. Plus Gonzales, the male member of the team of Gonzales and Gonzales. One eye is sticking out to here, and he's got a butcher's knife this long in his hand. His wife hadn't come home all night. He had gone around looking for her and found her in bed with Mungo and Lady Vine. The three of them. Mungo had hit him a shot and knocked him out into the hall and bolted the door. And, Christ, he's back there now with the butcher's knife to kill him.

We finally got everybody to leave, the soldiers dragging Gonzales away. Babe Hamberger, our all-purpose executive, smuggled Mungo out of the room and hid him down in the vegetable bin in the cellar. By that time the police had come back with warrants for Mungo's arrest and they were search-ing all over the hotel for him. Gonzales is prowling the hotel with his black eye and his butcher's knife. All you could hear, wherever you turned, was "Mungo . . . Mungo . . . Mungo." Meanwhile, Babe Hamberger was setting it up with the captain of the Pan-Am seaplane to fly him out. Somehow, Babe was able to smuggle him out to the wharf and had him crouching down between two big doors. As soon as the last piece of baggage was on the plane, the captain raised up his head. That was the signal. Hamberger yelled "Now!" and Mungo came out the door running. The police came running down the wharf behind him, blowing whistles, somebody threw a rope out of the plane, Mungo grabbed it, they pulled him aboard and he got out of Cuba.

I know Gonzales sued Mungo. I don't know what it finally cost.

But they wrote song parodies on it:

> Out the window he must go, he must go
> Out the window he must go
> To find Lady Vine

Johnny Allen asked for late leave before we broke camp the following spring, with almost equally disastrous results. Johnny was fired by both MacPhail and Rickey, as a matter of fact, although obviously only the last one stuck. His trouble with MacPhail came as a result of Larry's fondness for hiring detectives to trail the players. Now that we were pennant winners, he wasn't satisfied with just having them followed during the season. He had hired a private eye in Havana.

Since MacPhail left Cuba early, the final report was given to John McDonald. Unhappily for John, the detective took his gumshoeing so seriously that he identified his subjects by their uniform numbers instead of their names. Now, this was 1942. We were at war. The customs people in Miami found the report in McDonald's typewriter and immediately called in the FBI. Poor John had to do some fast talking to convince them that it wasn't a secret enemy code.

One of the reports was on "Number 15's" night on the town. Johnny Allen. MacPhail was handed the report when the team arrived in Daytona Beach and promptly went off into one of his tirades. On the spot, in front of everybody, he fined Allen and suspended him. It was awful. From what I heard, he achieved new heights of invective even for MacPhail. And when he wouldn't stop screaming long enough for Johnny to explain, Johnny, who had a pretty good temper of his own, stalked away and announced that he was going home and he wasn't coming back.

The first thing I did after I arrived, a couple of hours later, was to talk Johnny into unpacking his bags. The second thing I did was to go to MacPhail and tell him Johnny was unpacking, and that he really wasn't a bad kid. Larry must have gotten out of bed on the right side that day, because he then called a press conference, and when the newspapermen wanted to know how he could possibly reinstate a man he had just said all those terrible things about, Larry said, "Awwwwww, Johnny's not as bad as he's sometimes painted."

That was his apology.

By the next year, Branch Rickey was running the club. All the good young players were in the army by then, and Johnny was the best pitcher we had. I said that he had a temper. What I should have said was that he had a terrible temper. While he was pitching in Pittsburgh, George Barr, who was umpiring at second, called a balk on him that let in a run, and Allen went berserk. I don't mean he got mad; I mean he went berserk. Before I could get to him, he had a headlock on Barr and he was pounding him on top of his bald head with the ball. By the time I got up behind Johnny and put a bear hug on him, Barr's head was full of knots. I had wrapped my arms around him and lifted him off the ground, and I held on tight and practically carried him toward second. "Johnny . . . Johnny," I was saying. "This is Leo. Come on, Johnny. You can't do that. Gee, you're going to get suspended for life. Snap out of it, Johnny. . . ." We were all the way out to the dirt near second base before he began to relax a little and tell me that it was OK now, he was all right. So I let him down and—*shooom*—he's going for Barr again. *Boom!* Barr is flat on his back and now Johnny has him by his necktie. Barr was one of the umpires who wore those four-in-hand neckties, and I give you my word of honor that his tongue was hanging out and he was turning purple. He was choking him. *Choking* him! I also give you my word of honor that no umpire has worn a four-in-hand tie since; it took half the team to pull him away.

As luck would have it, Rickey was there, sitting in a box right behind the bench. After the game he was waiting for me in the lobby of the Schenley Hotel, right across the street from the ball park. When Rickey was really mad, his voice took on the rumblings of the briny deep. "Young man," he rumbled, "that was a disgrace."

What can I do, Branch? I pulled him off. I can't fight him.

"He will never put a Brooklyn uniform on again."

And he didn't. He was fined $1,000 and suspended for thirty days, which was getting off cheap. I guess they figured that if our boys were getting killed overseas, an umpire could stand to have his tongue hung out for airing. As soon as the suspension was up, Rickey put him up on waivers and the Giants claimed him.

Maybe five or six years later I was at the major-league meeting in Columbus, and there, half stiff at the hotel bar, was the familiar figure of Johnny Allen. "Hey, John," I said, "what are you doing with yourself these days?"

He said, "I've gone to umpiring." I like to fell off the chair.

After we had talked for a while about his philosophy of umpiring, I said, "Let me ask you something, Johnny. How much of a beef do you let a fellow have? Where do you draw the line?"

He said, "He can say anything to me as long as he don't touch me. He puts his hands on me, he's gone. He can call me anything, it's all right. But if he lays as much as a finger-tip on me . . ."

That's where I did fall off the chair.

I ONCE WON AN ARGUMENT
WITH AN UMPIRE

I NEVER QUESTIONED the integrity of an umpire. Their eyesight, yes. I always thought it surpassing strange that there has never been an umpire who needed glasses or whose hair turned gray. Ponce de Leon should have veered a little north when he hit the Atlantic Coast and applied at National League Headquarters for working papers. Perennial youth would have been guaranteed.

Every once in a while, though, the Great Scriptwriter in the Sky comes through for you. We were playing the final game of a series in Pittsburgh and the umpire was Bill Stewart, who will never be in the Umpire's Hall of Fame (unless they have a category for Most World Series Decisions Missed with the Cameras Popping). Stewart was a feisty little fellow, and he had been so bad all day that I observed, in the spirit of helpfulness, that it wouldn't be so embarrassing for a man of his age to wear glasses. "You'd see a little better," I explained sympathetically. "And you know you need them."

When he spluttered that he had never used them in his life, my astonishment was so clear, to say nothing of my vocabulary, that I got thrown out of the game.

I was living in St. Louis, and with an off day coming up, I grabbed a plane after the game to fly home. Now picture the scene. I'm sitting in the second seat of the second row with a newspaper in front of my face, and onto the plane strolls Bill Stewart. Sits down in the first row, without seeing me, unfolds his newspaper and reaches into his pocket for a pair of glasses.

Suddenly there comes a tapping on his shoulder, as of a gentle shower from above. *"Thought you didn't need them."*

The umpiring isn't as good today as it was when I broke in. One reason is that, with expansion, there are now so many of them, and another reason is that none of them are Bill Klem, the greatest umpire who ever lived. He called himself "The Old Arbiter," and he had what can only be described as a sense of majesty. To describe Klem's voice, you have to picture W. C. Fields playing a Shakespearean role, and sprinkle it with a slight Irish brogue.

Whatever he did was done with a great flourish. When he was calling you out on strikes, he would swing his arm and body around in a sweeping circular motion and bellow out "Striiiiikkke three!" and if you dared to protest he'd give that big motion again, yank off his mask and take a run at you. "Striiiiike threeee! I guess you didn't hear me, yew applehead, yew."

He never called you by name, he called you by position. If you were the kind of guy who squawked on every called strike, he just might establish some discipline by calling a third strike on a pitch that might have been a bit outside. And when you let out a scream he'd say, "Ah, shortstop, but *you* missed the first twoooo." You'd come to argue with him about a call he'd missed the day before, and he would draw himself up to his full height and intone, "Forty years I'm an umpire, and forty years I've never missed one. It's still a foul ball." What he meant by that was that it had been an honest mistake.

Like most of the umpires of that era, he'd let you give him a pretty good beef on a really close play. The one thing you could not do was call him "Catfish," a particularly ugly fish to which he bore a truly remarkable resemblance. You didn't have to use the word in an argument, either. Just yell it out—once—from the bench and he would pick you out with unerring accuracy. If he couldn't, he'd clear the whole bench. In one of the first games I ever played with Klem behind the plate, a fan sitting in the front row between our dugout and home plate was driving him crazy by chirping "Catfish" at him, plenty loud enough for him to hear but saying it so fast—hardly moving his lips, almost as if it were one syllable—that Klem was never able to turn fast enough to pick him out.

I came to the plate at the start of the sixth inning, and as I hit the plate with my bat, Klem walked around and pretended to be dusting off the plate. "Young man," he said, in as dignified a voice as an angry man can manage in that posture, "see if you can pick that fellow out for me."

I had picked the fellow out five innings earlier, along with everybody else on the bench. He was very easy to point out, too, because he had his topcoat draped on the rail in front of him. As Klem finished the whisking, I took a step back and kind of lifted my bat toward the guy. "He's right over—" Before I could say another word, Klem rasped, "Don't point . . . you . . . dummy . . . you. Or I'll throw you out of here."

What did he want from me? I'm trying to help him and he's going to throw me out of the game?

The next inning he called for the police and ordered them to throw the guy out. "Give him his money back and escort him from the ball park and see to it that he does not return."

I don't know where he got the authority to throw a fan out for exercising his right to free speech. He just did it, that's all. It wasn't the only time I ever saw him throw a fan out of the park, either.

I've got a million Klem stories because the Old Arbiter and Frankie Frisch loved each other, and the way they showed it was to fight and snarl and argue with each other all the time. Klem was a very fair guy that way. If he said something insulting to you first, he would allow you to call him anything in the world for the rest of the game.

There were only three umpires in those days, and the first-base umpire would position himself between first and second at the start of the game. Frisch greeted him with something about as inoffensive as "Hello," and Klem just gave him a look and let out a nasty laugh. "The Fordham Flash, huh? Fordham Flash, my ass!"

That was all it took, because now Frisch knew he had an invitation to the waltz. "Why, you catfish bastard," he said. "You no-good catfishing . . ." If I could have had a tape recorder on any game I've ever played, I know exactly the game it would be. For nine innings, they called each other everything they could think of. Without letup. Hardly stopping for breath.

Later in that same season, Klem forfeited a game on us in the old Baker Bowl in Philadelphia, when Dizzy Dean became so enraged during a rhubarb that he committed the unforgivable sin of heaving the ball against the screen. The next day, we were still so hot about it that it didn't take more than an inning or two before Klem had given Frankie the heave-ho. And there they were at it again. Now, Klem's great trick for putting an end to an argument was to scoot back and draw a line across the dirt with his spikes. "You cross that line, that's all you got to do, yew applehead! Cross that line and you're out of here!"

In the old Baker Bowl, the dressing room was out in center-field stands, just as it was in the Polo Grounds. Frisch started to leave. Klem was still standing back there, a good fifteen yards behind home plate, telling Frankie to be quick about it. Instead, Frankie wheeled around, took another run at him and came to a screeching stop with his toes right on the line. "Cross that line, and it will cost you some *money* now," Klem hollered. "Cross the line, yew applehead, that's all you got to do."

So Frankie wheeled around again, like the halfback he had once been, cut back sharply and came right at him. "Ohhh, that's going to cost you, yew applehead. Now you've done it."

I had kind of tippy-toed around to the side by then, so that I was already on the other side of the line, and now I came charging at him from his blind side. "You go with him," he said, pointing his mask imperiously toward the clubhouse. "Both of you, yewww appleheads."

Naturally, I began to scream that I hadn't crossed the line. I'd gone around it. "Saaame thing," Klem intoned, like ten John Barrymores. "Saaaame difference." His hand went flicking off toward some distant horizon; his voice descended to the lower depths. "When I draw a line it extends out to infinity."

In those days the umpires would always stand with their hands holding onto their lapels during an argument. That was another trick of Klem's, although I didn't discover it until after he had retired. I only wish I had found out about it sooner. The first thing the manager will do in disputing a decision is to ask the offending umpire to consult another umpire. As the senior member of any threesome he was in, Klem's instructions to his partners were to look to him. If they could see his thumbs, he was telling them they could either allow the manager to consult him or come to him themselves. If his thumbs were under the lapels, he was telling them they had called it right and to take nothing from them appleheads.

In those days they weren't afraid to consult the other umpire. They believed what it says in the rule book: "The first rule is: Get the decision right."

Which was great unless they reversed a decision against you.

Pound for pound, George Magerkurth was my favorite opponent. The Maje wasn't a very good umpire, but he would always let you have your beef, and I could get him so mad that his lower lip would turn blue and begin to quiver. (With one part of my mind I'd be screaming, and with the other I'd be watching his lip to see whether I could time it. *Any second now . . . any second now, any . . . there she comes. A little late this time, I must be slipping.*) At which point I would always say, "I'll punch you right in the nose," and he would never fail to answer, "I dare you . . . I dare you."

One day I had him so mad that I thought he was going to choke. The Maje was a giant of a man and he got right on top of me, like a big mastiff over a puppy. It looked as if he was going to take me up in his teeth and shake me. "I'll reach down," he was finally able to splutter, "and bite your head off."

Now, I am going to make a confession that it pains me to have to make. When it comes to the book on snappy repartee between manager and umpire, I am very well represented. I am also a bit of a fake. It has always been my ambition to get off a really good ad lib in the heat of an argument, but all of those immortal cracks of mine that you will hear at baseball banquets come under the heading of ad-libs-thought-out-well-in-advance. About two day later, naturally, the perfect answer came to me. I waited until we were in that situation again, with Magerkurth's lip turning a nice shade of indigo and vibrating away at about 78 rpm, and then I bellied right up to him so that he would be snarling down at me. And, sure enough, he said it again. "I'll reach down and bite your head off."

"If you do," I said, "you'll have more brains in your stomach than you've got in your head."

And I'm in the clubhouse.

The best of the Magerkurth stories came about because he always chewed tobacco, and when he got mad he'd get to spluttering and stuttering. A very dangerous combination when you're engaged in that kind of nose-to-nose confrontation. A couple of days before our most celebrated encounter, he had sprayed Billy Jurges so badly during an argument at the Polo Grounds that Billy had rared back and spit right into his face. The announcement had just come that Billy had been fined $250 and suspended for ten days. (The only reason he hadn't been suspended for the season was that the Maje had apparently been honest enough to list the provocation in his report.)

Before the game started, I had been ribbing him about it good-naturedly, and he had been predicting, perhaps good-naturedly, that I wasn't going to be around long.

During the game, he reversed a decision on us. What had happened was this: A ground ball was hit to Billy Herman, Herman flipped it to Pee Wee Reese, and as the ball hit Pee Wee's glove, Klem signaled that the runner was out and turned toward first to call the second half of the play. There was no second half, because Pee Wee had dropped the ball while transferring it to his throwing hand. Out of the dugout walked the Cincinnati manager, Bill McKechnie. The way he always did, with his arms crossed and walking real slow as if it pained him deeply to have to be doing this. Deacon Bill, we called him. He wore glasses, and he had a mild, reasonable way about him that allowed him to get away with murder. Every other manager I ever knew came running out there. Myself, I couldn't get there quick enough to get thrown out. I decided to try it McKechnie's way once, walking nice and easy, keeping my voice down, and I got thrown out, anyway. So what the hell was the difference?

Anyway, McKechnie got Klem to consult Magerkurth, and the next thing I knew everybody was safe. From the stands came the full-throated cry of the Brooklyn fan: "Leoooo!" Well, I'm not strapped to the bench. My people were calling, and here I come a-flying. "Why, you big ironhead you—" Before I could say another word, the Maje was all over me. "One more word and you're in the clubhouse."

"Not today you don't—not todayyy! You don't reverse a call on me and then shut me off. Not today." And I've got my hands in my pockets, like I always did, because I'm making sure I'm not going to lay a hand on an umpire. Crazy I may be, but not that crazy. But I'm bumping him pretty good. Every time Magerkurth tries to get by me, I move into his path and bump him some more. "Don't you bump into me," he says, and I keep bumping him and I say, "You're running into me, you oaf. Go around me." And everywhere he'd go I'd be in front of him. And when he does get past me and walks down the left-field line, I'm trying to step on his feet to trip him up because I'm really mad. Finally he wheeled on me and yelled, "That's all, you're out of the park." And when he said "park," the tobacco juice splattered me across the face like a summer monsoon. So I took a leap at him and I spit right in his face. Because, in case I have neglected to mention this, when I read about Jurges it had come to me exactly what Jurges should have said and I had it ready.

"That'll cost you two hundred fifty dollars and ten days," Magerkurth roared.

"For what?"

"You spat in my face."

"What the hell do you think this is?" I said, pointing. "Smallpox?"

With his great dignity, which was always so ridiculous in so big a man, he said, "Mi-i-i-ine was an accident."

Mimicking him to the letter, I said, "Not mi-i-i-ine. Mi-i-i-ine was intentional."

Every once in a while you get lucky and say exactly the right thing. "For telling the truth," Magerkurth said, "if you get out of here fast, I won't fine you and I won't suspend you."

"OK, Maje," I said. But, you know, I couldn't resist kicking a little dirt on him as I was leaving, and I got fined $50 for that.

The closest I ever came to a legitimate ad lib was when Beans Reardon, another favorite sparring partner of mine, didn't bother to call a ball fair or foul. Not that it mattered. What was really happening was that we were getting slaughtered by the Cubs, something like 11–0, in addition to which they had the bases loaded, in addition to which I was mad at everybody. Rickey had sent me a couple of young pitchers, Rex Barney and Hal Gregg, who were lightning fast and didn't have the control to throw the ball between a pair of swinging doors. His instructions were to just let them sit around for a while and watch before I used them, but in a game like this what difference did it make?

The batter was Bill "Swish" Nicholson, a big left-handed hitter who was the greatest hitter in the world if you put the ball from his belt on down, and helpless as a babe if you threw him fast balls up and in. The way we liked to pitch him was to get him thinking by starting him off with a slow curve that bounced in the dirt. Boy, he'd step out and pick up a handful of dirt and dig in with his left foot, looking for that slow curve which, of course, he was never going to see again. After that, we pitched him up, up and up. We'd throw him a fast ball across the letters and the whole park would go *Swish* as he swung and missed. The next pitch would be higher—*swish*—and the third pitch would be—*swish*—over his head. We struck him about three times a game, but if you ever made a mistake and got it down you were lucky if the ball only hit against the fence.

I brought Gregg in and explained how to pitch Nicholson. I'd hardly got back to the bench when Gregg threw a slow curve about a foot and a half off the ground, the only curve ball he got over the plate in two years.

Crack! A bullet down the first-base line. I couldn't tell whether it was fair or foul; all I could see was that Reardon had to skip rope to avoid being hit, three more runs have scored, and by the time the ball has stopped bouncing around the bullpen Nicholson is on third. And also that we're still waiting for Reardon to call it one way or the other.

"Leooooooo!" And here I come. As nastily as possible, I said, "Well, what was it, Beansie?"

He looked at me like I had forty-two heads for running out there. "What differences does it make?"

Beansie always had a little smile as if to say, "Aw, get out of here, you nut." And that was just the way he talked to you, too, as if you were wasting everybody's time and it was only through the sweetness of his nature that he was putting up with you.

But the fans were yelling, "Attaboy, Leo, give it to him." Which I could very well understand because there had been absolutely nothing else for them to cheer about all day.

So I'm running him all around first base. "I'm not leaving here until you tell me whether the ball was fair or foul," I said. "I don't know what it was, Beansie, but you certainly should because you had to jump out of the way or it would have hit you on the foot."

The smile became more like a smirk. "I guess it was a fair ball."

"You *guess*. . . ." Boy, I cut loose with some of my fanciest language and, as I was leaving, a couple I guess he had never heard before. Because as I was walking back to the dugout he was coming right behind me, hollering at me. And right at that point, there came to me the perfect squelcher, if only I could get him to feed me the right line. So I scurried along like a little kid to encourage him to keep after me and when I ducked into the little Brooklyn dugout in Ebbets Field I grabbed a towel and wiped my face, making sure that I was just kind of taking a peek to see if he was there.

"What did you say?" Beanie demanded.

"Didn't you hear me, Beansie?" I asked, brightly.

"I'm not sure."

"Well," I said. "*Guess* what I said. You've been guessing all afternoon, anyway."

That cost me $100 and a quick trip to the clubhouse, but

it was worth every cent because it was the closest to an ad lib I ever pulled off.

No, I did pull a brilliant ad lib once. And under the worst kind of pressure. But that was only because I didn't know how to speak Japanese. That's right, Japanese. I've managed to get into trouble wherever I've been. In foreign as well as domestic climes.

The plane had scarcely got off the ground on the Giants' first goodwill tour of Japan before Commissioner Ford Frick, who came with us, was telling me that he didn't want me to get into any argument and/or altercation with the umpires. "They have a tradition over there," he said. "They never argue with the umpires. Whenever they have to approach an umpire they bow."

We were bringing Larry Goetz along as our umpire, and he was sitting just across the aisle. "Never happen where I'll bow to Goetz," I said. "Never."

"Now, Leo," Frick said. "You'll start a third World War on us if you're not careful. Just keep remembering this is a goodwill tour. Don't let anything upset you."

We won the first few games we played, and it couldn't have been pleasanter. Before every game a little starlet would come up, present both managers with a bouquet of flowers and then cup her hands under her chin and bow. We would take one step forward, remove our caps, accept the flowers and bow back.

It was all very lovely, and of course it wasn't going to last. We had won every previous game but now we're in the sixth or seventh inning, and they were beating me, 3–1, with a very good left-handed pitcher who was known as the Japanese Satchel Paige. Men on first and third, one out, and the Japanese hitter hits a screamer down third base. Henry Thompson, our third-baseman, made an incredible diving stop, tagged the runner trying to slide back to third and threw to first for a double play.

The runner was still lying on the ground, about a yard short of the base, the little Japanese umpire was signaling safe, and I came running out of the dugout. I forgot myself. "You slant-eyed idiot, you," I screamed. "Where the hell were you looking?" The 60,000 people in the stadium had gone absolutely silent. The little Japanese umpire was backing up, just looking at me in disbelief. And I was all over him every step of the way giving him an elementary lesson in gutter English.

Out of the side of my eyes I could see Henry Thompson standing there, laughing his head off. "I'll give you a shot in the mouth too while I'm at it," I yelled at him. "What the hell are you laughing at?"

"Skip," he said, still laughing, "he don't understand you. He don't have the slightest idea what you're talking about."

I still didn't understand what I had done. The only thought I had was Yeah, what am I wasting my time for?

There was a huge foul area in the stadium, and as I walked back to the dugout, 60,000 people were standing up and staring at me like I was some kind of a four-headed monster. Not a word out of them, though. Not a sound. It was eerie.

We had a writer named Smith covering us for a Honolulu paper, and Smitty had been appointed my official interpreter. When I got to the dugout, he said, "Oh, my God. No one's ever done this, Leo. No one has ever questioned the umpire in the history of Japan."

"Well," I said. "What do I do now?"

How did he know? If nobody had ever done it before, there weren't any precedents to go by.

So now I'm thinking that I'd better do something fast to square myself. I hadn't been on the coaching lines up to then, so I walked out to show myself. In Japan, all the umpires carry a whisk broom, not just the plate umpire. Between every inning, each of the umpires brushes off his base, and the home-plate umpire also has the task of going to the mound and cleaning off the rubber. As I'm on my way to the coach's box, which is a good 40 feet from the dugout, my man was walking up the left-field line. "Hey!" I yelled.

And as he turned back to look at me, with the same wide-eyed expression, I stopped dead in my tracks, put my feet together and cupped my hands under my chin, just as I had seen the starlets do. And then I took my cap off and bowed to him. I'm sorry, I was saying. I hope you will forgive me. He, in turn, took his cap off, put his feet together and bowed back to me. Which meant that he understood and was accepting my apology.

A tremendous cheer went up from the stands. A mighty roar. They were forgiving me too.

The next day, Smitty brought the Tokyo paper to me and translated the headline. What it said, in letters about a foot high, was: DUROCHER BREAKS TRADITION IN JAPAN.

I wasn't quite so lucky in Cuba. It took a squad of soldiers to get me out of it there. That had happened when I was managing the Dodgers against the Cuban All-Stars. It happened, as I have already said, on the day before Mungo was supposed to pitch. Now, in Cuba, I had my own personal interpreter. Monchy de Archos. The first time I went to Cuba I had been on a delayed honeymoon with Grace, and this little kid came up to us, five or six years old, all dressed up in his Sunday suit, neat as a pin, to ask if he could have a baseball. He was so cute that I got him a baseball and autographed it for him. Every day after that a dozen roses were in our suite. His folks were among the leading citizens of the city and very wealthy. To jump way ahead, Monchy graduated Havana University with top honors, but he loved baseball so much that he became a scout for the Cleveland Indians.

At any rate, some guy bunted the ball up toward the pitcher's mound, and when Whitlow Wyatt came in to field it the guy ran about seven yards out of the base path and stepped right on his glove. Like to cut his hand off, and nobody called him out.

I came out there screaming at the plate umpire. I called him everything, and when I realized he couldn't understand me I called for Monchy who by this time was maybe twelve or thirteen years old.

"Tell the dirty sonofabitch, how can he do a thing like this?" I told him.

Monchy said, "Oh, Leo, I can't tell him that."

"*Tell him!* Do what I say."

He did, and the umpire took his mask off and started to hit me over the head with it. Monchy had told him all right. How was a thirteen-year-old kid to know I didn't mean *exactly?*

When he started to bounce his mask off me, I started to take a punch at him. I'm out of the ball game and here come Batista's soldiers with bayonets. The fans were yelling what sounded like "Go, go, go . . ." and the cushions were coming down, and the fans were whistling, which in Cuba is the same as a boo. The soldiers had to form a circle around me and march me the whole 600 feet to the clubhouse.

After the game Batista told Larry MacPhail that it was the greatest thing he had ever seen. "Tell Durocher," he said, "to do it again tomorrow." Batista couldn't believe that I had meant it. He thought from everything he had heard about me that it was my act.

It ain't no act. People are always asking why you bother to argue with an umpire when you know you can't win. Sometimes you'll do it to protect your player. You don't want him thrown out of the game, and you do want him to know that you're backing him up all the way. And there have been

times, I will admit, when I have tried to wake my team up
by whipping up a fight. But mostly it's because if you have
any competitive juices, you can't stand having somebody
take something away from you. You argue with the umpire
because there's nothing else you *can* do about it.

Do you know what the best way for an umpire to shut
you up is? Admit that he blew it. Babe Pinelli, who was a
very good umpire, used to do that. I'd come running out on
a bad call, and my first words would probably be, "Where
the hell were you looking? How can you miss a play like
that?" Whether he was right or wrong, Pinelli would always
get everybody away so that it was only you and him. When
he knew he'd blown it he'd say, "Wasn't that awful? I don't
know how I could have missed it, Leo. It was terrible." Now
what am I supposed to do? He's admitted he was wrong.
There's nothing for me to argue about. I can't go right back
to the dugout, though, without showing everybody in the
park that Pinelli has admitted he blew it. So I'd shake my
finger in his face and say, "How about a beer after the
game? I picked up the last check. This time it's your turn."

He'd put his hands on his hips and stick his jaw out and
snort, "To hell you did. You never picked up a check in your
life." After a while, he'd say, "I think that's long enough,
Leo," and I'd kick some dirt and walk away. "That's a boy,
Leo," everybody would be yelling. "That's how to tell him."

Lon Warneke, my old teammate with the Gas Housers,
became an instant umpire when he retired. I never thought
it possible anybody could be a worse umpire than Warneke
but there's a fellow named Mel Steiner around today who
in my opinion just might be. If I believed in reincarnation. . .
Most of the time Warneke wouldn't either defend himself
or admit he might have been wrong. He'd just stand there
with a little smile on his face and say, very timidly, "Well,
that's the way I saw it." If he'd have said, "Get out of here
or I'll run you out!" I'd have respected him more. "Well,"
he'd say, "you saw it one way, and that's the way I saw it."

I stopped going out to argue. I mean, there was nobody there to argue with.

There was one time in an exhibition game in Miami, though, where my man was a full stride across first base and Lonnie called him out. It was the kind of play that only Warneke could miss, and I couldn't restrain myself. "For God's sake, Lon . . ." He looked at me with that little silly grin and he said, "I know, Leo, I blew it. It was terrible." OK, I walked away. I was married to Laraine Day at the time, and as I got back to the dugout, there she was at the other end of the dugout screaming her lungs out at him. I said to her, "Sit down and shut up. Shut . . . up!"

The average fan could holler, that's what he paid for. I could holler, that's what I do. But I didn't like the idea of my wife hollering in front of thousands of people when she didn't know what she was hollering about.

And then, speaking of bad umpires, there was Frank Dascoli. The year I came back after my year's suspension, we took spring training in the Dominican Republic. Dascoli, who was just being brought up to umpire for the National League, was sent down to work all our games behind the plate. First day, and I have never seen anybody so bad. He was missing pitches you could have called from the bleachers. Up around the neck. Strike. Right down the middle. Ball. Where did they get this guy?, we were all asking each other. We were hollering everything at him.

After the game he came into my office. "I want to make it in the majors, Leo," he said. "I know I made a lot of mistakes, but when you holler at me and then the players holler at me, I get all excited and that only makes me worse. I think it would help me tremendously, Leo, if you just didn't holler at me." He'd take it as a great favor, he said, if I'd just tell the players to leave him alone and then sit with him after the game and try to tell him what he was doing wrong.

A guy asks you like that, what else can you say? I gave strict orders to my players. "Let the man alo-o-o-one." Every day I'd give him a post-game critique. I changed his whole stance around. His main trouble was that he had been positioning himself directly behind the catcher. The catcher would come up to catch the ball, and at the crucial moment Dascoli's vision would be cut off. The National League system, which he was going to have to learn anyway, was to position himself in the slot between the catcher and the batter and move with the pitch.

Now the season opens, and it's for the money. Dascoli has been assigned to the team that's opening the season at Ebbets Field, and on about the third day he's behind the plate. Can you see it coming? We're at bat, a ball is thrown that wasn't a foot off the ground and Dascoli called it a strike. "Come on, Frank," I hollered. "Bear down."

Off comes the mask and he's thumbing me out of the game. I went right to the clubhouse like a good boy, of course. Like hell I did. The things I called that man. Like: "You ungrateful dago. You miserable— For thirty days I worked with you and now I said 'Bear down' when you miss a pitch and . . ."

I had trouble with him from that day on. He strutted around like a big peacock. I wasn't the only one, either. Dascoli had his own phrase—like Klem's "Catfish" and Magerkurth's "Meathead"—that guaranteed instant expulsion. Frank hadn't been in the league all that long when he was careless enough to leave his shade up while he was entertaining a lady in the Stevens Hotel in Chicago. Right across the court from him, observing thoughtfully, were a couple of players from the visiting team. The first time he blew a pitch against them the next afternoon (which would have been along about the first or second inning) they yelled, "Hey, Frank, why don't you pull the shades down?" For as long as he remained in baseball those were the magic words that were guaranteed to get you thrown out of the game.

I once won an argument with an umpire, giving me a lifetime record of one win and 389 losses. The losing umpire
was Ziggy Sears.

I was coaching at first base. We had men on first and
second, and the count was two balls and one strike on the
hitter. The next ball was not that high off the ground, Sears
didn't make any motion with his hand that I could see, and
Ball 3 went up on the scoreboard. With a 3–1 count, I
wanted my men running, and I gave Dressen the sign.
(That was our system. I gave the signs to Dressen and the
players took them from him.) As the batter stepped back in
the box, I looked up to the scoreboard, and the count was
now 2–2. Well, I don't want them running on a 2–2 count.
So I yelled "Time," and started in toward the batter's box.
Ziggy Sears let me take maybe two steps and then he put
his hand up and ordered me not to come any further.

I had better explain that leaving the coach's box to kick
on a pitched ball calls for automatic expulsion. I hadn't said
a word, though. Just "Time." A few more steps, and Ziggy
was pointing his thumb toward our dugout, which meant,
"That's where you're walking, Durocher. Into the clubhouse." I kept coming, and when I got there he said, "You
automatically removed yourself. Keep going."

I explained exactly what had happened, and why it was
important for me to be sure of the count.

"It doesn't make any difference. You're out."

I said, "We will see about that, Mr. Sears."

For once, I had the advantage on an umpire and I was
going to . . . well, take advantage of it. I waited until the
notice came in that I had been fined, and then I went to
Larry MacPhail and told him to demand a formal hearing.

Ford Frick was the president of the National League at
the time. I asked him to read Ziggy's report to me. Sure
enough, he had written that I had kicked on a strike call.

Once I had been given permission to ask Mr. Sears some

questions, I said, "Ziggy, what was the count on the score-board when I had the men on first and second?"

"Well, at one time it was three and one."

"Yes, and then I looked up and it was two two."

"That's right."

"Then I left the coach's box, and what did you say to me when I got about three yards out?"

"I told you not to come any further, that you were through if you did."

"And what did I do?"

"You kept coming."

"Right. When I reached you, what were your first words to me?"

"I told you to keep going. That you automatically removed yourself from the game."

"That's right. At any time, Mr. Sears, did I say to you that the ball was low or high, inside or outside? At any time did I accuse you of missing the pitch? Did I open my mouth at any time about the strike?"

He said, "No, but I assumed that was what you were coming up to squawk about."

I looked over at Mr. Frick and he was tearing the report up. "You must never assume what anybody will do," he said. "And especially Durocher."

I found out later, although it was never publicized, that Sears was fined himself. Because Ziggy was very bitter about it. I always had a soft spot about Ford Frick because of that. I don't care what those $100-a-week typewriter reporters say about him, as far as I'm concerned he was a strong league president and a strong commissioner. Whenever I had anything to do with him he stood up just fine.

That's more than I can say for his successor, Warren Giles. When I was managing the Giants, I was thrown out of a game by Larry Goetz right at the time when we were beginning to move. The next day, after I had handed the lineup to the umpire-in-chief, I turned to Goetz and said, "You remember what I said yesterday? Well, it still goes."

And I'm out of the ball game. Another Durocher first. I had become the first manager to be thrown out of a game before it began. After the game, Arch Murray of the *Post* went to the umpire's room to ask him about it, and Goetz admitted quite openly that he threw Durocher and Stanky out quicker than he would anybody else. Then Arch came to me for my reaction. The next thing I knew I got a wire from Giles suspending me indefinitely for making derogatory remarks about an umpire. (That's an offense? I always thought that was as American as apple pie.) After a couple of days, Horace Stoneham, the owner of the Giants, called me into his office and informed me that I would have to apologize or I would never be able to put the uniform on again. All the newspaper boys were listening with their ears flapping.

"What do I got to apologize for? He admitted that he threw me and Stanky out quicker than anybody else. I got witnesses."

That didn't matter, as far as Stoneham was concerned. What mattered was that he was paying me to manage. A call would be coming from Giles momentarily, and I knew what I had to do.

In about two minutes the phone rings, and before I can open my mouth Giles is giving me hell.

"Wait a minute," I said. "I don't see how you can criticize me when your own umpire admitted it in the paper. I have the column here with me."

"Leo," he said, "you're right. I know you're right, but you just can't say things as tough as that about the umpire. You've got to say you apologize."

"OK, Warren, I apologize."

That wasn't the end of it, though.

"Then you are admitting that the umpires aren't out to get you," one of the writers said.

"Aren't out to get me?" I howled, waving the column. "You know as well as I do that—"

Stoneham almost had a stroke. "What are you guys trying to do?" he screamed. "Get my manager suspended again?"

I brought the column with me to Cincinnati, where Giles had his office, and he agreed to meet me underneath the stands alongside the visiting clubhouse.

Giles had already read it. Clips had been mailed to him from all over the country. "I handled that end of it, Leo," he said. "Don't worry about it."

How he handled it was none of my business, of course. I had a choice between taking his word for it and taking his word for it. It's the same old story—sometimes you sit down to a chicken dinner and sometimes they serve you up crow.

And sometimes you eat your crow with sore shins. After being out of baseball for five years, I came back, in 1961, as coach of the Los Angeles Dodgers. I wasn't back a week when I was suspended for engaging in a thrilling kicking match with Jocko Conlan. Jocko had already thrown me out of the game, and as I was taking my leisurely departure I thought it might be nice to kick dirt over the bottom of his trousers—one of the things about the Grand Old Game I had sorely missed. Jocko, unhappy at the thought of the cleaning bill, tried to kick some dirt back at me. Since umpires don't wear spikes, his shoe skidded off the ground and he kicked me right in the shin. Oooooh, that hurt. I kicked him back. He kicked me back. I kicked him back. And the band played on. Umpires, however, wear little shin guards underneath their pants to protect them from foul balls. They also have iron plates attached to the toes of their shoes. Every time Jocko kicked me, he raised a lump on my shins; every time I kicked him I bruised my toes. All at once it occurred to me that these were the lousiest odds I'd ever come up against.

You just can't win.

BOOK II

The Days of Trial and Glory

JACKIE

MY PART IN THE SIGNING of Jackie Robinson was zero. I read about it in the paper like everybody else. I never even saw him play until he came to spring training in Havana, the year after he had led the International League in hitting. And even then, Rickey kept Jackie with the minor-league squad, attached to the Montreal roster, through the entire training period. Mr. Rickey had some kind of pipe dream that as soon as the players recognized how much Jackie could help us, they were going to demand that he be brought up.

What happened was exactly the opposite. Early in the spring we went to Panama for a weekend series against a squad of Caribbean All-Stars. The Montreal club, including Robinson and three other Negro players—Roy Campanella, Don Newcombe and Roy Partlow—came to Panama too. The Dodgers stayed at the U.S. army barracks at Fort Gulick. The Montreal players had their own quarters on the other side of the Isthmus.

We had been there about a week when one of my coaches, Clyde Sukeforth, reported he was picking up talk that the players, led by Dixie Walker and Eddie Stanky, were getting up a petition to warn us that they would never play with Robinson.

I had seen Robinson in a couple of the Montreal exhibition games, and that was all it took to convince me that I wanted him. He was still playing second base with Montreal—he wasn't handed a first-baseman's mitt until the season was about to start—and you could see how he could move in the field and could run the bases. But most of all, you could see he was a really good hitter. And that nothing in the world scared him.

Since Mr. Rickey was due to join us in a couple of days, I decided to hold off and let him handle it. I was not completely convinced, understand, that the story was true. What did the damn fools think they were going to do—strike? To check it out, I spent the day testing some of the players. I'd turn the conversation around to Jackie Robinson and say, "Doesn't bother me any . . ." or "If this kid can play ball, boy, I want him on the ball club. . . ." The reactions, though somewhat guarded, were far from encouraging. The rumors were true all right.

As I lay in bed that night, unable to sleep, I suddenly asked myself why I was being so cute about it. Hell, I was getting as bad as Rickey. The thing to do, I could see, was to nip it in the bud, step on them hard before they had taken the irretrievable step of signing the petition and presenting it to anybody. Once the battle lines were drawn, it was going to become a very messy situation. And while they couldn't possibly win, the club couldn't possibly come out of it without being ripped apart, either. I made up my mind right there that there was going to be no petition. Not if I had anything to say about it.

I jumped right out of bed, woke up my coaches and instructed them to round up all the players and bring them downstairs. Still in my pajamas, I scouted around for a meeting place and stumbled across the perfect place. A huge, empty kitchen right behind the mess hall.

In came the players, some in pajamas, some in their underwear, some buckling their trousers. They sat on the chopping blocks and on the counters; they leaned sleepily against the refrigerator and the stoves.

I said: "I hear some of you fellows don't want to play with Robinson and that you have a petition drawn up that you are going to sign. Well, boys, you know what you can do with that petition. You can wipe your ass with it. Mr. Rickey is on his way down here and all you have to do is tell him about it. I'm sure he'll be happy to make other arrangements for you.

"I hear Dixie Walker is going to send Mr. Rickey a letter asking to be traded. Just hand him the letter, Dixie, and you're gone. *Gone!* If this fellow is good enough to play on this ball club—and from what I've seen and heard, he is—he is going to play on this ball club and he is going to play for *me*."

I said: "I'm the manager of this ball club, and I'm interested in one thing. Winning. I'll play an elephant if he can do the job, and to make room for him I'll send my own brother home. So make up your mind to it. This fellow is a real great ballplayer. He's going to win pennants for us. He's going to put money in your pockets and money in mine. And here's something else to think about when you put your head back on the pillow. From everything I hear, he's only the first. *Only the first, boys!* There's many more coming right behind him and they have the talent and they're gonna come to play. These fellows are hungry. They're good athletes and there's nowhere else they can make this kind of money. They're going to come, boys, and they're going to come scratching and diving. Unless you fellows look out and wake up, they're going to run you right out of the ball park.

"So," I said, "I don't want to see your petition and I don't want to hear anything more about it. The meeting is over; go back to bed."

That was that. I still couldn't tell you whether they ever got to the point of actually drawing the petition up. Mr.

Rickey got in the next morning, called the key players into his room individually, and laid down the law. I don't think I ever saw him that mad. Mr. Rickey was not only adamant about the question of any petition, he was equally adamant that they say not a word to the newspapermen. Since there weren't that many newpapermen in Panama with us, and they had all been comfortably asleep at the time of the meeting, the story of the aborted strike never got out—a minor miracle in itself.

It ended right there. The one player who didn't back off completely was Dixie Walker, who did send his letter to Mr. Rickey. I was told that a trade for him was in the works with Pittsburgh, but then Mr. Rickey reverted to type. He couldn't make the deal he wanted—Dixie, after all, was thirty-six—and so he called it off. It wasn't until the next year that Dixie was sent to the Pirates.

I wasn't with the Dodgers during Jackie's first season. I was suspended the day before he was brought up. But I have been told by several of the players that when Jackie joined the team, Eddie Stanky, always a stand-up guy, walked up to him and said, "I want you to know something. You're on this ball club and as far as I'm concerned that makes you one of twenty-five players on my team. But before I play with you I want you to know how I feel about it. I want you to know I don't like it. I want you to know I don't like you."

"All right," Jackie said. "That's the way I'd rather have it. Right out in the open."

By the time I came back the following season, Eddie was Jackie's greatest booster. By then, of course, the club had won a pennant. They knew him as a person and they appreciated him as a ballplayer. And they knew he had put money in their pockets.

Contrary to what has been printed, Jackie and I never had any kind of a quarrel during the half year I remained the Brooklyn manager. Not to my mind, anyway. He came

to camp hog fat, and I let him know I was unhappy with
him, the same as I would have done with anybody else.
What really made me mad was that he kept insisting he
wasn't overweight. When I finally was able to get him on
the scales, the needle went up to 216 pounds. The previous
year he had come in at 195. "Not overweight?" I hollered.
"Not much you're not!"

He was still a reasonably quiet young man at that stage.
I wanted him to stay that way, and as the season progressed
he became more and more combative. Because I was never
self-conscious about it, I told him, without pulling any
punches, that as the first Negro player he was bound to be
the subject of a great deal of resentment. "There's a certain
percentage of pitchers that are knocking you down because
of your color," I told him. "No question of that. But I got to
go the other way, Jackie. I got to say they're pushing you
back, most of them, because you're a great athlete and
they're afraid of you." My advice to him was to take it as a
compliment. "Just get back up and keep your mouth shut.
We'll take care of it. Let the rest of us handle it. It's the
same old sixes and sevens, Jackie. We can win without me
or one of my coaches, but we can't win if we lose you."

And we did protect him. One day in St. Louis, when
Eddie Dyer was managing the Cards, they threw behind
Jackie's back. Jackie bounced up so mad that he swelled up
like a porpoise. He looked like he was going to explode. I
was making zipping motions across my mouth from the
third-base coaching line and hollering, "Get to hitting,
buddy. We'll take care of it."

Now let me make it clear that no manager has ever told a
pitcher right out to throw at an opposing batter. He'd have
to be crazy to. Why? Suppose the pitcher hit him and killed
him. A firm suggestion is something else again. "Well," I
said to my pitcher on my way to the bench. "It looks as if
they're taking out after our boy. . . ."

I wish I could remember who the pitcher was, because

the next time Stan Musial came to bat he flattened him with the first pitch. His second pitch really undressed him. While Stan was unloading out of there, the ball hit his bat, and he was thrown out while he was still flat on his back.

Musial was what I call a double-professional. He knew this was part of the game and he wasn't going to complain. A couple of innings later, he stopped me on the field, and with that twinkle that was always in his eye he said, "Hey, Leo, I haven't got the ball out there. I didn't throw at your man."

"Stan, old boy," I said, "you better tell that man in there to let my man alone. As far as I know, I've got twenty-five players too. And Robinson is one of my best. You're the best player I know on the Cardinals. For every time my man get one, it looks to me like you're gonna get two."

We never had any more trouble with the Cardinals as far as Mr. Robinson was concerned.

When Roy Campanella came up later on in the season, he tried to tell Jackie the same thing. Stop carrying the flag. Have your say and then back off and let the manager and coaches take care of it. That's what Campy himself always did. It resulted in a strain between them that got worse and worse through the years. Having served out a year in silence, Jackie apparently felt that he had earned the right to assert himself. Before I left, he was asserting himself with a vengeance. I had no way of knowing that he was the kind of player who—like me—had to be diving and scratching and yelling to be at his best. Maybe he resented my trying to keep a rein on him more than he'd have resented it from anybody else. I don't know.

I do know that when I went over to the Giants, Jackie and I were always needling each other. And that the more I needled him, the more he killed me. Every time I looked up, it seemed Jackie Robinson was getting the late-inning hit that either tied the game or beat us. Him and Musial. It got to be an obsession with me. I'd run out to the pitcher's box and say, "Don't let this man beat us again. Anybody but him."

He beat me a thousand times in a thousand ways. Getting a base hit, making a play, making the double play, hitting the home run, stealing a base, stealing home, upsetting my pitcher with his antics on the bases. And instead of letting it alone, I kept trying to find some way to upset him, anything to get his mind off the game. Even at the end, when he had become a third-baseman, I'd be standing alongside him in the coaching box and I'd yell, "Hit one down to Fatso here. Old Fatso won't bend over." And sure enough, someone would hit a bullet down there and he'd make the goddamn-est play you ever saw, and then he'd look at me and laugh, you know, and then he'd walk up there and hit one. And always give it to me good. We were always giving it to each other back and forth, because by then he had become as bad as me.

Out of all the jockeying came the most vicious exchange I was ever involved in. I was coaching at third, and Jackie was playing second base. We had spent the day exchanging our usual pleasantries, with Jackie yelling things like: "Hey, Leo, is that Laraine's perfume you're wearing?" At the end of one particularly tasteful observation he shouted, ". . . and that goes for your Hollywood friends and that Hollywood wife of yours too."

I lost my head completely and went charging out on the field after him. Jackie, knowing very well he had stepped away out of bounds, was trying to laugh it off to show he hadn't really meant it. But by then it was too late; I was in an absolute rage.

You have to believe me when I say that I have no racial prejudice. Never. It may be because I have always hung around show people, where color has never meant anything. Still, I found myself calling him things that would have shamed the worst bigot. I found words coming out of my mouth that I would swear had never so much as passed through my mind before.

In the back of my head, a small voice was saying, *"What are you saying, Leo? Get ahold of yourself."* But the words kept flowing on. Pee Wee Reese had stepped in front of me to keep me away from Robinson and he kept jerking his head, very disturbed, and muttering "Leo . . . Leo . . . don't you see . . . ? Can't you see . . . ?"

As soon as I got control of myself I could have bitten my tongue off. I had never been so ashamed of myself in my life. I looked around and there on second base and third base were Henry Thompson and Monte Irvin, two of my own colored players.

I just thought, "Please, God, let a hole open up beneath me and swallow me up." I walked back to the coach's box, hanging my head, unable to even look at Monte Irvin, a man for whom I've always had an enormous respect. Cream and sugar. Nicest man in the whole world.

Monte must have seen exactly how I felt, because he did something I'll always be grateful to him for. He said, "Go get him, Skip. He had no right to say that to you. Anything you say goes double for me." Monte was telling me that he knew me well enough to understand that I had only been trying to hurt Jackie Robinson as much as I could by hitting him where I knew he was most vulnerable.

And then again, it might have been because Jackie had done something the previous day that was so uncalled for that everybody on the club wanted to kill him. The Giant pitcher on that occasion had been Sal Maglie. Otherwise it wouldn't have happened. Maglie hated Robinson. He hated everybody in the opposition uniform. With Jackie, the feeling was mutual. Sal always pitched him high and tight— brushed him back or knocked him down—then curved him low and outside. That's what everybody tried to do, of course. The difference was that Maglie did it successfully.

With everybody else, to throw close to Robinson was to make him a better hitter. That had been true when I had him at Brooklyn and it was just as true when I was with the Giants. Maglie had such pinpoint control that he'd come up tight with one pitch and then drop his curve ball, low-outside, on the corner. Sal was the one pitcher we had who could get him out consistently. Jackie just couldn't do a thing with him.

But still, every time Maglie threw close to him, Robinson was absolutely sure that it was my idea.

In the game in question, Maglie came off the mound to field Jackie's little nubber and flipped it to little Davey Williams, who had gone over to cover first. Jackie was out from here to the lamppost, but he came over the base full steam and gave little Davey a football hip that sent him flying twenty feet in the air. Knocked him right out of the ball game—Davey had a bad back anyway—and although we didn't know it yet, ended his playing career.

As soon as the players got back to the dugout, the seven other regulars went down into the hole and held a meeting. The first player who got to third, they agreed, was going to give it back to Jackie Robinson. Alvin Dark, our captain, hit a legitimate double and kept right on going. Robinson was waiting for him with the ball in his hand. Alvin, who had been an All-American running back himself, hit him with a block that jarred the ball right out of his hand. In fact, if Alvin hadn't left his feet just a little too soon, Jackie's career might have ended that day too. And when Dark got up he challenged him. Even from the dugout you could see that Alvin was choosing him right there on the ball field. Calling him everything. And that Jackie was taking it.

But that was Jackie Robinson. In the heat of competition he said and did things he didn't want to say or do. It was always Robinson against the New York Giants, and particularly Robinson against Durocher. In other words, he did to us exactly what I always tried to do when I was playing.

That was the great psychological advantage he always had over me. He knew that whatever I might yell at him, I admired him as a ballplayer and as a competitor. He was a Durocher with talent.

We were alike in another way, too. Mr. Rickey might not have been willing to say that Jackie had the ability to make a bad situation worse, but I don't think he would have said that Jackie ever went out of his way to make it any better either.

MR. RICKEY

I wasn't exactly worried about losing my job when Branch Rickey replaced MacPhail. To my way of thinking, Mr. Rickey had sent me to Brooklyn from St. Louis so that I could become their manager, and so when I heard that he was coming over too, I thought to myself, "Oh boy, I'm in." My only concern, really, was whether I would be able to get as large a raise out of Rickey as I had expected to get from MacPhail. Mr. Rickey, as a lay preacher, was a virtuous man, and he rated thrift among the greater virtues.

I was still living in St. Louis. Mr. Rickey had a magnificent estate, Country Life Acres, just outside the city. He phoned me at four in the morning, something I was going to become used to, to invite me over for breakfast. Mr. Rickey was a ridiculously early riser, and he saw no reason why his manager shouldn't be up and working alongside him. Always it would be the same. The phone would ring, and his low, rumbling voice be in my ear. "Hello. What are you doing?"

Invariably I'd say, "What do you think I'm doing? I'm bowling! I'm snowshoeing down the Alps. *I'm trying to sleep*, Mr. Rickey! It's still dark outside."

I had breakfast with the entire family and then accompanied the Old Man on a four-hour tour of his estate. We returned to the house, had lunch, and still not a word was spoken about baseball in general or my contract in particular. And, I tell you, the more we didn't talk about it the more I began to worry. It was mid-afternoon before he got into baseball and then he told me bluntly that Charlie Dressen was not going to be rehired as a coach. "He's a gambler," Mr. Rickey said. "He's a horse player. He spends all his time out at the racetrack."

Well, I came out of that chair about three feet. "Hold it right there, Mr. Rickey," I said. "Why, you're taking my right arm away from me. Invaluable this man is to me."

Invaluable. Charlie Dressen was the best coach in the business. His sense of timing was so perfect that we had been able to develop a system of absolutely undetectable signs. Billy Herman and Pee Wee Reese, two of the smartest ballplayers who ever lived, once sat right in front of me, within touching distance, and told me they were going to catch them.

"Anything on?" I asked them within a minute.

"No," they said.

"Well," I said. "It happens that I just put the hit-and-run on."

They both threw up their hands and gave up.

All I had done was move my head a fraction of an inch to the right and let my eyes drift in the same direction. If I had moved my head to the left it would have been another sign; down, still another.

So I said to Mr. Rickey, "Every manager needs help and I'm no different. I need this man."

Mr. Rickey looked me right in the eye and said. "Who said you were the manager?"

I collapsed right back into the chair. *So long, Charlie.* Now, I was fighting for my own life.

Rickey had heard there was a great deal of gambling in our clubhouse and on the trains, that bookmakers and other undesirables had free access to the dressing room, and that

I was not above sitting in on a friendly little poker game with the boys myself.

He asked me, straight out, whether his information was correct, and if I had lied I'm sure I would have been gone right there. We did have some lively games on the club. "Yes sir, Mr. Rickey." Lively enough so that you could win or lose a couple of hundred dollars without straining yourself. Of course, we'd had even livelier poker games on Rickey's own Gas House Gang when I was there. And I could name a few clubs today where the manager sets a sociable limit and the stakes go sky high as soon as his back is turned. Much of the glamorous life of a ballplayer is spent just killing time, and cards are as good a way as any to kill it.

I couldn't say that it had been done behind my back, though. I admitted quite readily that I could have held the stakes down and, just as readily, that I should have.

Nor could I deny that there might well have been some objectionable characters around the clubhouse. Ebbets Field was a small, intimate park with the special flavor of Brooklyn about it. Anybody could come into the clubhouse. The supposition was that you wouldn't be there unless you had good reason.

I promised Mr. Rickey the card games would come to an end—completely and absolutely—and that anybody he found objectionable would be barred from the clubhouse.

"Then you do want to manage this ball club?" he asked. Finally.

"Well, of course I do, Mr. Rickey. You know I do."

"The first thing I'm going to do," he said, "is cut your salary to twenty thousand dollars."

I was stunned. I had come looking for a raise and instead he was going to cut me fifteen grand. "For what?" I said. I reminded him forcefully that I had just completed two very successful seasons, wining the pennant and then finishing a very close second. Finishing second, we had won 104 games, enough to have won the pennant in all but a handful of previous years.

"You didn't let me finish," he said. "I am also going to put you in a position to make more money than any other manager in the history of the game."

The $20,000 was to be only the base salary. "If you draw half a million people, you'll get twenty-five thousand," he said. And slowly, mouthing the figures lovingly, he went right up the line, lifting my potential salary another $5,000 for every 100,000 additional people. "And if you draw one person over a million," he said to finish it off, "you will get fifty thousand dollars."

I tell you, my wheels were spinning: *Is it possible he's forgotten he's not in St. Louis any more? Doesn't he know we've been drawing over a million in Brooklyn every year?*

To make certain there was no loophole stuck in there anywhere, I made him repeat the offer all over again. Then I said, "Put it in writing." After it was down in black and white, I said, "Sign it."

That was my deal with Mr. Rickey. I made $50,000 every year I was with him. After the first two years we didn't even bother with the attendance clause.

I wasn't sure at first whether he had lost his mind, whether he thought that, with the war on, attendance had to drop, or whether he felt I needed some kind of special incentive to keep me in line. Like a piece of the action.

Before I left the farm that night, I had my answer. While we were discussing our personnel, Mr. Rickey paused over the name of one of our minor-league pitchers who had a reputation for being a real night rider. I didn't want any part of the guy. Rickey began to defend him, though, and suddenly he was saying: "Luke. Chapter Fifteen, verse eleven: 'A certain man had two sons . . .'" And, as I sat there, Mr. Rickey recited the parable of the Prodigal Son from beginning to end. Mr. Rickey, you must understand, was a biblical scholar. He could not only cite chapter and verse, he could tell you what page you could go to in your Bible.

I may not be a student of the Bible, but I didn't go to school just to eat my lunch either. I'd have had to be a fool not to know that he was talking about me, not some mediocre minor-league pitcher. Through our years together, Mr. Rickey recited the return of the Prodigal Son to me many, many times. Always in comment, ostensibly, about some other sinner or wastrel, but always at a time when I knew he looked on me as something less than the leading candidate for secretary of the YMCA.

But that was typical of Mr. Rickey, too. You had to know him to understand that he was a shy and, in certain ways, an indecisive man. Like most good men, he wanted other men to be better than they were. Unlike most good men, he found it unthinkable to intrude upon another man's private life. It would have been impossible for him, for instance, to come right out and say that he disapproved of sleeping with loose women on the Sabbath. Or even to allude to that kind of thing indirectly. Except for lecturing me about my debts and associations and exhorting me to become "more responsible," he never, in all our association, said one word to me *directly* about my other personal failings, which were, of course, enormous.

I knew he liked me. I knew he wanted the press and public to like me too; to see me not as brassy, opinionated and worthless, but as brassy, opinionated and worthwhile. If a majority of the press and public never quite came around to his way of thinking, I can't say that I blame them, because, frankly, I have never been able to understand what men like Rickey and Weil and Landis saw in me either. Or even why they put up with me.

Knowing as I did that it would take a major catastrophe to get me fired, I was able to take advantage of Branch in many ways.

There was, as an instance, the time I decided that there

were better ways to spend a summer afternoon than going to Olean, a small town in upper New York, to play an exhibition game. At the last moment I told Dressen, who had been rehired a couple of months into the season, to take over the club. I said not a word to anybody else.

Now, I didn't *know* Branch was going to be there with his whole family. I found out later from Branch, Jr., that the Old Man fired me the moment he got into his car after the game and didn't rehire me again until he had reached the approach to the George Washington Bridge.

The next day, Mr. Rickey dropped into my little office in the clubhouse. A little cubicle with a desk, a chair and a little two-seater divan. Rickey sat himself on the divan, I sat down on the step in front of the door. He just looked at me for a long time, the way he would, chewing on his cigar, to let me see that he was very disappointed in me again. As always, he started by way of Kansas City by delivering a lecture about responsibility, dependability and a few of the other essential qualities of a manager. At length he got down to the key question. "Where *were you* yesterday? *Why weren't you* at the exhibition game? *Where* did *you* go? What did you* have to do that was so important?"

Just as with Judge Landis, I was always afraid to lie to Branch Rickey because I was always sure he knew the answer before he asked the question. So I smiled my most winning smile and I said, "I went to the racetrack."

The words were hardly out of my mouth when he reached up with both hands, pulled his soft fedora down over his eyes and screamed, *"Judas Priest!"* With the hat still down over his eyes, he went barging right past me and out the door in a cloud of smoke. He didn't speak to me again for about two weeks.

No two men could have been more unlike than Larry MacPhail and Branch Rickey. Unlike MacPhail, who put a team together by patchwork, Rickey built his teams from the bottom up and built them to last. It was Rickey's Cardinals who had beaten us the previous season when his young team had jelled at mid-season, as Rickey teams had a way of doing, and won 37 out of their last 43 games. That was another hallmark of a Rickey team; they came on like gangbusters at the end.

The quality of his mind can best be demonstrated by the way he cornered the young talent after the United States got into World War II. Everybody else stopped signing kids. "They'll be going into the army," they said, "and who knows which ones will come back?" Rickey signed twice as many. "*Some* of them will be coming back," he said, "and we'll have them." The next year he was in Brooklyn doing the same thing. In 1946, the first postwar year, Brooklyn and St. Louis, the two teams he had built, battled each other into the first playoff series in baseball history. Unfortunately his old team beat his new one.

When it came to "putting a dollar sign on a muscle," as he liked to say, nobody could come close to him. When it came to trading his players "when they turned to money," as he also liked to say, he was in a class by himself. As a student of technique, he was simply unchallenged.

Our first training camp was at Sanford, Florida, and for one hour every morning Mr. Rickey would lecture on baseball fundamentals. How to field each position, the correct techniques for fingering a baseball and throwing it, for getting a lead off base, sliding. What it took to be a great hitter. Every phase of the game. On the second morning I hired a male stenographer, sat him down and told him not to miss a word. Other people gave instruction. Mr. Rickey *knew*.

The word was always out around St. Louis that Branch Rickey could have been governor if he had wanted to. For myself, I'd have felt perfectly safe if he had been running the country. He could have been a leader in politics, industry, anything; and he didn't care to involve himself in anything except baseball.

He didn't even care how he looked. Oh, every once in a while he'd come over to me at a banquet or something and ask where I had bought my suit. "That's beautiful," he'd sigh. "Just beautiful. Now why can't I look like that?"

"Forget it, Mr. Rickey," I'd tell him. "You could pay a thousand dollars for a suit and in twenty minutes you'd look like you fell out of bed."

Wearing clothes is as much a matter of attitude as of tailoring. You have to feel that clothes are important. Half the time he'd be at the park in an old pair of khaki pants and some beat-up loafers. Which was just as well. I've seen him come in looking as if he had just stepped out of a band-box, and if he saw a good-looking kid warming up, he'd take his coat off and throw it right down in the dirt. The kid was what he was interested in. Ten seconds later he'd shout, "Jane Anne!" and his secretary, little Jane Anne Jones, would come down from the stands with her notebook to take down his running commentary. The first thing he'd do was to take the boy's complete history. Age, mother, father, sisters, brothers. His whole background. He'd work with him for an hour, an hour and a half, and if the kid showed anything at all, he could give you back his whole history any time the kid's name came up.

And yet, it's funny. Here you had the most brilliant baseball man who ever lived, and before he let the kid go a silly look would come over his face, he'd call the catcher in about 30 feet and—while I was trying not to groan outwardly— he'd say, "All right, Jane Anne, now we're going to give him the aptitude test."

Worst aptitude test you ever saw in your life. Let me ask you something. How many fellows can take a baseball and hold it against their shoulder with the palm cupped inward and then throw it, with their arm coming straight out and over, so that it will go 30 feet? I've seen some of the great ones try it and on the first attempt the ball will always go straight up in the air. Also the second, third and fourth. I'd say to myself, "Poor kids, they want to do it so bad, and there's no way."

The idea seemed to be to see whether they could adapt themselves to a wholly unnatural way of pitching. To me, that made it an aptitude test in reverse. The worse they did, the better the pitcher they were sure to become. Every once in a while he would find someone who could do it and he'd say, "Ahhhh, got a good mind. Good mind. He's all right. He can pass the aptitude test, he's all right."

I'd write the kid off immediately, and Branch would never forget him. We'd be going over the Class D rosters a couple of years later and he'd pause over a name and say, "Got a good mind. Father's a pressman, mother used to teach school. Two older sisters and a younger brother. He passed the aptitude test, he'll be all right. All he has to do is find himself a girl and get married."

Yeah, he had passed the aptitude test, and he was in Class D with a record of 3–7. If he finds himself a girl, I'd be thinking, she'd better have a good job.

As a trader of ballplayers he was simply without peer. Over and over, when he was operating with that great St. Louis farm system, he'd throw two men at the other club, "Take your pick," and have it set up so they'd take the wrong one. You can still hear how he gave Pittsburgh their choice between Enos Slaughter and Johnny Rizzo, and Chicago their choice between Marty Marion and Bobby Sturgeon, and in both cases they picked the wrong one. It wasn't quite that simple, though, because it doesn't give either Rickey or the man on the other side of the table enough credit. Believe me, Rickey wasn't taking that kind of a chance of losing such great players as Slaughter and Marion.

Slaughter had been the best minor-league prospect to come along in years. But he was a left-handed hitter, and the Pirates were so overstocked with left-handed hitters, like the Waner Brothers, Arky Vaughan and Gus Suhr, that they had been seeing every left-handed pitcher in the league for years. The one thing they needed was a big right-handed bomb like Rizzo in the middle of their lineup. By throwing Slaughter into the pot—"Take your pick"—the Old Man was able to set a much higher price, and even upgrade Rizzo in Pittsburgh's mind. He was not only making it seem as if Rizzo was as valuable as Slaughter, but, really, that he was angling to save Rizzo for himself.

The Marion-Sturgeon choice was entirely different. The Cubs' great second-base combination, Billy Jurges and Billy Herman, had begun to slow up, and the Cubs had decided to break them up. They sure weren't going to trade Herman, and that meant they were looking for a young shortstop. They wanted Marion. Rickey, who had absolutely no intention of giving Marion up, set an all but prohibitive price on him, something like $150,000, but let them know they could have his other Triple A shortstop, Sturgeon, for $85,000. In the course of the conversation he confided to Pants Rowland, the Cubs' general manager, that the thinking in the Cardinals system was that Marion had been able to get away with playing such an excessively deep shortstop only because of the speed and agility of his second-baseman, a young man named Maurice Sturdy. Perhaps, Rickey suggested, Sturdy could do the same for Billy Jurges if the Cubs should decide to go with a young second-baseman and an aging shortstop, instead of the other way around. "Here's what I'll do for you," he said at last. "You can have either one of them for eighty-five thousand dollars. Sturgeon or Sturdy, take your pick."

Marion, the man they wanted, had been whisked out of sight. The choice he was giving them was between two other players. Now, Sturgeon and Sturdy weren't worth $85,000 if you put them together and threw in the team bus. It was only in comparison to the figure he had put on Marty Marion that the price didn't seem quite so outrageous.

That was always a favorite tactic with Rickey. Watch out when he threw out a string and pulled it back. If he had come to sell you a catcher, he would start by explaining why a second-baseman was going to solve all your problems. He would then hand you a list, price tags attached, of just about every second-baseman in his system. Starting at $200,000 for his best Triple A prospect and working all the way down to a giveaway $50,000 for some kid in Class C. The catcher's name is never going to be mentioned until you bring it up yourself. As, sooner or later, you will, because the catcher is who you want. Why else would Rickey have been there? At the first mention of his name, Rickey will either dismiss him with a contemptuous wave of his hand—"Not ready"—or give you what seems to be a valid reason why he has to hold onto him himself. (When he said, "Not ready," or even better, "I'm afraid I can't help you there; we're counting on him to fill our own needs very shortly"—*that* was the guy I always knew he was there to sell.) You're going to have to overcome all his arguments. And happily pay the price he has set after you have beaten him down and trapped him.

In Brooklyn, I sat in on several meetings with him when he dealt players, and what an education it was. During the war years we had a big, tall first-baseman, Howie Schultz, whom Rickey had bought from the minors for $52,000. He was exactly that, a wartime player. He was awkward and ungainly, but he could hit one every now and then and the thinking had been that he had to be more athletic than he looked because he had been a basketball player in college.

Lou Perini wanted him up in Boston, where they were in dire need of a first-baseman. And I couldn't believe my ears. For three hours, Mr. Rickey undersold this boy to Perini and his general manager, John Quinn. I want to tell you, the tears were streaming down my eyes. It made you cry to listen to this man talk. He didn't want to stick Boston with him. The boy couldn't field, couldn't hit, couldn't get out of his own way. The more he ran Schultz down, the more Perini's tongue hung out. When finally he coudn't stand it any longer, he jumped up and said, "Branch! Put a *price* on the man. I *want* him."

Mr. Rickey bit down on his cigar and said, "One hundred twenty-five thousand dollars."

Perini fell right back on the sofa. Ten minutes later they were out the door of the suite. Gone. I looked at Branch and I said, almost shocked, "Branch . . . how could you do that? I know you want to get rid of the fellow. You know you wanted to sell him. What are you doing, Branch?"

And he just bit down harder on his cigar and spat three words out: "They'll be back."

They were.

Howie was a wonderful kid, but he couldn't get all his co-ordination together.

It is well to keep the very special relationship between Mr. Rickey and myself in mind, as well as the man's genius for maneuvering, as background to the most critical period of my life: the eighteen-month period in which I was married to Laraine Day, suspended from baseball and transferred—through Rickey's sleight of hand—to our mortal enemies, the New York Giants.

A NIGHT FLIGHT TO COLUMBUS

MY ROMANCE WITH LARAINE DAY began, in faultless Class B movie style, with her hating my guts.

I first met Laraine when she came to New York on a War Bond tour with two old friends of mine, Allan Jones and Irene Hervey, who are probably best identified to the new generation as the parents of Jack Jones. I invited Allan and Irene, together with Laraine and her husband, Ray Hendricks, to dinner at the Stork Club. We all gathered at my penthouse apartment, my date included, for a drink. Laraine is a very strict Mormon. She has never smoked a cigarette or drunk an alcoholic beverage—or for that matter a cup of coffee—in her life. The boys said they'd settle for beer, but after we had gone into my little kitchenette and opened up a couple of bottles they let me know that they were really interested in Scotch. Every time they'd go in for another bottle of beer, they'd take another big belt out of the Scotch.

By the time we left they were both feeling pretty good. I was just feeling uncomfortable because Laraine was glaring at me.

During dinner, there was some talk about getting together at the New York Athletic Club for a workout, and when I phoned their hotel in the morning Laraine picked up the phone. To say that she was cool is to say that it gets a little brisk in Montreal around Christmas.

No, she snapped. Ray wasn't there.

"Well, is Allan there by any chance? His room didn't answer."

"No."

"Well, the boys said they wanted to play a little hand-ball . . ."

"They're not here!" And—boom—down slammed the phone.

Obviously she was not one of my greatest admirers. Frankly, I couldn't have cared less. Stuck-up broad!

Dissolve to the winter of 1946, a full year later. I am now taking my annual one-month vacation in California, living at my good friend George Raft's house and playing golf at the Hillcrest Country Club. An idyllic life, broken by a call from Branch Rickey instructing me to meet him in Governor Bricker's office in Columbus, Ohio, to discuss my contract.

The prospect of going to Columbus to talk about my contract would have left me something less than thrilled if something hadn't been involved. The ownership of the Dodgers was split four ways by that time. One of the pieces was supposed to be up for sale, and a New York jeweler named Roy Marcher, a close friend of mine, had asked me to act as his agent with the understanding that I would get something like 5 percent of the club as a finder's fee. I already had a certified check from him in my pocket to put down as "earnest money."

The first plane I could get was a midnight flight to Chicago. From there, I had to catch a train to Columbus. I rushed to the airport, only to find that the flight was going to be delayed three hours.

While I was in the restaurant killing time, Laraine walked in with her twin brother Lamar, her mother, her father, and her traveling companion, Ilene Germaine. A familiar face in an airport is like a familiar face overseas. You assume you're old friends. Laraine introduced me to her group and promptly disappeared. It wasn't until after we were married that she told me she had phoned some friends who lived in the Valley and gone over to sit out the early-morning hours with them, just so she wouldn't have to talk to me.

They didn't reserve seats on airplanes in those days—certainly not for midnight flights, anyway—and by the time she and Ilene reappeared there was a huge mob milling around the gate. I told them to stick close to me and edged my way up near the front. As soon as the gate opened I shoved a few people aside to open a path for them and—boom—they were through. Them, not me. When I started shoving I also became the shovee, which was fair enough, and got myself buffeted back and forth in the crush.

When I finally got aboard, Laraine was standing up in the middle of the plane, waving. She had held the seat across the aisle from her by throwing her mink coat over it.

Everybody else on the plane seemed to go right to sleep. Laraine and I talked all the way to Chicago, whispering back and forth across the aisle. She had become so furious with me in New York, I learned, because her husband had a drinking problem and had promised her that he wouldn't touch a drop on the bond tour.

She was on a last-minute errand herself. Rosalind Russell, the star of the picture *Sister Kenny*, had been taken suddenly ill, and Laraine was going to Minneapolis to represent the studio at the premiere.

We also discovered that we both planned to return to Chicago on Saturday and catch a Sunday-morning flight back to Los Angeles. I invited Laraine and Ilene to dinner Saturday night. But the studio had already arranged for her and Ilene to see the play *Dream Girl*, and so she invited me to join them.

When we landed in Los Angeles on Sunday, Laraine's mother, brother and her two adopted children, Michele, who was two, and Chris, who was a babe in arms, were waiting for her. By this time, we were all so friendly that they drove me back to George's house and invited me to drop over later for lunch.

A few days later, to reciprocate, I invited them all to dinner at Larue's. Including Ray. While we were dining, Laraine invited me to a sneak preview of her upcoming picture, *The Locket,* up at Pasadena the following week. This time, somewhat to my surprise, Ray wasn't in the car when they picked me up. Laraine told me he was going to join us at the theater.

The picture was a triumph for Laraine. She played an insane woman, one of the few times the studio had allowed her to get out of that nurse's uniform and show that she could act. When the lights came up, there, at last, stood Ray. He needed a shave, he was wearing a pair of dirty old white pants, and, I guarantee you, a sobriety test he had no chance whatsoever of passing. Behind him, at a discreet distance, was another guy, obviously his drinking companion.

"Well, where were you, honey?" Laraine said. "I saved this seat for you."

He just gave her a look and sneered, "Yeah, you saved a seat for me."

At that point, Laraine's mother nudged me with her elbow, and I quickly followed her out to her car.

When Laraine joined us, after a considerable length of time, she told us Ray was going to meet us at Will Wright's, a famous ice-cream parlor on Sunset Boulevard. Again he didn't show up. Lamar drove me back to Raft's house again, and that was that.

At three thirty in the morning, the phone woke me up. The first words to greet me—I will never forget them if I live to be a hundred—were: "Are you in love with my wife?"

Well, I was half asleep, but a question like that can clear your head in a hurry. "Who is this?" I asked.

"You know who it is. I repeat, are you in love with my wife?" By now, I could recognize the somewhat slurred and sloppy voice of Ray Hendricks. "Because if you are," he said. "You'd better get your ass over here."

The whole affair was really none of my business, and I suppose I could have hung up and gone back to sleep. But by this time I not only knew Laraine, I had become very friendly with the whole family. I said, "Is your wife there? If she is, put her on the phone. I'd like to speak to her."

Laraine was close to hysterics. I asked her whether she wanted me to come over, and she managed to tell me that she wished I would. I was there in a matter of perhaps twenty minutes. Ray let me in and walked away from me without a word. Laraine was sitting very quietly on one of the divans. She was no longer crying; she just seemed stunned. She had a robe on, and as far as I can remember she didn't utter one word from beginning to end.

Ray now began to pace around the room, bellowing, and from everything he was saying, it was perfectly obvious she had told him they were through.

I sat myself down on a divan on the opposite side of the room from Laraine, and jumped him at once to find out why he had called *me*.

"Because," he said, "I want to know if you're in love with my wife."

"What are you talking about? What's the matter with you? Has that whiskey gone to your brain or something?"

But Ray just kept walking and bellowing. He had only one thought on his mind and it was impossible to shake it loose. "If she were free," he said, "would you marry her tomorrow morning?"

"That's a pretty quick question," I told him, "and you seem to expect a pretty quick answer. I don't know."

"Are you in love with my wife?"

"That I don't know either."

The more he talked, the more belligerent he became. At last he bent right down over me, pushing his face so close to mine that I thought he was going to burn himself on my cigarette. "Durocher," he said, "I ought to punch you right in the nose."

I had remained slumped on the divan through it all, but, I tell you, I was tensed and coiled and ready for almost anything. As quietly as possible, I said, "I think that would be a bad move on your part, Ray. Number one, you're drunk. And even if you were sober, you're not man enough to do it. You never were and you never will be."

An odd little grin came over his face. "You know something," he said, "I think you're right."

"Then, if I were you," I said, "I'd just keep walking around the room. Say what you want, but don't you make any attempt to hit me. Because if you do, you and I are going to go around."

He resumed that nervous pacing again, but he was talking more softly now, first to himself and then to Laraine. He went off on a long and painful monologue about what a failure he had been, both in his career—he had been a singer at one time—and in his marriage. He talked about how he had fallen asleep with a cigarette in his hand and almost burned the house down, how he was working for something like $50 a week at an aircraft company while she was supporting him, and how they had not lived together as man and wife for the past two or three years. It was as if I weren't there at all.

By the time he had talked himself out, he had also talked himself almost sober. "You've always wanted a divorce," he said to Laraine, calmly and rationally. "Well, that's all right with me."

OK, everything was settled. I got up to leave. Ray walked me to the door, quite friendly now. "I'll tell you one thing," he said. "If you do marry her, you're getting yourself a hell of a fine girl."

"Ray," I said, "the unfortunate part of this whole thing is that it was all unnecessary. Number one, your wife and I have never been alone together for five seconds. More important still, you have two adopted children here and, as I understand it, the final papers haven't come through on Michele yet. This can turn out to be very unpleasant for them."

Now, this may sound strange, in the light of everything that had gone before, but Ray reached for my hand. Laraine had followed us to the door and, at the mention of the children, the three of us—Laraine, Ray and myself—found ourselves standing there with our hands clasped together. "There will be no trouble about that," Ray said firmly. "Laraine can have her divorce and there'll be no publicity. Above all, there'll be no unpleasantness, for the sake of the kids. Because that's the way *I* want it."

I had already begun to feel for Ray, almost in spite of myself, during his long rambling talk about the mess he had made of his life. As I was driving home, I was thinking that Mr. Rickey was right about people being basically decent. Any man who would be thinking of his children when he was as badly shaken up as Ray obviously was had to be essentially a good man at heart.

The next morning I was in the headlines. Ray Hendricks had accused Leo Durocher of breaking up his home. If I'd had a double-barreled shotgun in my hands at that moment and he had been standing in front of me, I swear to God I'd have killed him.

He even filed divorce papers naming me as corespondent, although I won that court case quickly enough when his lawyers discovered that Laraine and I had never so much as been alone together.

Laraine then filed for a divorce herself, and he didn't contest it. Well, there's nothing like being named corespondent to start a romance, I always say. After the first newspaper story, I was naturally invited to the house to discuss what we were going to do about it. Before long, Laraine and I, having already become good friends, became very close. So to all of you who have wondered what *she* ever saw in *him*, I must say that, in some degree, Hendricks brought us together.

(One last word about Ray Hendricks. After Laraine and I were married, I adopted Michele. The papers on Chris had come through shortly before the break-up, though, and before I could adopt him Ray had to sign some other papers. He signed them, all right. We gave him $1,500 for the privilege of adopting Chris.)

By the time Laraine went into court for the divorce trial, two months after she left Hendricks, we had decided we would eventually get married. Laraine was granted an interlocutory decree, which was to become final in a year.

The night of the divorce, we were all sitting around the house, Laraine, her family, and myself, and now that she was free, a year began to seem like an awfully long time. Especially when you considered that I would be going to spring training in a few weeks. As we talked about it, we all decided, almost on the spur of the moment, that there was nothing to prevent us from flying right down to Juarez, Mexico, which has no residency requirement for a divorce, then cross over into El Paso, Texas, and be married at once. We wouldn't be legally married in California, of course, but I wasn't going to be in California. As far as New York and the other forty-six states were concerned we would be perfectly legal.

We had hoped to avoid publicity, but by the time we crossed back to El Paso there were newspapermen and photographers jammed outside the office of the justice of the peace. After the ceremony, the justice told us we could duck them by climbing out of the window (no great problem, since it was a huge window, just barely above floor level), crossing over the low, flat roof and climbing down a fire escape on the far side. Having anticipated that we might have to run from photographers, Laraine was wearing flat heels, a black turtleneck sweater and a skirt. So that was no problem. The fire escape, however, was one of the kind that unfolds beneath you as you're descending, which made it kind of frightening. Laraine looked down, gulped and said, "Gee, I always wanted to be in a Harold Lloyd movie."

We ducked the photographers all right, but that turned out to be the least of our troubles. When we got back to the hotel, Laraine phoned her lawyer to break the news to him. He warned her that the judge who had granted the decree, Judge George Dockweiler, might not be too happy about it. Immediately I put in a call to him. My memory is that he had already heard about it, but whether he had or not, he flew into an absolute rage. As far as he was concerned, he told me, the marriage was illegal and he was personally going to see that it was annulled. If we lived under the same roof in California, he said, we would be committing adultery.

I kept trying to explain that we had no intention of living together in California, that I wasn't even going to be in California, and that we couldn't have really done anything so terrible if every other state in the country considered our marriage legal. I couldn't seem to get that point across to him, though, because he kept yelling "Adultery." So finally I said, "The least you can do, your Honor, is give me the courtesy of letting me come to your office and explain."

He gave us an appointment for the next day, and that was the end of our honeymoon.

There was a tremendous crush in the corridor outside the judge's chambers when we arrived, which did not do a thing to overcome my feeling that the judge was out to get all the publicity out of us that he could. To give you an idea of the state of my mind, I wasn't aware that any pictures were being taken until I opened the paper the next day and saw a picture of us sitting with the judge at his desk.

Eventually I was able to explain to him that I was living at the Miramar Hotel in Santa Monica (having moved out of George Raft's house for reasons I will go into shortly) and that I intended to stay there until I left for spring training. By the time the baseball season was over, the year would be almost up, but in any case, I gave him our word, absolutely, that we had no intention of living together in California until the decree was final. "And," I said, "if you say it is still not legal, then I will make it legal by remarrying her in California."

And, do you know, that seemed to make him even madder? As far as he was concerned, he said, we were committing adultery just by being married—which to my nonjudicial mind seemed to be a reversal of the usual procedure. "Let me ask you something, your Honor," I said. "Would you be making such a fuss about this if our names were Sarah Zilch and Joe Blow, walking along the street? Would you make this kind of commotion?"

And he said, "No, I certainly wouldn't." He couldn't be a watchdog, he said. He couldn't watch everybody. "But there's one thing I can do. I can make an example of you two."

"Ohhh," I told him, "in other words, you would *condone* what you consider adultery by two other people. But you're not going to condone it by us, is that what you're telling me? Maybe the only thing you're really interested in is a little publicity for yourself, is that it?"

And the good judge told us, sitting right across the able from us, that he didn't care whether we committed adultery or not. His only concern was with upholding the dignity of his court. We had made the court look very bad, it seemed, by getting married immediately following his decree instead of waiting a decent length of time, like two or three weeks. It would be a simple matter, he said, for us to restore the dignity of the court by setting aside the Mexican divorce. "Once that's done," he said, "you can go right ahead and live together as far as I am concerned. That part of it doesn't concern me one bit."

Well, now . . . you could have lit a cigarette on me, I was so hot. "Let me tell you something, your Honor," I said. "This is my *wife* you are talking about. I am *married* to this girl. You can do any goddam thing you want but I am going to stay married to her." And with that, Laraine and I got up and walked out of the office. For once, there was nobody to tell me I should have controlled my temper, because Laraine was every bit as angry as I was.

I was still so angry that when the reporters gathered around us, I told them the judge was "a pious, Bible-reading hypocrite," which is the kind of a phrase that comes easily enough to the lips when you're mad but makes you shudder when you see it in the newspaper the next day in cold black print. Especially since it gave everybody the opportunity to write that I had popped off at a distinguished jurist as if he were no better than an umpire.

Judge Dockweiler got so mad about it that he made the same mistake himself. The judge delivered such a diatribe against us, threatening to set aside the divorce decree on grounds of "collusion, fraud and bad faith" that a three-judge board removed him from the case for possible bias. Another judge, appointed to take his place, ruled that there were no grounds for setting aside the decree. A year later Laraine and I were quietly remarried in California.

By then I had been suspended from baseball. To this day, if you ask me *why* I was suspended, I could not tell you. Neither could any sportswriter who followed the case.

A HAMFAT POLITICIAN
NAMED HAPPY

A COUPLE OF DAYS AFTER the first unexpected blast by Ray Hendricks, I received a call from Happy Chandler, who had left the U.S. Senate upon the death of Judge Landis to become Commissioner of Baseball. We were still at war but Happy saw his duty and he done it. It was purely coincidental that the work was easier and the pay better. I know the call came on a Sunday afternoon because he reached me during the rehearsal of the Jack Benny radio show where I was portraying that argumentative fellow, Leo Durocher, a very taxing role. Happy had a few things he wanted to discuss with me and he suggested the most convenient time and place for him was at the Claremont Country Club in Berkeley the following Friday.

Only it wasn't a suggestion. "You'll be there, boy," he drawled, when I protested that he couldn't have picked a more inconvenient time for me. And there was something in his use of the word "boy"—or maybe it was in the drawl—that was ominous.

But still . . . Happy had always been a good friend. I used to run into good old Happy around the Stork Club all the time. Senator Albert B. "Happy" Chandler (D-Ky.) may have served his backwoods constituency well but that didn't mean he had to associate with them in non-election years,

did it? When he was running for the job of commissioner—
and no alderman ever ran harder or kissed more asses—he'd
give me his "Ah Love Baseball" routine and he'd put his
arms around my shoulders and he'd say, "If they ever ask
you, put in a word for me, willya, Leo old boy? You and I
always been such good friends. . . ."

And I did. I put in many a good word for Happy with the
newspapermen and club owners whenever the chance arose,
which only proves how right Mr. Rickey was—again—in saying that sooner or later we pay for our sins.

Friday turned out to be a dreary, drizzly day. But we had
a pleasant enough lunch together at the golf club and then
we walked three holes in a misty rain before we gave it up.
And it wasn't Laraine he wanted to talk about at all. Instead,
he pulled out a slip of paper which listed the names of a
number of presumed friends of mine whom he quite obviously did not look upon as forces for good within the community—or even, possibly, as acceptable contributors to a
Senator's campaign fund.

The reason Chandler would be so concerned about my
friends and associations wasn't that hard to figure out. The
basketball point-shaving scandals had just been uncovered,
and there was a story boiling up in the minor leagues about
games that had actually been fixed. The Attorney General
of the U.S., Tom Clark, had appealed to sportswriters for
help in cleaning up sports, and the sportswriters were climbing all over Chandler.

His first question to me was: "Do you know Joe Adonis?"

I had a nodding acquaintance with Joe Adonis. I used to
see him around the ball park, always with two or three guys
around him. Whenever he caught my eye he'd say hello, and
I would nod. When I was told who he was I was astonished,
because he looked far more like a banker than like a man
who was supposed to be high up in Murder, Inc.

I had never actually been introduced to Adonis, let alone

socialized with him, and I was happy enough to agree to stop nodding to him.

Bugsy Siegel was on the list. I had been introduced to him once in a barber shop.

Two of the other names on the list, though, were Memphis Engelberg and Connie Immerman. Engelberg was a close friend of Charlie Dressen's and a good friend of mine. He had been a bookmaker back in the days when bookmaking was legal in New York, and at the time I met him he was probably the best horse handicapper I had ever come across. Whenever I went to the track, which wasn't often, I'd have Memphis mark my card. So did all the players. And I'll tell you one thing: He did me a lot more good than harm. Engelberg was one of the men whose free run of our club house Rickey had most objected to, but if you had me swear on a stack of Bibles, I couldn't tell you whether he had ever bet on a baseball game or not.

Connie Immerman had run the Cotton Club back in my early days in New York. I had known him through the years, seen him occasionally, and I had always liked him. Chandler informed me that he was running a gambling casino in Havana, which, according to his information, was controlled by gangster interests. If I wanted to be smart, he said, I was to consider him out of bounds too.

Once the list had been taken care of, the commissioner told me that for my own good he was ordering me to move out of George Raft's home. On that he was emphatic. So emphatic as to leave little doubt that this was the real reason he had called me there.

Now that didn't come as a complete shock. Back in 1941, Judge Landis had kept Larry MacPhail and me in his office after the pre-Series meeting with the Yankees so that he could order me to get back the four tickets I had given George to my private box. He had information, the Judge said, that George had won $100,000 betting on baseball games, and no gambler was going to sit in my box.

I had been living in Raft's home for a month or so every winter and I had never heard he was any particular kind of gambler. I knew he played a lot of bridge and I knew that he was a teetotaler—he never took a drink in his life—and I also knew that he had a rich, and even fabled, social life. And that's about all. I know it's difficult to believe that I could have spent so much time in his home without really spending much time with him, but you have to understand the peculiar kind of life George led. He'd be up at five or six in the morning to go out to the studio, and I'd get up a few hours later and spend the day playing golf. He'd get home in the early evening and take a quick nap. The quickest nap in the West. George would walk into the den, sit down in his big leather chair and be sound asleep. An hour later he'd bounce up, and that was it; George was ready to go. Occasionally we'd have people over to dinner. Most of the time he'd go his way and I'd go mine.

It was a huge house, anyway. I had known George back in the days when he was a hoofer in New York, and when he first invited me to stay at his house he had assured me that the place was so big that we wouldn't even have to get in each other's way. Even the telephone system was set up so that my calls came in on a separate line.

I told Judge Landis that I didn't see how he could expect me to repay that kind of hospitality by insulting the man. Well, I went a lot further than that. "I gave the man the four seats," I said, "and he's going to keep the four seats." I'd get the seats back, Landis said, or I wouldn't put on my uniform the next day.

And through it all, MacPhail kept winking at me.

Judge Landis went so far as to take me back into his bedroom and talk to me like a Dutch uncle. "Now this isn't the first conversation we've had in here, son," he began. "You will get those tickets back...." And still I left there without having made any flat commitment.

As soon as we were out in the corridor, MacPhail turned

on me like he wanted to kill me. "What are you, blind or something?" he hollered. "Couldn't you see me giving you the sign to tell him Yes? I'll give him four seats in a box as good as yours. What difference does it make to him?"

It made a difference to him. Raft was so mad that he was going to sue Judge Landis for defamation of character or something, and for a while there it was touch and go.

A few years later, I was the one who was sore at Raft. That was the result of the celebrated "dice game" in my apartment, a marvelous example of the kind of hit-and-run reporting that has made me such an ardent admirer of the Great American Press. Years afterwards, the fans were still riding me about clipping some poor guy with loaded dice. And I wasn't even there.

Here is exactly what happened: Because of the transportation shortage during the war, all baseball clubs were barred from going anywhere below the Mason-Dixon line for spring training. The Dodgers were, therefore, "training" up at West Point, in three feet of snow, when Georgie called to ask me if it would be possible for me to come to the city and have dinner with him. Well, it was only an hour's drive, and frankly, I welcomed any kind of an excuse that would get me out of there. George's problem turned out to be the kind of problem we should all have. He was romancing one of the biggest musical-comedy stars on Broadway and he had a date with her that night. The problem? The problem was that he couldn't get her to walk through the lobby of his hotel, and he wanted to know if he could use my apartment. Sure, buddy. Glad to. The next day he was to put the key in an envelope and leave the envelope at the desk of his hotel so that I could pick it up when we came back to New York.

Seven months later, with the season over, I was in a military uniform at Fort Totten, just about to go overseas with a couple of other ballplayers to entertain the soldiers. I picked up the paper and—holy smoke—there I am in the headlines again. Some guy had sworn out a complaint that he had been cheated in a dice game in Durocher's apartment.

When you got down to the body of the story, you could see that the guy making the beef was claiming Raft had beaten him for $18,000, *seven months earlier,* by making thirteen straight passes with a pair of loaded dice. If you looked real close, you would also see that he had specifically stated that I hadn't been there and was absolving me from any possible blame. But it was my name in the headlines, not Raft's.

You try to do a guy a favor . . . I was so mad at George that I refused to speak to him for almost a year. And then one day we found ourselves sitting at adjacent tables at, I think, the Friars Club. A mutual friend brought us together, and George swore to me that the story wasn't true. He had used my apartment to play gin rummy with another guy, he said. A couple of other guys had come up to play gin too, and this guy, who wasn't in any of the games, had kept yelling that he wanted to shoot some craps.

The game had taken place, George said, in another room. And if the guy really had been taken, why had he waited almost seven months before making a beef?

There was no reason for me not to believe George. Especially since the case had just faded away after that one headline and sunk without a trace. When you came right down to it, I couldn't really be that indignant about his using my apartment for one night to play gin when I had been living in his home every winter for years.

I moved back into his home in California that winter, and it was only a few weeks later that Chandler was ordering me to move out again.

The talk with Chandler, let it be understood, was quite cordial. There were no threats and no harsh words. He was doing all this, he kept telling me, for my own good. But I had been around too many poolrooms in my younger days not to have an instinct for the fix. The sportswriters had been calling Chandler a clown and a political hack. He had made a lot of silly statements in calmer days about having the best job in the world because he was being paid $50,000 a year for going South in the winter and watching baseball in the summer. If Happy was setting up a scapegoat in case he had to prove he was really a cast-iron commissioner from the Landis mold, I knew whose head was being fitted for the horns.

If I had known a few things then that I didn't find out until years and years later, I'm not sure whether I would have felt better about it or worse. The man who had indirectly brought the meeting on was Westbrook Pegler. Pegler had been a great muckraking reporter in his day, and, while he still had his reputation, he was beginning to lose some of his marbles. If a man had dropped down from Mars and read nothing except Pegler's columns for a month, he couldn't help but believe the two great enemies of the Republic were Eleanor Roosevelt and Frank Sinatra. Eleanor Roosevelt because she was in some kind of mysterious plot to overthrow democracy, and Frank Sinatra because he was up there somewhere playing Advise and Consent in the inner councils of the Mafia. If you are old enough to remember Pegler in his declining years, you know exactly what I mean. If you're not . . . well, kids, there's no way to explain it.

Well, I was a friend of Frank's, the betting scandals were in the news, and so, unbeknownst to me, Pegler had set out to add my scalp to his collection. What he had done was to warn Branch Rickey that he was working on a series of columns exposing me for the moral delinquent that everybody knew I was but that before he went to press with it he was willing to give Rickey a chance to cleanse himself by firing me.

He told Rickey, speaking of the responsibility of the press, that I had been a character witness for Bugsy Siegel. When, where, why or how, he apparently wasn't able to say, probably because Eleanor Roosevelt and her cell of subversives were keeping it a secret. It was, of course, an absolute lie.

He also told Rickey that Brooklyn District Attorney Miles McDonald had put a tap on my phone and come up with some damning conversations between me and Joe Adonis. There was at least a flimsy basis of fact in that one. The DA had heard a conversation of sorts, Rickey had discovered, only it wasn't with Adonis. One of his friends, who I didn't even know, had come over to me one day to ask if I would donate some old balls and bats to a church charity Mr. Adonis was interested in. I told him I'd be glad to and forgot all about it until the same guy phoned after a couple of weeks to remind me. All I have to say is that if it was *my* phone that was being tapped, and not Adonis's, good luck to them. If that was the worst they could get on me, that I had donated some bats and balls to a church charity, I wasn't living as interesting a life as they thought.

While he was about it, Pegler had also imparted the information that I was involved in one of the big crime stories of the time, the Mergenthaler check-cashing swindle. When Rickey looked into that one, it turned out that a few of my checks had been routinely processed through a check-cashing house that was involved in the swindle, along with maybe a million other checks. It had nothing to do with me or even with the people I had made out the checks to. It had to do with nothing except the way banks conduct their business.

Although none of Pegler's charges had checked out, Rickey was still worried about one thing. If I was so clean, Pegler had kept asking him, how come I was living with George Raft, that good friend of Bugsy Siegel? Mr. Rickey had decided that it would be an excellent idea for me to move out of Raft's house before the Pegler columns appeared. Instead of laying the situation out for me and ordering me to move out or else, Rickey—with that way he had of doing everything by way of Kansas City—had sent his chief assistant, Arthur Mann, to Chandler's office to ask Happy to throw a fright into me. Arthur Mann had been sitting in the Commissioner's office when Happy called the NBC studio to set up the appointment at the Claremont Country Club.

When Pegler's columns about me appeared, three weeks after my meeting with Chandler, they were all implication and innuendo, linking me with Siegel and Adonis through my friendship with Raft. To show how accurate a reporter he was, he had me still living in George's house and he quoted Rickey as saying that I was "dumb as hell when it comes to figuring the consequences of an association . . . but entirely honest." I can easily imagine Rickey saying that I was irresponsible or naive, but nobody who knew Branch could possibly picture him using the word "hell" in anything other than a biblical context.

All this had taken place, you understand, before I married Laraine—another reason why it was so unbright of me to have popped off the way I did about Judge Dockweiler. The day we started spring training, the worst blow of all fell. The head of the Brooklyn chapter of the Catholic Youth Organization pulled his 50,000 boys out of the Dodgers Knothole Gang on the ground that I was "a powerful force for undermining the moral and spiritual training of our young boys." I had never claimed to be in any danger of sprouting wings but I had never considered myself a corrupter of the young either. From a very casual observation of the young men of Brooklyn, I had every confidence that they were quite capable of corrupting themselves without any help from me.

I had the Commissioner, the judiciary, the clergy and the crusading press watching every move I made. But do you think I was worried? Do you think I was running scared? You bet your sweet life I was.

The Dodgers were training in Havana. When I checked in to the hotel, who did I see in the lobby but Memphis Engelberg and Connie Immerman, two of the men I had been told to stay away from. When they came over to say hello, I ran, not walked to the nearest elevator.

Throughout spring training, I beat a narrow path from my hotel to the ball park and back to the hotel room. I had my meals sent up to the room so that I'd be in no danger of shaking the wrong hand or talking to the wrong person. Until Laraine finally came to Havana, after finishing her picture and tying up the loose ends of the divorce proceedings, I didn't even have anybody to talk to.

And then one day, I came home from a workout dead tired and decided we would give ourselves a treat by going back out into the civilized world and relaxing around the pool. While Branch, Jr., Laraine and I were lounging in front of the cabana, a complete stranger walked over, pointed to a group playing cards on the other side of the pool and told me he had a friend who was just dying to meet me. "He's a great baseball fan," he said, "and he's always admired you."

At this point, the President of the United States would have needed a security clearance in order to get a curt nod from me. This guy didn't get a second glance. He kept coming back, though, and to get him off my back, Branch, Jr., went over to find out who my devoted admirer was.

When he came back, he didn't look at all happy. "Who do you think wants to shake your hand, Leo?" he said, practically spitting. "Lucky Luciano."

I grabbed Laraine's hand and we ran upstairs without even pausing to get out of our bathing suits.

After all that care and caution, two incidents, both so minor that I never gave them a second thought, did me in. Worse, it was Larry MacPhail, a man who wished me no harm, who started the juggernaut rolling. MacPhail, having come home from the wars, had, as always, landed on his feet as co-owner and president of the New York Yankees. For reasons of his own, probably nothing more than publicity, he decided it would be nice to get a little feud going with his old friend and benefactor Branch Rickey. To get things started, he hired Charlie Dressen away from us—something I couldn't really object to. Charlie had managed for MacPhail in Cincinnati and coached for him in Brooklyn. Larry MacPhail was Dressen's Big Man, the same way that Branch Rickey was mine. For good measure, he then hired away my other coach, Red Corriden, who had also worked for him in both Cincinnati and Brooklyn.

The one thing he still didn't have was a manager. In Larry's one year with the Yankees, three managers had quit on him. Joe McCarthy, the most successful manager in baseball, had taken all of MacPhail he wanted after the first month. Bill Dickey, an old Yankee hero who had been hired to appease their fans, had quit with a few weeks left, and Johnny Neun, who had been one of McCarthy's coaches for years, had let it be known after about a week that he knew now what McCarthy and Dickey had been talking about and, by God, he didn't have to take that from anybody either. If it was possible for Larry MacPhail to be embarrassed, a highly debatable point, he was in a highly embarrassing position, and he rose to the occasion nicely by making noises all through the winter that he was negotiating with me. I kept needling him back by saying, in one way or another, that yes, Larry had tried to hire me but I wasn't interested in anything except managing the good old Brooklyn Dodgers. It was a lot of fun and it kept us in the papers during the off season. When Larry finally got around to signing Bucky Harris he kept it going by saying that he hadn't been trying to sign me after all, he had only been helping me to get a better contract out of Rickey.

Very cute. And also kind of silly to anybody who knew that I already had the best contract in baseball and had, in fact, made a handshake agreement with Rickey at the end of the season to come back.

Despite all the sniping, Rickey and MacPhail had arranged to train practically side by side in Havana. The one thing you have to give MacPhail was that he never took anything he said about somebody else personally. The exhibition season began, almost before we unpacked our baggage, with a three-game series between us and the Yankees. The first game was to be played, for reasons which I am sure were explained to me, in Caracas, Venezuela, and the final two in Havana. When we returned from Caracas, Walter O'Malley informed me that MacPhail was furious about a column I had written for the Brooklyn *Eagle*. More accurately, my name was on a daily column, *Durocher Says*, which Harold Parrott, our traveling secretary, was writing for me. Between you and me, since I didn't write it, I didn't always read it either, which seemed to balance the whole thing off nicely. I knew Harold would never write anything I couldn't stand behind and he hadn't. All he had done was to go with the winter publicity to make it seem as if the exhibition games against the Yankees were going to be for blood.

> This is a declaration of war . . . I want to beat the Yankees because of MacPhail and Dressen. [MacPhail] tried to drive a wedge between myself and all these things I hold dear. When MacPhail found I couldn't be induced to manage his Yankees for any of his inducements, he resolved to knock me and make life as hard as possible for me. . . . But surely people must recognize that it is the same old MacPhail. About Dressen, I cannot help but feel bitterly . . .
>
> One thing should be remembered: Dressen's only out as far as his Brooklyn contract was concerned was that he could sign to manage a major league club elsewhere. Has MacPhail promised Charlie this? What does this mean to Bucky Harris? Be sure I will ask these questions when we meet in Caracas tomorrow!

I read it and for the life of me I couldn't see anything for MacPhail to be mad about. As far as I was concerned, Larry was only trying to keep the thing going in the hope that it would help the gate. That was why he had started it, wasn't it?

In the first of the games at Havana, Rickey saw Engelberg and Immerman, two of the men he knew I had been warned about, sitting in one of the boxes assigned to the Yankees, right beside MacPhail's box. Back in the hotel lobby afterwards he had exploded to the newspapermen that if he had seen either of them in the Brooklyn ball park he would have thrown them out. "Yet, there they are as guests of the president of the Yankees. Why, my own manager can't even say hello to this actor, George what's-his-name. He won't have anything to do with these gamblers or any gamblers. But apparently there are rules for Durocher and other rules for the rest of baseball."

I hadn't even seen them there the first day, but on the following day Dick Young of the *Daily News* came into the dugout to tell me what Mr. Rickey had said and ask whether I agreed with him. Well, you know me. Ask me a question and you get an answer. I looked at them sitting there and, boy, it burned me up to think that while I had to run away from them like a scared rabbit it was perfectly all right for MacPhail to not only socialize with them but give them free seats. You're damn right I agreed with him! "Where does MacPhail come off flaunting his company with known gamblers right in the players' faces?" I said. "If I even say 'Hello' to one of these guys, I'd be called up before Commissioner Chandler and probably barred."

Nothing inflammatory about that. That's what Chandler himself had very strongly implied in our talk on the golf course.

Rickey's statement and mine apparently hit the New York papers like a time bomb. A week later, MacPhail counterattacked by demanding an investigation. What follows is the letter MacPhail wrote to Chandler, in full. The italics are mine.

I am attaching a summary of quotations attributed to Branch Rickey and a summary of statements appearing in the articles signed by Durocher.

These articles appearing in the Brooklyn *Eagle* are allegedly written and/or publication authorized by officials of the Brooklyn Baseball Club. Either the president of the Brooklyn Club made the statements attributed to him or he has been misquoted.

In any event, the charges are either true or false. If true, they should properly have been communicated to the Commissioner of Baseball. If false, their utterance and/or publication constitutes slander and libel and represents, in our opinion, conduct detrimental to baseball.

For these reasons the New York Club requests the Commissioner to call a hearing to determine responsibility of the statements and then whether they are true or not.

When these matters have been determined, the New York Club takes it for granted, in view of the publicity which has followed these charges, that *the Commissioner will make his findings public.* Mr. Will Harridge, president of the American League, joins me in making this request.

Two things: Not that it matters, but Mr. Will Harridge didn't seem to know that he had joined MacPhail until he read about it. More important, you will notice that Larry's sights are set on Rickey, not on me. It is Rickey's statement about Engelberg and Immerman he is objecting to, not mine. In bringing up the *Durocher Says* column he is trying to make the case—knowing very well that Parrott was writing them—that the "Brooklyn ball club," i.e., Branch Rickey, was responsible for them.

Just to set this straight right now, there was no doubt whatsoever as to the truth of Rickey's statement, a point the Commissioner studiously avoided in the hearing and totally misrepresented in his decision. Engelberg and Immerman were next to MacPhail's box. Their tickets had been left at the box office in the name of Larry MacPhail by Red Patterson, the Yankees' publicity man. All that aside, how smart do you have to be to know that nobody is sitting with MacPhail, in an attached box, unless he had invited them to sit there? And the *Daily News* had printed a picture, on the same day MacPhail filed his charges, showing him sitting there with them.

In the crazy-quilt training schedule Rickey had set up, we had flown right to Panama after the second exhibition game with the Yankees to set up our camp in the Canal Zone for the next two weeks. I was keeping myself so isolated that I didn't learn about the charges until Rickey flew in the day after they had been filed. Even then, he told me about it almost in passing because we had something that seemed far more serious to talk about, the players' petition against Jackie Robinson. Rickey spent the next day in his hotel, laying the law down, and then drove to the Atlantic side of the Isthmus to take a look at Robinson and the rest of the minor-league squad. As for me, I had to fly to Los Angeles on March 19 to respond to a show-cause order issued by Judge Dockweiler as to why he should not nullify Laraine's divorce.

Just before I left, I received a cable that the Commissioner, who, as everyone knew, owed his job to MacPhail, was holding a hearing on the charges in Sarasota on Monday, March 24.

Laraine, having finished her picture, flew back with me on Saturday. On Sunday, the entire Brooklyn contingent gathered together in Rickey's suite. And everybody treated the thing as a huge joke. Everybody except me. I could remember everything that had happened, starting with the call that brought me to the golf course in Berkeley. "I'm telling you now," I said, "there's been too much talk. When all the smoke clears away, the building is going to fall on me."

Everybody hooted. Our lawyer was former U.S. Senator George Williams, an old friend of Rickey's from Missouri.

Unless I am mistaken, he had retired from practice and just happened to be living in Sarasota. Williams hadn't even bothered to set up a defense. Based on the charges, he said, there was nothing to defend.

But that was what made me so nervous. If there had been something there, there would have been some logic to it. I mean, how could MacPhail argue that I had libeled him in saying that he had tried to hire me away, when I had only been going along with his own propaganda? Nothing about it seemed to make any sense. Except for one thing: On the same day that he had filed the charges Larry had also told Joe Trimble of the *Daily News* that Walter O'Malley and John Smith, two of the owners of the Dodgers, had given him permission during the season to deal with me if he wanted to. "At the time, this permission was given in confidence," he had told Trimble. "But in the light of recent statements by Rickey and Durocher that I tampered with Leo and Dressen, Smith and O'Malley have given me permission to reveal their consent to any dealing I care to do with Durocher."

At first glance, MacPhail merely seemed to be setting up his defense for all those statements of his that were on the record. You read it again and you had to ask yourself: "What the hell is going on here?" What did "in confidence" mean unless it meant that Branch Rickey, the man who was supposed to be running the club, wasn't supposed to know anything about it? I was Rickey's man, we were in the middle of a head-to-head pennant race with the Cardinals—*and they had given MacPhail permission to talk to me behind Rickey's back?*

And had now given MacPhail permission to use that secret conversation in his attack upon Rickey?

That put a whole new face on the matter, didn't it? It meant that there was a power struggle shaping up between O'Malley and Rickey for control of the club, and that Leo Durocher was caught right in the middle.

Nor was it the only newspaper report that had got my wind up. Only a few days earlier, Lou Smith of the Cincinnati *Enquirer* had quoted Chandler as telling him: "Somebody may wind up getting kicked out of baseball. I'm taking off my kid gloves and I intend to make things tough for the baseball people who won't toe the line and whose conduct I consider detrimental to baseball."

If I felt that the target had already been identified, it may well have been because Chandler had defended himself against the charges that he was a do-nothing commissioner by writing a Cincinnati sports editor who had been attacking him for his failure to discipline me on the dice game in my apartment that he had, in fact, followed up Pegler's accusations by questioning me "at length" at Berkeley. A clear implication—putting aside both the twisting of the dates and the breaking of his promise of confidentiality—that there must have been something to question me about.

"I've got a hunch," I told Senator Williams, "that the Commissioner is laying for me."

And then something happened to make me surer. One of the reasons we had never got down to a serious discussion in Rickey's suite was because Branch's brother-in-law had died the previous night, and Branch was preparing to leave for Ohio to attend the funeral. He had already asked the Commissioner to postpone the hearing until he got back and since it's rather difficult to hold a trial without the defendant, nobody had any doubt that it was going to be granted.

A few hours after he left, we received word that the request had been denied. Well, if Rickey wasn't going to be there, who was left? I looked all around me and I couldn't see anybody but Leo.

The hearing was held in the glass-enclosed penthouse of the Sarasota Terrace Hotel. I was put in an anteroom with the other witnesses: Ted McGrew, Charlie Dressen, Red Corriden, Harold Parrott and, to my astonishment, Augie Galan, an all-purpose ballplayer who had been traded during the winter. Augie kept asking me what in the world he had been called for.

"Hell, I don't know," I told him. "I don't even know why I'm here."

I was the last one called. I walked in and it was like a courtroom. The Commissioner was sitting there like a judge. The Yankees, represented only by MacPhail and Dan Topping, were on one side of the room. Three Dodger officials, Walter O'Malley, Branch Rickey, Jr., and Arthur Mann, were sitting with Senator Williams on the other.

A stenographer was seated at a table in front of the witness chair taking everything down.

"What's your name?" the Commissioner asked.

"What's my name?" *My name? You ought to know my name.* "I thought you were going to ask—"

But no, he wanted to know my name and who I managed and when I was hired and all that jazz. For the record.

"Do you write a series of articles, 'Durocher Says,' for the Brooklyn *Eagle*?"

"Yes, sir."

"Do you know what you said in this article?"

"Yes, sir."

At the direction of the Commissioner, MacPhail stood up and read the column through from beginning to end.

The moment he had finished, I said, "Well, Larry, as far as I'm concerned that's all baseball jargon. That's baseball talk, Larry. That's the way you and I have always talked."

I said, "Look, Larry, I didn't mean anything derogatory about you. I worked for you, and you fired me . . . how many times? You must have fired me sixty times and we were always friends. Maybe I have needled you a little bit in there, but to me it was nothing personal. Larry, if you think it's personal, if you think I've done something wrong here, I will right now apologize to you. And I also will apologize publicly if you want me to. Because I don't want you as an enemy of mine. We've been friends too long."

MacPhail just took the clipping he had been reading from and ripped it up into little pieces. He came up to the witness chair, put his arm around me and gave me a bear hug that practically lifted me out of the chair. "You've always been a great guy with me, and you always will be a great guy," he said. "Forget it, buddy, it's over."

I sat down. I'd been worried about nothing, just like everybody had said all along.

Only it wasn't over. The Commissioner turned to me and said, "Now let me ask some questions here."

And he took me off in another direction entirely. He took me down a road I had never heard about. The Commissioner said, "Is there any crap shooting on your club?"

What? I just stared at him.

"Do you shoot crap on the ball club? Do you carry dice on your ball club?"

"No, sir. There has never been a pair of dice in my clubhouse. There has never been any boys shooting crap on my club, in the clubhouse or, as far as I know, on the train, in a hotel room, anywhere."

"Well," he said, "that isn't the way I hear it."

"I don't care how you hear it. You're hearing it wrong. There has never been a pair of dice in my clubhouse."

"Do you have any card playing on your ball club?"

Card playing? Sure. Who doesn't have card playing? I explained that, before Rickey had ordered me to put a stop to it, we'd had some very interesting poker games.

Now I knew why Galan had been called. Augie had always been one of our most enthusiastic card players—he and Billy Herman had always been ready to gamble on anything—and Happy must have thought that now that Augie had left us he would have some wild and woolly tales to tell. I found out later that Augie had told him exactly what I was telling him. "We play a little gin now," I said. "A little fan-tan."

"That's not what I'm talking about. Do you play for high stakes with any of your players yourself?"

I could see now where he was leading me. I played gin rummy regularly with Kirby Higbe, and always managed to have him about $600 to $800 in debt to me. Of course, that wasn't saying too much for my game because Kirby couldn't beat your aunt from Duluth. Every time he won a ball game I'd leave a note in his locker telling him to deduct $200 from the bill. It was a marvelous system. It kept Kirby from losing real money to anybody else, and it gave him an extra incentive when he was out there pitching.

But, as I explained to Chandler, I had never taken ten cents in actual cash from Higbe in my life.

With all that inside information of his blown to hell, there was nothing left for Chandler to do but take up my quote about the gamblers in MacPhail's box. I told him that although I had never seen the quotes in the paper and couldn't remember exactly what I had said, word for word, I sure had spoken my mind. This was what I had been waiting for. I started to remind him that these were two of the men he himself had specifically warned me against associating with but the Commissioner cut me off, turned to Larry MacPhail and asked him rather abruptly whether I had ever applied for the job of manager of the New York Yankees.

From the time Larry tore up the column, Chandler's attitude toward him had changed from almost servile respect to scarcely concealed displeasure. Instead of answering immediately, MacPhail cleared his throat and asked Chandler for permission to have Dan Topping make some introductory remarks.

Topping told about meeting me at the ball park during the season and having a long talk with me. Could have happened, could have happened. To have a long talk with me, all you have to do is say hello. Topping never did say that the subject of managing his team had ever come up, though, and the question was never put to him.

Nor was it ever put to MacPhail again. Or, for that matter, to me. After Topping had finished, Larry gave a long, rambling talk in which he consistently avoided making any flat statement about offering me the job, one way or the other, or even about getting permission from O'Malley to talk to me. (I wish I had a copy of the transcript so that I could demonstrate how brilliantly he danced around it but I doubt whether any copies exist outside of Happy's vault.)

Having allowed MacPhail to get away without making anything like a direct answer to what was supposed to be one of the two questions we were there to answer, he turned back to me. "All right," he said. "You are hereby dismissed and you are hereby silenced."

I was half out of the witness chair when that last word hit me. I turned back to him, bewildered.

"That means," he said, "you cannot discuss one word of this with anyone. When you walk out of this door you are forever silenced."

I went downstairs to the lobby, and the first person I saw was Mrs. Chandler, who was a beautiful and affable and charming woman. "What's the matter with your old man?" I asked her. "Is he crazy or something?"

"Ahhhh," she said. "A little publicity, Leo. Nothing. Forget it. You going to buy me a drink?"

We went into the bar. She had a couple of drinks, and I had a couple of Cokes. Mrs. Chandler could see I was worried, and she couldn't have been nicer. "Relax, Leo," she said. "You know MacPhail. You know my husband. You should know better by now than to worry about those two."

That made me feel better. Chandler's wife didn't think he was out to get me, and who should know better.

The attitude of the Brooklyn officials was just what it had been earlier. The whole hearing, everybody felt, had been a farce. Harold Parrott sent a telegram back to the office saying: BROOKLYN WINS ANOTHER.

The day before the season was to open, we were all

Durocher and Frank Frisch, the captain and the manager of the Gas House Gang. They teamed together very well around second base and didn't do so badly when it came to ganging up on an umpire either. (ST. LOUIS POST-DIS-PATCH)

Right from the beginning, Leo was ready to speak his piece. Umpire Dolly Stark has given the first-year manager the thumb, and Leo is giving him the back of his hand. (N.Y. DAILY NEWS)

Three characteristic Durocher poses. The umpire is Lou Jorda. (three photos N.Y. DAILY NEWS)

A characteristic Durocher pose. The umpire is Dusty Boggess. (N.Y. DAILY NEWS)

Durocher restrained and Durocher departing. Everybody knew that Durocher and Eddie Stanky (no. 12) got the quickest thumb in baseball, but when Leo said it out loud he was ordered to apologize by League president Warren Giles. (both photos N.Y. DAILY NEWS)

Leo meets "Rookie of the Year" Jackie Robinson during a luncheon given in Robinson's honor in Los Angeles. Come the next spring, Jackie's coat jacket didn't fit quite so loosely and one of baseball's more exciting feuds was born. (UPI)

Leo was brought back into baseball the following year by Branch Rickey, the Great Man in his life. This picture was taken a month later when Durocher showed up to help drum up publicity for Rickey's announcement that the baseball club was taking over the operation of the Brooklyn football Dodgers in the All-American Conference. (UPI)

Horace Stoneham (left), the owner of the New York Giants, shocked the baseball world in mid-season by announcing that Leo Durocher, the most hated of all Giant enemies, was replacing Mel Ott (center), the most beloved of all Giant heroes. (N.Y. DAILY NEWS)

The public's attitude began to change when Chandler suspended Leo out of hand after a fraudulent assault charge had been placed against him. Some loyal Giant fans have come out early on the day the suspension was lifted to let Leo know they're with him. (N.Y. DAILY NEWS)

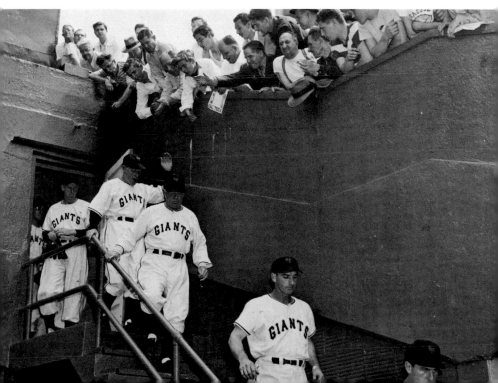

Sal Maglie, shown here in his later days pitching a no-hitter for Brooklyn, was discovered by Durocher one night in St. Louis when he had nobody else to pitch. Maglie promptly became the best pitcher in the National League. (N.Y. DAILY NEWS)

The Giants tied the Dodgers on the last day of the season in 1951 by defeating the Braves in Boston, 3–2. From left to right Larry Jansen, the winning pitcher, Stanky, Monte Irvin and manager Durocher. (UPI)

Bobby Thomson, the Hero, is being mobbed after THE home run. That's a hatless, hairless Durocher on the edge of the crowd in the upper right, a scene which he could scarcely recall later. Directly behind Leo is Clint Hartung, with Eddie Stanky coming in from the corner. (WIDE WORLD)

Battered, pummeled and almost choked to death, a dazed and only semiconscious genius manager is helped into the clubhouse a few moments later by Davey Williams and a special cop and a pair of welcoming hands. (N.Y. DAILY NEWS)

The world champions. The traditional picture on the stairs of City Hall and the traditional handshake from the mayor, Robert F. Wagner. (MAURICE J. SAKLAD)

Bobby Thomson was rewarded with a raise in salary for the following season. Leo and Chub Feeney (right), the Giants' general manager, weren't quite so friendly twenty years later when Feeney, as president of the National League, tried to fine Leo $250 for "breaking up a meeting" between his players and Marvin Miller. (N.Y. DAILY NEWS)

Manager Durocher is rewarded by a horseshoe of flowers and a shiny plaque proclaiming him to be "Baseball Manager of the Year." Handing him the plaque is old friend and good sport Charlie Dressen. (N.Y. DAILY NEWS)

(UPI)

Dusty Rhodes. He never doubted that he was the greatest hitter in the world and for that one year, 1954, he was. Having spread-eagled the league over the regular season with his pinch-hitting, Dusty (prophetically kissing his bat) is about to beat the World Series over the head and carry it home with him. (N.Y. DAILY NEWS)

"That's my boy." The greatest player who ever lived, says Leo Durocher about Willie Mays. Leo brought Willie up, coddled him, petted him and rode with him and the Giants to two pennants and one world championship. (N.Y. DAILY NEWS)

(right) Hail and Farewell. Having made an indelible impression by becoming the first man to have ever argued with an umpire in Japan, Leo is presented a scroll —and a bouquet of flowers—by a pair of visiting Nipponese beauties. Could it possibly read: In appreciation to a swell guy? (below) Having announced his resignation between the games of the last day's doubleheader in 1955, Number 2 walks out toward the center field clubhouse of the Polo Grounds for the last time as manager of the New York Giants. (both photos N.Y. DAILY NEWS)

Walter O'Malley, who played a curious role through Durocher's career, had brought him back to baseball four years earlier as coach of the Los Angeles Dodgers. (N.Y. DAILY NEWS)

On May 7, 1966, ten years after he retired (or was he pushed?), Leo Durocher returned to New York, the scene of his trials and his triumphs, as manager of the Chicago Cubs. (N.Y. DAILY NEWS)

But he wasn't around on August 17, 1966, to see Willie hit his 535th home run and establish himself (pre-Aaron) as the greatest right-hand home run hitter of baseball. (MAURICE J. SAKLAD)

A somewhat mellowing Durocher at an Oldtimers Game at Shea Stadium, New York, with old friends and foes—Enos Slaughter, Hank Sauer and Jackie Robinson. (N.Y. DAILY NEWS)

At Angels' training camp in Palm Springs, California, with his old first base-man (and current look-alike), Dolph Camilli. (CHARLES J. SCARDINA)

Leo's marriage to Lynne Walker Goldblatt in the middle of a hot pennant race in 1969 brought on some predictable and unpredictable problems. The friend on the left is Frank Sinatra. (CHARLES J. SCARDINA)

Robert J. Walker, the brother of the bride, served as best man. Walker was the chief investigator for the Illinois Crime Investigating Commission. It was a vague accusation directed at both Walker and Durocher that almost got Leo bounced out of baseball for a second time. A secret hearing in Scottsdale, Arizona, was called by the commissioner, Bowie Kuhn.

Lynne Walker Durocher

Commissioner Bowie Kuhn at work. This seems to be a good day. (N.Y. DAILY NEWS)

gathered in the Brooklyn office at Montague Street to discuss our playing personnel. Who to keep and who to send down. Mostly, the discussion had come around again to Jackie Robinson. Rickey was still holding to that dream of his for creating a demand for him. As a matter of fact, we were going to be playing an exhibition game against Montreal that afternoon at Ebbets Field, another of his plans for introducing Jackie Robinson to the fans gingerly. I was still holding to my position, which was to bring him up and stop being so cute about it. Right in the middle of it, the phone rang. Mr. Rickey's private phone. The minute he picked it up the whole room went absolutely silent. Just by his attitude we knew what it was about. His bushy eyebrows shot up the way they did when he was shocked; he ran his hand through his hair over and over the way he always did when he was upset. When he lit his cigar, the click of his lighter seemed to ring through the air. I remember very distinctly what his first words were. "You can't DO that!" he said.

After he hung up the receiver, it seemed like four days before he said a word. And then he said to Harold Parrott, "You have been fined five hundred dollars."

Another hour seemed to go by. You cannot imagine how heavy that silence hung. "The Brooklyn club has been fined two thousand dollars."

There was another dead silence, and I couldn't stand to wait through another hour and a half. "What happened to *me*?" I asked. "I know *I* didn't get away."

Very softly, Mr. Rickey said, "You have been suspended for one year."

I can still hear my next two words: "For *what*?"

Mr. Rickey, still running his hand through his hair, shook his head back and forth and said, almost blankly, "I . . . don't . . . know."

Parrott had been fined for writing "a deliberately derogatory column about others in baseball," and for violating the Commissioner's order of silence by sending that three-word telegram. While he was about it, the Commissioner ordered that the column be suspended forthwith. So much for freedom of the press.

The Brooklyn club and the Yankees were both fined for engaging "in a public controversy damaging to baseball."

Charlie Dressen, who had apparently filed a protest of his own at I-can't-imagine-whose behest, was rewarded by being suspended for thirty days. "The Commissioner is convinced by the evidence," the order read, "that Dressen agreed with Rickey to remain as coach for two more years although the formal contract had not been signed." You will notice that there is not the slightest hint that MacPhail might have tampered with Dressen, a finding which would have forced Chandler to discipline the man who had got him the job. No. The only implication a reasonable man could draw was that Charlie had gone to MacPhail and deliberately misled him.

The two issues the hearing was supposed to resolve were (1) the presence of gamblers in MacPhail's box, and (2) the nonsense about whether MacPhail had really tried to get me to manage the Yankees. Chandler handled them both by attacking along the flanks and distorting the facts.

He handled the first by reporting that Mr. Rickey had denied that he had said, "Apparently there are rules for Durocher and other rules for the rest of baseball." Mr. Rickey had done no such thing. In an off-the-record discussion after I had left the room, MacPhail had insisted that he would not be satisfied until there was a clear-cut decision on whether or not Rickey had made that statement. Well, if that was what the whole thing was about, you would have thought that, simple courtesy aside, Chandler would have given Rickey the delay he had asked for. And that MacPhail would have insisted upon it. On the other hand, if that was all it was going to take to put an end to the thing, Senator Williams, acting purely as a lawyer and choosing his words with care, had taken it upon himself to deny, on behalf of Rickey, that Rickey had made that specific statement. Well, if you wanted to be a lawyer about it, he hadn't. What had happened was that Herb Goren, a New York sportswriter who was representing the AP, had asked Rickey at the end of his diatribe whether he was saying there was a double standard, one for Durocher and one for everybody else, and Rickey had thundered that it most certainly was. It was a good try by Senator Williams, but that's all it was. Obviously, nobody could speak for Rickey except Rickey, and so the Commissioner ordered a second hearing to be held in his hotel suite at the Pennsylvania Hotel in St. Petersburg on Friday, March 28.

Given the chance to speak for himself, Rickey testified that if the specific words had been put in his mouth, they had expressed his feelings exactly and that he would stand behind Goren's quote in its entirety.

For Chandler to have taken that kind of testimony and stated flatly, in the only record that would ever be made public, that Rickey had denied the accuracy of the quote shows how slippery he was and also—it would seem—how anxious he was to protect MacPhail.

If that wasn't bad enough, he then went on to say: "Evidence produced at the hearing shows that the alleged gamblers were not guests of MacPhail and did not sit in his box in Havana." No such evidence was produced. The only other witness at the St. Petersburg hearing had been Red Patterson, and from what I heard, Patterson suffered an astonishing loss of memory about how the tickets had got to Engelberg and Immerman but had finally admitted that it was "conceivable" that he could have given them the tickets himself. Even forgetting that the assembled writers covering both the Dodgers and the Yankees had seen them in the box, there was hard evidence (the photo in the *Daily News*) that they were there with MacPhail. Evidence which Chandler had been able to ignore, for his purpose, by simply refusing to allow the Dodgers to introduce it.

When he came to the beef between MacPhail and me, he was just as tricky. Maybe even trickier. Get this: "MacPhail admitted refraining from announcing the signing of his manager, to give Durocher an opportunity to negotiate a better contract with Rickey; this could not be considered an act designed to engender a friendly feeling between two major-league clubs, and the Commissioner will not expect its repetition in the future."

You see what he has done here? Although he seems to be rebuking MacPhail, what is he rebuking him for except for giving me such a golden opportunity to shaft Rickey. What conclusion could anybody draw from that except that I, Leo Durocher, had gone to MacPhail and asked him to do me a favor and had repaid him by attacking him for trying to tamper with me. He didn't say that, of course. He didn't have to say it. What none of the sportswriters thought to ask the Commissioner was how much I had been able to black-jack Rickey out of. What better contract? I was getting paid the same as I had always been paid. Not only hadn't I negotiated, I hadn't even looked at the contract.

The ruling on me was kept very general and very vague. "Durocher has not measured up to the standards expected or required of managers of our baseball teams. As a result of the accumulation of unpleasant incidents in which he has been involved, which the commissioner construes as detrimental to baseball, Manager Durocher is hereby suspended from participating in professional baseball for the 1947 season."

The final paragraph read: "All parties to this controversy are silenced from the time this order is issued."

So much for freedom of speech.

In other words, you can distort the facts and twist the evidence to your heart's content as long as you have the power to order everybody not to blow the whistle on you.

One thing I must say. The Brooklyn club did not walk away from me. On the contrary, the whole organization gathered around me. George V. McLaughlin, president of

the Brooklyn Trust Company, appointed himself my legal
advisor, along with John Barnewall, another big man at the
bank. The first thing I had done when I returned to earth
was to call the Hotel Pierre, where I knew the management,
to reserve a suite. The second thing was to call Laraine and
tell her to clear out of our apartment before the press descended upon her. That night, we all gathered together
again at the Hotel Pierre to decide what we were going to
do. John L. Smith, the strong man among the split ownership, was there. There were also a couple of judges, including Supreme Court Justice Henry L. Ughetta, who was one
of the Dodgers' directors, and a handful of lawyers.

The first point they debated, to my astonishment, was
whether I should sue the Commissioner. In the end, they
advised me against it. "You'll win any suit," I was told.
"There's no question of that. But when you win, you'll lose."
The word "blackball" was never used but in my nonlegal
mind I could see that little black ball bouncing all around
the room. I wasn't primed to sue, anyway. It would never
have entered my mind to sue. It wasn't the Commissioner's
authority I questioned. It was his motives. His honesty. His
integrity. In other words, it would never have occurred to
me to go running to the court to challenge the structure of
baseball.

Their final advice was: Go back to California. Sit tight.
Let's see what happens. You will be paid your full $50,000
salary.

Back to California we went. I spent the whole year playing golf and clearing the ground for a new home we were
building.

While I was chopping down trees, I was also taking a
swing or two at Chandler. Because while he could silence me
publicly, he could not silence me man to man. My opinion
of Chandler, already rock bottom, kept hitting new lows.

When Branch Rickey came back to camp after the St.
Petersburg hearing he told me that Chandler had kept point-

ing to his breast pocket and telling him he had a letter from Justice Frank Murphy of the U.S. Supreme Court, a leading Catholic layman, demanding that I be expelled from baseball. Rickey assured me that Happy had just been fishing for his reaction, but still, I tell you, it put me into a spin. The Supreme Court was worried about Leo Durocher, baseball manager?

As soon as we got back to New York, I called Steve Hannegan, a good friend of mine and, I knew, an old friend of Justice Murphy's. "I don't believe one word of it," Steve said. "This is one of the finest men I know. He would never do a thing like that." Besides, Steve said, no Supreme Court Justice would be stupid enough to write that kind of a letter because it amounted to misconduct.

"Can you find out for sure?" I asked him.

Both Justice Murphy and Steve Hannegan are dead, unfortunately, but I will swear on a stack of Bibles that what I tell you here is exactly what Hannegan told me. If Chandler had said he had written a letter, Murphy wanted me to know, then Chandler had lied and he was going to let him know about it. Even more than that, Murphy wanted me to know that from what he had read in the papers the Commissioner did not have the right to suspend me for one minute, let alone one year. As a judge, he felt I had been deprived of about five basic protections of the Bill of Rights, including due process of law and freedom of speech.

I have no way of knowing whether Justice Murphy ever did give Happy a piece of his mind for using his name that way. I do know that during the season, the Commissioner sent for Harold Parrott. "You fined the club two thousand dollars," Harold told him. "That's like patting an elephant on the behind. But you fined me five hundred dollars and I'm trying to raise a family. And you suspended Durocher for a year."

The Commissioner told Harold, "I know I made a mistake, but it's going to stand. You just be quiet and you'll get your five hundred back." And shortly thereafter Harold received a check for $500.

Happy wasn't telling the whole wide world he had made any mistake. Oh no. Just the opposite. There were two men he didn't silence. One was Larry MacPhail, the most unsilenceable man who ever lived. Having set me up like a bull's-eye, Larry turned around, typically, and became my most outspoken defender. Right from the beginning he shouted that Chandler didn't have the right to suspend me for five minutes. I know for a fact that he even went to the Commissioner's office in Cincinnati to try to get him to rescind my suspension.

The other man the Commissioner didn't silence was, of course, himself.

The great majority of the writers may well have agreed with the Commissioner that it was about time Durocher got his, but since they were newspapermen first and moralists second, they were unhappy with the secrecy of the hearing, the silencing of the participants and the vagueness of the "detrimental to baseball" verdict. They wanted to know who, what, where, when and how.

The Commissioner, having nothing they didn't already know about, defended himself by doing the worst thing one man can do to another man. He said nothing and implied everything. He talked first about "my confidential and undisclosed file on Durocher." He said, "If I ever opened my private files on Durocher, the American people would say I acted too leniently." In short, my offenses were so shocking, shameful and vile that Chandler, having led the chaste life of a politician, had not been able to bring himself to make them public.

The first time I read about his "confidential file," I phoned the Commissioner. "What things can't we talk about?" I said. "There's nothing in my record we can't talk about. I challenge you to open your file on me. I challenge you to make your reasons for suspending me public. You have no reasons." I cursed him up, down and around. I called him everything that one man can call another man.

Happy kept reminding me, unhappily, that I had been silenced and, more to the point, that he had the power to make the suspension permanent. "Not to you I'm not silenced, you dirty punk," I told him. "Any time you make that kind of a statement about me you're going to get a call from me."

And any time I saw even a line in the paper, his phone was ringing. Oh, we had long, intimate talks for a while, Happy and I. Happy has a smooth, silken politician's voice, not unlike a faith healer's, but I'm afraid I tended to hog the conversation.

The last time I called, I told him, "One more popoff by you, and you can forget all about my being silenced. I challenge you to a public debate anywhere in the country you want to hold it. You haven't got the guts to, have you?" One more quote, I warned him, and I was going to start popping off too. "I'm going to challenge you to release the transcript of that hearing or, better still, to hold a new hearing publicly. For the record this time."

He made no more statements, and I was back the next year.

But I still wasn't through with Chandler. In the spring, immediately after I had come back, Branch Rickey was opening his new minor-league training park at Vero Beach. The Commissioner, that great lover of baseball and free speech, was out at home plate, along with the Governor of Florida and assorted dignitaries, to lend his presence to the dedication ceremonies.

I wasn't about to join them. No dugout having been built yet, I was sitting on a little wooden bench against a wire fence opposite third base. The ceremonies over, Mr. Rickey and the Commissioner strolled down the baseline and stopped right at the coach's box. Mr. Rickey hollered to me twice, "Leo . . . LEO." I didn't budge until he sent one of our coaches over to get me.

The first thing Chandler said to me was, "You didn't want to come out here, did you?"

I said, "No, sir."

"You don't want to let bygones be bygones then?"

Let bygones be bygones! That was the worst insult of all. I was not fit to associate with decent human beings; my sins were too horrible to be spread across the public records. But let's forget it, Leo? Just campaign oratory, Leo? Not *today*, Commissioner! No chance!

For his part, Chandler said, he was quite willing to forget our past difficulties, shake hands and be friends.

Sure he did. All I had to do was shake his hand before 10,000 people and I was admitting that he had been perfectly justified in suspending me, that everything he had implied about me was true.

Not that he didn't come very close to pulling it off. Branch Rickey, who seemed to be enjoying his role as the great peacemaker, had his arms around both our shoulders so that I was unable to pull away. While Happy had been making his pitch about shaking hands and becoming friends, he had reached for my hand and grabbed it. All I could do was grit my teeth and withdraw it. "Are you talking to me now as the Commissioner of Baseball?" I hissed. "Or are you talking to me man to man? There's a difference in what I have to say."

"I'm talking to you now—since you don't want to let bygones be bygones—man to man."

The minute he said it, I took off on him. "No, I don't want to let bygones be bygones, you dirty, no-good—" And I called him everything I had ever called him over the phone, plus everything I had thought of since, plus whatever new inspirational messages came to mind.

Well, the sun must have been beating down pretty heavy because the Commissioner got all red in the face. "You're a hypocrite and a cheap political hack," I told him. "From now on, don't you ever speak to me anywhere you see me. If you want me, you had better send for me. And it had better be about baseball."

Through it all, poor Mr. Rickey had been shaking his head and trying to quiet me. "That's the way it is with me, Branch," I told him. "I don't want to have anything to do with this man. He's no good."

I have to say one thing for the Commissioner. He's not an easy man to offend. It may even be impossible. Later that same year, after I had been bounced over to the Giants, Dick Butler, who was the Commissioner's assistant and a wonderful guy, came over to tell me that Chandler wanted me to come over to his box so he could shake my hand and commend me for the great job I was doing.

I said, "I told the Commissioner once before—and I tell *you* to tell him now—if he wants me, to send for me in his office."

Well, he did send for me. After the World Series, I had read that Fred Fitzsimmons was quitting as coach at Boston. I don't have to tell you how I felt about Fitz. Five or six weeks later, I offered him a coaching job with the Giants, and then it turned out that Freddie's resignation had not been filed with the Commissioner's office yet, a technicality I should have checked on.

During the winter meeting in Chicago, Chandler held a hearing to investigate the circumstances. I was fined $500 for "tampering" with Fitz, which was OK, but Chandler also announced that he was suspending Freddie for the first thirty days of spring training. Edgar Feeley, the Giants' attorney, showed him in the rule book where he had no right to do that. Chandler took the rule book from him, laid it down on the floor alongside his chair and said, "I make my own rules."

I was burning anyway because, as I saw it, Chandler was only punishing Fitzsimmons as a further way of getting at me. When he laid that rule book on the floor, as if he were the emperor of the world, I felt like belting him.

Still, I said to the Commissioner, quite calmly, "I'd like to speak to you, as man to man. May I?"

Once again, he told me to go ahead.

I waited until Mr. Feeley and Dick Butler were out of the room, and I took after him again. It was awful. I never gave him a chance to open his mouth. I lost complete control of myself and I yelled, "Lock both the doors! If you think you're a better man than I am, the best man walks out." Now the Commissioner was not a boy, he was a big man—well over six feet tall—and he probably could have taken me apart. But every time he tried to open his mouth I was all over him again. "I challenged you once before to a debate," I hollered. "I challenge you now to a physical debate. Just you and me here in this room. You're a no-good—" and I was off again.

It got so bad that Dick Butler, who could hear me all the way outside in the hall, came running in to pull me away and coax me out of there.

And those were the last words I ever exchanged with my good friend and benefactor Happy Chandler.

I heard from him once again, though. The next season was hardly underway when a fan named Fred Boysen, who had been giving me the worst going-over I ever received in my life, made a grab for my cap as I was leaving the field and then backed off fast. As soon as I recognized who it was I thought, frankly, that he had taken a swing at me, so I went after him. I hadn't taken more than two steps toward him before I was cut off by Freddie Fitzsimmons.

So naturally the guy sued me for assault. (He later admitted in open court that I hadn't come near him. His friends, he said, had told him that if he sued Durocher he'd be sure to get a settlement from the club.) As soon as Chandler read I was being sued, he suspended me. No hearing, no investigation, not even a phone call. And everybody in the park had seen I hadn't got within twenty feet of the guy.

This was where the Commissioner overreached himself.

This was where public opinion turned. Because there's one thing I firmly believe about the American press and the American public. You can knock a man out, and if they think he deserves it they're all for you. But if you then stand over him and kick him and spit on him, they're going to say, "Hey, wait a minute. What do you want from this man? You've knocked him down, that's enough. Let the man up; let him breathe."

The Commissioner, back-pedaling furiously, then made a complete ass of himself by trying to offer the excuse that since Boysen was a Puerto Rican it had been necessary for him to act quickly in order to head off a race riot.

I don't say his treatment of me was a major factor in losing Chandler his job. I do believe that it was a contributing factor. Because when his contract came up for renewal, three or four good friends of mine among the National League owners went out of their way to let me know they were going to get rid of him. Just to keep this straight, Horace Stoneham was not one of them. Not that I didn't raise hell with him. "How can you have Durocher as your manager and vote for that dirty hypocrite?" I'd say, pouring him another drink.

"That has nothing to do with it," he'd say. "I'm a Chandler man."

The end came for Albert B. (Happy) Chandler, most fittingly, in the Pennsylvania Hotel in St. Petersburg, the same suite, I like to think, where he had asked Rickey how much it would hurt him to have "your fellow" out of baseball. From what they told me afterwards about how he took it, I'd have loved to have been there when the special committee came in to tell him they were going to buy up his contract and kiss him off. I'd have liked to have been there not to see him beg—that's always a disgusting sight—but only so that I could have said, "Get up and walk out of here like a man. So you've been fired. So what?" Goddam, I'd have been willing to go back to California and chop down the whole forest to have been able to say that.

HELLO HORACE,
GOODBYE EBBETS FIELD

WHILE I WAS HOLDING those stimulating telephone conversations with Chandler during my year of penance I was not really in touch with the Dodgers. I was getting a telegram every day from the front office about the performance of the club—that was true enough. What I wasn't getting, despite the promise that I would be paid in full, were my pay checks. After about two months of this newsy poverty, I phoned George V. McLaughlin. "I'll tell you what to do," he said. "Send me a wire right now saying 'Please send $10,000 advance on my salary.' You phrase it exactly that way and I will see to it personally that the check goes right out."

I sent the wire. I got the check. I never got another.

Meanwhile, back at the other end of those telegrams, the Dodgers were showing how much they missed me by winning the pennant under Burt Shotton. If I asked you to define "mixed feelings" for me, you would probably give me that old joke about watching your mother-in-law go over a cliff in your new car. Never having had a mother-in-law I didn't like, I'll tell you what mine is. It's sitting in California all summer and watching *my* team—the team I had worked like a dog to put together—win without me.

Mr. Rickey did invite Laraine and me to New York to watch the Dodgers play the World Series against—yup—

269

MacPhail's Yankees. We sat in my old box, which put us about two boxes away from the Commissioner. Absolutely no pleasantries were exchanged.

In the course of a business meeting with the Dodger high brass after the first game, I mentioned to Mr. McLaughlin that except for that $10,000 "advance" he had got for me I hadn't been paid. Before McLaughlin could say anything, John L. Smith leaned back and roared: "What do you *mean* you've received no money? I gave orders the day you were suspended that you were to be paid in full *right now*."

The next morning I was called to the Dodger office by Mr. Rickey. He was waiting for me on the other side of the desk, with the check in his hand. "I had a tough time putting this through, Leo," he said, smiling, "but I finally got it for you."

It was as if I had caught my father out with another woman. It was the first time in my life I had ever been truly disappointed in Mr. Rickey. I took the check. I said, "Thank you, Mr. Rickey." I left. How could I embarrass him by saying anything more?

I thought, in fact, of something Laraine had said to me the first time she met Mr. Rickey. Because they were both such religious people I had been confident they would get along marvelously. Instead of the instant rapport I was expecting, there was instant non-rapport. "This man isn't your friend, Leo," she told me after he had gone. "I know you think the sun rises and sets on him, but he isn't what you think he is."

Laraine was a woman who had keen insights into the important people she was connected with, and she always spoke her mind. She'd say, "He never goes to the park on Sunday but he always calls to find out the attendance. How hypocritical can you get?" But he wasn't being hypocritical, I'd explain. When Branch first went into baseball, he promised his folks he wouldn't catch on Sunday, and he was simply holding to the spirit of that promise. He did have an interest in the ball game and in the gate receipts, though, and it would have been hypocritical of him, in my view, to have pretended otherwise.

"Well," she'd say, "he speaks with a forked tongue. I know the type. We have them in the Mormon church too." I'd say, "The only trouble with Branch is that if he was going from Minneapolis to St. Paul he'd take the night train to Kansas City. That's the way he is, hon. He's a real great man. He's the most brilliant man in the game of baseball."

It was like Freddie Fitzsimmons and Johnny Mize all over again. She didn't like him. Period. She didn't trust him. Period. He was no friend of mine. Period.

"If he's such a good friend," she was saying after the World Series, "why is he procrastinating about signing you to come back next year?" To that one I had no answer. I had assumed that the suspension would be automatically lifted at the end of the season. From what I read in the paper, there was pressure not to rehire me coming from both the Commissioner's office and the CYO in Brooklyn. The weeks wore on, and I heard not a word from anyone. They hung me up on a hook and left me to bleed for a while. Me call? I don't make that kind of call. Mr. Rickey was the president and general manager, and I was his manager-in-waiting. He still had his prerogatives and I still had mine. I never doubted that Mr. Rickey was on my side. When he wanted me he would send for me.

In late November, he sent for me to come to his farm on Chesapeake Bay. And it was like the visit to his Missouri estate all over again. We spend the first day traipsing over his 300-acre farm so that he could introduce me to his cows. It was awful. I had not brought along a wardrobe for that kind of cold, blustery weather, and I had to wear his old clothes, which were five sizes too large for me. I wrapped the pants around me and tied them with a string. I wore his old shoes, his old sweatshirts. Bundled up as I was in his fur-lined jacket, I looked like a five-year-old kid whose mother had taken him out for an airing.

Instead of revealing my fate to me, he lectured me on the joys of becoming a gentleman farmer. The neighboring spread could be bought, it seemed. Maybe I wanted to go over and meet the owner? "Mr. Rickey," I said, "the first time you can get me a piece of property and move it on top of the Waldorf-Astoria, I'm your boy." I said, "I'm a city man. I'm not a farmer, Mr. Rickey." In other words, it was a great place to visit but I'd hate to live there.

When at last he got down to cases, I discovered that nothing had been settled. He had been trying for months to get the Commissioner to commit himself one way or the other, and he had not been able to get so much as an indication. The ideal situation would have been for Chandler to say, "If you want to make Durocher manager, that's your business. We have nothing against this boy." With Chandler being so evasive, he was ready to settle for a simple clearance to hire anybody he wanted. No names mentioned. Or, if it came to that, for Chandler to look him in the eye and say, "If I were you, I wouldn't do that."

"What we don't want," he said, "is for me to name you manager and then have the Commissioner tell me behind closed doors that I made a mistake." Because that would put us right back where we had started.

Rickey had sent for me because he was about to spend two days with Chandler at his home in Versailles, Kentucky, and he did not intend to leave there without an answer. I spent those two days doing all the things I wouldn't be doing at the Waldorf-Astoria. I'm riding horseback. I'm walking around with a gun in my hand, for crissake, shooting at birds. I'm chopping trees. I didn't know whether he wanted them chopped down, but he had a lot of trees and I didn't think he'd miss them. Anything to keep warm.

At last, Mr. Rickey returned with the news that he had got the clearance he had been after. Chandler had finally shouted at him that he could do anything he damn well pleased, which from everything that Rickey had told me was about the best he could hope for. I signed my contract for 1948 at the same pay. With one difference. There was an extra little clause typed across the top which gave both parties—meaning them—the right to terminate the contract at any time. Since I had signed the contract, as always, without reading it, I didn't know it was there until Laraine pointed it out to me. "After all that procrastinating, and he puts that little ticking bomb in there," she said. "The first chance he gets, my boy, you're going to get the old heave-ho."

I didn't see it that way. If it meant anything at all, as far as I was concerned, it meant that Rickey had rehired me over the objections of some of his fellow owners and he had thrown that clause in there to keep them happy.

In view of what did happen, I want to make my feelings about Branch Rickey absolutely clear. The good I got from my association with Branch Rickey—and I'm speaking of far more than baseball—so far outweighed the bad that when you put it in the balance it comes out to nothing except good. Even when he found it necessary to get rid of me, whatever his reasons, he made sure—by maneuvering as only Rickey could maneuver—to drop me into another spot. I only wish he had let me know what he was doing, that's all.

The end with the Dodgers came, I believe, when Mr. Rickey called me to New York to settle a contract dispute with Eddie Stanky. If my memory serves me correctly, he was making $10,000 and holding out for $15,000. Rickey had offered him $12,500. I had interceded on Eddie's behalf the previous year to get him the raise he wanted, and when I found him sitting in the outer office I told him I'd do what I could for him again. And I did. Rickey pointed out to me that while I had been sitting out the season in California, Eddie had not been performing well enough to justify anything like a 50 percent raise. I pointed out right back that he was quoting statistics to me, and that when you were talking about a player like Eddie Stanky statistics meant nothing. It had been Rickey himself, I reminded him, who had said that Stanky couldn't hit, couldn't run, couldn't field and couldn't throw but was still the best player on the club.

"Branch," I said, "It's a difference of twenty-five hundred dollars. A few dollars. He's been a helluva ballplayer for the club. Let's keep him happy."

Before he called Stanky in, Branch made it very clear that he disagreed with me. Each of them presented a strong argument for his own position, and finally Mr. Rickey turned to me. "All right, Leo, I'll leave it up to you. Do you think he's deserving of the fifteen thousand?"

I said, "Yes, I do."

All right, they signed the contract. Mr. Rickey stood up, looked angrily from Stanky to me and said, "I won't forget this!"

It had finally caught up with me. At this stage of my career, above all others, Mr. Rickey undoubtedly felt that I owed him the same loyalty he had shown in giving me my job back. He had brought me all the way from the Coast to pacify Stanky, and as far as he was concerned I had knifed him in the back. I had known that my readiness to side with the player, for my own selfish reasons, was going to boomerang on me one fine day. Before it was over, both of them felt I had knifed them in the back, and I felt that both of them had knifed me. And all over a lousy $2,500.

But it wasn't the $2,500. One of the reasons Rickey may have been so reluctant to part with the extra $2,500 was that he had already decided to move Jackie Robinson from first base to second base, the position he had played at Montreal. Which made Stanky rather expendable. But the real reason was that Mr. Rickey was essentially a shrewd horse trader. That was what he did; that was part of what went into making him the greatest baseball man—no contest —who ever lived. In what he did, Mr. Rickey came to kill you, too. If he could get a player for five cents less than the player wanted, he felt he had accomplished something. He was a hard operator, no doubt about it. And I knew it, I knew it, I knew it.

We trained that spring in Ciudad Trujillo in the Dominican Republic, and from the first day the word was around that Stanky was going to be sold to the Boston Braves. As soon as I had verified it with Harold Parrott, I went to Rickey and used up whatever credit I had left to try to talk him out of it. I must have spent a whole week working on him. I couldn't budge him.

Finally I went running to Stanky. "It's up to you now, buddy. I want you on this ball club but there's not too much I can do about it. You're going to be traded. You're halfway to Boston right now. You better go talk to Mr. Rickey. He hasn't forgotten that contract."

"What do I got to do?" Eddie asked. "I'll tear up the contract and take what he wants to give me. Anything so I don't have to leave this club."

"Well, Eddie," I said, pointedly, "Mr. Rickey is the boss. I can't do any more than I've done. My shirt just has 'Manager' written on it. His says 'President and General Manager.' Don't tell me. Tell him."

That same night, Laraine and I were having dinner together on the terrace of the hotel. Stanky came over. Rickey was at another table with his family and several friends. "The time is now, Eddie," I said. "Tomorrow will be too late. Go on—go over there and see what you can do."

Stanky squared his shoulders and marched over. Before he could say a word, Rickey glared at him and barked, "When I want you, Stanky, I'll *send* for you."

The next day, Harold Parrott told me that the sale was going to be announced at midnight.

I went looking for Eddie and found him in bed with a touch of pneumonia. Ralph Branca, his roommate, was with him, and Ralph heard the entire conversation. I told Eddie I had tried to talk Rickey out of it right to the end. "You're going to be sold to the Boston Braves tonight and there's no way I can stop it, although I will keep trying." I told him that any time I had a club he could always play for me because I admired him for all the things he could do on a ball field. Eddie was terribly upset, though, and he seemed to be even madder at me than at Rickey. I hadn't done enough to keep him, as far as he was concerned. It didn't matter what I had done, I could have done more.

More? What did he think I had been telling him for three days except that my hands were tied. "I'm on thin ice around here too, Eddie. I'm not in too good graces with the boss myself. I might not be here very long, either."

I phoned Branch one last time that night and pleaded with him not to go through with the deal. I argued that Jackie Robinson was still so overweight that he couldn't possibly play second base. Hell, he couldn't move well enough, from what he had shown me, to play first. One word led to another, and we were both breathing heavily when we hung up. The next morning he invited me to his suite for breakfast and informed me that Eddie Stanky was now the property of the Boston Braves. "Do you want to tell him," he asked, "or should I?"

I looked him right in the eye. I'd tell him.

Mr. Rickey bit down on his cigar. "Do you want me to go with you?"

I sure did.

Rickey stationed himself right in front of Eddie's bed. I was sitting in a chair off to the side. Branca wasn't there. Eddie was still very belligerent, and I didn't blame him a bit. He was, in effect, accusing Branch of selling him out of personal pique.

"No deal is ever made on this club," Rickey said, "without the full consent and cooperation of the manager."

Nothing could have been further from the truth in this case, but I was too stunned to work up any real anger against Rickey. Stanky gave me a look, then turned back to Mr.

Rickey and said evenly, "Are you telling me that Durocher wanted me off this ball club?"

"Well, he's sitting right there," Rickey said. "Why don't you ask him?"

Stanky looked me full in the face. "Do you want me off this ball club, Leo?"

I didn't say one word. I didn't say yes, no, goodbye or go to hell. I just glared back at him, hoping he was getting the message, because what I wanted him to read there was: "What are you putting *me* on the spot for? This is the man I work for. You *know* I wanted you. You *know* how I fought to save you. You can't be saved now, Eddie. No matter what I say now, you'll still be the property of the Braves."

At length, Eddie turned back to Mr. Rickey, nodded curtly and said, "Well, that's good enough for me."

As for Rickey, he paused to shoot an angry glance at me as he got up to leave. I jumped up and went right out with him. We weren't two inches outside the door before he stopped dead in his tracks, put both hands on my shoulders, looked me right in the eye and growled, "You . . . embarrassed . . . me . . . in there!

I looked him right back in his two eyes and I said, "And *you* embarrassed me also." I could have told you right there that I was gone. I knew that from that moment on Mr. Rickey and I were going to be at loggerheads, that nothing I did was going to suit him. I knew then that it was only a question of whether I was going to be able to last out the year. I went back to my own suite and told Laraine, "For the first time in my life I kept my mouth shut and I think it cost me my job."

The next day, I read in the papers that Eddie Stanky had said I had stabbed him in the back.

Two years later, when I was managing the Giants, I got Stanky back, although I had to fight Horace Stoneham just as hard to get him as I had fought Rickey in trying to keep him. Stanky's first words on coming into my office were, "Look, Skip, I made a terrible mistake. I'm sorry."

I said, "Forget it, buddy, that's water over the dam. You're back with me and that's what I've always wanted."

All that happened was that the Giants won a pennant with him, just as the Dodgers and the Braves had. Because like Rickey had said, Stanky couldn't hit, run, field or throw. All Mr. Stanky could do for you was *win.*

My return to the Dodgers had turned sour from the beginning. Rickey and I knocked heads all through spring training, and not only about Stanky. With Jackie Robinson moving over to second base, we were going to need a new first-baseman. Branch wanted Pete Reiser there to keep him from running into any more fences, and so we sent Pete to Macon to work out under the guidance of George Sisler. Before he got back, I had a man of my own.

Now follow this: Clyde Sukeforth, an ex-catcher himself, had come over to me during the first week of training with his eyes glowing. "Leo," he said, "you got a fellow out here, don't ever let him get away from you. This Campanella is a great catcher. He's the best catcher in baseball *right now.*"

Great. With my catching set, I put a first-baseman's glove on our other rookie catcher, Gil Hodges, and told him to have some fun. Three days later I looked up and—wow—I was looking at the best first-baseman I'd seen since Dolph Camilli.

So Branch sent Campanella, the best catcher in baseball, back to the minors. I was told that it was because he wanted Campy to break the color line in the American Association. That's what I was told. Just coincidentally, it also put Hodges, my best first-baseman, back behind the plate.

I took a team that had won a pennant without me and sank right down into the second division. Not only didn't I have Campanella or a first-baseman, I set out on a Western trip with only six pitchers, which is like heading into the desert with half a canteen of water.

During the series in Pittsburgh, I had lunch with Frank McKinney, the Pirates' owner. What, Frank asked me, with a sly grin, was I doing in the West with six pitchers?

I was getting my brains knocked out, that's what I was doing. "Well," I said, "we're short. You know how it is. We'll come up with somebody."

"You're going to lose your job," he said, as if it was something everybody knew except me. "*That's* how it is. You're going to be fired. You wait and see, you'll be gone by All-Star time."

Well, I got to brooding a bit about that. I came back to Brooklyn and I raised the devil with Mr. Rickey. Without telling him anything about my conversation with McKinney, I told him I wanted Campanella right away, and I told him I wanted a couple of live pitchers. I got Campanella. I waited for the pitchers.

McKinney's timetable wasn't far off.

On July 4, ten days before the All-Star game, we were playing the Giants in Brooklyn. I had been thrown out of the game and I was in the middle of shaving when Harold Parrott came into the clubhouse and told me Mr. Rickey wanted me to resign. I said, "See that phone right there on the desk, Harold? That goes right up into Mr. Rickey's office. If he wants to fire me, let him pick up that phone and send for me so that he can fire me in person. You and I are old friends, so take this the way I mean it, but you tell him I am not going to resign and nobody is going to fire me by messenger."

The radio was on in the clubhouse, and while we were talking Campanella pulled it out for us with a ninth-inning home run, the turning point, ironically, of the whole season. We went on the road and won five of the next six games, which took the heat off me not at all. While we were in Philadelphia, Harold Parrott came into my room with another message. Mr. Rickey wanted me to come down to his farm. Mr. Rickey was sending for me, and for once I wasn't going. "You tell Mr. Rickey," I snapped, "that I'm not going to go all the way to Maryland to get fired. If he wants to fire me he can come up to Philadelphia."

He didn't come to Philadelphia. He came to St. Louis for the All-Star game and set in motion the most incredible three days of my life. Since the Dodgers were the defending champions, I had inherited the job of managing the National League team. On the morning of the game, Mr. Rickey came to my suite and told me that it had all been a mistake. He didn't want me to resign after all. We were going to forget the first half of the season and start out fresh. "Let me finish," he said, when I tried to interrupt him, "and then you can talk." We were scheduled to play a charity exhibition game in Cleveland the next day, but I was to skip it and fly right up to Toronto so that I could scout our Montreal farm team for the extra pitching I needed. Burt Shotton, who had gone back to his job as superscout, would be doing the same thing with St. Paul. Ray Blades, one of my coaches, would be taking over the team while I was gone.

Mr. Rickey talked on and on, painting a rosy picture of the future. Our little winning streak had brought us to only one game below .500, and with the Boston Braves, sparked by Eddie Stanky, running away with the race, we still had as good a chance as anybody of finishing second. And if the Braves should collapse, who knew?

On and on he talked, and I didn't believe a word of it. "Mr. Rickey," I said, "it's your privilege to fire me any time you want to, including right at this minute. But I am not going to be put in the position of jumping off a sinking ship, now or later, and nothing you can say will ever change that." And then I looked at this man who had always meant so much to me and I told him, "As far as I'm concerned, I'm through at the end of the year, anyway. I wouldn't work for you another day after all that's happened."

After the game, he came into the clubhouse with a slight change of plans. He had just learned that there were going to be 60,000 people at the exhibition game in Cleveland—

this was the year Bill Veeck was winning the pennant—and it wouldn't look good if I wasn't there. I was going to have to put off my flight to Toronto for a day.

All right. In due time I arrived in Toronto, got into a cab and told the driver to take me to the ball park. "What for?" he said. "There's nothing going on there." Montreal was playing Toronto all right. In Montreal.

All right. Planes fly into Montreal too. Waiting for me at the gate, with a cute little smile on his face, was Buzzy Bavasi, the Montreal general manager. I had known Buzzy since he was a little boy. "How are you, buddy?" he said. "Mr. Rickey called to tell me you were coming. He wants you to take the next plane back to New York."

While I was throwing a temper tantrum, and Buzzy was breaking up, who should come walking toward us but Branch Rickey, Jr. "Boy" had been sent to help me on the scouting expedition, and he had been chasing me all over the United States and Canada for two days. Including the same wild-goose chase to Toronto. Now that he had caught up with me, he couldn't have been happier. "Let's go to the ball park," he said.

Now it was his turn to blow up and my turn to laugh. He grabbed up the phone from the table right alongside us, put in a call to his father and screamed, "What is this? What do you mean, Leo's coming back to New York?"

Then his voice got quieter, "Yes . . . yes. . . ." And then very quiet. "Yes . . . yes. . . ."

He turned to me with a sheepish grin on his face and said, "And *I'm* to come with you."

I thought Buzzy was going to dissolve into a pool of water right there.

Mr. Rickey was waiting for us at the airport in a limousine. We stopped at a roadside inn for a quick bite. By the time we arrived at the Montague Street office it was late at night and pitch dark. There was nobody else in the building. There were no lights on in any windows of the neighborhood. Mr.

Rickey told Boy he could go home, and we went up to the office together.

Mr. Rickey settled into the upholstered swivel chair behind his desk. He put the usual cigar in his mouth, without lighting it now, because by this time he had been told to stop smoking. He chewed on the cigar and looked at me with those bright, penetrating eyes. From the time I had been given the message to fly back, I had assumed I was fired. Oh no, I didn't think he had called me back to kill any fatted calf this time.

Strange and wondrous things had been happening while I was flying all over Canada. Mr. Stoneham, he said, had asked him for permission to talk to Barney Shotton about managing the New York Giants. Rickey, of course, had given it. "And then," Mr. Rickey said, measuring me carefully, "I told him he could have his choice. I told him he could have either Shotton or Durocher." I could just hear him: "Durocher or Shotton, take your pick." The two strings, held out as always, and knowing all the time which string was going to be plucked. How many times had I seen him do it? Only this time one of the strings had been me.

"You mean I have a choice?" Stoneham had asked. "If I have a choice, Durocher is the man I want."

"I have Mr. Stoneham's telephone number right here in my desk," Rickey said. "If you're interested, you have only to pick up the phone and call him." He slid his chair toward me and leaned over until we were eyeball to eyeball. Very slowly and very emphatically, he said, "But . . . you . . . don't . . . have . . . to . . . go. You are the manager of this ball club."

Well, you know, I didn't go to school to eat my lunch. I was putting two and two together and it didn't come out three or five. It didn't add up to a vote of confidence, either.

I tell you, my wheels were spinning. I had told him I was never going to desert any ship that was sinking, and he was not only putting down the gangplank he was throwing me a lifesaver. Hell, he was putting me aboard an ocean liner.

How did I know I wasn't going to be fired tomorrow anyway? Right there, I made up my mind.

"Two questions, Mr. Rickey! One: Am I the manager of this ball club *now?*"

"Yes, *sir.*"

"Two: Will I be the manager of this ball club tomorrow, next week, next month and until the close of the 1948 season?"

And with that, he just looked at me and said, "Well . . ." And then he swiveled around and looked out the window into the pitch blackness. He chewed on his cigar. He said nothing.

"I don't know what the hell you expect to see out there!" I said, jumping up. "Where is that number?"

I called Mr. Stoneham and told him I would meet him at my apartment at 46 East 61 Street just as quickly as I could get there. Then I phoned Laraine. She didn't know Stoneham, and all I told her was that a gentleman would be coming to the door and I wanted her to make him a drink and keep him company until I arrived.

Laraine had never poured a drink in her life, and I hadn't had a drink in her presence since we'd been married. She literally did not know how to make a drink, but I had every confidence that Stoneham, who is a man who could find a drink in the Gobi Desert, would rise nobly to the occasion. He did not disappoint me.

Horace had come to the door with Carl Hubbell, introduced himself to Laraine and told her, "We're waiting for Leo to get here. He may be managing our ball club come tomorrow."

The Dodgers were playing in Cincinnati that night, and the play-by-play was coming over the radio. "Then what am I listening to this for?" she said, and clicked the radio off.

It wasn't that easy for me to click Brooklyn off. *Not* that easy for me, buddy. For nine years, I had been charging off the bench whenever that battle cry "Leooooo!" filled the

Brooklyn air. For nine years, I hadn't been able to drive up Bedford Avenue after a game without a knot of guys yelling at me from every corner to find out how we had made out. If we had won, they'd raise a cry of victory, and if we had lost they'd always say, *"Wha' happened?"*

For nine years, I had been Leo, the fair-haired boy of the Gowanus.

It wasn't that easy for the Giant fans to click off the old Giant-Dodger feud either. I received ample notice of that when I flew into Pittsburgh the next morning to hold a press conference before I took over the club. The conference over, I walked downstairs and bumped into Kenny Smith of the *Mirror*, an old friend whom I had been looking for among the Giant writers. There were tears in Kenny's eyes. "I wasn't there because I didn't want to be there," he told me. "You took my man's job. You and I have been friends for years, but that doesn't matter any more. I loved Mel Ott and I tell you right now I'm gonna knock your brains out." I couldn't help but admire him. I said, "That's good enough for me, Kenny. That's what I call a stand-up guy."

Now, if Kenny Smith, a friend, felt that strongly, you can imagine how the Giants fans felt. They hated the sight of me; they hated my guts. Durocher, their most despised enemy, in place of Mel Ott, their greatest idol? They like to booed me out of the park. "Ya bum ya," they yelled. "Go back to Brooklyn where you belong." It took them two years to learn to barely tolerate me.

That didn't surprise me so much. What did shock me was my return to Ebbets Field, Brooklyn, U.S.A. To *my* fans, my people. The first time I poked my head onto Ebbets Field, as the Giants manager, the roof fell in on me. As bad as it had been at the Polo Grounds, this was twice as bad. (Anything the Giants fan could do, the Brooklyn fan apparently felt he could do better.) The whole park stood up and booed me. *You bum you! You no good stinkin' traitor you!*

Who, me? Leo? Leo, the idol of Brooklyn? Oh no, you can't

mean me. Don't you remember how you yelled "Leoooooo!" Don't you remember all the laughs we had when I'd kick dirt on the umpire's pants? Don't you remember the parade down Flatbush Avenue after we had won the pennant? Don't you remember how you cheered? Wha' happened, fellows? Wha' happened?

I knew what had happened, all right. Today, you've got the word GIANTS written across your uniform, Durocher, you no-good, stinky traitor. You lousy, rotten crumb.

Let me tell you something about the Brooklyn fan. To get from the Brooklyn clubhouse to the bench, you had to walk along a long dirt runway which was separated from the main concourse by nothing but a high picket fence. Every day as you left the clubhouse, there would be maybe 300 fans lined up from one end of that fence to the other. The march to the bench was a triumphant processional. They'd reach through the iron fence to shake you by the hand or pat you on the back. They'd yell, "Durocher, you're the greatest manager in the whole world. Go get 'em, Pee Wee. Today's your day, Gil . . ."

You've played the ball game and you've got beat. What difference does it make what the score was? You got beat. There's no other way back, you know. You've got to go back the same way you came. The same 300 fans. They left in the eighth inning, they're waiting for you. Same faces. No sooner did you put your foot down on the dirt runway: "You stinking bum you, you couldn't manage nobody . . ." *Pfui!* They spat on you. They threw dirt at you, rocks, hot dogs covered with mustard. Anything. They sprayed you with Coca-Cola. They called you every filthy name they could think of.

Next day, you walked out of the clubhouse again. Same people waiting: "We'll get 'em today, Leo baby. Nobody can manage like you, pally . . ."

That was the Dodger fan of blessed memory. They came to root, and they never gave up. It was Brooklyn against the world. They were not only complete fanatics, but they *knew* baseball like the fans of no other city. It was exciting to play there. It was a treat. I walked into that crummy, flyblown park, as Brooklyn manager, for nine years, and every time I entered, my pulse quickened and my spirits soared.

You don't have fans like that any more. There will never be such fans again. Something went out of baseball when the Dodgers left Brooklyn, and not all the king's horses or all the king's men can ever put it back.

I have a philosophy, such as it is, about trouble and adversity. Everything that has ever happened to me has, I believe, happened for the best. I would change nothing. Laraine and I came under fire? It brought us closer together. Chandler picked me out to become his private whipping boy? It only helped him to lose his job and rally people around us. The Giants fans refused to accept me? I didn't say, "To hell with them; let 'em eat cake." I stiffened my neck and vowed that, like me or not, I was going to give them a ball club so exciting to watch that they'd come out in spite of me and in spite of themselves.

I had to fight Horace Stoneham to get 'my kind of team'? That only made the ultimate victory sweeter. And in three years, we won the pennant by tying the Dodgers with the greatest stretch run in the history of baseball—36 wins in our final 43 games—and ending the playoff series with the most dramatic single moment in the history of sports— Bobby Thomson's home run.

MY KIND OF TEAM

THERE'S A RITUAL YOU GO THROUGH when you are offered a managerial job.

I say, "Nothing I'd like more, Horace, but you already have a manager. Mel Ott, one of the nicest guys who ever put a shoe on."

He says, "No, Mel has already resigned. He wrote out a letter of resignation ten days ago." And then he says exactly what I have been expecting him to say. If I don't take the job, somebody else will be taking over the club in Pittsburgh the following night, anyway.

"That's different," I say.

But, you know, it's more than just an act. You do feel a little queasy about benefiting from another man's misfortune and you do want the owner to know that you are worthy of the high regard he so obviously has for you.

With Horace Stoneham, that kind of respect for tradition would have been especially important. In forty-five years the New York Giants had employed only three managers; John McGraw, Bill Terry and Mel Ott. Terry and Ott had played for no other team but the Giants, and they had both played under McGraw. That pretty much says all that has to be said about the kind of organization it was. A tight, clannish organization in which loyalty was the virtue prized above all others. If I hadn't known Horace for years around Broadway, I can't imagine that he would have hired me.

Horace Stoneham was an entirely different cup of tea than Larry MacPhail or Branch Rickey. Stoneham (along with Cal Griffith) is the last of a dying breed, the owner who has inherited the ball club, operates it personally and has nothing else going for him. Horace has only two occupations in life. He owns the Giants and he takes a drink every now and then.

Sober, Mr. Stoneham is the nicest man alive. Drunk he can become unmanageable. To say that Horace can drink is like saying that Sinatra can sing. We are dealing here with royalty. Horace can drink for three days and three nights and still remain standing while all around him are nothing but the fallen bodies.

There are two things that make it difficult to work for Stoneham when he's drinking.

(1) Sometimes you can't find him.

(2) Sometimes you can.

Not being able to find him for three days in the middle of trade negotiations can make the whole thing not only difficult but silly, because Horace runs his own team and makes all final decisions himself. But, you know, I wouldn't be surprised if Horace does it deliberately. Unlike MacPhail, he will never make a trade at the snap of a finger. He likes to sit on it, to think it over, to let it brew in his mind and settle out.

There are other times when Horace, far from disappearing, longs for the warmth of human companionship. Put in a slightly different way, that means Houdini couldn't get away from him.

Many times I've sat with him into the morning hours, and every time I'd make a break for it he'd say, "Sitsee."

"What do you mean sitsee, dammit?"

"You work for me, don't you?"

"Yeah."

"Sitsee."

"Sitsee, hell. I got to get up and manage the ball club in a few hours. You can lay in bed and watch it on television. Goodnight, Horace."

"You work for me, sitsee."

Once, when he had Frankie Frisch and me in his suite at the old Edgewater Beach Hotel in Chicago he sat on Frisch's coat all night, like the perfect host should, to hold Frank there. He had locked the door anyway, of course. He always locked the door and put the key in his jacket when he was in one of those moods. You'd just have to hope that he got so tired that he took the jacket off and wandered off to bed. This time he dozed off in the chair, and Frank and I were able to escape by crawling out through the transom.

The first thing Horace did after I had taken over was to ask me to write out a complete report on the club. The first thing I did was to tell him there was no way to know a team until you had lived with it on a day-to-day basis and found out what the players could do. I waited until the year was over and then I handed him a four-word report:

"Back up the truck."

In other words, you need a whole new team, Horace.

Horace couldn't believe I was serious. The Giants had set an all-time record for home runs the year before I got there and had easily led the major leagues again. "We can win the championship with this team next year," he insisted. "And you're the manager who can do it."

"It ain't my kind of team," I told him. We had Johnny Mize, who could hit the ball a mile and couldn't run. We had Walker Cooper, who could hit the ball out of sight and couldn't run. We had Willard Marshall and Sid Gordon, who could hit the ball out of the park and could run a little but not very much.

"Horace, you're throwing your money away when you pay me. A little boy can manage this team. All you do is make out the lineup and hope you get enough home runs. You can't steal, they're too slow. You can't bunt. You can't hit and run. I can't *do* anything. I can only sit and wait for a home run."

He thought he had a good defense. His organization was staffed by fellow Irishmen, the Feeneys, the Brannicks, the Sheehans and the Schumachers. So why wouldn't he love Buddy Kerr, his Irish shortstop who had set a fielding record for consecutive games without an error? "You think he's the greatest shortstop who ever put a shoe on," I'd tell him. "I know shortstops, and I think mediocrity is the word for him." He didn't make errors but he didn't make plays either. Bill Rigney, his Irish second-baseman, was frail, and he had been banged up so much that he could hardly move.

"This is a business you're involved in," I told him, "and you're talking like a fan. It makes my pitching look worse than it is because the defense is bad. It's bad, Horace. All you have to do is look at the figures. We don't make the double play."

We argued about it all winter and into the next season. I gave him the whole Rickey routine, which I knew by heart. Word for word, even to the Rickey inflection. "Horace, the arrow is pointing *down* with our club. As of the moment, *down*. The Dodgers are up here, we're down here, and our arrow is going to keep going down and the Dodger arrow is going to keep going up. But it isn't too late. *Stop* the arrow! Stop it somewhere and try to turn it around. Try to get it going the other way."

Before the end of the season he was convinced, and, boy, then he began to operate. He sold Mize, he traded Walker Cooper away, he really began to shake things up. He was still in love with Buddy Kerr, though, and we happened to be arguing about that during the World Series when Tom "Clancy" Sheehan, his favorite scout-crony-drinking companion, came into the box. "If you want a shortstop, Leo," he said, "Alvin Dark's available."

Alvin Dark? I couldn't believe it. "Horace," I yelped, "that's the man I want."

It's funny how things work out for you. Or maybe it isn't so funny. Alvin Dark had been the rookie of the year, a year earlier, when he had combined with the wise old head, Eddie Stanky, to lead the Braves to the pennant. But if there is one thing that should be clear by now, it is that baseball is a game played by human beings. Billy Southworth, the Boston manager, had been another of Branch Rickey's reclamation projects. Southworth had played for Rickey briefly in the late twenties and had managed for him even more briefly. He had become an alcoholic and drifted down to the minors, but Rickey had stuck with him and Billy had beaten it. Rickey rewarded him by bringing him back to manage the Cardinals, where he had put together the best three-year winning record in the history of baseball—admittedly under wartime conditions, when he had all the best young players. After Rickey left, Billy went over to Boston and proved he could win a pennant without necessarily having the best talent.

Under certain conditions, the final success can be the worst thing that can happen to a man. Billy had a big, handsome son, Billy Southworth, Jr., who was his pride and joy. A pretty good baseball prospect, too, before he joined the Air Force. I have already mentioned the Army bomber that crashed into Flushing Bay shortly after the war ended. Billy Southworth, Jr., was the pilot.

Billy had taken the blow and thrown himself into his work. Now that he had accomplished what he had set out to do and was being widely hailed as the best manager in baseball, it turned empty to him. He began to brood about the death of his son. The awful question: What did it all mean? The old answer: He went back to the bottle.

Now, Dark and Stanky were fierce competitors on the field, but they were also highly religious, rather moralistic young gentlemen and, given certain biblical injunctions about charity and compassion, rather presumptuous. They disapproved of a manager who came into the clubhouse drunk and they didn't keep their feelings to themselves. They had already become close friends, practically inseparable, and they now became the leaders of an anti-Southworth clique which had helped to wreck the pennant-winning team.

We opened negotiations with the Braves immediately with the understanding that we would get together at the winter meetings in New York and try to nail something down. The way Stoneham operates, he does not sit in on the negotiations. He had always left that up to his so-called general manager, Chub Feeney, who was also his nephew and not a bad little baseball man when he was given a chance to do anything. What that meant to me was that I was finally going to get a chance to sit in on the negotiations as a prime mover rather than as a mere observer. I had studied that course under the Master, and I could hardly wait.

The general idea we had already agreed upon was that they would get Buddy Kerr to replace Dark, and since Dark was unquestionably the superior player, something else in the bargain. My game plan, as I walked into Perini's suite with Feeney and Sheehan, was to solve my infield problem by getting a second-baseman to go along with Dark.

The reason I thought they'd be receptive was because they had Stanky, and they had just paid $75,000 for the Minor League Player of the Year, Roy Hartsfield, who was also a second-baseman. They also had Connie Ryan, a second-baseman whom Stoneham had sent them in a trade before I got there, and Sibby Sisti, a swift, solid, all-around infielder who had played brilliantly through their stretch drive in their pennant year after Stanky was injured. I could make myself look awfully smart here by saying I went in to get both Dark and Stanky, and don't think I'm not tempted to. But I didn't. Both of them? I didn't think there was a chance. Sibby Sisti was the man I was after.

Now you've got the picture. I was going to do what I had seen Rickey do so often. Ask for Hartsfield, who I knew I couldn't get. They would try to push Ryan on me, and I would turn him down out of hand. And then of course, *they* would bring up Sisti, and I would let them force him on me. "Oh, no," I would say. "I'm not interested in that man. . . ." Because I had come to realize that whenever Rickey said he wasn't interested, that was the man he was after.

OK. We began by settling upon Marshall and Kerr for Dark. And I said, "I've given up two men. If you were sitting where I am, Mr. Perini, would you consider that a fair deal?"

He agreed that he wouldn't.

Just as I expected, he vetoed Hartsfield and offered me Connie Ryan. "Ryan?" I had my answer all ready. "Stoneham got rid of *him*. He'd never take him back."

Everything clicking along exactly as I had planned. Now they would bring up Sisti. "Let's look the list over and see what we can do," I said, to encourage them. "Let's not blow the thing on this."

They looked over the list. Perini, his general manager, John Quinn, and Southworth. And instead of offering me Sisti, Perini said, "Well, Stanky. That's the only other second-baseman we've got."

Holy cats! I could get Stanky!

Southworth and Perini were conspicuously not looking at each other. Was it possible that they had a game plan too? Could it be possible that *they* had come here to force Stanky on *me*? Immediately, I substituted the name of Stanky for Sisti in my prepared response. "Not Stanky! I don't want no Stanky! He hollered that I stabbed him in the back when I sold him over to your club. I don't want no Stanky!" It was as if Branch Rickey was looking over my shoulder. No chance that I was going to take any Stanky.

Back and forth we went until they said, "Well, you're the one that wants a second-baseman. You won't take Ryan. Stanky's the only other one you can have."

Very reluctantly, I agreed to take Eddie Stanky. And then Mr. Perini said, "Now I'm going to ask you the same question you asked me. Dark and Stanky for Marshall and Kerr. If you were sitting in my chair, would you consider that a fair deal or would you insist that somebody else be put in from your side?"

"You were honest with me, Mr. Perini, I'll be honest with you. Yes, I'd insist."

It was agreed that we would go back and prepare a list from which they could take their choice. We came back with something like sixteen names, and we knew exactly who they were going to take. Sid Gordon, a man I hated to lose. But I wasn't going to blow it now by holding back on anything except our untouchables.

We had a deal, and we promised them that Stoneham would come to their suite and close it.

There was still that one problem to be overcome. The boss. As soon as we had got out into the corridor on the way back to my room to draw up the list, Feeney and Sheehan, who had spoken not a word through the entire negotiations, had let me know that Stoneham hated Stanky from all the way back to his days as the Brat with the Dodgers. "Hates him!" Sheehan said. "We're liable to blow Dark and whole deal if you just mention Stanky's name to him."

All right, we were just going to have to find some way of getting around that. "That's my department," Chub Feeney had said. "Leave the boss to me."

Sure enough, Stoneham hit the roof. "Stanky? Stanky!" Eddie Stanky was never going to play on his team. No chance at all. We worked on him—Feeney in particular—until he finally gave in. "All right," he said. "You can have Stanky *but you can't play him!*"

For chrissake, Horace.

"Well, you've got to promise me you won't start the season with him."

I promised I wouldn't start the season with him.

"Not just the opening game. The whole series. *The first two weeks.*"

Stoneham goes upstairs and he's up there for a long time. We were waiting down in the lobby when the word got to us, and I can't for the life of me remember how, that Perini had asked for another player and Horace had bounced out of the suite, steaming. I jumped into an elevator so fast that I was able to catch him in the corridor before he got back to his own suite. Mad? His face was a flaming red. They had asked for a pitcher named Red Webb. A mediocre pitcher, to begin with. On top of that, he had a bad arm. "Horace," I pleaded. "Don't kill this deal for Red Webb."

"Aaaaaah, they ask for a loaf of bread and now they want three pounds of meat to go with it." They had broken their word, and he wouldn't deal with people like that. The deal was off.

Now, when Mr. Stoneham gets that way it's almost impossible to change his mind. But I wasn't going to let him out of that hall until he did. "Horace, please. I'll jump into my car and drive out to the woods and get you a dozen Red Webbs. He can't *throw*, Horace. Believe me, he'll never pitch a baseball for the Boston ball club. He can't lift his arm. As long as they know this, Horace, give him to them. Don't let a waiver player stand in the way of this deal." I wouldn't let him past me. And do you know what the clincher was? Horace was always after me to drink with him, and I very seldom did. I said, "If you make the deal I'll have a drink with you. You go back in there, Horace, and I'll be waiting for you down at the bar."

When he came down he was still unhappy. "Wait and see," he grumped. "That's a bad deal."

"It's a hell of a deal," I kept telling him. "We've got the maneuverability and defense the Braves had, and they've got to play long ball like we did. Now you can talk about the pennant, Horace." From that time on, we had a tight infield—which improved our pitching 100 percent—and we had two guys who could do things with the bat, could run the bases and who came to kill you.

But do you know that 90 percent of the sportswriters saw it Horace's way? Everybody was writing the next day that the Braves had got so much the best of the deal that they had put themselves right back into pennant contention. What happened was that it won us a couple of pennants and wrecked them so completely that they had to move the team out of Boston three years later.

And, oh yes, Eddie Stanky was in the lineup on opening day. It took only three weeks of spring training for Stoneham to fall in love with him. "Send that fellow in to see me," he said. "Got to talk to that fellow. That little fellow's some ballplayer."

In all fairness to Horace Stoneham, he was a far more complicated man than comes out from this story. Going back to the Commodore bar at the time of the Stanky deal, there is a story that shows a side of Stoneham that was every bit as typical of him. After he got through grousing about the deal, he became very concerned about Sid Gordon, whom we had signed only a couple of weeks earlier. I say "we" because Horace had called me in to settle a salary dispute. Sid was asking for a raise from $15,000 to $30,000, Stoneham was offering him $27,500, and I told Sid I thought he was being offered all he was entitled to. "That's good enough for me," Sid had said, and reached for the pen.

"You know something, Leo," Stoneham said. "There's something that's been on my mind for a couple of weeks. Sid is always going to feel that we cheated him out of twenty-five hundred dollars."

There was nothing he could do about it; we didn't own his contract any more. So he called Mrs. Gordon, gave her a check for $2,500 and told her to go out and buy herself a mink coat.

You can say a lot of things about the man, and everybody did, and it becomes very easy to forget how warm and generous and loyal a man he could be. And also what a good baseball man he was. But that was mostly his own fault. Horace shunned publicity. He gave no interviews. No formal interviews, anyway. He traveled in his own narrow circles. He was not only uncomfortable with strangers, he was suspicious of them. I don't think any out-of-town writers or magazine guys ever got near him. The result was that I got all the credit for winning the pennant. Through the stretch run, the sportswriters began to call the Giants "Durocher's kind of team," and Horace, who deserved most of the credit for putting the team together, resented it. How much he resented it I discovered the night we won the pennant on Thomson's home run.

By the time I got back to the apartment after the riotous celebration in the clubhouse, there were stacks and stacks of telegrams and telephone messages from friends, and friends of friends. People were coming in from all over the country, they needed tickets—and the World Series was starting the next day. The list was so long—more than 500 tickets—that I had to hire a secretary the next morning and have her sit in my apartment to give them out as the people came filing in.

You think it was easy to get those tickets? As soon as I got everything straightened away, I went down to the Giants' office on Forty-second Street. It had to be getting on toward midnight by then, and I found Horace sitting there like Mahatma Gandhi with tickets piled high on his desk. Absolutely refused to give me any. Nobody was going to get any. They were his tickets. To hell with everybody. "Horace," I said, "sooner or later, you got to let loose of those tickets or there's going to be a lot of empty seats."

"Ain't gonna give ya ticket. No ticket."

"We just won the pennant, Horace. I'm the manager of your ball club. We won it, Horace! I got to have tickets."

Kicked me out of the office. "Geddadahere."

Chub Feeney and Eddie Brannick, the traveling secretary,

could go in and out and get a few here and there. A few of the players came in and were able to talk him out of a strip or two. Me? He wouldn't even let me back into the office to talk to him.

I was the most famous manager in the United States at that moment, my name was on everybody's lips. And do you know what I was doing to prepare for the World Series? I was hanging outside Stoneham's office at about two o'clock in the morning singing the old Joe E. Lewis song, "The baker got in, the iceman got in, the shoemaker got in, but . . . the . . . groom . . . couldn't . . . get . . . in." (If you don't know the song, you get the drift.)

I wasn't asking for free tickets, understand. I was trying to buy them. Every time the door opened, I'd wave my check and yell, "I got to have tickets, Horace. I got to have them."

It was three o'clock in the morning before Horace relented and let me have my tickets.

HOW TO BECOME A
MIRACLE MANAGER

IN 1951, WE SWAPPED training camps with the Yankees. They trained at our camp in Phoenix, and we trained at theirs in St. Petersburg. We had the best spring I had ever had, and I felt that I was going to New York with the best team I'd ever had. Before we broke camp, Laraine and Freddie Fitzsimmons' wife, Helen, dragged us down to a numerologist in the lobby of the hotel. Laraine took that kind of thing very seriously, and I'm so superstitious that I'll try anything. Not that I believe in anything like that, oh no . . . just for the fun of hearing what they say. Oh yes. . . .

An indistinguishable, middle-aged woman. She told Fred to change the number of his uniform from 6 to 5. And also that he should wear something purple. And then she got to me. I was going to get off to the worst start I had ever had, she told me, and she was right. We didn't lose our first eleven games, as I keep reading; we won our opener and then lost eleven straight. The first half of the season was going to be so bad, she said, that when I came up to my birthday we would be half a step from falling into last place. She was right. On July 27, we were half a game out of the cellar. After my birthday, she said, things would change and I would go on to have the greatest season of my life and end up winning everything.

Freddie and I went up, laughing at the girls. How could we have that miserable a start with this good a team? Well, the eleven-game streak came to an end when Freddie changed his number and started to wear purple shorts. From there, it was like we were following a script. Superstitious as I am, I did everything to find that woman. We wrote to the hotel and they couldn't even tell us her name. Just an indistinguishable, middle-aged woman. It was hard to even describe her.

People are always telling me that the biggest thrill in my life must have been watching Bobby Thomson's home run go into the bleachers. They are wrong on only two counts: (1) I didn't see it. (2) I wasn't thrilled, because I went into complete shock. The mind, I learned that day, can be a very strange and frightening thing.

We went into the last half of the ninth inning trailing the Dodgers, 4–1. As I started out of the dugout to go out to the coaching lines I could see Laraine standing up in her box at the end of the dugout, with tears in her eyes. She shook her fist at me, and I knew she was telling me, "Don't be down on yourself. You've done a great job and I want you to walk out of here with your head high."

So I stepped back down and waited for the players to come in. "Fellows," I said, "you've done just a hell of a job all year long. I'm proud of every one of you. We've got three whacks at them, boys! It's not over yet. Let's go out there and give them all we got, and let's leave this ball field, win or lose, with our heads in the air."

The players responded, all as one, in a chorus of yells! "Yeah, they still got to get us out. They haven't got us out yet." And the last thing I heard as I was going up the stairs was Eddie Stanky yelling, "Let's win it for Leo."

I felt good when I went out to the coaching line, but that doesn't mean I didn't think we had lost it. I'm an optimist, but I'm not a nut.

But the first two men singled, and now I become goose-pimply all over, and, boy, my wheels are spinning now. Monte Irvin, my best hitter, is coming to bat. Man, I got to get me another knock here. But I'm way ahead of it. If Irvin hits it out, the score is tied. But if Irvin singles, I have a run in and the tying runs on base, with Whitey Lockman coming to bat. Am I going to play it conservatively and let Lockman bunt, or am I going to cross them up and go for the whole ball of wax? Irvin immediately takes that decision out of my hands by fouling out. I really need another little knock now. I got to get that tying run on. Lockman lines a high outside pitch into the left-field corner for a double, scoring Dark and sending Don Mueller to third.

But something else has happened here. Don Mueller is laid out at third base and his ankle is twisted, the oddest injury I have ever seen at a time like this. It turned out to be only a bad sprain, but from the look of him while Doc Bowman, our trainer, was examining it I was sure it was broken. Now, the last thing in the world you want when you have a pitcher on the ropes is to give him a chance to compose himself, and so I'm also screaming insults at the Brooklyn pitcher, Don Newcombe. Not that I needed any encouragement. The truth is that I had been trying to get into a fight with Newcombe from the time we tied the score in the fourth inning. After every inning, I had waited for him to pass me on his way back to the dugout so that I could let him know what a choke-artist he was. Inning after inning, Don had just walked on by and given me the kind of winking look that says, "Keep trying, Leo, but it ain't going to work." And inning after inning, he had just grown stronger and stronger. It had been the Dodgers who had broken through in the eighth with three runs against Sal Maglie.

You can imagine how I'd been giving it to Big Newk after each of the hits. Everything I could think of. As he was waiting for the stretcher to take Mueller off the field, he was giving me the kind of look that wasn't filled with cool amusement any more.

One of the favorite trivia questions is: "Who was on base when Bobby Thomson hit his home run?" The trick part of it being that there was a runner for Mueller. I looked down my bench and for some reason or other picked out big Clint Hartung, who was six feet five and very far from the best or fastest runner on the team.

Just as the game was about to resume, Charlie Dressen, the Dodgers' manager, came out to the mound to talk to Newcombe. Another delay. I'm screaming everything at him now, and it all turns out to be wasted effort when Dressen waves to the bullpen and in comes Ralph Branca.

As Big Newk left the mound he started right for me. "Well here I go again . . ." I said, and Hartung, who was standing right alongside me, said, "Let him come over here, I'll take care of him." That's when I knew why I had picked Clint Hartung. He was the only man in the ball park bigger than Don Newcombe.

Newk took a couple of more steps toward me before he got ahold of himself and swerved sharply toward the clubhouse, with all the people waving their handerchiefs at him as he went up the runway.

There was another delay coming up. Branca indicated that he was ready, Thomson started back to the plate, and, as my mind was wrenched back to the ball game, I remembered something. The last time Bobby had faced Branca had been in the first playoff game, and he had hit a home run off him. I called time and ran up to the batter's circle to remind Bobby that the pitch had been a curve or a slider, probably a slider, which meant that he wouldn't be seeing that pitch in this spot.

"What do you think?" Bobby said.

I said, "I think he'll throw you a fast one. High and tight like they always try to pitch you. Be ready for it, Bobby! Go to ripping at it! Get me a base hit here!"

So the first pitch came right down Thomson's alley, right where he liked it, and he took it for a strike.

Bobby looked at me, his eyes lifted in disgust, and I hollered, "Come on! He'll throw you another one."

I'm not thinking of a home run; a home run never occurred to me. This is the last inning, *we've got to get that tying run in,* that's all I'm thinking about. Now, when the ball left Thomson's bat I knew it was going to hit the wall, but it didn't occur to me that it was going over. There were very few home runs hit into the lower deck at the Polo Grounds, because of the overhang from the upper deck. Only a line shot—a rising line drive—ever went in there. This one was far too low to hit the overhang, and it was a *sinking* line drive. I can't remember any ball hit like that ever going in before. (The fans out there told me later that it got over the fence by no more than the width of the baseball.)

Remember, I'm coaching at third. I've got work to do. As soon as I saw the ball was up in the air, I automatically yelled for Hartung to tag up. A split second later, I could see the ball wasn't going to be caught and I'm screaming for Lockman to come on.

Lockman came on, and that's when I turned to pick up the ball again . . . and all of a sudden there was no ball.

And that's the last thing I really remember. I would have bet my life I would have kept my head in any kind of crisis, but I didn't. I blanked out. The last picture I have in my mind is of seeing the fans reaching and jumping in the left-field bleachers, frozen and unmoving, like a still photo. Lockman is halfway down the line, caught in full stride and —as improbable as it sounds—Pee Wee Reese is still in his normal position at shortstop, with his hands on his knees, looking back over his head, his mouth open in surprise. All of it frozen, you understand, like a picture. Like one huge mural.

Now, I knew that couldn't be right. Logic told me that Pee Wee had to have gone out to take a possible relay. Still, that's what I saw then, and that's the picture that is still stamped into my mind.

That same fall, I went to a big luncheon for Pee Wee in Louisville and, to my utter astonishment, Pee Wee told me I was probably right. His own memory was that he hadn't been able to move. Pee Wee had gone into shock too. "When I walked off the field," he said, "and we were in the club-house, I just sat in front of my locker and I said to myself—" and his voice grew soft and dazed as he relived it for me— "I said to myself, 'It's not so. They just called time for a minute. We're going to go back out and play. They . . . can't . . . do . . . this . . . to . . . us. They can't beat us with one swing of the bat like that after we were in front by thirteen and a half." And then Pee Wee told me, "I sat there in front of my locker for I don't know how long, stunned. 'It's not over. I don't believe it. It's not so. We're going out in a few minutes to finish the game. They just called time for a minute. They've called time. . . .'"

When Pee Wee told me that, I could remember one other thing that surprised me. In that one frozen moment, I had felt sorry for Pee Wee and Gil and Campy and all the rest of my old boys. Not that I wouldn't have wanted to kill them if they had beaten us, but, still, I knew what they were going through and I shed a couple of tears with them in memory of the old days we had spent together in Brooklyn.

After that, it had been all bits and pieces for me. All I could remember when I tried to fit the picture together were a series of flash images, surrounded by empty spaces. I could see myself doing a couple of somersaults out of sheer exuberance. I could remember running over to Laraine's box and kissing her. The next thing I could remember I was in the middle of a mob scene out in center field being at-tacked. Some big 250-pounder had clamped a headlock on me and forced me down to one knee, and I was fighting for breath. I was sure that a crazed Brooklyn fan was trying to kill me—not the ecstatic Giant fan that it was—and being joined by other disappointed Brooklyn fans who were whack-ing me in the back and short ribs as they came galloping past. By the time two policemen tore him away from me he had completely cut my windpipe off. I couldn't breathe. And then I was being pushed and carried up the clubhouse stairs, gasping for breath every step of the way. Through the entire victory celebration, which must have lasted three hours, my throat was so raw that I couldn't talk above a whisper, a hell of a spot for me to be in at a time like that.

More than anything else, however, it was the vivid memory I had of kissing Laraine that showed me what a mysterious thing the mind can be. And it took moving pictures to convince me. Driving out to the game, I had said to Laraine, "If we win this thing, honey, I will rush over to the box and give you a great big hug and kiss in front of the whole crowd. Because what a triumph this will be for us. What a comeback."

I would have bet every dollar in the national debt that I had done exactly that. And Laraine kept saying, "You didn't. You never came near the box."

"I did," I said. "I know I did. What's the matter with you? Are you trying to tell me I'm crazy or something?"

Maybe three or four nights later, we caught the pictures of it on television. And I never went near the box. The camera caught Stanky leaping up on my back like a monkey on a stick. (That accounted for the flip-flops. I would have sworn I'd done them on my own.) The camera moved to home plate to pick up the players mobbing Thomson, and when I came into sight again I was standing on the pitcher's mound, having my cap stolen, and trying to get to Thomson, as the whole mob, myself included, moved out toward the clubhouse into center field.

That was "The Miracle of Coogan's Bluff," and after it was over I was being widely acclaimed as all the great managers rolled into one. I'll show you what a genius I was. The team caught fire after I moved Whitey Lockman in to first base, where he had never played before, and Bobby Thomson, who had lost his regular spot in center field to Willie Mays,

in to third base. Brilliant moves, right? Let me ask you
something. If I was such a genius, why didn't I do it earlier?
I was tripping over them all year. The truth is that I almost
blew the pennant by waiting too long before, out of sheer
desperation, I made those brilliant moves.

Sal Maglie won twenty-three games for us. I had taken
Sal out of the bullpen a year earlier and made him a starting
pitcher, right? Well, not exactly. Sal had come back to the
Giants organization after he had jumped to the Mexican
League, and we had been forced to take him back on orders
from the Commissioner. "That dirty jumper's not going to
be around here long," Mr. Stoneham told me. "He isn't going
to be getting my paychecks." Durocher, the peerless manager, was ready, willing and eager to bounce him too. But
I was shoveling for pitchers in spring training, and Frank
Shellenbach, my pitching coach, told me that Maglie might
make a very fine relief pitcher for us. I'll play an elephant if
he can do the job, so why shouldn't I play a jumper?

But I was the genius who saw what a great starter he
would make, wasn't I? Sure I was. The season was more
than half over when I found myself stuck for a pitcher in
St. Louis. So I threw Maglie in, and from that day on he was
the best pitcher in the League.

It does your reputation no great harm to have Willie
Mays on your side either. I've said it a thousand times and
I'll say it again. Players make the manager.

What can I say about Willie Mays after I say he's the
greatest player any of us has ever seen? Well, I can say
plenty. From the first moment I saw Willie, he was my boy.
After all the fathers I'd had watching over me in my own
career I had finally got me a son. A baseball team is a
fairly haphazard collection of twenty-five individual players,
of varying—and if you don't watch out—conflicting personalities, habits and temperaments. Before you can even begin
to appreciate Willie Mays, I have to give you some idea of
what Willie did for the club, not only on the ball field but in

the clubhouse, on the bus, in the plane, in the hotel lobby.

Willie was not only the star of the team, he was everybody's pet. He'd take out his pocketbook in the bus and, in his high, piping voice, he'd say, "Man, I'm empty." Then he'd hand it to the guy behind him and say, "Boys, put a little somp'n in." Well, they'd spit in it and put cigarette butts in it, and by the time it came back around to him there'd be three pennies and an indescrible mess. Willie would look in happily, and with that big sunny smile of his he'd say, "Ev'y little bit helps."

Just to have him on the club, you had 30 percent the best of it before the ball game started. In each generation there are one or two players like that, men who are winning players because their own ability and their own—what?— no, luck isn't the word. The word is *magnetism.* A personal magnetism which infects everybody around them with the feeling that this is the man who will carry them to victory. Babe Ruth had it, and so did Dizzy Dean, Jackie Robinson and Pepper Martin. My definition of Willie Mays walking into a room is the chandeliers shaking. And what made him even more appealing was that he didn't know it.

Spencer Tracy, who I was very close to, always used to come into my clubhouse in New York. The first time he saw Willie Mays, he just stood back against the wall and watched him cavorting around, kidding and being kidded, as one great performer watching another. After about twenty minutes, Spence came back to my office, and in a hushed voice, he said, "Isn't he marvelous?"

I first heard about Willie Mays when Eddie Montague, a Giant scout who had been sent to look over a Negro first-baseman in Birmingham, came back with a report that said, "I don't know about the first-baseman, but they got a kid playing center field practically barefooted that's the best ballplayer I ever looked at. You better send somebody down there with a barrelful of money and grab this kid." The Giants bought him for something like $13,000, and then

Willie said, "I didn't get nothing," and Mr. Stoneham gave him another $5,000 and a Chevrolet.

They sent him to Trenton in the Interstate League, and the next spring a kid we had scouting around that area told me that I hadn't seen anything until I saw a kid named Willie Mays play center field.

Well, I'm pretty broad-minded. Two scouts out of two tell me we've got the greatest player who ever lived on our hands, I'm willing to take a look at him. And I couldn't get the Giants to bring him to camp. Not ready. After all, he had not yet turned twenty. "OK, he's not good enough. OK, he's just a baby. OK, I can't have him. At least let me see him play, will you? Let me see the kid play!"

So they arranged to play a special game for me at our minor-league camp in Sanford between our two top farm clubs, Minneapolis and Ottawa. Mr. Stoneham, Carl Hubbell and I drove down at 9 A.M. and sat in the bleachers along with a scattering of fans who had drifted in to see what was happening that early in the morning. I could tell you every move Mays made that day. He made a couple of great catches in the outfield. He threw a guy out trying to go from first to third on a base hit into left center. A shot. Threw another guy out at the plate late in the game. A shot. Hit a bullet into right center for two his first time. Struck out on a sidearmed curve. Popped up. The last time he came up, Red Hardy, a good veteran pitcher, tried to get him with the sidearmed curve again, and Mays hit it over the clubhouse in left field, about 370 feet away.

"Not ready, huh?" I said, "Not much he's not ready. I want him."

I couldn't have him. We got off to that horrible start, and after every game I screamed a little louder. How many did they want me to lose before they gave me any help?

"Can't have him," Stoneham kept saying. "The boy's going into the service any minute."

"He's going into the service and he's not ready," I yelled.

"And he's only hitting .477 at Minneapolis. Let him come up here and hit a few of those for me before he goes, huh?"

So, finally, I got him. He joined us in Philadelphia for our thirty-fourth game, arriving in the clubhouse after we had dressed and gone out onto the field. And I saw something then that I had never seen before in my life. The Philadelphia ball club was warming up on the sidelines getting ready to take infield practice when Willie stepped into the batting cage for the first time, and every player there stopped dead in his tracks and watched him. He hit balls on top of the roof, into the upper deck, the lower deck, all over the park, and everything he hit was a screamer.

The only trouble was that he didn't hit in the game. In the first two games, he had to face Curt Simmons and Robin Roberts, two of the best pitchers in the league. He went 0 for 12 in Philadelphia, and 24 straight times at bat without a hit in all. After the last of the hitless games, which we lost, 1–0, I went back into my office, kicked off my shoes and contemplated the various ways of committing suicide.

While I was wondering whether it was really so painful to slit your wrists, my two coaches, Fitzsimmons and Herman Franks, came in looking somewhat embarrassed. "You better do something about your boy," Herman said.

"What's the matter?"

"Well, Leo, he's in front of his locker, crying."

I went running out there and, sure enough, there was Mays sitting in front of his locker, just sobbing away. I crouched down alongside him, put my arm around his shoulder and asked, "What's the matter, son?"

Willie has a high tenor voice. When he first came up, he'd get so excited that he'd begin to talk faster and faster, and his voice would go up, up, up, until he was chirping away like a canary. He never called me Mr. Durocher or Leo or Skipper. It was always Mis-a-Leo. He said, "Mis-a-Leo, I can't help you. I can't even get a hit. I know I can't play up here, and you're gonna send me back to Minneapolis. That's where I belong. I don't belong up here. I can't play up here . . ." And his voice went right up the scale and clear out of sight.

I just patted him on the back. "Look, son," I said. "I brought you up here to do one thing. That's to play center field. You're the best center fielder I've ever looked at. As long as I'm here, Willie, you're going to play center field. Tomorrow, next week, next month. As long as Durocher is manager of this ball club you will be on this ball club because you are the best ballplayer I have ever seen. Forget it. Go home and get a good night's sleep. Tomorrow is another day."

The next day, he hit the first ball Warren Spahn threw to him clear over the lights. And from that day on, he just carried us on his back.

With Willie, you just had to keep patting him, keep rubbing him. I went to all my other players, and I told them, "Look, there's something about Willie Mays. I don't know whether you see it, but I see it. He's a young boy, he's a baby. But he's got more talent in five minutes than the rest of us will ever have in our lifetime. It doesn't mean that I don't like you fellows equally well. But I think it does something for Mays if I keep telling him, 'You're the greatest, no one can carry your glove, nobody can put your shoe on.' I think it makes him a better player, and as long as it does, buddy, he puts money in your pocket and mine."

Without exception, my players said, "Just keep rubbing him, Skip. He's our boy, too."

That's all a manager can do. Bring out the best in the talent he has. Each player has to become part of a twenty-five-man squad, but each player also has to be taken on his own terms. I learned that from Miller Huggins. Willie, you just kept rubbing. There were players, like Alvin Dark, you never had to speak to at all. Sal Maglie you had to stay after. You had to needle him, you had to make him mad. In 1954 we had a chance to clinch the pennant by beating Brooklyn on our last game at Ebbets Field, and I wanted very badly to win it. Maglie went out to the mound and, pitching easy, not bending his back, he walked the first two men.

Like I've said, I'm not strapped to the bench, I came barreling out there. "Get a pitcher ready!" I hollered. "Let's go! You're through, Maglie! Out."

Oh no. I wasn't taking *him* out of that kind of a game after two batters.

"Like hell I'm not. I don't *need* you. I got eight other guys out here who want to *win* this game. Out."

"Get back in that dugout, Durocher! You manage! I'll pitch!"

"You will, huh? I'll tell you what you'll do. You'll bear down on this next one. You'll bend your back and shake your ass, or you're through."

Sal was so mad he waited until I got back into the dugout so that he could give me the Italian salute. (One of the photographers got a picture of it. Maglie looking into the dugout with his hand on his crotch. They didn't dare to print it, of course, but they presented me with a copy which I had for a long time and finally turned over to that great Italian art lover, Dean Martin.)

I didn't have the slightest intention of taking him out, of course. He got the next man, and then Snider hit into a double play and we were out of the inning. Sal marched right to the water fountain, filled his mouth, stopped right in front of me and spat it out all over my shoe. "How do you *like* it?" he scowled.

I liked it just fine, but I didn't let *him* know. This was still the first inning, so I cussed him up and down some more.

After the game was over and he's won it easy, I was going from player to player, congratulating them. When I got to Sal, he said, "You dirty ——. You get me so mad I could kill you. I know what you're doing, and that's what makes me so mad. I tell myself I'm not going to let you do it to me again, and then I *still* let you get under my skin."

I learned something else from Huggins. I can say the same thing to two different players and by my tone and my inflection and my attitude have them mean entirely different things.

Watch: I'm talking to Mays because he's pulled a boner. My attitude is one of bafflement but never angry. My tone is wheedling. A question mark hangs over every word I say; I can't understand what happened.

You play like my *kid*. What the hell's the *matter* with you? *Bear* down out there. How the hell can *you* make a mistake like that?

Same words with Maglie. My attitude is that he's dogging it so bad I can barely stand to talk to him. My tone is gruff and disgusted. My voice is bullying; my inflections harsh.

You play like *my* kid. What the *hell's* the matter with *you*? *Bear down out there.* How the hell can you *make* a mistake like that?

In both cases, they'll be so keyed up to get out onto the field that they'll make a new door for you. Sal can't wait to shove your words down your throat and laugh at you while you're choking on them. Willie is eager to confirm your high opinion of him.

Although Willie didn't hit that much for average the first year, he won game after game for us. With his hitting, with his fielding, with his arm and with his base running. Especially at the end.

The last two days of the season we're playing in Boston. After being 13½ behind we've tied it up, and I want to tell you something, I was tight. A lot of times, you'll see a ball club make a big move and come up to a tie, and then somehow relax and tail off. It was Maglie against Spahn, our best against their best. All the blue chips were in the pot.

The first time Willie's up, he gets a base hit off Warren Spahn. Now, I had a sign with Willie that first year that if he wanted to steal he would nod his head just enough so that the bill of his cap would bob. If I then wanted to give him the go-ahead I would show him the palm of my hand. I look over to first and I almost seem to think I see the bill of his hat bob. Now, Warren Spahn had the best move to first base anybody has ever seen. You didn't steal second base on Spahn, you just tried not to get picked off. But sure enough, the bill on Willie's hat jumps again. He not only wants to run against Spahn, he wants to run right now.

I tell you, it was just as if he had cut the tension with a knife. I'm sweating, and this rookie, all he wants to do is run? You want to go, son, here's the palm. Go ahead. Boom! He stole second base clean as a whistle, dusted off his pants and the cap is going up and down again.

He stole third just as easy, and scored on Don Mueller's single. We scored two more runs before the day was over but the game was won right there. He took the pressure right off the whole club. Especially their dandy little manager.

The next year was a complete reversal. When the army finally grabbed him, after 34 games, we were in first place by 2½ games. Ten days later, we were out of first place for good and the arrow was pointing straight down. The following year, without Willie, we dropped to fifth place, 35 full games behind Brooklyn.

Then Willie came out of the army and we won another pennant.

If I live to be a hundred, I will never forget the return of Willie Mays. We were out on the field playing an intra-squad game early in spring training, and the first I knew he was there was when one of the writers yelled, "Hey, Leo, here comes your pennant." He had got out of the army a couple of weeks before we expected, taken a plane right to Phoenix, gone right to the clubhouse and put on his uniform.

I rushed over and gave him such a hug that I almost put

him out of commission. "As long as you're going to win the pennant for me," I yelled, when I let go of him, "you might as well get out there in center field where you belong."

It was like it was written in the stars. First batter hits a tremendous drive. No chance whatsoever to get it. You know very well what happened. Willie got it. First time up he hits a single. Before it's over he wallops a home run. All I did was sit there and smile. "It's only 240 days to World Series time," I said, grinning. "In order to avoid the last-minute rush, let's start printing the tickets now."

Led the league by hitting .345. Hit 41 home runs. Knocked in 110 runs. Won the Most Valuable Player Award. Fielded like only Willie Mays could field.

That great catch off Dick Wertz in the World Series. When the ball was hit, I hollered, "Stay in the park, he'll catch it." He caught it like a ballet dancer over his head. The hardest catch in the world, even for an infielder. When the ball game was over, Frank Gibbons of the Cleveland *Press* said to me, "Leo, that was some great catch."

"Routine," I said.

The sportswriters, gathered around me, couldn't believe they'd heard me right.

"Yeah, routine. I've seen him make so many catches better than that I knew he had it all the way."

Aw, come on, they said. "It's got to be the best catch you ever seen. It was the ball game."

I hadn't said it wasn't a great catch. I hadn't said it wasn't the ball game. All I had said was that it was a routine catch for Willie Mays. "Look," I said, when they kept hammering away at me. "What are you asking me for? I didn't catch it. There's Mays right over there. Why don't you ask him?"

Now, Willie wasn't highly educated. He could hardly read or write when he came up, you know. But I wish I could have thought to have said what he said to them. "Willie," they asked, "how do you compare this catch with other catches you've made?"

"I don't compare them," Willie said. "I catch 'em."

He had that inborn talent to say exactly the right thing with exactly the right timing. The first speech he ever had to make was in Hackensack, New Jersey. I had got him into it, and when I went to pick him up at the house he was staying at on Coogan's Bluff, I was scared to death for him. I drove up in my Cadillac and found him talking to about a hundred people. Sonofabuck, he jumped into the back seat, leaned back and said to me, "OK, chauffeur, drive on." It broke me up. I collapsed.

After we got to Hackensack, he did the same thing to the audience. Some little colored kid got up in the back of the hall to ask him a question but he was so far back that we couldn't hear him. "Have him come up here," I said. "Bring him right up here." Try to visualize this, now. This little colored boy comes right up the center aisle and stands there, looking straight up at Willie with his big, worshipful eyes. "Willie," he says, his voice trembling just a little. "Who's the greatest center fielder in baseball?"

Willie just looked at him, deadpan. "You's looking at him, son," he said.

I grabbed his coattail and said, "Sit down. You got 'em now. You racked 'em up right there. Don't worry about a thing, you don't have to say any more."

Everything about him delighted me. In fact, we had a little act on the road that delighted us both. He'd come up to me at night in the lobby of the hotel. "What is it now?" I'd say, faking impatience. "For crissake, what do you want now?"

"Mis-a-Leo," he'd say, his voice way up there. "I'd like to go to the picture show."

"Why don't you go?"

"Man . . . Man . . ." By the second "Man" his voice was an octave higher. "I'm empty." He'd pull out his pockets. "I'm empty."

"Well, what do you want from me?"

"Well, I know you loaded. You loaded, man."

"Awwww, for crissake." I'd take my money out, and there would always be a twenty on top. The minute he saw it, he'd grab it and he'd be gone.

The next day I'd say to him, "Where's my change?"

"Oh, I had to stop to get something to eat. A little ice cream. Had some of the boys with me. Had to have a little dessert."

"Twenty dollars worth????" I'd scream.

I guarantee you. I don't know how many twenties I gave him, but he put them back ten times over. Some kind of boy.

Halfway through my last game as manager of the New York Giants, I motioned for Willie to come into the little toilet we had at the far end of the dugout. Two men could barely squeeze in, so we were standing nose to nose. "Now, son," I said, "I want to tell you something. You're just great. You're the best ballplayer I've ever looked at."

I said, "Willie, you know I love you, so I'm prejudiced. There are other great ballplayers, there have been some fine ballplayers in our time. But to me you're just the best, the best ever. Having you on my team has made everything worthwhile."

I went on to tell him to take care of himself and listen to his new manager. "You know I'll always be looking out for you." I said. "If there's anything you ever want or ever need, all you have to do is call on me."

Willie put both hands on my shoulders and, with tears in his eyes, he said, "Yeah, Mis-a-Leo. But you won't be here to help me."

"You don't need any help, Willie. You've forgotten more than all those other fellows will ever learn, because with you, Willie, it's God-given."

And Willie leaned over and gave me a big kiss on the cheek. I tell you, I had to get out of there before I started to bawl myself.

In 1954, we not only won the pennant again, we swept the World Series in four straight games. "The Little Miracle of Coogan's Bluff." Once again I was a genius, and just in the nick of time too, because for two years I'd been just another bum. Just in case there are any skeptics in the house I can prove what a genius I was by the saga of Dusty Rhodes, the night rider from Matthews, a small town in the deep South.

At the end of the 1953 season, the Giants went to Japan on a goodwill tour. We arrived in Tokyo on a Thursday afternoon and were scheduled to play our first game the next day. Friday morning, I came down to the lobby to catch our bus to the stadium, and there, in almost living color, was Dusty Rhodes. His shirttails were hanging out, his hair was all mussed up, he was just barely able to stand. If the Japanese had any kind of sobriety test, Dusty was a mortal cinch to flunk.

"Are you coming," I said, "or going? Where the hell have you been?"

"Was over to shee my shishter."

Now I'd heard it all. "I know ballplayers generally have a lot of sisters in a lot of cities," I scowled. "But I didn't know you could find one so quick in Japan."

I said, "The bus leaves in a couple of minutes. You be on it."

Goodwill tour, huh? Not *today*, Dusty. I put him right into the starting lineup and sat back to watch him suffer. To really infuriate me, he wobbled up to the plate and hit . . . I don't remember whether it was two or three home runs.

I couldn't wait until the ball game was over so that I could take a quick shower and run down to Mr. Stoneham's suite to demand that he get rid of Rhodes.

Who do you think opened the door for me? Right, Dusty Rhodes.

What was he holding in his hand? Right, a drink. Dusty was in there drinking with the boss.

I started to scream. "Get this guy out of here, Horace." But Dusty has poured me a drink and he's trying to force it on me while Horace is doubled over with laughter.

By the time I pushed Dusty out of there—a matter of no more than twenty minutes—I was so mad you could have heard me back in the States. "Get rid of the bum! He's a drunk!"

In due time, I calmed down enough to realize that wasn't exactly the most damning indictment that could be made to Mr. Stoneham, who had been known to take a drink or two himself. "Horace," I said, "we've got a good ball club here. We might win the whole ball of wax this year. But I can't win it with this man on the club. He's a rotten apple, Horace. I want him out of here."

"Now, Leo, you're all excited . . ."

"I'm not excited, I'm mad! It's Durocher or Rhodes, make up your mind. I don't want him on this club!"

From that moment on, we tried to trade him and we couldn't even get a nibble. Everybody else had heard about Mr. Rhodes too. Any club could have claimed him for a dollar bill. Thank the Lord none did.

In 1951, as I said at the time, the Giants caught lightning in a Coca-Cola bottle. In 1954, Dusty Rhodes trapped the thunder in a bottle of bourbon. Every time we needed a pinch hit to win a ball game, there was Dusty Rhodes to deliver it for us. Confident? The average fan may think a manager has to fight his men off when he's looking for a pinch hitter. Don't kid yourself. You look down the bench and more often than not every eye is averted. Not Dusty Rhodes's. Dusty would always be up on his feet, at the far end of the dugout, hefting a bat. "Ah'm your man," he'd call down. "What are you waiting on, Skip? Ah'm your man!"

He thought he was the greatest hitter in the whole world, and for that one year I never saw a better one. The best pinch hitter, no contest, I ever looked at. In only 164 times at bat, he hit 15 home runs and had 50 RBI. And batted .341. He was also the worst fielder who ever played in a big-league game. Any time you see a fielder get under a ball and pound his glove—even in the Little League—you know he's going to catch it. I have seen Rhodes pound his glove and have the ball fall twenty feet behind him. I have seen even more balls fall into his glove and fall right out again. Didn't bother Dusty one bit. He'd come running in at the end of the inning with a big grin on his face. "Better get me out of theah, Skip. Ah'm going to get kilt. You know I can't ketch the ball."

Before the summer was out, I was leading him around the bars and buying his whisky. Training rules? They were forgotten where Dusty Rhodes was concerned. He never took another player with him, and he never lied to me. If I asked him what time he had got in, and he had got in at four o'clock, he'd tell me four o'clock. And he was always the first one dressed the next day and ready to play.

In addition to everything else, he was the kind of buffoon who kept a club confident and happy. Between Willie Mays and Dusty Rhodes there was nothing but laughter in our clubhouse all through the season. Pressure? They spit at it.

I have already told how Dusty bailed me out when I sent him up to bat for my only catcher. While I was telling the newspapermen that I'd have found somebody to catch if I'd had to, Rhodes, who was always on the ear, came walking by. "You don't think ah'd leave the boss on that spot, do ye?"

The very next day, we were in the same situation again. Brooklyn had me beaten by a run, the bases were loaded and there were two out. The only difference was that it was the thirteenth inning and Billy Loes was the pitcher. I looked down the dugout and there was Rhodes again, pumping a bat. His hat, as always, cocked at a rakish angle. "Ah'm your man."

It was a carbon-copy situation, and he won it with a

carbon-copy of the hit that had won the previous game. A line drive into center field.

Naturally, I felt that Dusty deserved some kind of token reward. The Giants always kept a plentiful supply of liquor in my office for the newspapermen. Also on hand was the world's biggest Dixie Cup, which had been kicking around the office for weeks. I filled it almost to the top with straight bourbon, the only drink Dusty had any use for, dropped in a piece of ice and then added just enough Coke to color it.

Dusty turned away in disgust. "Soft drink," he said, appalled. "Poison ye . . . poison ye . . . ruin a man's stomach."

I signaled my coaches to keep after him, though, and just as he was turning into the shower room, he apparently took a sip. Because suddenly Dusty came leaping back into the clubhouse, holding the Dixie Cup aloft and screaming, "THE GREATEST COKE EVER MA-A-A-A-A-ADE!"

After he had spread-eagled the regular season, he took the World Series, beat it over the head and carried it home to hang in his trophy room. In the opening game, I sent him up for Monte Irvin in the tenth inning, with the score tied, 2–2, and runners on first and second. Bob Lemon's first pitch was a slow curve on the outside corner just where the book said you were supposed to pitch him. Dusty didn't exactly strike a mighty blow. He hit a lazy fly ball down the right-field line, which, at 258 feet, was the shortest fence in baseball. The ball kept drifting back, the Cleveland right fielder leaped, and the ball just barely dropped into the stands. Dusty Rhodes had a home run and 3 rbi to show for his five seconds at the plate, and we had our first victory.

A Chinese home run? What are you talking about? A Chinese home run is a pop fly hit by the *other* team.

After the game I got so sick of hearing the Cleveland writers moan about what a tough game it had been for Lemon to lose on a cheapie like that that I finally hollered, "What are you taking it out on Dusty for? They didn't move the fence in when he came up to hit. Why didn't one of your guys hit it over?"

Dusty—on the ear as always—came wandering by, winked at me and said, "I measured it off just right, Skip."

The next day, Early Wynn was beating us, 1–0, in the last of the fifth. Two men were on and nobody was out when once again I sent Dusty in to bat for Monte Irvin. This time the ball dropped into center field and the score was tied. Before the inning was over, we were leading, 2–1.

Lucky Rhodes, huh? Sure. Lucky Rhodes went out to left field in place of Irvin, and in the seventh inning he hit one of Wynn's knucklers so hard that the ball was still rising when it splattered against the upper facade, 350 feet away. The Giants won, 3–1, and Dusty had knocked in two of the runs and put the other into scoring position.

That wasn't the end of his day's work. When the Cleveland writers came marching into our dressing room, Dusty was waiting with a cigar in his mouth and a beer in his hand. "I guess that was a cheap one, too?" he said.

In the third game, I used him even earlier. In the third inning, we were ahead of their third 20-game winner, Mike Garcia, 1–0, but the bases were loaded and I couldn't see any compelling reason to sit back and wait when I had a chance to break the game open right now. Dusty swung at the first pitch and slashed a wicked line drive into right field for two more runs.

Adding it up, Dusty was now four for four and had driven in seven runs—including seven of the last nine we had scored. While he was at it, he had broken or tied four World Series records for pinch hits.

And that wasn't the only thrill he gave us. Because, remember, I had to put Dusty out in left field after he pinch-hit for Irvin. I had a standing rule with Willie Mays. "Any time a ball goes up in the air, don't let him get tangled up with it. Go around him, if you have to, but you catch it."

The second game ended with the tying runs on base, and Vic Wertz was at bat. And all Wertz had been doing was powdering everything we threw up to him. He started by hitting two long fouls over the right-field fence, and then he hit one a ton into left center. A monster of a drive, but it's in the park and all is right with the world because Mays is racing over. And then, all of a sudden, I see Rhodes coming into the scene, pounding his glove and driving Mays away. *Oh no!* I dropped down on my knees and covered my head. I wouldn't look. I couldn't bring myself to open my eyes until my coaches were grabbing me and screaming into my ear that he'd caught it.

When I got to the clubhouse door, Dusty was waiting for me with a big smile on his face. "What were you worried about, Skip? I had it all the way."

Just don't think that becoming a genius is all milk and honey.

But, you know, I never learned. The next spring, after we broke camp, we came up to Los Angeles to play an exhibition game against Cleveland. The night before the game, Laraine and I threw a party to end all parties for my players. Everybody who was anybody in Hollywood was there. We tented the place in and had 293 people sitting down for dinner. Humphrey Bogart and Dusty Rhodes had to take only one look at each other to realize that they were kindred spirits. Very quickly, they retired to a convenient corner, each carrying his own bottle. Before both bottles were emptied, Bogie was betting Dusty a noisy $100 that he wouldn't get a base hit, and Rhodes—no man to quibble over details— was betting him an even noisier $100 that base hit, hell, he'd hit a home run.

I was coaching at third base, and somewhere around the seventh inning I could hear Bogie yelling at me from his box behind the dugout. From the look of him it was surprising he was able to talk above a whisper. As for Dusty, the last I'd seen of him he had been snoozing in a corner of the dugout. Nor was he the only one. We'd had to pour the players in the bus to get them to the hotel. "When are you going to let that bum go up and hit?" Bogie was yelling.

Jeez, I'd forgotten all about it. I stopped the game and sent Dusty in for a guy who was already in the batter's box, and goddamned if he doesn't hit the scoreboard for a home run. Bogart fell right into the aisle.

P.S. I learned later that Dusty did have a sister in Japan. She was married to a serviceman who was stationed there.

THE EYE-TALIAN STREET SINGER
AND A COUPLE OF
OTHER HEAVY HITTERS

ALMOST FROM THE MOMENT I got bounced out of Brooklyn, the late, great Manny Sachs—a dear friend—had been offering me a job at NBC, where he was a vice-president. "You'll make twice the money with me," he kept saying, "and you won't have to worry about chasing that little white ball around."

Manny knew I had a lot of friends in show business and he saw me doing public relations and goodwill work among them for NBC, with perhaps some performing and sportscasting thrown in for good measure. But from the time I was a kid I had five ambitions. I wanted to be a big-league baseball player, to play on a World Championship team, to manage, to manage a pennant winner and to manage a World Championship club. Four of those ambitions were in the trophy case, I told Mannie, and I was going to hold out for a clean sweep.

By the time we clinched the pennant in 1954, word had already leaked out that I was ready to sign with NBC. During our victory party after we had swept the World Series, Horace called me over to his table to ask me what it was all about. Since Horace had been known to fire me when he was in one of his moods, I said, just as a joke, "Quitting or getting fired, Horace, what difference does it make?"

Horace reminded me abruptly I had another year to go on my contract. All right, I haven't walked out on a contract yet. If he wanted me, he had me. "But," I said, "let me tell you something before you get too many drinks in you. This club isn't as good as you think it is. Everything went our way this year, Horace. Next, year, we're going to have to fill four big holes."

Well, that wasn't exactly what Horace wanted to hear in the middle of a victory celebration.

The celebrations continued apace. When I went on to California, the boys at the Hillcrest Country Club decided they would honor me with a stag dinner. The place was jammed to absolute capacity. George Jessel was the MC. The dais was the most glittering I have ever seen: Danny Kaye, Frank Sinatra, Bob Hope, Danny Thomas, George Burns, Milton Berle, Dean Martin . . . you name him, he was there. Ten million dollars worth of talent.

Danny Kaye was scheduled to be the last speaker before me, and I noticed he had been gathering a lot of empty bottles and dishes on the table in front of him.

Danny stood up—his shirt pulled out, his pants unzipped, his hair all disheveled—and went sprawling across the table, sending all that crockery flying. He drew himself up, wavered back and forth, screwed up his face and said, "Where can a guy take a piss?"

From there, Danny did a take-off on Stoneham and me having a rather spirited argument, with Danny taking both roles himself. I was the one who was being roasted, not Stoneham, and the theme of Danny's dialogue was that Stoneham, drunk as he was, was the real brains behind the team and I was nothing but a loudmouthed errand boy. It was nothing but good, clean fun, and by the standards of a show-business stag—as anyone who has ever been to a Friars dinner can attest—fairly mild stuff. By which I mean he sometimes managed to get through a full sentence without using a four-letter word.

Danny's imitation of Stoneham was so funny that *Variety* gave it a review, and Stoneham got mad all over again. "You and your Hollywood friends," he growled at me.

My Hollywood friends? Danny Kaye had been a close friend of Horace's for years. He followed the Giants all over the country. "Horace," I said, "it was a stag affair. If you'd have been there you'd have loved it. You'd have died laughing, what else can I tell you?"

Well, that wasn't the best thing I could have said. Horace scowled at me as if to say, *Yeah, I heard you almost died laughing.*

A few more victory celebrations and Horace would not only have canceled my contract, he'd have probably had me barred from the Polo Grounds. As it was, it took Horace years to forgive Danny Kaye. I don't think he ever felt quite the same about me again.

A day arrived when I was called up to Mr. Stoneham's office. "Leo," he said, "we're going to make a change next year. Bill Rigney is going to be the manager."

I didn't tell Horace, he told me. In my book, that means I was fired. Because why kid myself? If he had asked me to reconsider I would have probably jumped at the chance to come back.

The Hillcrest stag was a great affair, though, and it ended with one of the nicest things that has ever happened to me. After I made my speech, George Jessel very quietly handed me a set of automobile keys, along with a slip of paper containing ten names. "The boys thought you might enjoy this," he said. "It's outside." Ten of my close friends had chipped together to buy me a white Cadillac. No fuss. Just the list of names so that I could write each of them a note.

I have always been a fan of entertainers. I like being around celebrities. I find the people of show business exciting, and the world of show business glamorous. Most of my close friendships date back to my playing days with the

Yankees and the early years as manager of the Dodgers. When Danny Kaye was in his first supporting role on Broadway, I used to bring gloves and baseballs to the theatre so that Danny, Benny Baker, Nanette Fabray and I could go out in the alley, between acts, and play catch.

Danny and I were so close that he talked me into going to Japan with him for the USO right after the war—just him, me and his pianist. You've got to watch out for these people, though—they're a treacherous and shifty lot. Before I knew what was happening, Danny had me doing a song-and-dance routine with him that had every GI from Brooklyn—and it seemed that *every* GI was from Brooklyn—threatening to run me out of that noble borough as their first act in civilian life. To give you a rough idea, our opening number, written by Danny's wife, Sylvia, began:

> How, how, how, how, how do you do, boys
> How, how, how, do you do-o-o
> Everything is kosher with Kaye and Durocher
> We hope to hear the same from you-ou-ou

Unless you have had the unforgettable privilege of hearing my voice, you cannot possibly appreciate how revolting I was. And even then, I'd have to ask you, "Ah, but have you ever seen me dance?"

In other words, I loved every minute of it.

Spencer Tracy was another great baseball fan. And as dear a friend as I ever had. I'll tell you what kind of a fan he was. He was on his way to make a picture in Europe, in 1954, when he stopped off to spend a couple of days with me. We were just going into the winning streak that clinched the pennant, and I was able to keep him with us for the next two weeks by convincing him that I needed his advice. "How could you leave me now?" I'd say every time he pleaded that they were waiting for him in Europe. "I can't possibly win without your help."

I kept him in New York while we were winning the first two games of the World Series and was aghast when he suggested that I would have to go the rest of the way without him. "There's no possible way that you would not go to Cleveland with me," I said. "You wouldn't dare!"

He came to Cleveland, and after we had won the fourth game, he screamed, "Now can I go?"

OK, Spence. Now you can go.

Another of my closest friends through the years has been Frank Sinatra. I can remember Frank *before* he was with the Dorsey band. I can remember when Frank would run out to the Rustic Cabin in Jersey to sing for his supper.

I can also remember Frank playing the Paramount, after he had made it so big that the police had to put up barricades to hold the customers off. Playing across the street to empty houses was a fat comedian named Jackie Gleason. One night when I was in Frank's dressing room, Gleason called across to ask, "Am I hurting you, Frankie? Am I hurting your business?"

Frank was a Dodger rooter when I was with Brooklyn, a Giant rooter when I bounced to New York, and he continued to shift his allegiance to whatever team I was associated with. But he does such terrible things to me, who needs him? Like the time I went all the way to Miami to catch the opening of the Summit Conference—Frank, Dean Martin, Sammy Davis Jr., Joey Bishop and Peter Lawford—at the Fontainebleau Hotel. Frank graciously called me to the stage to introduce some of the ballplayers in the audience, and while I was trying to oblige him, he and Dean kept graciously pouring water into my jacket pockets.

In Los Angeles, his box was right off the corner of the bench, not more than ten feet from where I liked to stand. His children were still very small in my first years there, and he brought them with him whenever he could. Well, on this particular night, we had been accusing the Milwaukee pitcher, Lew Burdette, of throwing spitters, and the um-pires—who knew Burdette was throwing spitters and also knew that they weren't going to do anything about it—had ordered us to shut up.

From ten feet behind me, a voice which sounded remark-ably like mine hollered, "Why don't you give him a bucket of water?"

The umpire spun around and pointed at me. "That will be enough out of you."

Who me? I didn't say nothing!

A couple of pitches later: "Send for the lifeguards! There's a man drowning out there!"

This time the mask came off. "I'm not going to warn you again, Durocher!"

A few minutes later, we're out on the field, our pitcher winds up to throw and Frank yells, "Stick it in his ear!"

I'm out of the game, and Frank is on the floor, laughing.

He told me afterwards that his children had asked, "Daddy, why did they make Uncle Leo leave?"

There was another time when Frank and Dean were listening to the game in a London bar over one of those transatlantic radios. We had a pretty good lead, but Roger Craig was getting belted around pretty good, when all of a sudden the telephone in the dugout rang. The only direct line is between the dugout and the bullpen. The switch-board is under strict orders to put no other calls through. I don't know whether Frank sung "The Second Time Around" to her or what, but Joe Becker was holding the phone and saying, "Hey, Leo, it's for you."

"How long you going to leave that bum in there?" the voice said. "Going to wait until they get ten runs?" As soon as I recognized who it was I hung up.

Everybody was looking at me. "It was Frank Sinatra," I said. "From London."

There wasn't a man there who believed me.

You can hear almost anything you want to about Frank Sinatra, I suppose, but I can tell you, as one who knows, that I have never seen him go looking for trouble, and I have often seen him go to almost superhuman lengths to avoid it. I don't think people realize what a man of Frank's stature has to go through every time he goes out. Autograph seekers, especially women, are always pawing him. And Frank can't stand being touched. Worst of all, he can almost never go out without having some drunk challenge him to a fight.

This may sound strange, but you get so you hate to go into the men's room of a public place, because any drunk looking for trouble always seems to follow you in. You can walk into a men's room and get into a fight and nothing more will ever be heard about it. But let Sinatra do the very same thing and three lawyers will come jumping out of the urinals.

While we're talking about Frank, let me take another few lines to tell you about this rare friend and gifted man. It's no secret to anyone who knows me that I've fought my way out of more than one Hollywood party defending Sinatra, and I guess that's because Hollywood is the kind of town it is, because Frank is the kind of guy he is and because I'll always go to bat for the best hitter on the team.

Frank is two things in my life. He's an artist. But more than a performer who sings and much more than a personality who punches people. He's without a doubt the greatest single entertainer of the twentieth century. And he is my friend. Looking back over our years together, I'd say Frank has been as good to me as he's been to humanity. Which means he's my best friend, too.

If I were down and out, Frank's the one I'd dial. And he's the guy who'd take my call in the middle of the night just as he's answered countless cries of "Help" from friends and strangers alike over the years. Only with Frank, you don't have to cry for help; he rings your bell.

And now while the gossip columnists who never knew Frank and who will never understand him or give him his due dip their pens in poison, let me tell you something about this guy called Sinatra.

He's a public man who cherishes his privacy and resents those who take it away from him for their own advantage.

There isn't a man alive who can beat him to the check whether it's for lunch or an operation.

He'll give you the shirt off his back and come around next day to see if you need it rinsed out.

He resents injustice of any kind, as you do, but because of his status as a public figure he can do something about it. And does.

During those two years when he retired from performing, Sinatra never retired from his good works, which included putting in his two cents' worth and then some, for anything and everything he strongly believed could right a wrong. Your wrong or his; it makes no difference.

I guess you could say Frank is the average guy who nearly died at birth and continues to spend the rest of his life trying to pay rent for his spot on earth and chipping in for a lot of others. He saw his dream early in life and followed it until he landed in the pot at the end of his rainbow. Sure he did it by singing. And a lot of you sing in the shower, and what's so hard about getting up there and singing for that kind of money? Well, my friend, if it were that easy, there'd be no one left driving the trucks.

I have no idea what Frank is worth, but he's worth every million of it. He earned it the hard way—his way. He supports an army of people with his charities and a couple of states with his taxes. Still, with some people, Sinatra can do no right. If you slug a guy in a saloon because he's bothering you or your friends, you get applauded by the gang in the neighborhood. If Frank does it, the press says it's his Mafia connections who taught him how.

Mafia, my ass.

Frank, like a lot of performers, came up the hard way through the nightclub circuit. And you can count the nightclubs which don't, or didn't, have Mafia connections on the fingers of one hand and probably get your thumb shot off while you're doing it.

But I'd better get off Sinatra and start putting myself back into this book or they'll have to change the title.

Just let me say . . . I'm sure once in a while on a quiet day in Heaven, the good Lord must say, "It's pretty dull up here today. Take a look down there and see what Francis is up to."

BOOK III

The New Breed

HOW I DIDN'T BECOME
MANAGER OF THE
ST. LOUIS CARDINALS, ETCETERA

IN THE 1964 WORLD SERIES, baseball was faced with what could have turned into a monumental mess. Although it could not have been known to more than half a dozen people, Johnny Keane, the manager of the St. Louis National League team, had already agreed to replace Yogi Berra, the manager of the New York American League team, the following season. When the dust had settled, you will be happy to hear, only one person got hurt. A passing stranger named Leo Durocher, who had been happily serving out his fourth year as a coach with the Los Angeles Dodgers.

I got my head stuck into the thing, all unawares, while I was being interviewed by Harry Caray, the Cards' announcer, during the Dodgers' last trip to St. Louis. Not unexpectedly, the conversation turned to the great job being done by Gene Mauch, whose Philadelphia ball club was romping to the pennant. Mauch had come up to the majors with me as a nineteen-year-old kid and, as Harry was quick to point out, was only one of nine of my former players currently managing in the big leagues.

"What about Leo Durocher?" Harry then asked. "You're not a Number Two man; you're a Number One man." Would I be interested, he wanted to know, if somebody offered me a managing job?

I guess I must have been feeling humble, because after I had given him the automatic answer about how happy I was in Los Angeles, I went on to tell him that during the days when I was being offered managerial jobs regularly I had got too greedy and asked for a piece of the club, and now that I was willing to manage on any terms, I wasn't exactly being deluged.

All things considered, a reasonably truthful answer.

While I was at NBC I had received several offers, including the best offer ever made to me or, I would suspect, to anybody else. When Frank Lane was running the club at Cleveland, he offered me a three-year deal that would have netted me $53,000 a year *after taxes*, considerably more than I was able to keep on a $100,000 salary. Sportswriters around the country were expressing some skepticism that I was offered the job at all, let alone at anything like the figures I am about to cite. I could afford to sit and smile because I had the offer in writing from Nate Dolin, the head man of the Indians, on the stationery of the Penn-Sheraton Hotel in Pittsburgh.

To start with, I was to get $35,000 a year plus an expense account, nontaxable, of $10,000. What made the deal so attractive, though, was that they were going to allow me to purchase $360,000 worth of the club's debentures for $270,000 —and arrange the bank loan for me themselves. I quote now from the offer: "At the end of 3 years we would purchase your Notes at the face amount of $360,000." In other words, I would have a capital gain of $90,000. In the meantime, the dividends on those debentures—minus the interest I would have to pay on the bank loan—would have netted me another $3,700 a year.

How could I possibly have let a deal like that slip away? You play the hand that is dealt you. I have other abilities, you have to remember, besides the relatively simple one of making a bad situation worse. Given the best deal ever offered a manager, I had to try to make it better. I had heard that there were $750,000 of those debentures around, and I couldn't see why I shouldn't be allowed to "buy" $600,000 worth, and have a capital gain of $150,000. The Indians seemed to think I was being unreasonable and so I turned them down.

After I left NBC, I just loafed around for a year playing golf. I was an unemployed amateur golfer, and, quite frankly, I was beginning to go nuts.

Early in 1961, Horace Stoneham, who thought he had a pennant-winning ball club in San Francisco, asked me to take a look at the club and try to find out what was wrong and, particularly, whether there was any serious dissension among the white players, the colored players and the Latin players. I watched them through a series in Milwaukee and, after getting permission from Bill Rigney, gave them a kidding-on-the-level pep talk to try to fire them up.

The main thing wrong with the team, if the truth were known, was that Bill Rigney couldn't get along with Willie Mays. I had told Rig that the one thing he must never do was holler at Willie, and so Rigney had stopped play during the club's first workout in spring training to chastise Willie for throwing a ball to the plate too high to be handled by the pickoff man. And had spent the rest of spring training telling the newspapermen that Willie was only one of twenty-five as far as he was concerned, which comes right out of the Old Managers Book of Wise and Pithy Sayings and should have been left there. Apparently he was out to show the other players that Willie Mays wasn't going to be treated as a privileged player any more. All he succeeded in doing was to convince Willie that he didn't like him personally and didn't think very much of him as a player.

I didn't tell that to Chub Feeney when I delivered my report, though. Number one, I didn't want to appear to be doing a hatchet job on Rigney, and number two, I considered it privileged information. Willie had got married not long after I left the Giants, and although I had never met his wife, she called me shortly after the season began to tell me that Willie had come back from spring training terribly depressed. From everything she had heard Willie say about me, she felt that I was the one person who might be able to snap him out of it. I called Willie—just to see how everything was going, you know—and did my darndest to convince him that although Rigney's methods might be different than mine, he appreciated him every bit as much. Actually, I thought that Rigney was being stupid. But I didn't tell Willie that and—you can look it up—I was never asked about Rigney that I didn't say what a fine job I thought he was doing.

I told Chub Feeney the same thing. That Rigney, who had them in second place, had them as high as they had any right to be. The only thing really wrong, I told him, was that Mr. Stoneham, as usual, thought his team was better than it was. When Rigney was fired a short time afterwards and replaced by Tom Sheehan, of all people, I was shocked.

About a month before the season ended I was in New York. Toots Shor, who was probably Horace's closest friend, told me the boss was in town too, and wanted me to call him. I didn't. If he had anything he wanted to say to me, I felt, he knew where he could reach me.

A couple of days later, Mr. Stoneham called me at my hotel to ask whether I was committed to manage any other team, either verbally or in writing. I answered, quite honestly, that I didn't have so much as a nibble. Putting my hat in my hand, I said, "Horace, if you think I can do you any good, all you have to do is ask me. Don't let salary worry you. All you have to do is tell me you want me and I'll work for nothing."

As we were saying our goodbyes, I put it to him even plainer. "I'm not very happy playing golf every day, Horace. I feel that I'd like to get back into baseball, where I belong. It's been my whole life and I guess it's in my blood. So if

you think I can help you, I'm as close to you as the telephone."

Hat in hand? I did everything but crawl for the job.

Horace assured me he'd get in touch with me. And he did.
At the end of the season, just before the Giants were leaving
for an exhibition tour through Japan, he called to tell me not
to make any commitments while he was away. "I'll get in
touch with you," he said, "the minute we get back."

In Japan, he announced that Alvin Dark had been made
manager. Fine. Alvin was one of my boys. I didn't think
Horace could have made a better choice. I did feel he had
owed me the courtesy of sending me a cablegram or something before the announcement was made. He obviously
hadn't felt it was necessary.

What really griped me was what happened after he returned. The newspapers had been reporting all along that I
was the leading candidate for the job, and when Horace
returned he was asked whether he had considered naming
me. Horace was quoted as saying, "Sure, I was interested
in Durocher, but if he was interested in the job why didn't
he apply for it?"

A month later, Los Angeles was officially granted one of
the new franchises in the American League. Fred Haney,
a close friend of mine through the years, became general
manager. From the first moment the franchise became more
than a possibility, the Los Angeles writers had been touting
me as the perfect choice for manager. (If newspapermen
could hire managers, I'd have been managing twelve different clubs, including eight that never asked me.)

As soon as the Autry group was voted the franchise, Frank
Sinatra came to me and said, "Whatever you do, don't let
salary interfere with this. Because, first of all, I'd like to see
you back in baseball. But, more than that. I keep reading
where they might need a little more financing there. You
got yourself half a million dollars in the bank right now,

buddy, to buy yourself half a million dollars worth of stock."

A few days before the new clubs were to draft their players, Fred Haney called. He wanted to see me.

I said, "I'm a very busy man, Fred. Is five minutes from now too soon for you?"

He made an appointment to meet me at my penthouse apartment the following morning.

What would you have thought? The players were about to be picked. The papers were saying the manager was going to be named momentarily. And my old friend, Fred Haney, couldn't wait to talk to me.

I can remember the scene vividly. It was a Saturday morning, one of the coldest mornings of the year. Fred came in with his topcoat over his arm, carrying a little portfolio. Out of the portfolio he pulled the confidential list of the players who had been made available for the draft.

I sat with him for a couple of hours, giving him my opinion of all the players on the list I was familiar with. When we got to the end I sat back, with my tongue hanging out, confidently waiting to be offered the job.

Haney said, "I just want you to know that we have decided on our manager. We're going to announce that Bill Rigney has been signed."

Again, fine. It was Fred's club; he was entitled to name whomever he wanted. It would have been a little more considerate to have told me why he was coming up. We weren't strangers; I'd have been very happy to have gone over the players with him. At worst, I felt he should have told me he had a manager when he walked through the door. Fred knew why I thought he was there.

On the way out to the elevator, he told me he was flying right down to Palm Springs to set up a training site. As he pressed the button he said, "Look, Leo. If any newspaperman calls you or anything just tell him that, you know, that yes, I did come here to see you but you weren't interested in the job."

Before I could utter a word, the door opened, Fred stepped into the elevator and he was on his way down.

Well, I went back into my penthouse and I just sat there and looked at the four walls. What do you mean I'm not interested in the job, Fred? You sat right over there and watched me drool.

In the afternoon I went out to Hillcrest to play a round of golf, and the moment I put my head into the locker room fifty members jumped me.

"What's the matter, you think you're too good to manage the Angels?"

"Why didn't you take the job when Haney offered it to you?"

"What do you want, the whole world with a fence around it?"

Just before I walked in there, Fred had been on television from Palm Springs saying that I hadn't been interested in the job. Now he wasn't only deciding what I should say, he was taking it upon himself to say it for me.

Between the two of them, Stoneham and Haney had fouled me up good. Since it was now established beyond doubt—it was in the papers and over TV, wasn't it?—that I didn't want to manage in either San Francisco or Los Angeles, the clubs closest to my home, every other baseball operator had to assume that I didn't want to manage anywhere. My chances of getting any offer now were just about nil.

They had fouled me up even worse with my friends. I had been telling the fellows at Hillcrest I was anxious to manage the Angels, and now they were sure I had been conning them. Frank Sinatra had committed himself to put up half a million bucks for me, and it looked as if I were telling him to go jump.

What right did Stoneham and Haney have to put me in that kind of a spot? I hadn't contacted either of them. They had contacted me.

When Mel Durslag of the Los Angeles *Examiner* asked me about it, I popped off good. I gave him the rough details of what had happened with both Stoneham and Haney, and to make sure it didn't get lost among the racing results I told him that I thought it possible I was being blacklisted. If nothing else, my friends would know what had really happened and baseball would know I was available.

I didn't have to wait long. Out of the blue I got a call from Buzzy Bavasi. "This is doing you no good, Leo," he told me. "Just don't say anything more. I want to see you; can I come right up?"

To my amazement, he asked if I would be interested in a coaching job with the Dodgers. He had talked to both Walter O'Malley and Walter Alston, he said, and they would both love to have me aboard.

I was more than interested. I was genuinely touched that Buzzy was that concerned about me. Lord knows, nobody else seemed to be. When he warned me that a coach's salary would hardly be what I had been getting, I told him that I couldn't discuss salary or anything else with him unless I could get Mr. O'Malley's permission to talk. "I'll leave that," I said, "entirely up to Mr. O'Malley."

It never fails to happen. As soon as I had a job the offers came in to manage. Charley Finley called one morning to offer me a three-year contract. The Athletics were playing the Yankees at Kansas City that night, and all Finley wanted me to do was hop right on a plane so that I could sign and be introduced to the press before the game started. Kansas City? What the hell was I going to do in Kansas City? I tried to be a little more diplomatic than that about it, but when Finley refused to believe that I was turning him down I brought the conversation to an end by saying, "If I want a steak that bad, Mr. Finley, I'll send for it."

Before the year was over, Paul Richards left the Baltimore Orioles to become the general manager at Houston. Lee MacPhail, the Baltimore general manager, consulted his father about a replacement. "You know where the best manager in the country is," Larry MacPhail told him. "Go get him."

Although I made it clear to Lee that I wasn't interested, he insisted upon flying out to Los Angeles to talk to me. I met him at the Statler Hotel and repeated that I didn't want to leave my home in Los Angeles. "When I was out of work," I said. "Nobody offered me a job except Mr. O'Malley and Buzzy Bavasi. There's a certain point where gratitude has to enter into it."

In other words, I didn't want to live in Baltimore, either.

Or Cleveland. Paul Richards was going to the front office in Houston to replace Gabe Paul, who had left Houston during the 1961 season to take over the Cleveland Indians. Not long after he took over, Gabe caught me at the bar of the Sheraton Palace in San Francisco, told me he had permission to talk to me and offered me $50,000. That same night we were returning to Los Angeles and when I went up to my apartment I found him sitting outside my door. He left somewhere around midnight to catch a plane back to Cleveland, vowing that he was never going to give up. And he didn't. Right smack in the middle of the controversy about the final playoff game the next year, he started to call me again.

So when I told Harry Caray that nobody was interested in having me manage for them, I really meant that nobody was offering me any jobs to manage a team I'd want to manage.

Later that night, Harry called me at the hotel to tell me that Gussie Busch had heard the show and wanted to talk to me. Harry was going to pick me up at eight in the morning, not in front of the hotel but two blocks down on Lindel Boulevard where nobody would see us.

St. Louis was something else again. I had lived in St. Louis for so long that it was like my second home town. And I had known Gussie, as a friend, all the way back to the days when I was the shortstop for the Cardinals. I don't think I have emphasized strongly enough that I have not lived my entire life in the dugout. Through a couple of close friends, I had become a member of the Bastard Club, a very small and exclusive club with a membership consisting of perhaps twenty-five of the most distinguished businessmen and bankers of the city and . . . well, me.

The Bastard Club had only one function. A dinner was given every week, on a rotating basis, with he whose turn it was to be the Bastard taking over one of the better restaurants or private clubs and picking up the tab for a sumptuous meal. Each of the members, in turn, had to wrack their brains to present you with something you wouldn't already have and see to it that it went on his bill. Not anything extravagant. A really expensive gift would have been considered in bad taste. It was the thought that went into it, the research. Did you smoke cigars? Somebody would be sure to present you with a box of cigars imported from Cuba. What kind of whiskey wouldn't this week's Bastard have? Go out and get him a case. After dinner, we'd shoot crap, play poker. Have ourselves a ball. That was my relationship with Gussie Busch.

When we arrived at Mr. Busch's estate at Grant's Farm, Harry said that he'd wait in the car. A servant opened the door and took me the distance of a couple of city blocks to the living room. Then we went through a couple of more rooms and out to a screened-in porch where Gussie was having his breakfast. It was a very hot Sunday morning, and his kids were riding back and forth outside on their ponies. I had a cup of coffee and a sweet roll with him. The small talk was kept to a minimum. Gussie wanted to know whether I would be interested in managing his ball club next year if the job should become available.

The job, as everybody knew, was going to become available. Busch had fired his general manager, Bing Devine, a couple of weeks earlier and it was common talk that Johnny Keane had been kept on only because it hadn't been considered good policy to let both the manager and general manager go in the middle of the season.

When he had finished breakfast, he took me on another long hike back to his office. It was a little bit of an office, and the floor was almost completely covered with mounted heads of animals waiting to be hung. We must have talked for an hour, and then he stuck out his hand and said, "You're the manager of the ball club. Don't worry about the salary."

The last thing I said before getting up was that it was going to be very hard to keep our agreement out of the newspapers. "How do you think Johnny Keane is going to feel when he hears about this? Because you're not out of it yet, Gus. You're only seven and a half games out, you could win this thing yet. Anything can happen in this game."

Harry Caray was waiting outside in the car, and the day had turned so hot that although he had been doing nothing except sitting there, he was covered with sweat. Harry was simply overjoyed when I told him what had happened. He couldn't have been happier.

Oh yes, he could! Harry, who is one of the great rooters of the airwaves, became downright ecstatic, I'm sure, as the Cardinals went on a winning rampage over the last two weeks of the season and, with the Phillies going into one of the great collapses of baseball history, won the pennant on the last day.

And where did that leave me?

Unemployed, that's where.

The first thing I had done upon returning to Los Angeles was to tell Mr. O'Malley about my conversation with Busch. He already knew about it; Busch had phoned him. The best thing for me to do, we agreed, was to hand in my resignation immediately.

But that was only the beginning, folks. I didn't only lose the job; I lost it twice. Johnny Keane, who knew the job had been offered to me, had made a secret deal of his own with Ralph Houk a couple of weeks later to manage the Yankees, and then the Yankees had also come on late in the season—if you can follow this—to win a pennant which their front office had also given up on.

After the Cardinals had beaten the Yankees in the World Series, Keane let Gussie Busch call a press conference to announce that he was signing him to a new contract and then walked in and handed him his resignation. I'm not so sure that Johnny Keane had tried to stick it to Busch for hiring me behind his back, as the press reported. I mean, what are you going to do if you're managing one team in the World Series, and you have already agreed to manage the team you're playing against? Yon keep quiet about it, that's what you do. If it was me, I'd have ended up out of baseball. If it was Johnny Keane, you ended up as the hero of the multitudes, the little man who had told the big man where to head off. The press, who preferred the human-interest story over the real story, went to superhuman efforts not to dig it up.

However you wanted to read it, the end result was the same. The job had become available, and Gussie Busch had a handshake agreement with me.

A few days later, he called me. Right from the beginning I didn't like the way the conversation was going, mostly because it wasn't going anywhere. All hemming and hawing, and not a word about managing his ball club. I could understand the fix he was in. Poor Gussie had finally won his first pennant after thirteen years, with a World Championship thrown into the bargain, and before you could say "A bottle of Bud" he had become the laughingstock of the country, something I never expected to see equaled until Charley Finley won his first two World Championships in a row and managed to come out of it looking like a horse's ass.

I'm not going to try to kid anybody. I knew Gussie couldn't afford to hire me. The popular view in St. Louis was that Gussie had done something underhanded in hiring me, which also seemed to mean that I had done something underhanded in being hired. "Gussie," I said finally. *"Tell me.* Just give me the facts." *Tell me and let me get mad or be a sport about it. But tell me and let me do something.* "Apparently what you're trying to tell me is that you can't make me manager of your ball club. Is that what you're trying to tell me?"

"Yeah," he said. "In sort of a way."

"Hell, say so. It's perfectly all right. Forget the handshake. Forget you gave me the job. Forget that I'm the manager of the ball club. I understand the fix you're in. If you don't mind me saying something here, I think you've got one of two choices. It's got to be a real popular man in St. Louis, and that means either Stan Musial or Red Schoendienst."

I read afterwards that Busch had given me $50,000 to $100,000 to call the deal off. Uhn-uh. Number one, I wouldn't have taken it. Number two, he didn't offer me a penny. I mean he didn't even give me a chance to be noble about it. I was so sure that he was going to say he wanted to make it up to me, or something like that, that I was all set to say, "Well, I'm a peculiar kind of a fellow that way, Gus. I've always said that any owner has a right not to want me to manage for him, but nobody can pay me not to manage for him. So let's just forget it and part friends, huh? And next time I see you I'll buy you a drink."

Jeez, I was entitled to that much, wasn't I?

He said, "Thanks very much, Leo. I knew you'd understand the predicament I was in." *Click.*

And there I sat with the telephone in my hand. . . .

SOMETHING GOOD IS
GOING TO HAPPEN TOMORROW

LIFE IS FUNNY, BOY. It was a year later, during the World
Series between the Dodgers and the Minnesota Twins, that
I really was hired to become the manager of the Chicago
Cubs, the one job in the history of the major leagues where
you didn't have to worry about replacing anybody. The
Cubs hadn't had a manager for five years. Phil Wrigley, who
has a mind of his own, had been experimenting with a
system of rotating "head coaches" and the attendance had
just hit a modern low (640,000) and the red ink had hit
$1,200,000.

But I've got to say it. When John Holland, the Cubs'
general manager, came to my home from out of the blue, I
was tremendously surprised. But only because I had never
expected that I would be hired by the Chicago Cubs. Except
for that one period after I had been tossed around by Stoneham and Haney, I had never doubted that the time would
come when some owner would turn to his general manager—
as Phil Wrigley had turned to Holland—and tell him he
wanted a manager who knew the game and wasn't afraid to
take charge. And that the general manager would say—as
Holland did say: "There's one man who answers that description. Leo Durocher."

Actually, it was Herman Franks, who had become the

manager of San Francisco, who had recommended me. I was working for ABC Game of the Week, telecasting a ball game every Saturday and holding forth on an hour-and-a-half call-in radio show five days a week in L.A. It was a pleasant enough life, I was making more than I had ever made in baseball, and so naturally I couldn't wait to put the uniform back on.

Holland placed a contract on the table in front of me and told me I could fill in my own terms. What did I want, and for how many years? Two years? Five years? All I had to do was name it.

"The length of the contract doesn't matter to me," I told Holland. "I don't operate that way. If the contract is for five years and I work for one, you can tear it up." As for the money . . . well, that was a very secondary consideration with me too. "It's the people you're working for that's important," I assured him. "And how happy you are working for them." I picked up the contract and handed it back to him. "You take it back and have Mr. Wrigley fill it in."

Let me tell you something: If you are going to be running something for a man where you have a number of men working under your supervision—whether it's a ball club or a shipyard makes no difference—you will always come out better if you wave the question of salary aside and tell him to fill in the terms himself. I'll tell you why. He's afraid to cheat me. I'll make him say, "Well, maybe I should put fifty or sixty thou in there. Gee, maybe he ought to get more than that." He'll be making better arguments for me than I could be making for myself, because he knows better than I do what he wants me to do for him. I guarantee you that I'll get the top dollar he was prepared to pay, and maybe a little extra just to make sure.

Especially with Mr. Wrigley. After I found out what kind of a man Mr. Wrigley was, I was almost ashamed of myself. "You tell me that man said that?" Wrigley asked Holland. "That whatever I say is all right with him?"

So I went to Chicago, and he gave me the best contract I had ever had. But, really, the contract was only to keep the lawyers and the accountants happy. As far as Mr. Wrigley is concerned, the handshake is the deal. When I left after six and a half years, which was a year after I should have, Mr. Wrigley argued with me right to the end. "How can you leave?" he said. "We've got a handshake."

I have never worked for a bad owner. They have all been good to me: Barrow, Weil, MacPhail, Rickey, Stoneham, Wrigley and Hofheinz. Some of them I fought with, sure. That's part of the price you pay for working for strong, colorful men. Also part of the fun. It just so happens that of all the owners, in my opinion, Mr. Wrigley treated me the best. Phil Wrigley is simply the finest man to work for in the world. The most decent man, probably, I have ever met. Although the performance of the club was a terrible disappointment to both of us that first year, there was never a word of criticism. Quite the opposite. "I've had a lot of managers work for me," he would say. "They used to stop by every time they won and I never saw them when they lost. You're the only manager I ever had who keeps coming by when we lose."

He was full of surprises. For one thing, he was the most available of men. He would be sitting in his office with his jacket off and his shirtsleeves rolled up, smoking a cigarette, and anybody could drop in without an appointment. For another thing, he is a great mechanic. If he hadn't inherited the Wrigley Company from his father, there is no question in my mind but that he would have been another Henry Ford or Thomas Edison. Give him the worst motor in the world and he's in heaven. He'll rip it apart and put it back together so that it purrs. Give him the best one you can find, and he'll make it run even better. Well, I'll tell you. When his son bought a new European sports car, the first thing Mr. Wrigley did was to take the motor apart for him and put it back together so that it would be perfect to the nth degree.

Not by the manufacturer's standards, but by Mr. Wrigley's.

From Tuesday to Thursday, he takes care of the giant corporation he built from his father's gum company. On Friday, he drives up to his place in Lake Geneva, Wisconsin, to pursue his real love, which is tinkering. Whenever I'd go up there I'd find him in his coveralls, working in the tremendous garage he built along his lakefront. He's an old navy man, you know, and every tool is hung just so, in its proper niche, along the wall. The whole place is so spotless that you could eat off the floor. TV sets are spotted all around the place so that wherever he happens to be working he has only to glance up to see what is going on.

One of the great misconceptions about him in Chicago is that he is not interested in baseball. That, in fact, he hasn't gone to a game in years. Not true. I don't know what it is with Mr. Wrigley. He's not a shy man in private; he'll tell you right to your face what he thinks of you. But he has such a horror of flaunting his wealth and position in public that he can't seem to bring himself to sit in his private box. His wife, who is one of nature's noblewomen, would be sitting in the box with his own children or his grandchildren. Mr. Wrigley would be out in the bleachers, anonymous and invisible.

During my first year there, he would go to the upper deck of the grandstand, which was always practically empty. By the second year, we were beginning to draw big enough crowds so that the usher would come along and ask for his ticket. If it was me, I'd have had a cigar in my mouth—even though I hate cigars—just so that I could blow out a stream of smoke and say, "It's all right, son. I own the place. Keep up the good work."

Mr. Wrigley would just apologize and walk around to the bleachers.

For the rest of my stay, I could chart him to perfection. I would keep my eyes on the bleachers from the opening pitch, and within a batter or two I'd see him walking up the ramp and disappearing into the crowd. When the ninth inning started, I'd look up again and watch him walk down the runway and out the gate where his chauffeur would be waiting with the limousine to drive him home.

The great disappointment of my career is that I wasn't able to win a pennant for him. We did come close, though. We gave him some thrills. By the second year, we were not only in the black, we were in third place, the first time the Cubs had been in the first division in twenty years. In the third year, the attendance went over a million. In the fourth, the sweet and sour year of 1969, we broke all attendance records. The Cubs play only in the daytime, the park seats only 36,667 and Mr. Wrigley's concern for the fans is so overpowering that 22,432 of those seats are always held out for the day of the game. And still we drew 1,674,993 fans, breaking not only the Cub record that went all the way back to 1929, but the all-time Chicago record that had been set by Bill Veeck's pennant-winning White Sox in 1959. And continued to go over 1,600,000 the next two years. Excitement? The boys were playing such exciting baseball by then that when I came to the park at nine thirty in the morning the long lines would already be forming outside the park.

To give you an idea of our relationship, I never called him anything except Mr. Wrigley, and he never called me anything except Leo or son. That's right, son. Mr. Wrigley is twelve years older than I am, and so if I was sixty in my first year in Chicago, he had to be seventy-two. Still, he could understand that whatever it might say on my birth certificate, in my mind I was twenty-eight.

Nothing shows how loyal he was, and how well he understood me, than the time I celebrated my sixty-third birthday by playing hooky. Although, to be frank about it, I had the terrible feeling when I was summoned to his home two days later that I was about to go into the Guinness Book of Records for pulling off two impossible feats at the same time:

1. Being fired by Mr. Wrigley.
2. Being fired while I was in first place.

Because he should have fired me.

I had got married again in the wonderful year of 1969. My new bride was Lynne Walker Goldblatt, who had been conducting a television interview show in Chicago shortly before I arrived upon the scene. My marriage to Laraine had broken up after thirteen years for the same reason, when everything is said and done, that my marriage to Grace Dozier had broken up. Two careers that had kept us apart over too long a period of time. I am a very domestic person at heart. I am never happier than when I have the warmth of a family around me. My worst enemy (a hotly-contested category) will admit that I fall over dead for kids, and Lynne had a son and two daughters from a previous marriage. My new stepson, Joel Goldblatt, was twelve years old, and I loved him. I had known Joel for four years, but in the five weeks since I had married his mother he had been away to a summer camp in Wisconsin.

With parents' weekend coming up, I had been trying to explain to him over the phone that there were very few days off in baseball, and never on Saturday or Sunday. I could understand his disappointment. I was Leo Durocher, manager of the Chicago Cubs, and he wanted to show me off to his friends.

There was still another complication. My birthday was falling on that Sunday. Lynne's plans were to go up on a charter plane Saturday morning and although she hadn't said anything about it I suspected that she was torn between staying with her son for the whole weekend or coming back on the Sunday afternoon plane to spend at least part of my birthday with me.

On Friday night, as we were going to bed, I said, "You know what they say. You never can tell what Durocher's going to do. You just might see me up there before you leave."

When I got to my office in the morning, I changed into my uniform, sat down at my desk and there, staring me in the face, was the telephone. On the spur of the moment, I picked it up, called home and told Lynne to cancel out the morning flight and make an extra reservation on the afternoon charter.

At the end of three innings, with the Cubs leading 1–0, I put Pete Reiser in charge of the club, changed into my civilian clothes, got into my car and drove to Megs Field, a private airfield on Lake Michigan.

And I felt great about it. Free as a bird. It took a little more than an hour to make the trip in the little Beechcraft, and we were able to listen to the game on the plane's radio. Los Angeles had tied the game up, but the Cubs won it in the eleventh. That put us five games ahead of the New York Mets, and everybody knew that by the end of the year the Mets, who hadn't finished anywhere except last in their entire seven-year history, would be back where they belonged.

Well, Joel was in heaven when he saw me. All the kids were Cubs fans, and if their parents weren't they became Cub fans of the moment. Overnight, we stayed at a hotel in the little town, Eagle River, and when we came down in the morning they had a banner hanging across the street:

WELCOME LEO DUROCHER

That I could have done without. Nobody at the camp was going to blow the whistle on me, I was sure. But still . . . I'm a hunch guy and if there is anything you're not looking for while you're on the lam it's a welcoming committee and a brass band. I decided that if we took the early charter back, I could get to the park for the start of the game and nobody would be the wiser.

And that was the biggest mistake I made all weekend. The weather was terrible. Not raining, but a very dark, dreary day. When we got over Lake Michigan, the little plane began to bounce around like a rubber ball. We couldn't land, there was no visibility. All we could do was fly around at low level, getting sicker all the time, until we were finally able to put down during a brief break in the weather.

It was too late to get to the park by then, and I was too sick to care. My loyal coaches, as I later learned, had told the sportswriters that I had become ill on the bench. A chronic stomach condition, Reiser had explained. Well, maybe I didn't have anything wrong with my stomach when I left, but I sure did when I got back.

Happy birthday, Leo.

Believe me, I felt every one of my twenty-eight years.

When we picked up the papers that night, we discovered that I had been found out. A truant officer named Jim Enright who masqueraded as a sportswriter for Chicago *Today* had been tipped off by some apple polisher in Eagle River. The story was spread all over the papers with appropriate comments on the maturity and sense of responsibility of a manager who would abandon his team in the middle of a hot pennant race. Phil Wrigley, old navy man that he was, was quoted from Wisconsin as observing that it was impossible to run a ship without a rudder. "In view of the all-out effort everybody in the organization is making to win the pennant," Mr. Wrigley had said, "I feel Leo owes an apology to the players."

The Chicago sportswriters, sensing my demise, were sniffing around like the jackals that most of them are. Fortunately, I was able to ignore their questions when I got to the park on Monday because I hadn't been talking to them for weeks. Even more fortunately, we won a very thrilling ten-inning ball game from San Francisco by scoring two runs off Juan Marichal, whom we hadn't beaten in years.

It was the next day, upon Mr. Wrigley's return to Chicago, that I was summoned to his apartment on Lake Shore Drive. I found him waiting for me in his library. He leaned back, looked me in the eye and said, "Why, Leo? Explain it to me."

"Well," I started, "I promised my boy I would come up to see him . . ." And then, realizing how lame that sounded even to my ears, "I have no excuse, Mr. Wrigley. I can't sit here and say that I have a reason. I just did it. It was a terrible thing to do, and I know it was wrong. *Now* I know it was wrong . . . *now* I wish I hadn't done it. But I did."

Quietly, almost conspiratorially, he leaned forward and said, "Leo, I . . . don't . . . mind. I don't mind if you wanted to go see your son. But we got a lot of bad publicity. All you had to do was pick up the telephone and say to me, 'I want to visit my son.' If you wanted to visit your son for a week, it would have been all right with me. Just let me know where you are. Tell me what's going on so that when the newspapermen called I could have said, 'I know where he's at. He called me and I told him to go ahead.' " So what could they write? he asked me. "Nothing."

When a man treats you like that, what can you do? I know what I felt like doing. I felt like crying. *How could I do this to this man?*

"If the job gets to you," Mr. Wrigley was saying. "If you get aggravated and want to take a week off, that's all you ever have to do. Call me."

Why did I do it, Mr. Wrigley? I was thinking. Because every once in a while, Mr. Wrigley, I do stupid things. Haven't you read my life story? I mean, didn't you find out anything about me before you hired me?

I mean, doesn't everybody in the world shake his head from time to time and say to himself, "Did I really do that? How could I be so stupid? What am I, crazy or something?"

But, do you know, by the time I was back in my car and driving to the ball park in the warm summer air, I was feeling just great again. I'd had a great day, I'd made Joel and a lot of kids happy, and now I'd have all those jackals who thought they had me on the run grinding their teeth. Especially the Unholy Six led by big Jack Brickhouse (you can speak plainer than that, Leo) who had got together to try to run me out of Chicago. Up yours too, Brickhouse. Screw you, Enright.

The real reason I had gone, if I wanted to be honest with myself, was because I knew I'd feel better about myself if I went than if I didn't. At sixty-three, my philosophy was no different than it had been at twenty. If you feel like doing it, do it, and it will all come out right in the end.

Except that it didn't come out right, in the end, on the ball field. We had come out of the gate kicking and scratching, winning eleven of our first twelve games, and on August 7, we had a lead of nine and a half games. And then the Mets went crazy, getting the kind of pitching, day by day, that had never been heard of before or since, while we stopped hitting completely. (How many people remember, I wonder, that Jim McAndrew, the Mets' number 5 pitcher, had consecutive wins of 1–0, 2–1, 6–0, 3–0?) To my way of thinking, it isn't fair to the Mets to say we lost it. The Mets won it.

One month later, on September 8, when we came into New York to play our final two games against the Mets, we were still holding a two-and-a-half game lead. All we had to do was win one of them and we would leave in pretty good shape. We lost the first one on a very bad decision at home plate. We got murdered in the second one.

I sat there on the bench during that second loss, and the New York fans really gave it to me. "It couldn't be happening to a nicer guy," was the kindest thing they yelled at me. Good luck to them. I had been ridiculing their Mets all season, and they were entitled.

We were still in first place by half a game when we left for Philadelphia. Twenty-four hours later we weren't. I hadn't touched a cigarette for more than seven months. When I got back to the clubhouse I yelled to Yosh Kuwano, our clubhouse man, to get me a pack. Yosh, who came with the Chicago franchise and will probably die with it, is a power unto himself. He pleaded with me not to start smoking again. *Get me some cigarettes, Yosh!* When you hear how we lost the next night's game, you'll wonder why I didn't scream for poison.

The Phils had men on first and second, two men were out and Richie Allen was the batter. The count goes to 3-and-2, and that means the runners are going to be going. Got the picture? Okay. Dick Selma, our pitcher, goes into his stretch, takes his foot off the rubber, looks to home plate and lobs the ball to third base. A perfect throw to nobody! *What in the world* . . . ? One runner scores, the other goes to third, and that's the ball game.

I made a game effort to argue that since Selma had committed a balk by throwing to an empty base, the runners should be sent back to second and third. Two things were against me: the umpires and the rules.

So we're back in the clubhouse, and somewhere along about the fifth cigarette I asked Joey Amalfitano, one of my coaches, to find Selma, who seemed to have disappeared, and ask him what had happened. The locker room in old Shibe Park was so tiny that the trainer's room was up a flight of stairs, like a kind of indoor porch. Selma wasn't on the training table, but Joey spotted a pair of feet sticking out from underneath the clothes in one of the narrow lockers right behind it. "Dick," Joey said to the feet. "Leo wants to know what you were thinking about?"

Actually, Selma's thinking had been pretty good. He didn't want to pitch to Allen, and who could blame him? Selma, who was a great one for trick plays, had worked out the "balk play" with Santo for exactly that situation. Men on first and second, two out, and a 3–2 count on a batter he would just as soon put on base. His theory was that he just might be able to catch the umpires off guard, and if he didn't . . . well, the runners would advance to second and third on the balk and he'd put the dangerous batter on first.

The natural question for Joey to ask under the circumstances was, "Have you got a sign with Santo on it?"

He sure did. The sign was for Selma to yell over, "It's two out, knock the ball down." Which is baseball shorthand for "Guard the line. With two out and the tying and go-ahead runs on base, our main concern is to keep the ball in the infield. Dive if you have to. Block it any way you can, but don't let the ball get by you."

A very well disguised signal, as you can see, because it is exactly what a pitcher would be likely to yell over in that situation. That was the trouble with it. It was too well disguised. What they had done was to work up the same signal for two different plays that could be used in the same situation. Already you can see the seeds for disaster.

It gets worse. Santo's answering sign was to yell back "Yeah." After which he would move over toward the third-base line and be in perfect position to break for the base to take Selma's pick-off throw.

You see what they had done? Selma's sign was what he would be normally saying in that situation anyway, and Santo's answering sign was what he would naturally say without thinking. A very bad answering sign. It should have been something that he normally *wouldn't* be doing. Hit the belt buckle. Pick your nose. Anything in the world except "Yeah."

When he came back down to the locker room, Joey asked Santo whether he had the balk-move play with Selma. "Yeah," Santo said. "We talked about it a while back."

"Know what the sign is?"

"Yeah, he tells me to knock the ball down."

"Did you answer him?"

"Holy cow," Santo groaned, realizing for the first time what had happened. "I answered him."

And that's how it goes when everything is collapsing around you.

From there the collapse was total. Everybody stopped hitting, and then the fielding disintegrated, and finally the pitching turned spotty. And, of course, everybody second-guessed me and invited me to second-guess myself. I had stayed with my regular lineup. Shouldn't I have rested them? Well, if I had known what was going to happen I'd have given everybody a rest for three days and played nine pitchers. The way we were getting beat, it wouldn't have made any difference if I had played nine girls. You can only play what you've got, though. You've got the same twenty-five men you've had all year. You can only bear down so hard on them, and they can only bear down so hard on the field. It's too late to plead with them or blame them. There's only one person to blame, and that's the manager. Whether anybody else could have stopped the slide is beside the point. All we do know is that I wasn't able to.

I was on a pregame call-in show in Chicago after we had been eliminated, and in answering a question about our collapse I intimated that the players had run out of gas. My pen pals in the Chicago press claimed that I was trying to shift the blame from myself to the players. As it happened, they were wrong. Not for the first time. The players knew exactly what I was referring to, and it had nothing to do with their play on the field.

We had come to Montreal, during that disastrous road trip, three and a half games behind but still in it. The schedule called for a night game followed by a day game. We lost the night game, and as I was coming down the next morning to catch the bus to the park, Pete Reiser was waiting to tell me he had run a bed check. Now that's something I absolutely forbid my coaches to do. In my spring-training speech, I tell my players that I am not going to put my coaches in the position of being stool pigeons by sending them around to knock on doors at two in the morning. "I'll do it, if I feel like it," I tell them. "But it will be me and nobody else."

Now I'm no fool. If Pete had felt it necessary to run a bed check, against my orders, it could only mean that some of them had been cheating on me right along. But even then, if he had told me that he had caught three or four of them, I'd have bawled him out.

Know how many of them had been out? Thirteen. And a couple of them were young kids we had just brought up. I don't think I have ever been more discouraged in my life. It hit me so hard that I felt as if the plug had been pulled out of me.

I got them together in the clubhouse, and they thought I was going to rip into them. But what good was that going to do at that stage of the game? It was my job to motivate them, and I had failed. I just sat there in my civilian clothes, smoking a cigarette and looking at them. And then I said, "You know, we're playing for a lot of money. We're playing for the championship, and you guys are telling me you really don't care about it. You fellows don't care whether you win or not. So if that's the way you feel about it, there's nothing either of us can do about it. That's the way you feel."

I got up, went back into my office, put on my uniform and went out onto the field.

We won that day. We actually won two straight. And then we stopped hitting again and began to lose, lose, lose.

Something bad just seemed to happen every day.

MISTER CUB

"ONE THING I CAN TELL YOU," I had said at the press conference at which I was unveiled to the Chicago newspapermen.
"This is not an eighth-place team." The Cubs thereupon sank
like a stone into the cellar, giving every card-carrying member of the Baseball Writers Association of America the
chance to write, "Durocher said it wasn't an eighth-place
team, and he was right. It's a tenth-place team." Made the
whole season for them.

The fact of the matter is that while I hadn't thought the
team was as good as I had been trying to convince the players it was, I hadn't thought it was that bad either. When you
thought of the Chicago Cubs, there were three names that
came immediately into your mind. Ernie Banks, Ron Santo,
and Billy Williams. Three great hitters. You never know a
team, though, until you've lived with it. After I had lived
with the Cubs for a couple of months, it had become very
clear to me that you needed more than a scorecard to tell
the strengths from the weaknesses. Right in the middle of
the lineup I had two men who couldn't run. Santo and Banks.
It was the New York Giants all over again; I couldn't make a
move. I had this kid second-baseman, Beckert, who worked
like hell to improve himself. Made himself into a great
player. Another Eddie Stanky. The leadoff man would get

on, Beckert would move him to third on a hit-and-run, Williams would get a knock, and then it was Santo and Banks and pray for a long ball.

I gave Mr. Wrigley the whole routine about "Our arrow is going down. What we have to do is reverse the arrow. . . ." I explained Mr. Rickey's theory to him. What we had to do, I felt, was trade Banks and Santo for some young players who would turn our arrow around and get it pointed upwards.

I couldn't trade either of them. I couldn't trade Banks because he was a civic monument in Chicago, and Mr. Wrigley's personal favorite. I couldn't trade Santo because nobody would give us anything for him that wouldn't have looked like a joke to the Chicago fans. So I tried to get my young players by trading Billy Williams. I still shudder whenever I think about it.

Because of the clubhouse explosion that erupted around Ron Santo later, I want to make it very clear that there is nothing personal in anything I say about him. When I took over the club I looked upon Santo as one of my great assets. I had seen him from the other side of the field, remember, for four years. He was the best fielding third-baseman in the National League, and he knocked in his 100 to 110 runs a year. But right from the first, other baseball men whom I respected began to tell me that I was never going to win a pennant with him. *What are you talking about?* "Sooner or later," they would say, "Santo is going to come up with the game on the bases and nine times out of ten he's going to kill you." Five runs ahead, and he'd knock in all the runs I could ask for. One run behind and he was going to kill me.

They were right. The kid never had anything but good to say about me. He was so happy to have a manager who would take charge that he became my greatest booster in the clubhouse. For my part, I made him my field captain to try to instill more confidence in him. A great kid. Gave you everything he had. That was one of his problems, he tried too hard. He'd get into a slump and press so bad that he became helpless. And then the fans would get on him and his fielding would fall apart too. A very emotional kid. He'd get so mad that he'd come in and tear the bench apart. He'd hit the door with his fist. He'd pull the bat rack down, and we'd have to send for the ground crew and have them build us a new one during the game. There was this one loud-mouthed guy who had Ron so crazy that he was ready to go after him. It got so bad that I finally decided to have the park police hold the guy under the stands after a game so that I could talk to him. You know, sometimes I think fans are crazy. Was he a Cub fan? Sure he was. He loved Ron, he loved me, he loved the Cubs. Nothing he wanted more than to see the Cubs win. *Then leave Santo alone.*

By the time I had Holland and Wrigley convinced that we had to trade him to get some speed onto the club, nobody was interested. The first time I saw Doug Rader at Houston I liked him so much that I tried to trade Santo for him, even up. Spec Richardson just laughed at me. I offered to put something else in our side. He wouldn't even talk to me.

It wasn't until the winter meetings of 1971 that we even had a discussion going, and what a farce that was. Bill Rigney, who was managing at Minnesota, came to me out of the blue and told me that he wanted him. What did he have in mind? Well, he could give me Tom Hall, a skinny colored relief pitcher.

"Not for Santo," I said. "For chrissake, Hall can't play third base. I need a third-baseman. Tell you what I'll do. I'll give you Santo for Tovar."

No, he couldn't give me Tovar. "A name like he's got? As popular as he is in Minnesota?"

"What do you think Santo is, a piece of cheese? He's only been an All-Star third-baseman for six-seven years." I had to get Tovar for him. If he'd throw in Hall, then I'd put in something to even it up.

I'm sitting at the Biltmore about three in the morning with

the whole Cub family and our wives when Rigney came over to announce that he was ready to make a deal. "Tovar and Hall for Santo and Decker." Decker was one of our better young pitching prospects. I looked at him for a full minute and then I stuck out my hand. "You got a deal." Immediately, he pulled his hand back.

He still insisted that he wanted to do something for me, though. He knew I needed a left-handed relief pitcher, he said, and he wanted me to have Hall. "Just leave it to me, and I'll get back to you."

I got up the next morning and read in the paper that Hall had been traded to Cincinnati for Granger, even up. They had traded him to a team in my league and my division, and he hadn't even given me the courtesy of a phone call. But that's another of the changes that has come into baseball now that it has become a full-fledged industry. A man's word doesn't mean what it used to.

Where Banks was concerned, I could never get permission to even try to trade him. Except for once, very briefly, after I had been there for three years. And even then, not really. During spring training, Mr. Holland said, in the course of a casual conversation, "You can trade any player on this team if you think it will improve us, and you have Mr. Wrigley's permission." I took that to include Ernie Banks. Within the week, I was told that it didn't. Ernie was too popular with the fans.

What do you say about Ernie Banks? Well, you say: He had bad knees but he did the best he could under the circumstances. You say: He was at the end of the road and I guess he knew it as well as anyone else. But he gave you all he had when he was playing, and he was a great player in his time. You say: It was too bad the Cubs didn't have nine Ernie Bankses. Know what I mean? Praise him.

The only thing true about it is that he was a great player

in his time. Unfortunately, his time wasn't my time. Even more unfortunately, there was not a thing I could do about it. He couldn't run, he couldn't field; toward the end, he couldn't even hit. There are some players who instinctively do the right thing on the base paths. Ernie had an unfailing instinct for doing the wrong thing. But I had to play him. Had to play the man or there would have been a revolution in the street.

Ernie Banks owns Chicago. He's Mr. Cub. All the players on the Chicago Cubs have said it themselves. "Ernie Banks could come to bat and make a gesture telling everyone in the grandstand where they could go and they'd *r-i-i-i-i-se* up as a man and give him a standing ovation."

How does he do it? You could say about Ernie that he never remembered a sign or forgot a newspaperman's name. All he knew was, "Ho, let's go. Ho, babydoobedoobedoo. It's a wonderful day for a game in Chicago. Let's play twooo." We'd get on the bus and he'd sit across from the writers. "A beaooootiful day for twooo." It could be snowing outside. "Let's play three."

Jim Enright, who was his pal, wrote a book with him, which was called "Mr. Cub." All the writers in the country rushed to write what a great book it was, and all of them said in private, "If he wanted to write a book, with all the goodwill he has going for him, why didn't he get himself a writer?" I don't know why it is, but where Ernie is concerned everybody is always ready to fall over and play dead.

As a player, by the time I got there, there was nothing wrong with Ernie that two new knees wouldn't have cured. He'd come up with men on the bases and if he hit a ground ball they could walk through the double play. To do me any good he'd have had to hit 70 home runs and knock in 200 runs. In the field he was very good at one thing. I never saw anybody who could dig a thrown ball out of the dirt any better. But that was where it ended. If the ball wasn't hit right at him, forget it. He'd wave at it. Two feet away from him—whoops—right under his glove. But did anybody in Chicago ever write that Mr. Cub couldn't get off a dime? Never. Criticizing Ernie Banks doesn't sell papers; the best it's going to get you is a ton of abuse.

I'd tell Holland and Wrigley, "He can't do it any more. I love him as well as you do. I love him as much as the fans do. But I've got to have somebody there who can play. Balls are going by there this far that should be outs or double plays."

With every other player, we had the usual signs, an indicator followed by a combination. With Ernie we had to have flash signs. One sign. Like the Little League. Ernie, you're always hitting unless we flash something at you. If I tip my hat, now you're taking. Pull up my belt, it's a hit-and-run. In my first year, when he could still run a little, I'd sometimes want him moving on a 3–1 count with Santo at bat to break up the possible double play. From the bench, you could see his whole body just rear back and he'd look at the coach as if he were saying, "You got to be kidding." Your little boy knows that it's percentage baseball to get a runner moving on a 3–1 count under those conditions. But not Mister Cub.

In all fairness, I want to say this about him. He did love to play; that part of the Ernie Banks legend is true. As badly as he was hurting, in the four years before his knees gave out completely he didn't miss more than a handful of games. He was also a great man to have in the clubhouse. Always full of life. Always ready to kid or be kidded. Never a troublemaker in any sense of the word. He knew I wanted to get rid of him and it didn't affect our personal relationship a bit. But, then, why should it?

By his last year as an active player, his left knee had got so bad that it would blow up on him like a balloon. They were draining water out of it twice a week; he could hardly walk. And every time I didn't play him, the sportswriters were all over me. At first he would tell me when he couldn't play, although he would never tell the newspapermen. After a while, when it got to be a constant issue with his pal Enright, he would never tell me. Enright had his book coming up, and they seemed to think it very important that Ernie still be an active player when it came out.

Before the game, the writers would ask him how he felt. "Great." Could he play? "Yeah, I can play." Then he'd tell Doc Sheuneman, the trainer, that he couldn't play, and I'd write him out of the lineup. "How come you didn't play today, Ernie?" the newspapermen would ask him. "The knee bother you?" He'd shrug and give them a significant look. "The man says I play, I play."

Aha! Leo Durocher doesn't want Banks to play because Leo Durocher has decided that it would be a wonderful day in Chicago to lose a game or two, scoobedoobedoo.

Every time they asked Doc Sheuneman about it he would tell them Banks couldn't play because Banks couldn't walk. So they stopped going to Doc Sheuneman. Some of the other players went out of their way to tell the writers there was no way Ernie could have played. Not once did Ernie ever defend me. If he did, they certainly didn't print it.

A couple of times I said to him, "I ask you if you can play and you're always ready to play a doubleheader, a tripleheader if we'll let you, but you get into the clubhouse and I see them wrap your knee and it's that big. I know you can't play, and I don't play you and I catch hell from the newspapermen about it. Ernie, if your knee hurts, why don't you tell them?"

"Well," he'd say, "you're the manager, Leo. I don't think it's my place to tell you who to play."

There was no way of winning. I could have put his name in the lineup every day until he couldn't walk. Until he begged to be taken out. And then they would have written, "That dirty sonofabitch Durocher broke him down. If Durocher had picked the spots for him, he could have prolonged his career three or four more years."

They'd have attacked me every day in the paper for that, and instead of ignoring the fact that Ernie was limping back and forth from the dugout when he did get to play, they'd have *booed* me every time he limped back and forth.

Do you know how true to form these things run? In Houston, I had a traveling secretary named Art Perkins, who was born with a bad foot. I don't know what it's called, but you've seen it. His foot is turned in, and it flops back and forth when he walks so that he has almost no control over it. Bad foot and all, Art just loved to grab a first-baseman's glove and work out around the bag during batting pactice, and since you have to admire a guy like that I sure wasn't going to stop him. Well, one day a ball is thrown into the dirt and skips past him, and while Art is running after it this leather-lung yells, "Durocher, you dummy, are you trying to *cripple that man?*" You could hear him all over the park, I couldn't believe it. I looked up, and Judge Hofheinz was laughing and Spec Richardson was laughing, and all the players on the bench were laughing. It's my fault. I'm trying to cripple him.

The showdown finally came in Atlanta. Banks's knees were so bad that he hadn't been playing for about a week and the newspapermen came in wanting to know when I was going to put him back in the lineup.

As soon as he could play, I explained patiently. "One knee is almost normal, the other is still twice the size. I'm not a doctor. I'm just the manager of the club."

A while later, in comes Ernie. He wants to play both games.

"All right," I said. "All right. Let's have an understanding then. I'm sick and tired of taking the abuse. You want to play? You're playing. You're playing until you take yourself out."

I called in the newspapermen. "Banks just asked to play, and he's playing. A doubleheader tonight. Both games!"

By the sixth inning of the first game, the knee had blown

up so much that they had to give him a shot of Novocaine. He could hardly make it from first base to the bench. Between games, Doc Sheuneman came to me and said, "This guy can't make it any more, Leo."

Oh? And what made the trainer think he was the medical authority around here? "Did Ernie tell you he can't make it?"

"That's what I'm telling you, Leo. Ernie told me he just can't go any more."

Don't you think the writers came bombing in afterwards wanting to know why I hadn't played Banks in the second game like I'd promised?

"Because the man can't walk. Why don't you ask him? Can't walk! Go look at his knee."

That wasn't what Ernie said. All Ernie knew was that the manager hadn't written his name on the card. Shrug, smile, what-are-you-gonna-do?

The next day we had to put him on the disabled list. When he came back a month later, the newspapers reported, in sheer joy, that he hadn't slowed down a bit. The first honest report they made on him all year. He couldn't run before and he still couldn't.

But, of course, whenever the fans came to the park for the rest of the season, they wanted to see Mr. Cub on first base. They didn't care if we had to roll him out in a wheelchair. Every time he came to bat, they still expected him to hit a home run. So I played him every once in a while when he felt good, and they loved it. All they had to do was hear his name announced and they'd *holler* and they'd *cheer*. He'd hit a pop fly and they'd cheer him all the way back to the dugout. And every once in a while he'd hit one out of the park, and it didn't matter that we'd still be losing, 10–3, it was as if we had just won the championship of the whole wide world.

Billy Williams was everything that Banks was supposed to be, although it took me awhile to appreciate him. He hadn't had a particular good season that first year but he was a solid ballplayer and eminently marketable, and so when I found that I couldn't trade Santo or Banks I got permission to trade him.

Baltimore was the obvious place to go for young ball-players. The Orioles had just swept the World Series in four straight games, and they had more good young players in their farm system than they knew what to do with. We got together with them during the winter meetings to hammer out a 5-for-1 deal. The key player on their side from the beginning was Mike Epstein, who had just finished his second great year in the high minors. Charley Grimm, who had scouted him for us, called him "the greatest young hitter in the next couple of years in the minor leagues." And Charley wasn't alone. The only reason he was available was because Baltimore already had a powerful left-hand-hitting first-baseman in Boog Powell.

Hank Bauer, the Orioles' manager, and I were shunted off to the corner with a bottle of whiskey while the front-office men played put-and-take through the night and into the morning. John Holland handled the negotiations for our side. Harry Dalton, the Baltimore farm director, handled it for them along with Frank Lane, who had just joined the organization as a special adviser.

At four o'clock in the morning, they finally settled upon the other players to go with Epstein. Two pitchers, Eddie Watt and Tom Phoebus; an outfielder, Sam Bowen; and Curt Blefary, who had a couple of pretty good years behind him and was going to replace Williams in left field.

Harry Dalton thought Baltimore was giving up too much. Lane fought to make the deal. He really fought for it. In front of all of us, he told Dalton, "There's no way in the world you can sit here and not make that deal. You're going to get one of the best four or five left-handed hitters in baseball, and he's young enough and he can run and he can field." How many times, he asked Dalton, did he think that kind of a ballplayer came around?

All that remained was to get the approval of the Baltimore owner, Jerry Hoffberger. Dalton went out to make the call and came back with the word that Hoffberger wasn't willing to let go of Epstein. There were never many Jewish players around, and Hoffberger was sure he was going to be a great player for them and also a great gate attraction.

Frank Lane said to Dalton, "Boy, you're going to regret this. Frank Robinson and Billy Williams in the same outfield, and you're letting it get away. I can't believe it. This is the biggest mistake you could have made."

I'll tell you how funny life can be. The wheel keeps turning, and five years later it was the Cubs who almost had them both in the same outfield. Baltimore had Frank Robinson on the market, and how I wanted him! In all the years I had been in Chicago we had never had a right fielder, and here we had a chance to get Frank Robinson. "By accident he'll hit 35–40 home runs in our ball park," I told Holland. Not to mention the other things he could do for us. Leadership on the field and in the clubhouse. A clutch hitter.

We made an appointment to meet the Baltimore people at the hotel bar at two thirty in the afternoon. Frank Cashen, their new general manager, Earl Weaver, and a couple of others. The first thing we had to do, as we knew we were going to have to, was refuse to let them have Bill North. After that, Baltimore began to ask for young pitchers. They asked for Jim Colborn. "You got him." They asked for Earl Stephenson, a left-handed pitcher who was having trouble with his arm, and for Brock Davis, an outfielder. "You got them."

And then they asked for two more of our young pitchers, Bonham and Decker. "Wait a minute," I said. "Hold it." They were asking five for one. Four for one was more like it.

They could have either Bonham or Decker, but not both of them.

After a couple of more drinks, Cashen said, "I'll talk to you later, but I'm sure we've got a deal."

Mr. Wrigley has a home up on the hill in Phoenix, and Baltimore had taken it over that night to give a victory party. During the course of the evening, the word got around that they had traded Frank Robinson to the Dodgers for a couple of relief pitchers.

To make it perfect, it was the same day that Rigney had backed out on the deal for Santo and then promised me Hall. I grabbed Earl Weaver in a corner and I said, "You dirty, no-good—. You're sure we've got a deal, huh? You didn't even give us the courtesy of a phone call. You didn't have the simple decency to give us another chance."

But Frank Lane was absolutely right about Billy Williams. It turned out to be the best deal I never made since I had been unable to get anybody to take Dusty Rhodes off my hands. I had underestimated Williams to begin with, and he kept getting better and better every year. A manager's dream. For six years I was able to walk into my office and start the day by writing his name in the #3 slot of the lineup card. Never had to say a word to him. He'd be out on the field early every day practicing. Like clockwork. He set his own time schedule and he never wasted a minute.

Another double professional. He set a National League record by playing 1,117 consecutive games, a streak that had begun two years before I got there, and ended in September 1970. Actually, we had tried to end it earlier. Billy had got to be thirty-two years old, we were right in the middle of another pennant fight and the streak was wearing him down. Emotionally as well as physically. Finally, I called him in and I said, "Bill, what do you want to do?"

"I want out of it," he said. "It's getting to be a monster." Good. We made the announcement that the streak was coming to an end, and I told him to go home. He didn't. Jack

Brickhouse wanted him for his post-game show, so he hung around in the clubhouse. We fell behind early in the game, and while we had a rally going in the fifth inning Billy came out to the dugout. In uniform. When I looked down the bench for a left-handed pinch hitter and saw him sitting there . . . well, who else would I want? "Come here, pal," I called. "I want you to hit." He got the hit that tied the ball game, and we went on to win it.

A couple of weeks later he came to me on his own and said, "Leo, let's break this thing once and for all. Let's get it over with."

"There's only one way I know," I told him. "Don't come to the ball park tomorrow. If I don't see you, I can't use you." Billy went right to the newspapermen and told them he had asked to be taken out. Took all the pressure off me.

Cream and sugar. Billy Williams is in a class all by himself.

THE SANTO EXPLOSION

IT WAS ONE OF Santo's slumps that led, indirectly, to the worst argument I ever saw in a clubhouse. The only thing that didn't fly was fists, and for a while there it was a very near thing. And it wasn't Santo's fault. I have nobody to blame but myself. As a bow to the modern ballplayer, I had formed the habit of holding open meetings. "OK, boys," I'd say, after I had spoken my piece. "Now we'll forget that I'm the manager, and let's hear what's on your mind." Keep asking for it, buddy, and you're going to get it.

The real culprits were Milt Pappas and Joe Pepitone, a pair of renegades we had picked up during the previous season. Pappas I will never forgive. All I did for Pappas was save his life after he had done everything but crawl on his knees to me. He started on me in Acapulco in the winter of 1969 while my wife and I were sitting in a restaurant. Pappas was a great friend of our traveling secretary, Blake Cullen, and he came over to our table to say hello. "Goddam, get me, Leo," he said. "I want to pitch for you."

Now, Milt could pitch, but he had a reputation everywhere he had ever been of being one of the great clubhouse lawyers of our time. That's why Baltimore, his original club, had let him go; it was, from everything I heard, why Cincinnati had let him go; and it was probably why he no longer felt he had a glowing future in Atlanta. That didn't bother me at all. I always felt that I could handle the renegades.

I didn't think Atlanta was going to give him up that easily, though, and I told him so.

The following summer he wooed me. Early in the season we played three games in Atlanta, and he came to me three different times. The first two times he came over while I was on the field watching batting practice to let me know Atlanta wasn't using him and he definitely could be had. Just what I needed. To begin with, there's an antifraternization rule. You're not supposed to even talk to a player in the other uniform, let alone be talking about making a deal for him. The last day, I was told that he was waiting for me at the bus outside our clubhouse. "Get him out of there," I yelled.

Same thing when Atlanta came to Chicago a week later. And all the time he kept telling Blake Cullen how much he would like to be with the Cubs, and Blake would come to me and ask whether I thought Pappas could help us.

There was no question that he could help us. We needed another starting pitcher bad, and you only had to look at the box scores to see that Pappas was right in feeling that his future did not lay in Atlanta. So I talked to John Holland about him. John wasn't crazy about the idea, but—lucky me —I finally was able to talk him into it.

The guy could pitch, all right. But he always wanted to spit the bit out, that was the other part of his reputation. He'd give you a great six, seven innings, and if he had a one-run lead he was through. If he won it, fine, he got credit for the win. If you lost, he was off the hook. If he was a run behind it was a different story; he'd really be bearing down. The time that tore it, he was pitching against Cincinnati after he had been with us about a month, and he was pitching just great. (A couple of weeks earlier he had shut the Reds out, the only time they were shut out all year.) This time, I made the mistake of sending Joe Becker, my pitching coach, over to ask him how he felt, "Aahh, I'm all in," Milt said. "I'd get a new pitcher in there." I took him out. My fault.

Cincinnati tied the game in the eighth and beat us in the ninth. If that wasn't bad enough, he threw a temper tantrum in the clubhouse when he heard the score had been tied. My coaches came to me in a body to tell me that I should never do that with Pappas. "I know," I said. "I wanted to be sure."

I sat everybody down and I said, "I want to apologize to the rest of the team. I screwed up today." And then I turned to Pappas and told him he was never going to do that to me again. "You're going to start and you're staying in there until I take you out, and nobody's going to ask you. Quit looking over your shoulder at me. I blame myself because I should know better."

From that day on, he never got to talk to me. He'd come into the dugout looking for me, and wherever he went I'd go the other way. He'd look into the dugout from the mound, and I'd put my head down. It didn't matter what he said to the coaches. They were under instructions never to relay any of his complaints to me. I made him stay nine. Pitch, I'd say to myself. You ain't going to get out of there today; you're pitching too good. They're going to get a couple of men on, and somebody's going to get a base hit before I take you out now. Tired or not, you're pitching too good. The same year we had the blowup, he won more games for me, seventeen, than he had ever won before in his life. And pitched more innings.

But he was always agitating. He became the player representative when Randy Hundley quit, a job nobody else wanted and Milt always loved. He had also been the player rep at Baltimore, Cincinnati and Atlanta. Worst thing that could have happened. Once he was the player representative, he was holding meetings all the time. Practically overnight, all harmony disappeared from the Chicago clubhouse.

And it wasn't that the players looked on him with any particular affection, either. There was one time during a road trip that we were going from someplace or other to Cincinnati. We had been playing horribly, and since the first day in Cincinnati was open, I had Blake Cullen reroute us to Chicago. And not to give the players a day with their loved ones! "We're going to work out at Wrigley Field," I told them, "and everybody is to be there."

Milt Pappas didn't show up. His wife called up to say he was sick. As soon as the other guys saw he wasn't there, they just stood around on the field hollering, "Where is Pappas? Where is Pappas?" I was so mad about it myself that I sent everybody back into the clubhouse and told them they could go home. "See you tomorrow in Cincinnati." That was our workout. That was what we had made the trip to Chicago for.

Milt showed up about three days later with a note from his family doctor.

Pepitone was another kettle of fish entirely. I knew exactly what I was getting when I got him. A couple of days before Ernie Banks went on the disabled list, Pepitone had left Houston, wailing that he couldn't stand (1) Harry Walker, the manager; (2) Spec Richardson, the general manager; (3) anybody else who tried to tell him what he had to do. "I can't stand a million rules," Peppy had said—and a beautiful example was the awful thing they were trying to do to Peppy in Houston. They had actually tried to assign him a roommate on the road, like everybody else. Pepitone had gone home to his hair-styling salon in Brooklyn to brood about man's inhumanity to man, and he was nothing if not available.

He didn't come cheap, either. Although it was announced as a straight sale, it wasn't. We had to agree to give up a minor-league player at the end of the season, and the player was going to be Roger Metzger, who we really hated to lose.

It was a calculated risk we were willing to take because we were fighting for the division title, and Peppy was another guy who could play. He was a good hitter, he could run, he had a good arm. He knew how to play ball. He was the best first-baseman we had, and he was also the best outfielder. He could do everything. It was just a question of how much of it he was willing to give you on any particular day.

It was a crime, watching a guy like that wasting all that talent. Because basically Peppy was a lovable guy. He could charm the birds out of the trees. No matter how mad you might be when you started to talk to him, you'd go away thinking, "He's his own worst enemy, poor fellow. Too bad." Which, I guess, was exactly what Peppy, poor fellow, wanted you to go away thinking.

Training rules? Forget it. No training rules where Joe Pepitone was concerned. What were you going to do, fine him? He was in debt up to his eyeballs when he came to us. He always owed the club half of his year's salary before the year started. Gratitude? You're kidding. His attitude, like most of them, was "I'm entitled to it."

A shining example of the new breed. Mod all the way.

I came into the office one day, and right outside my door there's a Harley-Davis motorcycle. I called Yosh to find out whose it was. Listen, it didn't have to be Peppy's. We had another nut there, Ray Newman, who used to ride to the park from the Executive House, ten or twelve miles away, on his bicycle. That was my left-handed relief pitcher. One day he ran it right into a bus and almost killed himself. Had to get rid of the bicycle. Him too, while we were at it.

Peppy couldn't understand why I would object to having a motorcycle in the clubhouse. It seemed reasonable enough to him. "Every time I try to get on it out on the parking lot, the kids bother me."

We tried to put him on a budget. See you later, pal. He'd

go into Cincinnati and visit Dino's, a fancy haberdashery, and the next thing you knew you'd walk into the clubhouse and he'd be putting on a fashion show.

"Joe, who's paying for this?"

"They took a check."

If you're thinking that Pepitone was sent to me in just retribution, and that somewhere the ghosts of Sidney Weil and Branch Rickey were laughing uproariously, I have to admit that the same thought occasionally crossed my own mind.

If you have picked up the impression somewhere along the line that Joey Amalfitano is very important to me, you are absolutely right. Joe came to me in the spring of 1954 as an eighteen-year-old bonus boy who had just been signed by the New York Giants. Just what I didn't need, an untried kid I had to keep on the roster. But he hustled all the time, was very bright and he got 120 percent out of his talent. After I left the Giants he was sent down to the minors, but I always stayed in contact with him and used whatever influence I had to get him back there. He lived with his parents in Long Beach, California, in the off season, helping with the family fishing fleet. He is a good son, and he is highly religious. Or wouldn't you say that a man who has got up with the dawn a minimum of four times a week all his life to take communion is highly religious?

I will never forget one Sunday in Mexico when I took Joe and a couple of other people to the bullfights in Acapulco. It was a little after seven at night, and we had barely started to drive back to the Racquet Club when Joe said, "Let me out."

"Let me out for what?" I yelped. "We've got five miles to go yet. How are you going to get back?"

He'd take a cab.

"Wait a minute, where are you going?"

To church.

"What church? Where's there a church?"

Up in the hills, he said. There was an open-air church up there that had a seven thirty evening mass. "I'll walk up."

Don't you know, we went up with him in the burning heat? Worst-looking church you ever saw in your life. All open air. Kids running in and out. Mosquitoes everywhere.

But Joey wasn't going to miss mass.

By a stroke of luck, Joey was playing for the Cubs when I got there. Right away, I made him one of my coaches. If I hadn't, we probably never would have got Jim Hickman, who also had a role to play in the explosion.

We were making a deal with Los Angeles for Phil Regan, the relief pitcher I needed, and as the deal was worked out we agreed to send a pitcher from our minor-league club in Tacoma to their minor-league team in Spokane. To even it off, Bavasi was going to send someone from Spokane to Tacoma. He gave us a list of four players we could choose from, and Hickman, who had been one of the original members of the New York Mets, was on it. "Grab him," Joey said. "He always hit well in Wrigley Field." A year later he was up with us, and in 1970, the guy who had been one of four names thrown into a minor-league deal won the All-Star game for the National League with a hit in the thirteenth inning. What a year he had for us! He played the outfield for us, he played first base in a pinch, and when he wasn't starting he was hitting home runs as a pinch hitter. He hit 32 home runs and knocked in 115 runs. He won game after game for us to keep us in the pennant race.

A very quiet, soft-spoken young man from Hennings, Tennessee. "My hillbilly," I called him. During spring training the following year, he was sitting morosely at a table in the Pink Pony, having a drink, and doing his best, in his polite way, to get rid of some girl who was bothering him. Yosh came over to where Lynne and I were sitting. "Better go over and talk to Hickman."

I went over to the table and told the girl to get lost. "Jim, what's your problem, buddy? Anything I can do? Anything you want to tell me about?"

"Well," he said. "I don't want to bother you. You've been so good to me."

I finally got him to tell me. He had asked for $46,000 because that was what he thought he deserved, and all Holland had wanted to give him was $40,000. "I wanted to play for you," he said, "and I don't like to hold out so I signed for the forty thousand." He just didn't like to get into a big fight over money, it went against him, but that didn't mean he didn't feel he was being cheated.

I said, "I wish you'd have told me about it, Jim. I wish I'd have known about it before you signed." I didn't know if I could do him any good now that the contract was signed, I told him, but I sure as hell was going to try.

I bided my time until Holland was in a particularly good mood, and then I said, "You know we've got a very unhappy player on this club." I sketched in the background for him very quickly. "Couple of thousand one way or the other doesn't make any difference, but there's a six thousand dollar difference here. It's entirely up to you, John. But he's been a hell of a guy on the club. Cost us nothing and done a great job since he came here. Very popular with the fans. Drew people in the park. I think he's an outstanding player on our club. I hate to see him unhappy."

"What are you asking me to do?"

"That's an unfair question, John," I said, laughing it up a little. "I'll just leave it up to you."

"Send him in to see me," John sighed.

I sent him in and Holland gave him the $46,000.

And Jim Hickman never forgot it.

Now you have the main cast of characters. Pappas, Pepitone, Amalfitano and Hickman. And Santo.

The whole thing started, really, when we arrived in Atlanta late at night on the last stop of a road trip before returning to Chicago. Santo got on the elevator with me, just the two of us, and asked if he could talk to me in private. When we got to my suite, it developed that he wanted to talk about the Day they were giving him the second Sunday after we got back. "I never wanted a Day to begin with," he said. "And now I'm going so lousy that the fans are going to be on me. I just wish you'd talk to Holland about calling it off."

No way, Holland told me. Too much had already been done. It was a hell of a time for him to be asking that it be called off, John said, especially since it had been Ron himself who had asked for it. *Ron had asked for it?* Yeah, while they had been negotiating his contract, Ron had argued that since Banks and Williams had been given a Day, he was entitled to one, too. Now in fairness to Ron, I want to add very quickly that Ron was a diabetic, something he had kept entirely to himself up to then. The principal beneficiary of Santo Day, as the plans were worked out, was to be not Ron himself but the Diabetic Association. In fairness to myself, I should say that I didn't know this—I'm not sure anybody outside of the front office knew it—until it came out during the actual ceremonies. I hadn't even known there was going to be a Day until Ron told me about it in my suite in Atlanta.

In the course of that same talk, Ron had also asked if it would be all right with me if he didn't take batting practice. Just, you know, to see if it might help him shake his slump. Sure, Ron. Good idea. Might be just the thing. He had done pretty well for two days, too. And then he had gone into an even worse slump. When I called the meeting on August 23, we had been home for three days and Ron had not had a base hit in twelve times at bat. And he still wasn't taking batting practice.

To complete the background, we were still very much in the pennant race: 4½ games behind Pittsburgh with 37 games left to play. We had lost two straight to Houston, though, the last loss coming when Doug Rader doubled off Pappas on an 0–2 pitch, the unforgivable sin for a pitcher.

That was one of the things I brought up in the course of the meeting. We weren't hustling, I told them. We weren't bearing down. We were slipping back into the sloppy, uncaring ways that had beaten us for three straight years now. I said, "The guy in left field, Number twenty-six, I write his name in the lineup every day and forget about him. He's out there taking batting practice. He's out there early fielding and throwing." I said, "I got a guy over here, Beckert, busting his rear end. He's having a super year. Challenging Clemente for the batting title. He's out there every day. He works on his hitting, he works on his fielding. He works on all his weaknesses. He made himself into a hell of a player."

But there were some of them, I said, who didn't seem to care. "I'm out there watching the workout, Ronnie, and you're not even there during batting practice. You're coming out late."

"Well, in my case," Ronnie said, "I don't care to hit some days."

"Well, that's what I'm trying to say, Ronnie. Maybe if you came out there and practiced, you wouldn't get into these slumps you get into periodically."

And that's where Ronnie started to blow up. He was different than Beckert, he said. I had given him permission not to take batting practice, and now I was jumping all over him. "You say we're all the same to you, and we're not all the same. It doesn't matter what I do, you're right on my ass . . ."

Well, this wasn't what I wanted at all. "Wait a minute," I said. "The only thing I'm trying to tell you is that you got to go on the field and practice. If nothing else, the fans come out early to see you, and you don't hit, you're not even there, and they're disappointed."

It might have ended right there, except that Pappas had to open his mouth. "The whole trouble in this locker room," he said, "is that you don't know how to handle us."

I had to sit there for ten minutes and listen to Milt Pappas lecture me on the proper way to handle ballplayers, something Milt Pappas knew all about from never having managed.

"Listen, Pappas," I said, when he was finished. "I brought you here from Atlanta. I've given you the ball. I don't know what you've got to complain about. You've been winning more games the way I've been handling you than you ever won in your life."

Pepitone's locker was right next to Pappas', which was a mistake right there. "I want to say something," Peppy said. "You know, I played for the Yankees with some very good clubs, and Ralph Houk is just a super guy. He lets you play. The trouble with this club is if a guy makes a mistake on the field you talk about him on the bench. Houk never did that."

He held the floor for about ten minutes too, telling me what a great manager Ralph Houk was, what a super guy. The only thing he didn't tell me was why Houk had finally thrown up his super hands and practically given him away. At the end, Peppy yelled at the top of his voice, "Hell, I can take it. Hell, I've been down that road before. But Ronnie can't take it. You got to rub Ronnie. You got to pat him."

"Are you through?" I asked him. Yes, he was through. "OK, now I'm going to speak. Nobody wanted you, Pepitone. We took a chance and brought you here. Who in the hell sets any rules for you? You can come and go as you please. Do you mean to tell me that when you screw up in the ballgame I don't have the right to criticize you? Who the hell are *you?*" Now Joe started to pipe up again, and I had to remind him that I had asked him whether he had finished. "I'm going to do the talking now," I said.

Oh no, I wasn't. Santo was yelling again. They had got him all worked up, and as emotional as Ronnie is, he was accusing me of all kind of things. And he wasn't alone. I had lost control of the meeting, it was out of hand. They had me backed against the wall, and when my back is against the wall I hit back. "Wait a minute," I said. "Let me ask you something, Ronnie. Isn't it true that you came to my room in Atlanta to talk to me about calling off this Day that's coming up Sunday?"

Yes, it was.

"Didn't I tell you we couldn't do that, Ron?"

Yes, I had.

"Isn't it also true that you had a problem signing a contract this year and wanted a stipulation that the Cubs would have a Day for you because they gave one to Billy Williams and Ernie Banks? You told me you never wanted the Day, and that was an erroneous statement on your part, wasn't it?"

The room went absolutely quiet. "That's a lie!" Ron screamed, and took a leap across the room at me. I thought he was going to belt me one, that's how mad he was. If he had, there would have been a fight for sure, and I'd have probably been killed. He didn't swing at me, though. He just stood nose to nose with me and kept yelling.

"Do you want me to get Mr. Holland down here to clear that up, Ron?" I finally asked.

Yeah, why didn't I just get Mr. Holland down and clear it up?

I went over and picked up the phone. "John, we got a bit of a problem. I think you should come down here."

To keep things cooled down while we were waiting, I went up to my office to get some cigarettes. The office was up a little flight of stairs and through the equipment room. I'd hardly got there before I heard a racket. Santo had started after me. My guess is that he wanted to ask me to call Holland back or, possibly, to intercept Holland before he got to the locker room. There's no way of knowing. Some of the other players had grabbed him at the top of the steps, and I could hear Milt Pappas yelling, "Let him go. Let him do what he has to do. Let him go get him."

And Jim Hickman, who had just got out of the hospital, was yelling back, "Why don't you sit down, Pappas, and shut up. Just for once in your life, shut up!"

Holland was there within the minute. Without saying a word to him, I took him back down the steps into the dressing room. "I just want you to answer one question for me," I told him. "Yes or no. Isn't it true that the idea for this Day for Santo was brought up by Ron?" I put him on the spot, no question about it. "Didn't it enter into your discussion when you were trying to sign his contract? That's all. Just yes or no."

"Well, yes," he said. "In a way he did. When he signed his contract."

Santo blew up again. A lie. It was a goddam lie!

And poor John said, "Well, it seems to me that it did enter into your conversation that you desired to have a Day, Ron. It was so long ago that you probably don't remember. It was brought up casually but you did bring it up. Not that you're not deserving of it, Ron."

Ron let out a scream. "Ooooohhh, my God! Ohhh, Jesus Christ." And then he was back at me. "I heard about you but I didn't want to believe it."

Now Pepitone piped up again. "That's the most horseshit thing I've ever seen. You see what you've done! You've destroyed him. What kind of a manager are you?"

And Pappas is right in there agreeing with him. My heavenly twins. Look what I had done. I had destroyed Ron Santo.

Holland was trying to quiet them down. But I was burning. "Wait a minute," I yelled. "Let me say something." I told them I was sorry this had all come about. "I didn't know there was this much hatred for me on this ball club. So I've got a solution to the whole thing. *I'll see you later!*" I turned to Holland. "You can take the uniform and shove it up your ass. Just get yourself another manager."

I was stalking through the equipment room, with my shirt already off, when I thought of something else and came running back down the stairs. "One more thing," I said. "And all I need is a yes or no on this too, John. Is there a player on this club that I didn't fight with you and Mr. Wrigley to get more money? Every player on this club. Didn't I always fight with you when you asked me? More money, more money, more money. Fighting for the player when I should have been on the executive side?"

"That's right. You were in the middle of it, always fighting for the player."

"Yeah," I said. "I think we've all done pretty well since I been here." I went back upstairs, took off the uniform and went into the shower.

What was happening down in the clubhouse while I was showering I heard about later. Holland talked to the players and told them if they let me walk out of there under these conditions they were going to go down in history with the Cleveland Cry-Babies, who had petitioned the front office to fire their manager, Ossie Vitt, for being so mean to them. Well, that had happened in 1940, before most of our players had been born. Holland had to explain to them how the Cleveland players had become the laughingstock of the whole country.

After Holland was through, Jim Hickman said, "We've gotten this far with him, we can't let him go. He's helped us all and we need him."

When some of the others, who had previously been silent, began to express the same sentiments, Pappas jumped up and yelled, "Let's take a vote on it."

Holland didn't say a word. It was Joey Amalfitano who jumped up on the equipment trunk and took over. Addressing himself specifically to Santo, Pappas and Pepitone, he said, "I'm asking each one of you, has anybody ever told you three guys what to do in your careers? You think you're going to tell that man what to do? Leo's a personality all to himself. He's been here before you, and he'll be here after you're gone. This isn't a guy that walked off the street. He knows what he's doing. And you think you're going to change him? Mr. Holland can't even change him. If you think we got a chance to win the pennant without him, you're crazier than I think you are."

With nobody saying a word, Joey looked straight at Santo. "You want him to come back, Ron?"

And Santo said, "Yeah."

"Then get your ass up there with me." Which is strong language for Joey Amalfitano.

I had taken my shower and put on my street clothes when Amalfitano came in with Santo. The first thing he said to me was that Ron hadn't meant it. "What you said, Leo, I don't think you should have said. And the names you called him, Ron, you shouldn't have said, either. Now if you're two adults, like I think you are, you got to apologize to each other and shake hands."

"Ronnie," I said, "I haven't got a thing in the world against you." As we shook hands, Ronnie, who was just emotionally drained, threw his arms around me. "I didn't mean to say the things I said, Leo," he said. "You know how I get. How hot-tempered . . ." I had a cigarette in my hand and I was shaking so bad I could hardly hold it. "Ronnie," I said, "I'm not mad at you. Hell, you got a right to your feelings. You had a right to pop off. It was an open meeting. So did I. Forget it. But those other two bastards . . ." I was never going to forgive them.

And I wasn't going to put the uniform back on, either.

"No, no," Joey said. "You've preached all your life you can't stand a quitter. And you're going to quit? You're just going to walk out of here and leave us by ourself?"

"I've had enough, Joe. I'm tired."

"Bullshit!" It was a swearing day for Joey.

Nothing he could say was going to change my mind. I was through. After Joe and Santo had left, Peanuts Lowrey, my other coach, came in to plead with me. And then, to my surprise, Ernie Banks, who was a player-coach by then, came up. "Please, Leo," he said. "Don't quit. We want you here. We need you. Don't go doing something you might regret."

"Well, I think I've had enough, Ernie. I've had enough of this."

While all this was going on, Jim Hickman had taken charge in the clubhouse. He started by telling Pappas and Pepitone what ungrateful bastards they were, and then he ate the rest of them out for the way they had turned on me. I guess it was the longest speech my hillbilly ever made in his life. There were three or four of them who never spoke to Jim Hickman again. What really surprised me when I heard about it was that J. C. Martin, my reserve catcher, and Chris Cannizzaro, who had just joined the team, were supporting him. "I've been around for a long time," Martin told them, "and this is the worst thing I've ever seen."

As for John Holland, he had come up to my office right behind Ernie Banks. Same plea. Same answer. "All right then," he said. "If you won't do it for me, do it for Mr. Wrigley." After everything Mr. Wrigley had done for me, there was nothing I could say to that. And John knew it. I looked at my watch; the game was starting in seven minutes. I put the uniform back on and walked through the locker room as if nothing had happened. We won 6–3. Santo had two doubles and a single, and knocked in three runs.

The story broke all over the papers the next day. Which was to be expected. Everything that happened in the locker room was always all over the papers the next day. Dick Dozer of the *Tribune* told me straight out, "I don't care whether I ever go into your clubhouse or not, Leo. I don't have to. Ten minutes after the door opens I know every word that was spoken in there."

So what else was new? Every writer who covered the Cubs had his private source among the players. Sometimes their information was even accurate.

The controversy continued to swirl around our heads for more than a week. Durocher was through again. You can't fire twenty-five players but you can fire the manager. When

Mr. Wrigley finally let it be known that he was standing solidly behind me, he did it, with his customary flair for the unusual, not by calling a press conference but by taking out a paid advertisement in all of the Chicago papers.

What follows are some selected excerpts from that advertisement:

Many people seem to have forgotten, but I have not, that after many years of successful seasons . . . the Cubs went into the doldrums and for a quarter of a century were perennial dwellers of the second division in spite of everything we could think of to try. . . .

We figured out what we thought was needed to make a lot of potential talent into a contending team, and we settled on Leo Durocher, who had the baseball knowledge to build a contender and win pennants, and also knowing that he had been a controversial figure wherever he went, particularly with the press because he just never was cut out to be a diplomat. He accepted the job at less than he was making because he considered it to be a challenge, and Leo thrives on challenges. . . .

In his first year we ended in the cellar, but from then on came steadily up, knocking on the door for the top. . . .

Each near miss has caused more and more criticism, and this year there has been a constant campaign to dump Durocher that has even affected the players. . . .

All this preamble is to say that after careful consideration and consultation with my baseball people, Leo is the team manager and the "Dump Durocher Clique" might as well give up. He is running the team and if some of the players do not like it and lie down on the job, during the off season we will see what we can do to find them happier homes.

(signed) Phil Wrigley

P.S. If only we could find more team players like Ernie Banks.

I have my own P.S. I kept handing Milt Pappas the ball. I never will forgive him. Pepitone? Ahhh, Pepitone. Peppy is like me. He has made a career of being forgiven.

He had this little bar, called Peppy's Thing, only a block from where I lived. (The bar went under like everything else. I heard that Santo lost some money on it, too.) I dropped in one morning a couple of weeks later, just as I had been in the habit of doing earlier. Yosh and a couple of the other players were there, and so Peppy called me in back so that he could tell me how sorry he was. "I wish I had a knife," he said, "so I could cut my tongue out."

Peppy's always sorry. Ten seconds after I walked up the steps that day he was buttonholing my coaches to tell them that he was sorry. In the newspaper stories the next day, Joe Pepitone was my greatest defender. He didn't get around to apologizing directly, of course, until after Wrigley's ad had appeared.

But if he was conning me, he did a magnificent job at it. Over the winter, Bill Wrigley wanted to know whether I'd give Peppy a two-year contract if I was the owner of the club. It was another way, you understand, of helping him to work out his debts by giving him a guaranteed income over a period of time. Work out his debts? The combined resources of the Bank of England and the Bank of America couldn't get him out.

After everything that had happened, I went to bat for him again. Yeah, he had the talent. Yeah, he could do it all. "Yeah," I said. "I would."

They did.

He appreciated it so much that he came down to Scottsdale for spring training with this eighteen-year-old girl he was living with. As soon as Holland heard about it he ordered me to tell Pepitone to get her out of there. "We can't stand that kind of thing! Can't have that on this club!"

Peppy was already half into his salary by then, and we

hadn't got out of Scottsdale. "If she leaves," he told me, "I leave."

I said, "That's probably the way it's going to be. Because I was told by Mr. Holland to tell you."

Immediately, he changed his tune. "Leo, I got this girl down here with me because I'm in love with her. I'm so much in love with her I'm home with her every night. If she wasn't here, I'd be out with some broad tonight. And every night I'd be out with some broad."

Which did make sense. Isn't it better that I'm going home every night instead of chasing around? Isn't that what you want from me? Stability. You've got to admit that it made better sense.

Guys like that always make sense. Once that kind of guy sees he can get around you, he'll con you right out of your shoes.

It was out of my hands, I told him. She had to leave. "But," I said, taking the first step backwards, "if you want to talk to John, go ahead. I won't stand in your way."

I guess he gave John the same treatment, because when he came out he was able to hand me the glad news that John was leaving it entirely up to me. "You're the boss, Leo. Whatever you say."

And *again* I let him. I let him keep the broad down there, and it was wrong. Wrong, wrong, wrong . . .

Right to the end. Leo the Lamb. I'm tough to play for, huh? If you couldn't play for me, you couldn't play for anybody.

Pepitone? He lasted about a month into the season, and then we traded him to Atlanta for a minor-league first-baseman. A couple of months later, he was playing in Japan. The last I heard he wasn't happy there, either. The Japanese people were very inconsiderate. They insisted upon speaking Japanese.

Give Peppy a couple of hours with the Emperor, and the country will go bilingual.

IT CAN'T BE HAPPENING
TO ME AGAIN

WHEN I SAY THAT I put the uniform back on because there was nothing I wouldn't have done for Mr. Wrigley I am not speaking idly. Wrigley had stood by me, like the Rock of Gibraltar, in the spring of 1971 when I became the target of a setup that had me on the verge of being tossed out of baseball again. Wrigley not only stood by me personally and publicly, but offered to commit a fortune to my defense if necessary.

The last time it had started with a phone call ordering me to come to a golf course in California. This time it started in Chicago with my wife, Lynne, waking me from a nap in our apartment on Lake Shore Drive to show me a picture. I can place the approximate date very easily because it was in the evening just before Christmas and I was in bed under doctor's orders with the flu. All I had to do was look at the guy in the picture and the first word that came to mind was "hoodlum." After I had told her that I had never seen the guy before and that his name meant nothing to me, she asked me whether I had ever been in a certain restaurant in Chicago. The restaurant had an Italian name starting with "P," and I had never heard of it before.

"That's all I want to know for the moment," she said. "I'll fill you in on this when I come back."

Before it was over, I was into a situation that was unreal. It was as though I had stepped into a time capsule ("Let's go back twenty-four years, Igor") and was reliving that part of my life. My marriage was involved again, an incredibly flimsy charge of association with a gambler was involved again, and the Commissioner of Baseball was carrying the ball again. The principal difference was that Happy Chandler had been carrying his own ball, while this commissioner had been handed a ball by a few bitter enemies of mine in the Chicago sports press.

The other differences were that political stakes were involved this time, and Lynne was far more intimately involved than Laraine had ever been.

I met Lynne soon after I came to Chicago at a dinner party given by mutual friends. As a matter of fact, I was doing a show on WGN-TV, the *Tribune*-owned station, with Jack Brickhouse, who was broadcasting the Cubs games that night. I asked Lynne if she cared to come with me. After the show we stopped at Maxime's for a drink. Lynne had tea, which is the equivalent of a cocktail for her. A few days later I called her, and we started to go out together.

I have always liked intelligent, capable women. Independent women. I make all the decisions I want to make at the ballpark; when I get home I don't want to be bothered. I'd just as soon leave the domestic decisions to my wife, even to deciding what restaurant we're going to. In addition to which, I like women as people. I've always had enough confidence in myself so that I don't need to have my male ego massaged. Grace and Laraine both remained such good friends after we were divorced that I have to wonder whether I don't make a better ex-husband than husband.

Lynne, besides being physically attractive, is a very capable woman, as Bowie Kuhn, God bless him, later discovered. Before her first marriage, she had been an actress under contract to Sam Goldwyn in Hollywood, as well as a singer, and she had been married for fourteen years to Joel Goldblatt, former president and part owner of Goldblatt's Department Stores, a large chain of stores in the Midwest. At the time I met her, which was three years before we were married, she had already been divorced, and on her own for four years. Her television show, Lynne Walker, Woman on the Go, was not the usual show for a woman. It was a hard-hitting interview show which went into all phases of life including politics, which is played for keeps in Chicago. At one time she had been working on an exposé of one of Sheriff Ogilvie's lieutenants, and in Cook County the sheriff's office is uniquely powerful. She had witnesses who were ready to appear on TV and tell how the lieutenant had allegedly been working with organized crime in pressuring little bookstores all over the city to sell pornographic literature. He would walk in and plant the pornographic material, according to her information, then flash his badge and tell the owners that if they wouldn't sell it for him he would arrest them for selling it, using as evidence the material he had just planted.

At this time, Lynne's brother, Rob Walker, was the chief investigator for the Illinois Crime Investigating Commission, a completely autonomous body set up by the Illinois State Legislature with the power to investigate all organized crime and possible misuse of office by any public official from the Governor of Illinois on down. When Rob heard she was about to bust the thing wide open, he told her to drop it fast.

"We know about it," he said. "We are investigating it. Stay away from this as far as you can, because, remember, you have kids and these people play rough."

The lieutenant eventually went to prison for one of his other capers, and Ogilvie himself unseated the Democrat incumbent to become the Governor of Illinois.

One other thing. During the time Lynne was married to Goldblatt, among their closest friends had been the Don Maxwells. Don Maxwell was editor in chief of the Chicago *Tribune*, the most powerful newspaper in the Midwest. Out of that friendship, Maxwell had offered himself as a go-between to try to bring Joel and Lynne back together. When Lynne told him the marriage was beyond saving and she didn't care to talk to him about it, he did what no friend should ever do. He took sides—Joel's side.

Back to the picture. What had happened is this. Three guys had pushed their way into our Lake Shore Drive apartment. Our apartment was on the 48th floor and visitors were so carefully screened that it was almost impossible for anybody to get up without our knowing it. Lynne had been on the phone in the den, though, and the elderly Filipino who had worked for her for years had always had his problems with the house phone. Once the guys were up there, they had pushed right past him, walked into the den where Lynne was sitting in her robe, and demanded to see Leo Durocher.

"Who," she asked, "are you?"

One of them was from the Better Business Bureau, the second was from the Internal Revenue Service. The guy who had demanded to see me said, "My name is Jones."

When Lynne demanded to see their credentials, the IRS and BBB men produced them immediately. But Jones only said, "I am with the *Tribune*."

"You're a newsman," she said, immediately suspecting trouble. And when they refused to tell her what they wanted to see me about, she was sure of it.

All three of them got very belligerent, Jones more than the others. He was going to see me whether I was sick or not. Come hell or high water!

They were *not* going to see me, come anything, Lynne assured them. And if they didn't leave quietly she would have them forcefully ejected. The other two were ready to back off at that point, but Jones wasn't budging until he had seen Durocher.

"All right," the others finally told him. "Show *her* the picture."

The first thing they wanted to know was whether Lynne

had ever seen the guy before. No, she hadn't. "Who is he?"

They wouldn't tell her. "We just want to show Leo the picture and find out whether he knows him."

And now she knew it was a frame. They would show me the picture, I would tell them I didn't know him and the headline in the *Tribune* the next morning would read, "Durocher Denies Knowing Hoodlum." And, well, you can take it from there.

A secondhand denial would mean nothing. So Lynne told them she would consent to show me the picture. "But before I leave this room," she said, "you will tell me who this man is and what you want to know. I will take the picture in and ask Leo about it. But you will not talk to him."

Well, he was a hoodlum-gambler, and it had been reported that she, her brother Rob Walker and I had been seen having lunch with him at the Italian restaurant, which Lynne herself had never heard of although she had lived in Chicago all her life. She understood so well what was going on that before she left the room she couldn't resist saying "You're telling me this man is a hoodlum. I don't understand what you are doing here. If you fellows are on a police investigative case, why don't you talk to my brother? He's the policeman."

When she returned after showing me the picture they still wanted to see me. "We have cooperated with you as far as we are going to cooperate," she told the IRS man. "We didn't have to, but we have been raised to respect the law." But now, she said, they were leaving. "You," she told Jones, "can't in any way explain to me your presence here."

"Well, I'm investigating."

"You're a newspaperman trying to get a headline," she said. "That's what you are. You are a disgrace to your profession." She walked to the door and opened it, leaving them no alternative but to follow her. "And a Merry Christmas to you, gentlemen," she said just before she shut the door behind them.

And then she called her brother. Rob had never heard of the guy either, as far as he knew, but he had so many investigations going on that he would have to check on his files to be sure. The next day he called her back. "We've tagged this guy a couple of times," he said, "because he's a smalltime gambler. But only in relation to something else that we were working on."

No, he said, when Lynne asked him, he had never had lunch with the guy personally. Although, here again, it was always possible that one of his investigators had, because they all worked undercover.

It was only then that Lynne told Rob the story. Immediately Rob said, "It's a setup. There's two things going on and I'll warn you about them right now."

With the changeover from a Democratic to a Republican administration in Springfield, politics was the name of the game. Now that Ogilvie was firmly entrenched in power he appeared to be out to get rid of the Illinois Crime Commission and establish his own investigative agency. At a minimum, he seemed to be out to get rid of Rob, who had been investigating him from time to time, for years.

"It's the Commission they're really out to discredit," he said. "If they can tie us together, using Leo's name and my name, the press will do the rest of it for them and kill two birds with one stone."

The *Tribune* had backed Ogilvie. He was their man, and if they could get their hands on anything at all they would go all the way with it.

The beauty of it, as who would be able to see better than me, was that they wouldn't have to prove a thing against me. All they had to do was throw enough mud around and the Commissioner could suspend me out of hand. (Durocher was tied up with gamblers again, was he? Wasn't there something about him and a gambler a while back? Yeah.) Once you saw it, the very insignificance of the bum they were trying to frame me with became frightening. A low-grade hoodlum who would say anything they wanted him to say, either to get a favor or square a rap.

As far as the Chicago *Tribune* was concerned, the personal feelings coming out of Lynne's divorce and my feud with Jack Brickhouse, the sportscaster for the *Tribune*-owned Chicago TV station, merely contributed to what had become a very dangerous situation for me. Purely coincidental, an unlucky break, yes, but we all know that personal feelings can become at least as important as political ones. At any rate, three or four of Lynne's friends close to the *Tribune* let her know that the word had been passed down from the top. It wasn't an active campaign to "Get Durocher." It was, "If you can get Durocher, get him." In fact, a sportswriter with the Tribune came to me and told me confidentially that he knew about the story. "I wouldn't touch it with a ten-foot pole," he said, "because I know there's no truth in it."

So there it was. We also suspected that our phone was tapped. No doubt about it. Hell, you could hear you had company every time you picked it up. The Cubs General Manager, John Holland, even warned me to be very careful about using the private line in my own office. "I wouldn't even touch the thing if I were you," he said.

About a month into spring training, John Holland called to tell me that Commissioner Bowie Kuhn wanted him and me to come to his suite at the Executive House in Scottsdale, Arizona, as soon as our practice session was over. The first thing the Commissioner did was to throw the same picture at me. "Do you know this man?" he asked.

"No, I don't know him. I never saw the man before in my life, and the first time I saw that picture was when it was brought to my Chicago apartment by a newspaper man."

Had I ever had dinner with him, alone or with anybody else?

No!

Kuhn opened up his portfolio, took out a long list and began to throw a lot of questions at me. After each of my answers, he would make a sweeping check mark.

"When was the last time you were in Las Vegas?"

"It was just this spring. About three days before we went into spring training."

"Do you gamble?"

"Yes, sir."

"Do you ever gamble for big money?"

"Yes, sir."

"Did you gamble for big money this time?"

"Yes, sir."

"Did you win this time?"

"Yes, sir."

"How much?"

"Twenty-five thousand."

He made his check mark and I wasn't going to wait for the next question. "And for your information, Harvey Wineberg, my business manager, declared it on my federal income tax."

He said, "Yes, I know." And made another check mark.

After he had gone over the stuff about the alleged luncheon again, he let me go. I was telling Lynne about it when John Holland called, not to speak to me but to speak to Lynne. The Commissioner wanted all of us to have dinner with him at Joe Hunt's Restaurant in town that night, and he had stated specifically that he wanted Lynne there as well as me. By making the point of relaying the Commissioner's request directly to Lynne, John was making it clear that the club was not endorsing any view Kuhn might have that Lynne was under the Commissioner's jurisdiction. Which was just as well because Lynne was going to make sure that the Commissioner was under no illusions about that either.

You couldn't have kept her away.

That evening at our table were John Holland, Mrs. Holland, and my good friend Monte Irvin, who was affiliated with the Commissioner's office. Lynne was sitting between the Commissioner and me and he kept asking her questions about our association with various people. Not the guy in the picture, but just people in general. Every time anybody would stop by to say hello or pat me on the back—which is something fans have a way of doing to kind of show they recognize you and wish you well—he would ask her, "Who was that?"

"I have no idea," she would say.

Nine times out of ten I wouldn't have the slightest idea either. Then he would say to me, "What are you talking to them for? Why are you answering them?"

"Well, it seemed to be the polite thing to do."

He didn't want me to do that any more. "You could be talking to anybody. It could be a gangster and you wouldn't know it. Then he could go out and tell people he was talking to Leo Durocher."

"Look, I go into a restaurant. I'm waiting for someone. While I'm waiting, maybe six or eight people will stop by. A couple of them will sit down. What do you want me to do, order them away?"

"That's right. Order them away. Tell them to go away."

"You've got a great case, Bowie," I said. "I'm known to people all over the world. The only way I could stop it would be to stay in my room."

He told Lynne that from now on it was up to her to protect me. "Don't let people come up and talk to him like that."

"Wait a minute," she said. "I don't think I heard you correctly. If a man comes up to the table, like this man right now, and he says something to Leo, what do you expect me to do?"

He said, "I expect you to see to it that he sends the man away. You protect him from anybody coming up to the table or anywhere else."

"Commissioner," she said, "in case you haven't noticed it, he's the man and I'm the lady. Even if he would let me do it, which I'm quite sure he wouldn't, I don't think I'd be capable of doing it. And I have no intention of even trying.

I mean, literally, if I could physically draw someone away from Leo, you'd want me to go that far?"

"Yes," he said.

It isn't uncommon for people to want to buy me a drink when I'm out for an evening, and this time the waitress came over with a big tray of drinks for everybody at our table.

"What is this? Who sent these?" Kuhn asked.

There was a card on the tray and I just threw it down in front of him. He read the name off. "Do you know him?"

Never heard of him.

Kuhn thought about it for a minute. "We're going to accept these drinks. But from now on you can't accept a drink like that from anybody. You do know what's going to happen now, don't you? Now that man will go around telling everybody he had a drink with Leo Durocher and the Commissioner of Baseball. And he didn't actually have a drink with us."

At first, Lynne had been giving me the kind of look that said *I don't believe this!* But by this time she was looking at him with such open contempt and disbelief that I was trying to kick her under the table.

John Holland was sitting on the other side of the table, and although I couldn't hear what John was saying I could see that he was becoming openly hostile.

"I'll tell you what I want you to do," Bowie Kuhn finally said to Lynne. "Tomorrow morning I want to have breakfast with you and Leo at the Executive House."

"Let's see," she said, as if she were trying to think whether she could fit it into her schedule. "Tomorrow morning? Well, I think I can make it. But I'll have to check with Leo."

He looked at her the way God would have looked at Moses if Moses had told Him he thought he might be able to make it up the mountain to receive the Ten Commandments.

She pursed her lips thoughtfully. She was putting him on while I was dying. "Oh . . . that's . . . right," she said at last. "You're the Commissioner. I guess he'll have to make it."

My wife never gets up before noon, if possible, and he

wanted us to be at his suite at 8:30 A.M. "You've got to be kidding," she said. "Would you believe eleven o'clock?"

She got him up to nine o'clock, but he wouldn't budge another minute.

"All right," he said. "Now we'll take your breakfast order."

All we could do was stare at him. "Now?"

Of course, now. We were going to clear the decks, get everything in order. The Commissioner is a very efficient fellow when it comes to matters of no consequence. So what was there to do except tell him we'd have coffee and eggs?

We left with Holland, who was really angry. "What you don't know," he informed us, "is that I told the Commissioner that I talked to Mr. Wrigley tonight and he wants Kuhn to know that if he tries to blackball his manager he will have Mr. Wrigley himself to contend with." Mr. Wrigley also wanted us to know that we had his backing 100 percent and that if it became necessary to go to court to defend our reputations he was prepared to do it even if it cost him a fortune.

When we got home that night, I got a call from Dr. Murray Saklad, a long-time friend of mine in New York. Murray is a dentist and has a lot of celebrity patients. Joe Garagiola is one of them. Garagiola, who was still on the Today show, had called to tell Doc that he had been alerted to keep the lines open at NBC the next day for some big news that would be coming out of Scottsdale about Durocher. Joe had wanted to know whether Doc had any idea what it was about. Murray just thought I might want to know about it.

My wife may have been coy with the Commissioner at Joe Hunt's Restaurant, but she was all killer instinct the next day. In the first place, she had to get up at eight o'clock in the morning to catch her brother before he left for work, and that meant she was mad to begin with.

"Look, buster," she said. "You had better be leveling with me because we're going for broke today. If you've forgotten anything of importance you had better come up with it right now!"

It was his reputation that was at stake too, he reminded her. If she wanted him there, he was ready to get on a plane and be there within a couple of hours, he said. Lynne didn't think that would be necessary. All she wanted Rob to do was to stand by the phone in case she found it necessary to call him.

Kuhn was at the corner of his hotel terrace, waving at us and shouting directions. To get to his suite, we had to cut through the tall wet grass, and Lynne was wearing sandals without any stockings. The Commissioner said, "Good morning," and that's all he got a chance to say.

"What's good about it?" Lynne shot back. "I wouldn't get up at nine in the morning to see Washington crossing the Delaware and you got me shlepping through wet grass up to my ankles."

We were seated at a table, Lynne directly opposite Kuhn and me in the middle—really in the middle—because after breakfast when things really got hot I was too far from Lynne to kick her under the table.

Bowie Kuhn went into the next room for his papers, and when he left the door open upon his return, Lynne and I exchanged a glance. We suspected that the conversation was either being monitored or taped. I hope it was. I hope a transcript exists somewhere because it would be a classic. In the three hours we were there with Kuhn, I'll bet I didn't say a hundred words. It was all Lynne and the Commissioner. They went at it hammer and tongs. There was some kind of a lawyer in the room that day, and it wasn't Bowie Kuhn. Lynne turned the tables on him completely.

The Commissioner began in complete control. He had the folder opened up in front of him again, and he began to shoot questions at us like the high-priced corporation lawyer he was supposed to be. Lynne gave him the whole background of the case, both the political stakes and the *Tribune* feud and my running feud with the Chicago sports press, making it clear that she was giving him the benefit of the doubt in assuming that he was hearing nothing he hadn't already known about, and even making a glancing reference to "you and your police-state tactics in getting information."

The Commissioner kept going back over the same ground, rephrasing what were essentially the same questions, throwing in some extraneous questions here and there to throw her off the track and always managing to sound as if he didn't believe a word she was saying.

When Kuhn finally referred to an association on her part, as well as mine, with a known hoodlum she blew sky high. "Now you've gone too far! You are now attacking my family's reputation. My brother is waiting for a call from me right now. Do you want me to get him down here?" She started for the phone and stopped. "Wait a minute," she said. "I'm not going to do that because it isn't necessary. This is a conspiracy from beginning to end, and you know it. I don't really think there's much more that has to be said. Do you?"

"I'm not sure," he said. "That's why we're still here."

"Why aren't you sure? Are you saying you don't believe us? Is that it?"

Well, the Commissioner's job as he saw it was to protect the integrity of baseball by keeping a check on the associations of the people involved in the game, etc., etc., etc.

They went back at it again with Lynne getting madder and madder. And all of a sudden she really got hot. "I'll tell you one thing, Commissioner," she said. "When we leave this room that folder will be closed. And this case will be closed. And I mean it will be *closed!* We're not even going to discuss it any more. I want to hear from you now that you believe us and there will never be any more discussion regarding this incident."

She stared down at the folder and he didn't make a move. Now *he* was mad. He didn't know whether he was convinced completely, he said sharply.

"All right, Commissioner," she said. "I've tolerated this

nonsense up until now to clarify something in your mind. This is an obvious setup. I know where you got the information. I told you where you got the information. I've given you the reason and so has Leo. Now, I want to tell you another thing. You may be able to control Leo and even throw him out of baseball forever, and at this point I don't care if you do! But you had better keep in mind, you have absolutely *no* control over me!"

I'm trying to kick her under the table. *Jesus, be quiet, I'll be suspended for life!*

Coldly and concisely she went on. "I am so angry now that I am ready to not only sue the news media for libel, I'm ready to sue baseball! And I've got news for you. You think the *Tribune* and these other papers in town don't have a part in this affair? I know they have a part, and you know they have a part. But I have a couple of other friends on other newspapers in Chicago. If we're going to play those kind of games, I can play them too. Not only will I start a suit immediately against you and baseball, including your head of security and the people who sent you this material, but my family will start a suit against you also!"

The Commissioner is a very large man, but my wife stands five feet nine herself, and when she draws herself up and gives you a look of disdain she can wither you. "That you, Commissioner, would put a man of Leo's achievements, of his standing in life, through the scene that you have and not say by now, 'OK, I've done my job, I've heard your story, the books are closed . . .' How dare you! Leo knows more about this game than anyone else in baseball probably will ever know, and his word alone should be enough for you. Evidently it isn't, because I don't . . . see . . . that . . . file . . . closed . . . yet!"

The file remained open. The Commissioner made an attempt to resume his questioning but she wouldn't let him. "I don't understand something, Commissioner," she said, very nastily. "I really don't. Who hired you?"

He didn't answer.

"I asked you a question. We've been getting the interrogation. Now it's your turn. Who gave you your job?"

He still didn't answer. Just a steady, guarded look.

"I'm rather new to baseball," she said. "But I'm under the impression, somehow, that the owners hired you. Is that correct?"

That seemed safe enough. "Well, yes," he said.

"I see. I'm also under the impression that as Commissioner of Baseball it is your duty and obligation to the people who hired you to protect their people in baseball. Is that correct?"

"Well, yes. And also to see that baseball is protected."

"But part of your function is to protect the people in baseball from just this kind of thing I'm talking about. Or am I wrong?"

No, she wasn't wrong.

"Well, where is our protection? Who do we go to for help in a situation like this? Obviously not to you!"

He stared silently, never taking his eyes off her.

"We've good reason to suspect our phone lines have been tapped and we're sitting here being interrogated like a couple of common criminals. And you are taking the unsubstantiated word of the press against one of your own people, the man you are supposed to be protecting, and putting us through all this humiliation. Frankly, you are not doing your job."

"Well, now, that's going a little far.

"I repeat," she said, "if you want an all-out battle on this, you're pushing me too far. Just remember, I have a few resources of my own if I have to go to court and I am *not* afraid of the *Tribune*. Now, do you want to continue this discussion?" All of a sudden, she shot the last question at him. "Commissioner, are *you* afraid of the *Tribune?*"

My hand to God, he looked at her and he blurted, "You know they could do the same thing to me that they're doing to Leo!"

Lynne's hand came down on the table in front of the folder. "There's your answer," she said triumphantly. "You've proven our point! *Now* will you close the file?"

A startled look came over his face as he realized what he had said. His face turned brick red. And do you know what he said? He said, "Well, they could *do* that, you know."

"So you're afraid of the newspapers," she said, pronouncing judgment. She turned to me. "I don't think Judge Landis would have been afraid of the newspapers or anybody else. Do you, Leo?" Turning back to the Commissioner, she said, "And you had the gall to put my husband and me through this humiliation, suspecting it was a frameup from the very beginning. Is the file closed, Commissioner? Because as far as I'm concerned this discussion is over."

He didn't want to do it but there was nothing else he could do. He looked at her and then he looked at me and very slowly and reluctantly he closed the folder.

"All right," he said. "But I would like a commitment from you that this discussion will not get to the press."

Lynne still wasn't completely satisfied. "Before we leave, I want to hear you say it, Commissioner." As if she were prompting a child she said, "You believe what we have told you and you know the story to be a total fabrication. And you will protect us from this sort of thing in the future. Is that our understanding before we leave this room?"

Bowie Kuhn, the Commissioner of Baseball, said, "Yes."

When we saw John Holland that evening he was laughing. Bowie Kuhn had walked into John's office not very long after we had left his hotel, and had sat down looking as if he were in shock. Holland asked him if the file was closed and Kuhn didn't answer him. He just sat there and stared at the wall behind Holland's desk for five minutes. Finally, he said, "Lynne Durocher is quite an exceptional woman." Only it wasn't meant as a compliment. The way he said it he was making it clear that he considered her some kind of female monster who had risen up out of the briny deep.

THE DIMINISHING MANAGER

IT ISN'T THE GAME I used to know. In the first place, there are the players. They're a different breed. Everything has to be done their way. Who are we kidding? It isn't a sport any more—if it ever was—it's an industry. They've got a union, headed by Marvin Miller, and they're carting their money away in bushel baskets. You can't tell them what to do. They have to be consulted; they want to know why. Not *how* but *why*. The battle cry of today's player is: *I don't have to*.

And do you know something? He doesn't. What are you going to do with a guy making $60,000, fine him? He'll laugh at you. I look at some of these guys getting $60,000 and I think, "My God, if he's a $60,000 player, what's a $50,000 player?"

He's thinking, "I'm making $60,000, I've got to be damn good." Or he's looking at some other player who's getting $75,000, and thinking, "If he's a $75,000 player, I'm worth $90,000 easy."

Expansion and the rise of the other professional sports have put him in the driver's seat. You can't fine him because it's a waste of time, and you can't bench him because you've got nobody to put in his place.

On top of that, you have the rebellion against authority

which pervades the whole society. Every time you want to send a player down you've got a fight on your hands. They're all perfectly willing to tell you right out that they're better than anybody you've got on the club. I had a guy at Houston named Al Jutze who thinks he's the best catcher in the League. He's a mediocre catcher. A triple-A catcher in my book. He comes to me and says he ought to be the number 1 catcher. "When do I get a chance to catch?"

I reminded him that the St. Louis organization hadn't thought he was that good or they wouldn't have let him go. "All of a sudden you come over here, now you're going to run this club."

"If you don't let me catch, I'm going to go home."

In the olden days, with a player with twice the talent, you'd have said, "Goodbye. Thanks for dropping by. See you later." All I could do was tell him if he wanted to catch regularly, I'd give him his chance by sending him down. So I sent him down and he went home. The club brought him back. Mediocre catchers aren't so easy to come by these days. He says, "I'm a star," you say, "Okay, you're a star. Anything else you want to be? Do you want to be a lamp? Or a breadbox? Or a pen-and-pencil set?"

The other slogan of the day is *I'll do it my way*. The prevailing attitude is that they've got everything coming to them. Not by accomplishment but just because they're alive. No concern for the owner of the club at all. We had a pitcher at Houston who had a bad arm all year. Before I left, the club was trying to get him to go to the winter league for a month to find out if they could count on him for the next year. If he could pitch like he can, they were going to have a good shot at the division title. If he couldn't, they were in trouble. He wouldn't go. Why? Well, he had just got a divorce and he was going with another woman. The club was perfectly willing to have him bring her along at their expense. Naw, he didn't want to. It would interfere, apparently, with the development of his new relationship. The club had given him a fortune when they signed him. Now he was going to do everything his way.

The manager's authority has been whittled away from everywhere. From above and from below. The front office runs everything. If the manager is going to be respected, the players have to know that they cannot go to the front office without your permission. At Houston, Spec Richardson was always around the clubhouse where the players could gripe to him at will. When I told Spec I was leaving, he asked me what was wrong with the club. As much as I like Spec, and as good as he had been to me, I had to tell him, "You're a great guy, Spec, but you make the players afraid of you. They think you're going to jump on them. If you really want to know what's wrong, Spec, it's you."

And then there are my old friends, the umpires. If they won't let you show your players you're battling for them, they're cutting away at another source of your strength. In the old days, you used to be able to use some language. The minute you get there now, they say, "Don't you open your mouth!" And right away, that's a challenge. What do they think I came out there for? Do they think I'm going to say, "Oh, I'm sorry . . ." and turn away? You open your mouth and you're gone; their eyesight might leave something to be desired, but they all have 20-20 hearing. Since the owner isn't paying you to find out how many games you can get thrown out of, you find yourself laying back.

Of course, if I was as bad as most of today's umpires I'd want all the power I could get, too. The umpires today, they're ridiculous. They've got an umpire in the National League they call The Puker. Paul Pryor. He was umpiring behind home plate one night at Dodger Stadium. Johnny Roseboro bent down to give the sign and—whoooooops!— Pryor threw up all over him and the hitter. Green! Green beer. When we got him back to the bench he threw up all over the place again. Had to wash him up, give him some smelling salts and give him something for his stomach. That's how he got his name: "Hey, Puker, you drink that nickel green beer it's bound to make you sick all the time. That green beer will do it, Puker!"

Mel Steiner, he couldn't umpire up an alley. He's bad on balls, he's bad on strikes and he's bad on the bases. And that's the only consistency he has. Some say he's the worst umpire in the National League, and we've got some bad ones. (Hi there, Satch Davidson.) But that's expansion, too. It's like you had a player who couldn't hit, couldn't run and couldn't field but you keep him because you say, "Well, it's hard to get players these days."

Any new rule just gives Steiner another opportunity to be wrong. Like when they came out with a rule that said you had to pitch within twenty seconds when there was nobody on base. We're in Chicago and Mel Steiner is umpiring at third base. Just as the game is getting started I see him take his watch out of his pocket, give it a look and put it back again. And I let out a *shry* from the bench: "Well, I only know one thing. They put a new rule in today, and you can bet me a new suit of clothes the first one to screw it up will be *you!*"

Would you believe that he had the nerve to be insulted?

Within an inning or two, our pitcher throws the ball over to first base, gets the ball back and begins to fiddle around. And here comes Steiner running up the third-base line yelling "Ball!" The three other umpires immediately threw up their hands and tried to wave him back. I'm standing on the top step of the dugout, so close to him that all I had to do was smile and say, "Doesn't count with a man on base, does it, Mel?" And then, while he jammed the watch back in his pocket, I howled, "I knew it! The first day! I told you you'd be the first to screw it up."

There wasn't much he could do about it right there, but don't think they're not out to get you. There's this little fat guy, Brucie Froemming. He turned into a very good umpire, I've got to admit, except that you couldn't talk to him. He was another of them that was going to be the big cheese. He was working the last series in Los Angeles after I had gone to Houston at the end of 1972, and two days in a row he's after me. The first day, when he was umpiring at first base, he came running over to the dugout screaming at me. I hadn't opened my mouth. Everybody on the club was hollering at him that I hadn't said a word. Even the plate umpire came over to defend me.

The next night Froemming is behind the plate. I had gone out to talk to Augie Donatelli, the first-base umpire, between innings, and the first thing you know, Brucie had come a couple of steps up the line, real mad, screaming for me to get out of there. Donatelli just waved him back in disgust, as if to say, "What are you making a federal case out of it for? Go on back and umpire, and he'll be on his way."

In the Los Angeles clubhouse, the umpire's shower is right next to the visiting manager's shower, with only a thin wall —and an open vent—in between. You could hear them as plainly as if they were in the same room. Little Brucie was all over Donatelli and screaming at him. "You embarrassed me, you dago. I got that one sonofabitch with that club (meaning Harry Walker, whom I had replaced), and I'll get this sonofabitch before the summer is out too."

"What the hell are you talking about?" Donatelli was saying. "We weren't even talking about you. It was a personal conversation."

I had half my ball club in the office. "Listen to that bullshit going on. You gonna tell me they don't lay for you?" Here's a guy who was admitting he was laying for me, and even if I had a tape recording of it, it wouldn't have done me any good. He'd have said it was just a manner of speaking, he didn't really mean it, and that would have been the end of that. Like hell he didn't mean it. They lay for you and they lay for you good.

Protesting to League headquarters is a waste of time; you'd be just as well off if you put your protest in a bottle and threw it into the sea. They've got that one word in the umpire's vocabulary that covers everything. "Judgment." It doesn't matter how bad they blew it. It was the umpire's judgment. I had the classic of all time in Chicago in 1969, while we were in first place and fighting to stay there. We were a run behind the Giants in the last of the eighth. With a man on first base and Beckert at bat I called for the hit-and-run, and Beckert hit the ball into the hole. The Giants' shortstop, Hal Lanier, had to reverse his field and make a backhanded stop; he had no play at second because Kessinger was around the base and his off-balance throw to first went into the dugout. The umpire had already signaled that Beckert had beaten the throw and the official scorer gave him a hit.

The way the rule book reads, a base runner is awarded two bases if all the base runners, including the batter, have advanced at least one base when an infielder makes a wild throw. The umpires didn't dispute that both runners had reached their target bases. Nevertheless, they sent Kessinger back to third base, and Beckert back to second. We lost by a run. My protest was turned down. And this wasn't even a judgment play; it was a rule-book interpretation.

Nine days later, we're trailing the Dodgers in Los Angeles by two runs and up comes a rerun of the same play. This time, it's Willie Davis of the Dodgers who hits a slow chopper into the hole on the hit-and-run. Willie Crawford is around second, Davis has the throw beaten at first and the ball goes into the dugout. The same play exactly. And the same umpires.

And they allow Crawford to score.

Wellll . . . "Oh, no you don't. I can't lose both of them, boys. That's the same play in Chicago where you told me the man stops at third."

I couldn't wait to wire my protest in. A wire came back the same day disallowing it. I grabbed the phone and called Giles at League headquarters in Cincinnati. He wasn't there.

He was in Los Angeles. I didn't know that Giles was right there in the Biltmore Hotel with us. I hadn't known he had been at the game. I was screaming so loud that at least a dozen people told me afterwards that you could hear me all over the hotel: "I can't lose both of them, they're both the same play! You ruled against me once, I got to win the other one! I must win one of them, Warren. I cannot lose both!"

He said: "You're right, Leo. It's the same play but the umpires interpreted the rule different."

Huh? Now he was telling me that a rule-book interpretation was also subject to the umpire's judgment. There is no possible way you can win. I kept screaming at him, and he kept telling me I was absolutely right but he still wasn't going to overrule his umpires.

The next day I carried the rule book with me to home plate. I read the rule off and then I said, "Now I am going to explain to you what this rule means." Very carefully, I ripped the page out, tore it up into little pieces and threw the pieces in the air. That was my explanation. "In fact," I said, "this whole book doesn't mean a goddamned thing." I tore the whole book up in front of them and let it all go flying.

While the paper was falling all around us I pulled out the lineup card, handed it to the plate umpire and said, "Let's have a good night, huh, gentlemen?"

When have you ever read in the newspapers that an umpire was reprimanded or fined? Never.

Warren Giles was a man I'd always had a great deal of respect for when he was running the Cincinnati ball club. There's just something about the job of League president that turns anybody who steps into it into a jellyfish. It's a nonjob for which they get well paid, and when you have a well-paid nonjob that you can't lose unless you do something horrendous you're just not going to do anything. Chub Feeney, who succeeded Giles, had trained for the job by spending a full career working for Horace Stoneham. That's why they hired him, I guess. They want someone who knows where the power lies and isn't going to get any bright ideas. As I had occasion to find out when I found myself in a dispute with the real power in baseball, Marvin Miller.

We had a Player Association long before Miller came along, you know. It was started right after the war. Even though I was a manager, I was still on the active list and so I was included in on it, with full seniority. That gave me a vested interest, of sorts, in Miller when he came on the scene in the spring of 1966, the same year I became manager of the Chicago Cubs. In one way, I benefited more than anybody else. I'm the only member who gets the full pension because I'm the only member who waited until I was sixty-five before I took it. I never cared for the guy, though. He'd bother you those first years with nits and nats. Better shower heads, improved accommodations, the kind of thing you were ready to give him automatically. He drove Randy Hundley, my fine young catcher, so crazy with his daily bulletins and phone calls that Randy quit as player representative. Miller probably thought I asked Randy to quit, and I won't say I didn't encourage him to.

And when he was threatening a player strike, it was the Cubs, along with the Pirates, who took the most intransigent line. "Put a lock on the door," Wrigley said. "And that will be that." I just told my players, "Who do you think is going to eat better, boys, you or Mr. Wrigley?"

Every spring, Miller would tour the camps, holding meetings with the players. Which is fine. I'd tell the player representative to ask Miller how much time he wanted, and when he wanted it. He wants an hour from nine to ten? Fine. I wanted my players to be dressed, spikes and all, so that they'd be ready to walk out of the meeting at ten sharp and go right out onto the field. When ten o'clock came, I'd step out of my office and announce, "Time's up, boys. Let's go." Maybe other clubs did it different. That's the way I did it.

He could have held his meeting just as easily in the evening, of course, and had all the time he wanted. But who's kidding who here? Part of the power play of union bosses is to do it on company time. I wouldn't let him, and maybe he resented it.

During my last training camp with Houston in 1973, Miller was touring the camps to explain the new three-year agreement that had been signed with the owners. His schedule didn't call for him to stop at our camp in Cocoa, Florida, though. He was going to talk to the Montreal club at their camp in Daytona Beach, 60 miles up the road, and then go right past our door, to the Texas Rangers camp at Pompano Beach, which was 165 miles away. We were playing Texas on Monday, and he was going to talk to both teams before the game. We were told to be there at ten thirty, and the bus company informed us it was going to take four hours to make the trip.

While I was telling the players that the bus would be leaving at six thirty in the morning, Doug Rader, our alternate player representative, jumped up and said, "Leo, I was at the Miami meeting while the agreement was being worked out. I have all the information. It's not compulsory that the players hear it direct from Miller. Nobody has to go unless they want to."

"All right," I said. "Let's do it legal-like." Two sheets of paper were pinned on the wall. Those who wanted to attend the meeting were to sign for the six thirty bus; those who didn't care to attend would sign for the seven thirty bus.

There were 38 players in the room. Every one of them signed for seven thirty.

As the manager of the club, I have an obligation to pick the ball club that I want to play on any given day. On Sunday, we were going to Orlando to play the Twins in the first exhibition game that was going to be televised back to Houston. I played my regular lineup for the full nine innings, and since I didn't want to make them travel again the next day,

I took only four or five of the players who were members of the Association to Pompano Beach. The others were kids I wanted to look at. That's what spring training is supposed to be about. The only one who did ask to make the trip was Larry Dierker, our player representative. He wanted to tell Miller that he was resigning his post, and he didn't feel that he should do it by phone or letter.

When we arrived, somewhere around ten forty-five, we saw that Marvin Miller had the Texas club sitting out in center field. Dierker got the players together, they dressed real quick and ran out. Members and nonmembers alike.

At eleven thirty, I was talking to Red Smith of *The New York Times* and another newspaperman. Preston Gomez, one of my coaches, came over to tell me we were going to be hitting in ten minutes. "We'd better get a pitcher warmed up," I said, and Gomez and I went to center field. "I'm sorry, Mr. Miller," I said. "This meeting is over as far as my club is concerned. We got ten minutes to get ready to hit. Any of you who are members of the union that want to stay here, stay right here. All the rest of you, come on." They all got up. Every one of them.

Miller said, "You can't do that, Leo."

Dick Moss, the Association's attorney, said, "It's a breach of contract. Our agreement gives us ninety minutes at any time we want."

I told him to take that up with Mr. Richardson and Mr. Hofheinz. "I got to get my players ready."

Whitey Herzog, the Rangers' manager, told me afterwards that he wished he'd have had the guts to do it.

You want to talk about making a federal case out of it. Miller not only accused me of breaking the baseball agreement but of violating the national labor law. That wasn't what made me so mad. Labor lawyers have their jargon, the same as ballplayers. You press a button and you know exactly what is going to come out. But do you know what that creep had the nerve to call me? He called me a free-rider and a Johnny-come-lately. I had been in the game for forty-eight years, and he'd been in eight. And I'm a Johnny-come-lately?

The next thing I knew I got a wire from Chub Feeney, fining me $250 for breaking up a meeting. The same old crap. Never called me, never asked for my side of it. "A pincushion," Mr. Rickey would have called him. "A mollycoddle." Well, I had been around too long to get whacked around by politicians and lawyers again. If lawyers had become such an important part of baseball, I was ready to get one of my own. I announced on the spot that I wasn't going to pay it until somebody gave me a hearing and then showed me in black and white where Feeney, Kuhn or anybody else had the power to fine me when I had a paper signed by every player on the team which said, in effect, that they didn't want to attend the meeting.

Although Spec Richardson was solidly behind me on the principle of the thing, he took the attitude, as a practical measure, that I should let the club pay the fine for me and forget about it. No chance, I told him. Never. I would resign as manager of the club first.

My own opinion was that Miller had set me up. Why would he be holding his meeting in center field unless it was to get me to do what he knew I was going to do, out in the open where everybody would see me? He knew that our players had voted not to attend, because Spec Richardson had decided to protect himself immediately after the vote by informing Chub Feeney. Maybe his feelings were hurt. The way I see it, he was out to show the players that it didn't matter what they wanted to do, they had better do what Marvin Miller told them to do from now on because Marvin Miller was all powerful. The baseball officials he didn't have to worry about. All he had to do was crack the whip and they'd come crawling.

If that was what he was after, he sure did have an ally in Red Smith. As soon as the meeting was over, I had seen

Miller and Smith locked together in conversation out near the gate by the clubhouse. The next day the lead in Smith's column read: "Leo Durocher threw a wrench into baseball's labor relations today by pulling his Houston Astros out of a meeting with Marvin Miller."

He went on to say that Miller was so furious at this violation of a written contract that the players were not going to ratify the agreement "until the matter was cleared up." Whether or not the season was going to open on time depended upon the action taken by "the responsible people in baseball." Meaning the two League presidents and their labor negotiator.

Two days later, Smith was at it again: "The men who hammered out baseball's three-year peace treaty put too much time and effort into the job to let one man's arrogance and another man's stupidity ruin it all. Otherwise, Leo Durocher, the practically peerless leader of the Houston Astros, and Spec Richardson, the Houston general manager, might be taking bows for one of the clumsiest efforts of sabotage this side of Watergate."

Who is arrogant? I wonder. A manager who wants to get his players on the field for the game, or a labor leader who uses it to make an issue over what is, as anybody with any common sense would have to admit, nothing? Or could it be a sportswriter who goes on to write what amounts to a legal brief for a powerful union boss while pretending that he is on the side of the underdog? "Not many people in baseball are as abrasive as Durocher," Smith wrote, "and most of them are smarter than Richardson, but the current dust-up is, unhappily, an example of the way some minds in this game work. It was a case of two small men determined to show Marvin Miller he couldn't dictate to them."

And now get this: "Durocher said Larry Dierker, Houston's best pitcher, went down to resign as player representative. There is no evidence here that he was coerced into resigning." Since one good disavowal deserves another, I want to say straight out that there is no evidence that Red Smith is on Marvin Miller's payroll.

And finally: "Miller got in touch with John Gaherin, the owner's labor negotiator, who assured him of full cooperation from all clubs. The responsible people in baseball—there are a few—were aghast that two bungling obstructionists should jeopardize the game's hard-won peace. Chub Feeney is the most amiable of men and he proved that again by assessing a token fine. That $250 is one-tenth of the monthly pension Durocher draws from baseball, thanks mostly to Marvin Miller."

On second thought, maybe I'd better not be so fast with my disavowals.

Fines are payable before the season opens, and when we got back to Houston, Reuben Askanase, the Astro president, came down with three letters for me to sign, each of them giving a different reason why I was sending in the $250 under protest. "No, sir," I said. No chance.

Askanase got good and mad. Feeney was a good friend of his, and he didn't see why we should be giving him all this trouble.

After I had told him what Feeney could do to himself, I barked, "Get him on the phone."

Feeney's first words were, "What the hell are you trying to do to me, Leo?"

What was I trying to do to *him*? "What are you trying to do to me? You fined me two hundred and fifty dollars and you only got one side of it. You never asked me a question. And then you got the guts to come up with other statements since then saying that I wanted a hearing and even if I got a hearing I was going to get fined two hundred and fifty dollars. What kind of a jury are you?"

The only way I'd send him a check, I told him, was if it was put in escrow, pending a hearing. Otherwise, he could suspend me and wait to hear from my attorney.

With that understanding, we wrote still another letter and I sent him the check.

The first time we got to San Francisco, where he had his office, I called him. He gave me his word I'd have my hearing by All-Star time. A month before the All-Star game we were in San Francisco again. He came down to our bench and promised me I'd have the hearing before the season was over.

The only thing I got was another blast from Red Smith. Four full months after it had happened, he brought the whole thing up again. "For this petty exercise in obstruction," he wrote, "Chub Feeney, president of the National League, fined Durocher $250, which was cheap but not as cheap as the offender. Durocher vowed he would quit baseball before he would pay. He paid."

As much as I hate to dispute the authority of Red Smith, I did not pay. Not then. Not ever. With the season almost over, I phoned Chub and told him he had a dead piece of paper in his office. "You've broken your word to me twice about the hearing. If you're just trying to whitewash the whole thing and let it die, that's OK with me. But I want to know. Just like I want you to know that I've instructed my accountant and the bank that if that check comes through to send it back."

The last time we were in San Francisco, he finally called me up to one of the offices in Candlestick Park and let me explain what had happened.

"Well," he said. "Miller said that you were hitting fungoes into his meeting in center field."

A lie. "I never picked up a bat."

Well, maybe it had been somebody else.

Nobody. If it were true, didn't he think that Red Smith, the friend of the downtrodden union bosses, would have said something about it? The fact of the matter is that I had instructed my pitching coach, Hub Kittle, to hit fungoes across the field from the right-field line toward the left-field line, and then stationed four players in front of the meeting to make sure that no stray ball went in there.

Feeney sent for Doug Rader, and Rader told him the same thing. Word for word.

"Jeez, Leo," he said after Rader had left. "You know Miller and all the trouble he can cause to the owners and everybody else. What do you want to do, stir it all up again after we got him quieted down?"

"What is baseball all of a sudden so scared of?" I demanded. "Has he got you people crawling on your knees or something? If you're that frightened, why don't you give up and go home? Why don't you just lock up shop, turn the keys over to Miller, and go home?"

And that's where it ended. The check was never cashed. I paid no fine.

WHATEVER HAPPENED TO SIT DOWN, SHUT UP AND LISTEN?

WHEN I LEFT THE CUBS, I was sure my baseball career was over. A month later my wife and I were lying in bed, with the television set on, planning our itinerary for a trip through the Far East. We had our passports and we had taken our shots. The phone rang, and it was Spec Richardson, an old friend. "Come on," he said. "You're not going to retire, are you? I want you to manage my ball club." Could I get on a plane and be there the next morning?

I told him I'd call him back. Then I looked at Lynne. "Seoul . . . Honolulu . . . Tokyo . . . Bangkok . . . Singapore . . . HOUSTON?" she said.

If Houston had been the kind of club I had taken over at Chicago, a second-division team in need of rebuilding, I wouldn't have even considered it. But it was a good club. They had made some good trades over the previous winter and had been favorites to win their division. I asked myself only one question: Can I win with this club *next year*? My answer was yes. They were a solid ball club, it seemed to me, and they had the best young ballplayer in baseball, Cesar Cedeno.

I went down to Houston and told the players that I was just going to sit there and make notes for the final four or five weeks and try to figure out why the club hadn't done better. Never opened my mouth. We finished second, which was where they were when I got there, but when it came time to vote their World Series shares, they cut Harry Walker out and gave me a full share. You have to communicate, but Walker had apparently overcommunicated. Yacking away at them all the time. I had to warn them that the Commissioner was going to reverse their vote and award Walker a full share anyway. I even begged them to give him the share they had voted me, and eventually they changed their minds and cut Walker in.

The next year, I decided I was going to do something I had never done before. I would be one of the boys. A pal. A buddy. The times had changed, and you had to change with them. I was going to do it their way. I'd play cards with them for half an hour before we went out. Spin stories; listen to theirs. I was always there to be communicated with. Rib me, call me anything. I had one of the best spring training camps I ever had, and by the time the season started I had communicated away all my authority. "One of the boys" means they are going to walk all over you. Give them an inch means they are going to take a yard.

I tried to keep a bandage across my lips. When a player screwed up, I'd go down in the little room behind the dugout, light up a cigarette and mumble to myself. Didn't do a bit of good. The guy's roommate would be sitting there and he'd tell him I was mumbling about him.

Not that they were bad kids taken as individuals; some of them were great. Jimmy Wynn. Lee May. Doug Rader. The only one who was real trouble on the Houston club was Jerry Reuss, the asshole of all time in my opinion. As good an arm as you'd want to see. All his trouble was in his head. If you asked anybody on the Houston club what was wrong with Reuss, they'd have told you, "Well, there's not too much wrong with him, he's just a little crazy." Half the time, his wife would take the road trips with him, traveling from town to town by commercial plane. Any trips she didn't take with us, there he'd be, two or three days before the trip was over, telling me he wanted to go home. "It's my wife, she's going to the hospital to be operated on."

My goodness, Jerry, what's wrong with her?

Well, she had an infected foot or a displaced kidney. Who can remember? Maybe once or twice he finished a road trip with me, and if his wife was operated on one time I never heard about it.

Gratitude? Hell, no. He was always mad at me. I gave him the ball and let him pitch. He won sixteen games for me, more than he had ever won anywhere in his life. Why shouldn't he be mad at me?

He was willing to admit openly that he was the best left-hander in the league. Probably the best left-hander ever.

"You're forgetting a left-hander named Koufax. He was pretty good."

"I can throw as good as Koufax could ever throw."

Then why aren't you winning like Koufax, Jer? (If you could throw like Koufax could throw, I'd be thinking, you'd have a record of about 18–5 with about two months to go yet and you'd probably win 27–28 games. Every year.)

Guess what? That was my fault too. We're playing in Montreal and we got seven runs for him in the first two innings—four in the first and three in the second. Montreal gets four of them back in the second, and now we're going into the bottom half of the third. The first guy up hits a line drive—Christ, it looks like a blur. The next man up hits a line drive—holy gee, another blur. "Christ, get somebody warmed up, he hasn't got it tonight. Get somebody ready." Next man up hits a line drive right at my left fielder, a shot—like that!—he never moved. If it had been up in the air it would have been into the seats.

"Get him out of there!"

Now he's so pissed off at me that he isn't going to pitch for me any more. We're in the clubhouse and he's not going to dress for the second game. He's quitting. "Why did you take me out?"

Why did I take him out???

"Let me show you," he says, "why I can't trust you. I just can't trust your reasoning."

My reasoning? You were getting the shit hammered out of you, Jerry, that was my reasoning. It was an act of elementary humanitarianism. But you've got to communicate, so all I said was, "Well, I know what my reasoning was, Jerry. I want to hear your reasoning."

He said, "My reasoning is that if the next man up hits a home run, the score is still seven–seven. You didn't give me a chance to battle my way out of it."

"Give you a chance?" I had to laugh. "I didn't want the married men in the infield killed. Christ, they were hitting bullets off you. I thought I'd try to save the three-run lead as long as I could."

I missed the whole second game of the doubleheader talking to him in my office. I said, "I think you've got a good arm. I think you forget how to pitch out there. You're just a thrower, and throwers are a dime a dozen. Until you learn how to pitch you're going to be in trouble."

He reminded me that he was the best left-handed pitcher in all of baseball.

"All right," I said. "I'll tell you what I'll do with you. Next time, I'll let you go out and go all the way."

The next time out, he got the living shit hammered out of him. I let him stay there until they got a five- or six-run lead on him. I stayed with him and I stayed with him, and when it came to the point where he couldn't get anybody out I figured I'd have to break my word and take the consequences.

Whenever a pitcher is coming out, I always say something to encourage him. "Stay with 'em, Jerry," I said, as he came into the dugout. "These things happen."

What do you think he said to me? He looked right at me and he said, "What the hell took you so long?"

You look at a guy like this and you think: *You know, you're daft.*

So over the winter, I read in the paper that Jerry Reuss called me a dummy. Well, I'll tell you one thing. This dummy don't throw the balls, that other dummy on the other end of the wire is throwing the ball. I couldn't have been such a dummy when he won. I must have left him in pretty good, I must have made some right guesses, because sixteen was the most he had ever won anyplace.

But that's expansion too. You'll go a long way with a good enough arm because you'll say to yourself: *Who am I going to bring in from the bullpen with that much stuff?* So you try him a little longer and the next thing you know you've got beat.

They do it *their* way. I've had some of the best drinkers in baseball, and some of the best drunks. Some of them I'd loved, and some of them I'd laughed with. The difference was a difference in attitude. In the olden days, it was fun and games. It was "Catch me if you can." Today there's a meanness about it. It's "Who are you to tell me not to drink?" and "What are you going to do about it?"

One night we were at the airport coming home to Houston. I'm in the front seat of the bus. My coaches and the newspapermen are sitting right across from me. Everybody's in except maybe three or four guys, and here comes big Don Wilson. We had taken a commercial flight back, and the drinks had been limited, so what the hell, we had won the ball game, we had an off day coming up, so I had told them they could go ahead and have a couple of extra drinks on the plane. Maybe they had a bottle of their own that I didn't know about, too.

Now, a couple of times in spring training Wilson had broken training rules, and I had not only overlooked it, I had covered up for him with the front office. Why? Because he was rooming with a hell of a nice guy, Jimmy Wynn, who had insisted upon playing for me when I got to Houston the previous year despite a bad elbow.

So here comes Wilson and he looks right at me and says, "Leo Durocher, you motherfucker, you." And walked on by with a little wise-guy grin on his face.

Jimmy Wynn was right behind him. Jimmy held up two fingers and whispered, "Peace, Skip."

"Is he talking to me?" I said more to myself than to anyone else. "Is he kidding?" If he's kidding, fine. If he . . . But I knew better. Maybe he was half-drunk, but there was no doubt he had been serious. I got so goddam mad I jumped up and started toward the back of the bus. As soon as he saw me coming, he jumped up too. I yelled, "Were you talking to me? Did you mean that, what you said?"

He said: "Who the fuck did you think I meant?" And it wasn't any half-smile now, it was that meanness.

"You no-good sonofabitch," I yelled. I was ready to fight right there. Big Lee May had the aisle blocked. Lee May. Cream and sugar. Played with knees so bad he could hardly walk. Played hurt all the time.

I was never madder. I said, "You drunken bum, you. I'll take care of you tomorrow. That will cost you three hundred dollars right now. And more later if I got anything to do with it."

Spec brought the fine up to the $1,000 limit, directed me to call a meeting in the trainer's room, and ordered Wilson to apologize to the whole club for the way he had talked to me. And to apologize to me personally.

I said, "Perfectly all right, Don. Go about your business, it's all right."

He didn't have anything against me. He just felt like telling me off in the foulest way he could think of. That was his thing at the moment and these guys are going to do their thing.

I started to think right there that I'd had about all I needed of the modern player. It was Cesar Cedeno who made up my mind.

Let me say about Cesar that he is not a bad kid at all. He's a good kid. That and a nickel won't get you on the subway any more. Cesar Cedeno also happens to be the most talented ballplayer in the game today. I had managed only two other players in the same class. One of them, of course, was Willie Mays. To me, there will never be a baseball player as good as Willie Mays. Why do I say that? Because I'm prejudiced, that's why. Of course I am. If somebody came up and hit .450, stole 100 bases and performed a miracle in the field every day I'd still look you right in the eye and tell you that Willie was better. He could do the five things you have to do to be a superstar: hit, hit with power, run, throw and field. And he had the other magic ingredient that turns a superstar into a super Superstar. Charisma. He lit the room up when he came in. He was a joy to be around.

The other player was Pete Reiser, who was every bit as good as Mays. *Might have been better.* Pete Reiser just might have been the best baseball player I ever saw. At the age of twenty-two, he hit .343 to lead the League in batting. The next year he was hitting .380 in July when he ran into the fence in St. Louis and busted himself up. He had more power than Willie, *lefty and righty both.* He could throw as good as Willie—at least as good—and he could throw right-handed and left-handed. You think Willie Mays could run in his heyday? You think Mickey Mantle could run? Name whoever you want to, and Pete Reiser was faster. You want to talk about your Brocks and your Russells and these guys? They couldn't get out of the box with him. He ran down to first base consistently in 3.6 and 3.7, and, believe me, there has never been anybody before or since who could do that. And knew how to run the bases. In an era when there wasn't that much stealing, he stole home for me seven times in one year. He'd throw his body out toward the pitcher's mound as he went by the plate, and the catcher would have nothing to tag but the tip of his hand.

Pete Reiser had everything but luck. Willie Mays had everything. It was the chance to end my career by managing another Willie Mays that was behind my decision, in the end, to go to Houston. Natural talent? Cesar Cedeno has it to burn. Willie Mays had come to the Giants at the age of twenty-one. His total batting average when he went into the army a year later was .265. Cedeno had come to Houston at the age of nineteen. The year I got there he was twenty-one years old and at the end of the season was hitting .320, with 55 stolen bases, 22 home runs and 82 rbi. He could cover center field just as good as Mays, too, which was absolutely vital at the Astrodome, where anything hit into the hole scooted off the synthetic grass and went all the way to the fence.

So now I'm managing the Houston ball club, and I can see that the talent is there, but he is not like Willie Mays. Every day with Mays I would come to the ball park, pick up the lineup card and write his name in. Willie Mays was never sick, he was never hurt, he never had a bellyache, he never had a toothache, he never had a headache. He came to the park every day to put on the uniform and play.

I never knew when I came to the park whether I'd have Cedeno. With Cedeno it was: Me no feel good today, me got tummy ache. Me got headache, I dunno if I can play. He had a very high susceptibility to injury and a very low threshhold of pain. Even when he was playing, he was complaining. "Me play, but me no feel good."

All Mays did to loosen up for the game was get a rub on his arm, chase fly balls and get into a pepper game. Cedeno was in the outfield every night stretching his legs back and forth. Doing situps.

Every day, Spec would point down to the field and say, "If I catch any more of your players laying down . . ."

I'd say, "He's not laying down, Spec. He's doing his calisthenics."

"Calisthenics, my ass," Spec would say.

Amen to that, I'd think. *Calisthenics is the only way you can lay down on a ballfield and make it look legitimate.*

It kills you. You spend your life looking for the great talent that comes along about once a decade, and you have to sit there and see it being thrown away. I'd look at Cedeno and think, "How do I get to this kid? How do you tell a twenty-two-year-old kid who's out of an entirely different culture that you can see him looking back twenty years from now and telling himself, *I had it all, and I threw it away.*

And then there was his temperament on the ball field. I never saw Mays throw his helmet. I never saw him get mad over a called third strike. I've yet to see him throw his bat. Did you ever see DiMaggio do anything like that? Or Ted Williams? Or Stan Musial or Hank Aaron or Mickey Mantle? In other words, I never saw Talent do that.

The Pitchers Union always complains that the Williams, Musials, DiMaggios and Aarons get a fourth strike. You're damned right they do. Especially in the clutch. The umpires respect their ability so much that if it's a close call on, say, a 2–2 count they'll give them the benefit of the doubt. *If it was a strike, Ted Williams wouldn't have let it go by.* The dumbest thing anybody with that kind of an edge can do is to get the umpires down on him.

Cedeno was getting called out on pitches that were outside by this much. He'd come back to the bench still screaming, and heave his helmet and bat. The umpires are looking. Not only the plate umpire, the ones on the bases. The umpires are watching and, don't kid yourself, they're all keeping score. I can tell you that just as sure as 2 plus 2 equal 4, I saw Cedeno steal second base so cleanly that he was sliding and on the way up. Out! One series, he was called out three straight times on bases he had stolen so cleanly that you could have umpired from the bench.

I'd try to tell him he was hurting himself. "Cesar, when the umpires need hollering at, that's my job. We have guys sitting on the bench that can take care of it, Cesar." You're getting a raw deal, Cesar. We all know that. They're waiting to see if you've learned your lesson.

He never did.

That was *his* way. How dare anybody criticize anybody for doing it their way.

When Mays was breaking in, all I had to do was move my knuckle an inch or two and Willie would start moving in the outfield, never taking his eyes off me until he saw my signal to stop. Cedeno would move if he saw me.

We were in Los Angeles with a month to go in the season. We're leading by one run in the eighth inning, men on second and third, two men out, and I look over to the Dodger dugout and see a skinny kid I'd never seen before coming out to the batting circle, swinging a couple of bats. So I turn to the players on the bench to find out if anybody knows who he is.

A couple of the guys knew him. "Alvarez. He played at Waterbury."

I want to find out if he has any power.

"Nothing. A Punch-and-Judy. Just bloops the ball over the infield."

I'm trying to get Cedeno's attention so that I can bring him in. My coaches and I are waving towels to signal him to come in. Cedeno paid absolutely no attention to us.

Fortunately for us, Bob Watson in left field saw what was going on, moved way in and over and, just exactly like the players had told me, Alvarez hit a little blooper into short center field. If Cedeno had been where he should have been, it would have been a routine catch. As it was, it took a great catch by Watson, just off the ground, to save the game.

I'm waiting for Cedeno to come in. Now, Cedeno never lost an opportunity to case the grandstand; he hadn't looked into the dugout all year before he hit the top step. Half the time he'd fall into the dugout, with his eyes still up in the stands. I said, "Come in here, Cesar. Don't be looking up in the stands. I want to speak to you."

After he had admitted that he had no idea who the last hitter had been, I explained to him how we had been trying to move him in, and how lucky it had been that Watson had seen us. I said, "You know, you got to look in here once in a while, Cesar, or we can't help you. Maybe we'll be trying to get your attention to move you around a little bit like all clubs do. Didn't you see us waving the towels?"

No, he had been watching the batter.

"But, Cesar, we were waving towels long before the batter was announced."

He looked me right in the eye and said, "Fuck you. I can't watch you and the ball too." Not unpleasantly, either. Cesar just wanted me to know where he stood on the question of whether a player had to look into the dugout for instructions.

Wellll . . . I said, "That last 'fuck' cost you two hundred dollars. Now get up that runway and take your uniform off. Get it off! You're indefinitely suspended!" I'm right behind him every step of the way, getting madder all the time. All he had to do is say one more word and it's going to be $400, $600, $800. I'm praying for him to open his mouth just once, so that I can go all the way and let him protest it to the Commissioner, the Supreme Court and all the way up to Marvin Miller himself.

He just went to his locker and sat there, not particularly perturbed, just kind of ignoring me while I was calling him everything in the book.

The game isn't over five minutes before Spec Richardson, who had been listening to the game back in Houston, calls to ask me what I could have been thinking of to take Cedeno out with a one-run lead. When I told him, he said, "Send him in when you get back in the morning." Spec fined him a thousand.

I'm not sure the fine was ever collected. What good would

it have done? The next day Cedeno came to the park early, and when I came out into the clubhouse he walked by and said, "Hi, Skip." Just as if nothing had happened. As far as he was concerned the only thing that had happened was that the Skip had got himself all excited about something or other.

I reiterate, he's not a bad kid. When he got into the trouble in Puerto Rico, I called Spec to tell him that if it would do any good I'd be glad to go down there at my own expense as a character witness.

But I made up my mind right there. I'm used to the olden days when a manager would hop all over a player who was caught out of position, and the player would keep his mouth shut and listen. By my rules, the manager is the boss, and you respect him and you play like hell for him. If they weren't playing by my rules any more, I didn't have to play by theirs.

I told Jimmy Wynn, Doug Rader and a couple of the other club leaders that I wouldn't be back. And also Preston Gomez. It was in my mind even then that if they asked me to recommend anybody—which is exactly what did happen —I would say, "No one but Gomez. You've got an awful lot of Latin ballplayers on the club, good ones. I think Gomez will do as good a job as anyone in baseball."

Gomez has a good mind and he's a hard worker. He thinks and talks baseball twenty-four hours a day. He is also bi-lingual. I had called an open meeting in Atlanta earlier in the season and turned it over to him, and it was the best meeting we had all year. It went back and forth, in English and Spanish both, and when he was finished everybody applauded. His theme was that the mental and physical sides of baseball were inseparable; that if they had enough pride in themselves and what they were doing they would be anxious to take care of themselves physically. Which was something they hadn't been doing and were willing to admit, at that moment, they hadn't been doing. All I had to say when it was over was, "That's it, boys. He said it all right there."

Putting everything else aside, Gomez was the logical choice, I felt, if only because he had a better chance than anybody else to get Cesar Cedeno to play for him. And, boy, if Cedeno is ever willing to give a manager everything he has he could just carry that club on his back.

I hadn't told Spec I would be leaving, though, and until you've told the head man you can always change your mind. The day after the season ended, I walked into the front office and told them I was through.

I still loved baseball. Baseball has been good to me. And I had never been surer that I was doing the right thing. It's a different breed, boy, and they're going to keep right on doing it their way. *Well, I'm a guy who has to do it my way.*

Whether you like it or not.

INDEX

439